Qanemcit Amllertut

Many Stories to Tell

Published by
University of Alaska Press
P.O. Box 756240
Fairbanks, AK 99775-6240

Cover design by Dixon Jones
Interior design by Leon Unruh

Cover animal images from the USFW (top to bottom): Cackling Canada goose brood, ID 50E3D3A1-65BF-03E7-2E79A6BACAC438AA; Raven in hand, ID 65CF8304-EF78-6E45-45442820B9CA6698; Pacific walrus, ID 5390891034_cd-b1134e47_b; Bull moose, ID 1D921E5D-FE9C-4F32-6F0E1EC2793EB0B2.

Library of Congress Cataloguing-in-Publication Data
Cover people images (top to bottom): Paul John, Elsie Tommy, and Michael John by Ann Fienup-Riordan; Nick Andrew and John Phillip by Mark John.

Names: Rearden, Alice, translator. I Meade, Marie, translator. I Fienup-Riordan, Ann, editor of compilation. I Alaska Native Language Center.
Title: Qanemcit amllertut = many stories to tell : traditional tales and narratives from southwest Alaska / transcribed and translated by Alice Rearden with Marie Meade ; edited by Ann Fienup-Riordan.
Other titles: Traditional tales and narratives from southwest Alaska I Many stories to tell, traditional tales and narratives from southwest Alaska
Description: Fairbanks : University of Alaska Press ; Alaska Native Language Center, [2017] I Includes bibliographical references and index. I Identifiers: LCCN 2016056627 (print) I LCCN 2017019343 (ebook) I ISBN 9781602233379 (ebook) I ISBN 9781602233362 (pbk. : alk. paper)
Subjects: LCSH: Yupik Eskimos--Alaska, Southwest--Folklore. I Tales--Alaska. I Yupik languages--Alaska, Southwest--Texts. I Alaska, Southwest--Folklore.
Classification: LCC E99.E7 (ebook) I LCC E99.E7 Q24 2017 (print) I DDC 398.209798dc23
LC record available at https://lccn.loc.gov/2016056627

QANEMCIT AMLLERTUT

MANY STORIES TO TELL

Traditional Tales and Narratives

from Southwest Alaska

Transcribed and translated by Alice Rearden with Marie Meade

Edited by Ann Fienup-Riordan

University of Alaska Press and Alaska Native Language Center
2017

Kalikam Imai

The Book's Contents

Tarenrat Nunanguat-llu

Illustrations

Quyavikelput

Acknowledgments

In this book, we are happy to share some of our favorite stories. Marie Meade and Alice Rearden have listened to some since childhood, while I only began to hear them as a grown woman with children of my own. Some, like the adventures of the wily Raven, are well known in southwest Alaska and told to this day. Others are rarely heard. Most are old stories, true *qulirat* (traditional tales), but some are more recent, like the story of Atertayagaq, the one who drifted away on ice as a young man but who came home and told his own story. All are part of a great narrative tradition, shared and treasured by Yup'ik people into the present day.

Although a number of bilingual Yup'ik story collections have been published over the last twenty years, all either concern a particular person (Shield and Fienup-Riordan 2003; Andrew 2008), a particular topic (Meade and Fienup-Riordan 1996, 2005; Rearden, Meade, and Fienup-Riordan 2005; Fienup-Riordan and Rearden 2016), or a particular community (Orr and Orr 1995; Orr et al. 1997; Rearden and Fienup-Riordan 2011, 2013, 2014). The present collection, for the first time, showcases a variety of Yup'ik orators from throughout southwest Alaska speaking in detail about their history and narrative traditions.

In 2012, Calista Education and Culture (CEC, formerly the Calista Elders Council) received a grant from the National Endowment for the Humanities (NEH) to work on two bilingual books sharing new translations of historical narratives and traditional tales recorded with elders from throughout the Yukon-Kuskokwim delta. The first book, *Anguyiim Nalliini/Time of Warring*, was published in 2016 and included dozens of accounts of the bow-and-arrow wars fought in southwest Alaska into the early 1800s. This second volume focuses on what are known as *qulirat*, old stories from distant times, most probably told by men and women in southwest Alaska long before the wars began, let alone ended.

A large part of this book is composed of new transcriptions and translations of audio tapes that I made with the help of Yup'ik friends and colleagues while living on Nelson Island in the late 1970s and early 1980s. It is sometimes said that an untranscribed tape is useless, while a transcribed tape is priceless, and we believe this to be true of these older recordings. The early tapes provided the basis for my first book, *The Nelson Island Eskimo*, published in 1983, but the narratives themselves re-mained unavailable. Thanks to Alice and Marie, readers now have the opportunity to understand not just what elders said but how they said it.

As most of these early recordings came from Nelson Island, we have added re-cordings made with elders from the Yukon and Kuskokwim rivers to give regional breadth to this collection. Work with Joshua Phillip in 1988 was carried out as part of the Yupiit Nation Traditional Law and Governance Project. Beginning in 1992, Marie and I talked to a number of elders in preparation for the Yup'ik mask exhibit, *Agayuliyararput/Our Way of Making Prayer.* Working with the Calista Elders Council since 1999, Alice and I have also had the opportunity to listen to expert orators like Paul John, John Phillip, and Nick Andrew.

All of the stories in this book were told in Yup'ik by men and women who heard them from their own parents and grandparents as part of an oral tradition thou-sands of years old. Each story text is both less and more than the original. Yes, we have lost the pitch and tone of the speakers' voices, their smiles and scowls, their hand motions, and the comfortable smells coming from the kitchen table, around which many of these stories were told. At the same time, writing the stories down gives both Yup'ik speakers and non-speakers access to this unique narrative tra-dition. And for all audiences, we have provided the original audio recordings of some stories, along with text, as part of the Yup'ik Atlas at http://eloka-arctic.org/communities/yupik/. Smartphones and inexpensive video equipment were not available when most of these stories were recorded, but the elders' voices come through loud and clear.

The translators—Alice Rearden and Marie Meade—are two of the most experi-enced working with the Yup'ik language today. While their styles and approaches differ, they are alike in the respect and awe with which they approach these stories. Neither of them takes these stories for granted, nor do I. Elders shared them with us because they knew we would enjoy them and because they trusted us to treat them with respect.

Sharing knowledge is highly valued in southwest Alaska, but with this comes the responsibility to share in turn—accurately and acknowledging both one's sourc-es and the limits of one's own knowledge, memory, and experience. We are here as editors and translators, not as authors. We are proud to take our places in the long line of storytellers who have, through sharing them, kept these stories alive for so many years.

Because the stories were recorded as part of so many projects over more than forty years, we have many organizations and individuals to thank, including the Alaska Humanities Forum for originally sending me to Nelson Island in 1974 and for their support of the Nelson Island Oral History Project between 1985 and 1987; the Smithsonian Urgent Anthropology Fund, National Museum of Natural History, which provided my only fieldwork funding while on Nelson Island ($1,000); the Yupiit Nation's Traditional Law and Governance Project in 1988 and 1989; Eliza Orr for recordings she made with Tununak elders in 1976; Robert Drozda for sharing the recording he and Bill Sheppard made with Jack Williams in 1991; the Coastal Yukon Mayors' Association, the National Endowment for the Humanities, the Rasmuson Foundation, and the Anchorage Museum of History and Art for support provided in preparation for the Yup'ik mask exhibit between 1992 and 1996; the National Science Foundation, the National Park Service, and the Administration for Native Americans for supporting elder gatherings organized by the Calista Elders Council between 2000 and 2012; CEC staff members Mark John, Rea Bavilla, and Dora Moore, as well as the Calista Corporation; the ELOKA project, especially Peter Pulsifer and Chris McNeave, for creating the Yup'ik place name atlas and website; Kurt Riemann of Surreal Studios for turning our audio recordings into videos, combining the speakers' voices with Yup'ik text and translations; James H. Barker, the Moravian Archives (Bethlehem, Pennsylvania), Anna Mossolova, and the University of Alaska Museum of the North for sharing photographs to enrich the text; Patrick Jankanish and Michael Knapp for the book's maps; and the National Endowment for the Humanities, Scholarly Editions and Translations Program, for funds to put this book together. Our work would not have been possible without the continued encouragement and support of our NEH program officer, Lydia Medici, a tireless advocate for including an audio component to this project.

For overseeing the publication of our book, we are indebted to the fine staff of the University of Alaska Press, including Krista West and Amy Simpson, as well as freelance editor Lesley Bolton. Thanks to Walkie Charles, Robert Drozda, Theresa John, Larry Kaplan, and Phyllis Morrow for their thoughtful and insightful comments on earlier drafts of the book. Special thanks to Leon Unruh of the Alaska Native Language Center for another fine book design and to Dixon Jones for ensuring that the cover of our book is as compelling as its contents.

Our biggest debt is to the men and women who shared these stories, including Tim Agagtak, Simeon Agnus, John Alirkar, Dick Andrew, Nick Andrew, Dick Anthony, George Billy, David Chanar, Wassillie Evan, Theresa Hooper, Lucy Inakak, Raphael Jimmy, Michael John, Paul John, Andy Kinzy, Paul Kiunya, Sophie Lee, Martha Mann, Mary Napoka, Stephanie Nayagniq, Dennis Panruk, John Phillip, Joshua Phillip, Roland Phillip, Magdalene Sunny, Elsie Tommy, Frances Usugan, and Jack Williams. Their dramatic and lively contributions eloquently make the point that so-called traditional stories are never anonymous. They are the authors of this book, and as translators and editors, our role has been to share their narrative performances so that they may be enjoyed for generations to come.

Qanemcillret

Those Who Told Stories

This list reflects Yup'ik protocol. Names are ordered by community, running north to south along the Bering Sea coast and upriver to Bethel. Within each community, individuals are listed by age (eldest to youngest); their Yup'ik names are in italics. In the text the first occurrence of each speaker's name is followed by place of residence, e.g., Paul John (November 2000:81) of Toksook Bay. The gathering date and transcript page number of the statement follows the elder's name in parentheses.

	Residence	Birthplace	Birth Year
Nick Andrew Sr. / *Apirtaq*	Marshall	Iquarmiut	1933
Andy Kinzy / *Qut'raacuk*	St. Marys	Qissunaq River	1911
Jack Williams Sr. / *Uyuruciar*	Mekoryuk	1911	
Elsie Tommy / *Nanugaq*	Newtok	Kaviarmiut	1922
Michael John / *Qukailnguq*	Newtok	Cevtaq	1931
Theresa Hooper / *Ackiar*	Tununak	Umkumiut	1936
Lucy Inakak / *Negeryaq*	Tununak	1916	
Stephanie Nayagniq / *Ceturngalria*	Tununak	1905	
Frances Usugan / *Piyuuk*	Toksook Bay	Up'nerkillermiut	1915
Paul John / *Kangrilnguq*	Toksook Bay	Cevv'arneq	1928
John Alirkar / *Allirkar*	Toksook Bay	Cevv'arneq	1929
Ruth Jimmie / *Angalgaq*	Toksook Bay	Nightmute	1951
Cathy Moses / *Keggutailnguq*	Toksook Bay	Kotlik	1952
Tim Agagtak / *Akagtaq*	Nightmute	1903	
Magdalene Sunny / *Missan*	Nightmute	1915	
Dick Anthony / *Minegtuli*	Nightmute	Cevv'arneq	1922

Simeon Agnus / *Unangik* — Nightmute | Nightmute | 1930

Dennis Panruk / *Panruk* — Chefornak | Cevv'arneq

Paul Kiunya / *Kayungiar* — Kipnuk | Pengurpagmiut | 1930

Roland Phillip / *Anguteka'ar* — Kwigillingok | 1927

Martha Mann / *Mass'aluq* — Kongiganak | Qipneq | 1906

Julia Azean / *Anglluralria* — Kongiganak | Urutaq | 1918

John Phillip Sr. / *Ayagina'ar* — Kongiganak | Anuuraaq | 1925

George Billy / *Nacailnguq* — Napakiak | Nanvarnarrlagmiut | 1922

Wassillie Evan / *Misngalria* — Akiak | Napaskiak | 1930

Joshua Phillip / *Maqista* — Tuluksak | Akiachak | 1912

Mary Napoka — Tuluksak | 1916

Rachel Sallaffie / *Maayaaq* — Tuluksak | 1965

Dick Andrew / *Apaqutaq* — Bethel | Kayalivik | 1909

Sophie Lee — Anchorage | Alakanak

Raphael Jimmy / *Angagaq* — Anchorage | Kuiggarpak | 1924

David Chanar / *Cingurruk* — Anchorage | Umkumiut | 1946

Marie Meade / *Arnaq* — Anchorage | Nunapitchuk | 1947

Ann Riordan / *Ellaq'am Arnaan* — Anchorage | Virginia | 1948

Mark John / *Miisaq* — Anchorage | Nightmute | 1954

Alice Rearden / *Cucuaq* — Anchorage | Napakiak | 1976

Kalikam Ayagnara

Introduction

Long ago, the elderly men told *qulirat* to put people to sleep, when we would go to sleep in the *qasgi*. . . . I do know different kinds of short *qulirat*. I enjoyed some. The ones I enjoyed, I tried not to fall asleep listening to them. . . .

And [a story] about grandchildren who weren't weak when it was time to catch animals. These stories that gave me the desire to be strong, I still haven't forgotten them today. . . .

There are many stories to tell, there are actually many to tell, including *qulirat.*

—Dennis Panruk, Chefornak, 1987

The stories in this book come from the Yukon-Kuskokwim region, a lowland delta the size of Kansas that was the traditional homeland of the Yupiit or Yup'ik people. The region's population of over 23,000 (the largest Native population in Alaska) lives scattered in 56 villages, ranging between 200 and 1,200 persons each, and the large regional center of Bethel (population 5,800). Lack of commercially valuable resources (including whales, fur bearers, and mineral deposits) meant that the region attracted a resident non-Native population relatively late compared to other parts of Alaska. The first non-Natives to settle in significant numbers were Christian missionaries beginning in the 1840s (Oswalt 1963, 1990; Fienup-Riordan 1988, 1991). Through the 1930s, most people lived in small settlements (ten to thirty residents), divided between a *qasgi* (communal men's house, plural *qasgit*) and separate sod homes for women and children, where residents spoke the Central Yup'ik language and engaged in traditional harvesting activities. Some settlements, such as Qissunaq, Naparyaarmiut, and Qinaq were larger, including one hundred or more residents and more than one *qasgi*.

Both late contact and lack of commercial resources have meant that the Yup'ik region has retained many social patterns and a traditional knowledge base lost in other parts of the United States. This continued cultural vitality has contributed to the position of Yup'ik people as among the most traditional Native American groups, actively working both to retain the best of their past and carry still-vital traditions into the future. Today, the Yup'ik language has the largest number of speakers of any Alaska Native language.

The Yup'ik language continued strong through the 1990s, with an estimated 18,000 speakers. By 2000, that number had dropped to 14,000, with language shift accelerating in many communities. Although children still grow up speaking Yup'ik as their first language in seventeen lower Kuskokwim and coastal communities, few young people speak the language in Yukon and Nushagak river communities. Many recognize that the continued vitality of the Yup'ik language cannot be taken for granted (Krauss 2007). The complex grammatical constructions and rich vocabulary used by older speakers in the 1970s and 1980s are rarely heard today and not always understood by younger community members. Even expert translators like Alice Rearden and Marie Meade find some older terms and turns of phrase baffling. We have explained and expanded meanings whenever we can, and in fact elders themselves have provided their listeners with explanations of some terms, such as the use of *"eng"* as an expression of empathy (p. 148). This collection thus has the potential to enhance the reader's ability to understand the stories with clarity. While discussions with elders can answer some questions, some words remain a mystery and are transcribed in Yup'ik without translation in the text.

Storytelling was common in the past. In the evening before bed or after a good meal, elders often told stories, both in the *qasgi* and home. Audiences included adults as well as children. Boys often heard stories from their fathers and grandfathers while falling asleep in the *qasgi*, but girls heard these stories as well. Elsie Tommy (June 1992) of Newtok recalled: "Ap'ayagaq . . . would tell [stories] to us girls in the evenings sometimes when we wintered in places where they had no *qasgi*, down below Kayalivigmiut." Small groups of young women and children also told stories to one another through "storyknifing" outside their homes. As she spoke, the narrator would illustrate her story by drawing pictures in the mud or snow with an ivory storyknife or one of her mother's butter knives, erasing each episode before drawing another (Oswalt 1964; Ager 1971). Even though storyknifing has disappeared and tales generally are told less often, elders continue to retell the old stories in new contexts—community halls, school classrooms, regional gatherings. People used stories to communicate with listeners in the past, and this dialogue is not done. The written stories that follow descend directly from this venerable tradition.[1]

Two broad story categories exist within Yup'ik narrative tradition (Jacobson 1984; Morrow 1994; Woodbury 1994; Fienup-Riordan and Kaplan 2007). The first are legends or tales told by distant ancestors and passed down from generation to generation—what James Ruppert and John Bernet (2001:9) call distant-time stories. Most Central Alaska Yup'ik speakers refer to legends as *qulirat* or *quli'ir* (*qulirer* in Cup'ig). Cup'ig speakers from Nunivak Island, as well as Central Yup'ik speakers from the Yukon area and Norton Sound, also sometimes use the term *univkar* or *univkaraq* (lit., "that which is left behind") for a legend or traditional tale. These include origin stories, especially accounts involving Raven, and tales of the time when the earth was thin and humans interacted freely with animals and other nonhuman persons. A number concern heroes, many of whom begin as "poor boys" (usually orphans). Many of these stories describe the self-reliant individual who overcomes adversity to ultimately succeed. Another common theme is the selfish or overbearing hunter or shaman whose cruelty and disregard for others ultimately results in his undoing.

The second broad story category consists of historical narratives related by known persons, labeled *qanemcit* (from *qaner-*, "to speak") by Central Yup'ik speakers and *qanengssi* among Cup'ig speakers. The words *qalamciq* and *qalangssak* (from *qalarte-*, "to talk, to speak") also mean "story" for Yup'ik speakers living in the Bristol Bay area, where *qanengssiit* (from *qaneq*, "mouth," or *qaner-*, "to speak," the same base as *qanemcit*) is used to designate stories from distant times.

Whereas *qulirat* are part of the experience of very ancient ancestors and never involve particular individuals definitely known to have existed, *qanemcit* are grounded in the experience of a particular person, whether that person is living or dead. *Qanemcit* include, among other things, detailed accounts of the bow-and-arrow wars that occurred in Alaska into the early nineteenth century, encounters with ghosts or *ircenrraat* (other-than-human persons), past events involving known people, and personal experiences.

The Yup'ik distinction between legend and historical narrative is sometimes equated with the Western distinction between fanciful myths or fairy tales and factual history. In fact, legends and historical accounts are considered equally reliable sources of information, simply referring to different time periods—the distant past and recent times. As such, legends and historical accounts exist along a continuum and are not mutually exclusive. For example, at the close of "Pamalirugmiut," Elsie Tommy recalled: "It's like a *quliraq*. The late husband of Laakautarkaq . . . in the evenings *qanemciurautellra* [he told that *qanemciq*]."

Yup'ik stories are not owned or inherited, and any knowledgeable person can tell them. It is, however, important to acknowledge one's source, as when Dick

Anthony of Nightmute began his account with the words, "Let me tell you the story that was told to me by a man from Nunivak Island." Elders such as Dick Anthony, Paul John, and Elsie Tommy were well-known and respected tradition bearers who knew and told many stories. Others have one or two stories that they particularly enjoy telling and may do so whenever asked. Raphael Jimmy of Mountain Village ended his shaman story saying, "This is the only [tale] that I don't forget, this *quliraq* that Nanuq told." Before sharing a story with Marie Meade when she visited him in his home in Tuntutuliak, Nick Lupie (March 1992) said: "That person [Makalli, Carl McCall] is the one who used to tell that legend. It was the only legend he would relate. And even though I am not very smart I know it pretty well because he used to tell it over and over again. When they'd ask me to tell a legend, this is the only one I used to relate." It is also not unusual for storytellers to apologize for the limits of their knowledge, downplaying their memory, as Nick did when he said that he was "not very smart." Ben and Eliza Orr (1995:371) wisely point out that such disclaimers reflect modesty rather than lack of competence.

When she was living on Nunivak Island in the 1930s, anthropologist Margaret Lantis (1946:264) was told that myths were not supposed to vary and storytellers were not to add or reorder events. Elders had been taught to attend to the words of parents and grandparents and not to repeat what they did not know from their own experience (including what they heard). Joshua Phillip (June 1988) described his experience:

> When one of the people was relating a legend, he said, "I have
> forgotten some of it. It is okay if I don't relate this legend."
>   Then I said to him, "Go ahead and insert anything you think
> in the parts that you don't remember."
>   The one who I asked [to insert portions] quickly answered me,
> "Well, if I just added anything to the story, a legend will no longer
> be a legend; it will no longer be."

Although plots are stable, the prose is neither memorized text nor rigid repetition, and stories vary considerably in how they are told. Each telling is unique to the storyteller and his or her audience. While the story "episodes" or sequence of events remain the same, the way they are described can vary a great deal. Experienced storytellers can and do embellish and enlarge events and character interactions to great effect. To show readers just how flexible storytelling can be, we have included several versions of the well-known cycle of Raven stories.

Linguist Anthony Woodbury noted that despite careful transmission, no immutable legend canon exists: "Repertoires and stories vary, not only from region to region but among storytellers in the same village" (Woodbury and Moses 1994:18).

Elders recognize this. Dick Andrew (August 1992:3) of Bethel recalled: "The ways of the people are not the same from village to village. That's the way it is from what I know. And their stories, though they are similar, they change from place to place. The story would change slowly as it went." Chefornak elder Dennis Panruk agreed: "Since I enjoy it, sometimes when I tell that story, the ones [listening] smile a little, looking at me. It's because I tell it like I heard it. These stories were also told differently. When another person told it, some part of it would be different." What varies less often, Woodbury continued, are standard themes, settings, and characters: "It is these characteristics, as much as the individual stories, that constitute the inherited tradition" and shape the listeners' understandings of the stories (Woodbury and Moses 1994:18).

The stories in this book, like Yup'ik stories generally, deal with all kinds of human interaction, including that between spouses, parents and children, siblings, and especially grandparent and grandchild. As important, stories bring to life human interaction with the world around them, including all manner of nonhuman and other-than-human persons—animals, ghosts, *ircenrraat*, and the dead. Many stories include explicit moral direction, and the consequences of both appropriate and inappropriate action, such as Martha Mann's story, in which the admonition never to bother swallows is followed by a story of a boy who didn't listen and experienced the consequences. A typical story progression might involve a young man or woman who disobeys his or her grandmother and as a result confronts peril, which he or she overcomes. In Dick Andrew's story of Qanikcaartuli, for example, a young man ignores his grandmother's warning never to pick berries in a certain spot, and as a result is captured, starved, and almost killed by the evil Qanikcaartuli before he is helped to escape and finally returns home. Alternately, as in Lucy Inakak's story, "One Who Changed the Weather," a mischievous grandson lies to his grandmother, telling her nothing has changed when in fact the world around them is growing hotter and hotter, until finally fire consumes their home and both are transformed into weasels with singed tails. In both cases, breaking the rules creates suspense, making the listener anxious to know what will happen.

Yet as many working with oral tradition today wisely note, storytelling is first and foremost a social activity, not an intellectual exercise conceived in isolation. Those who tell stories are talking to people—grandchildren, children, peers—and what they say is for them. As is the case with words generally, nonhuman persons are also part of the unstated, invisible audience. Storytelling is always part of these wider relationships.

೫ *Qanemcilallrat Qulirilallrat-llu* ೫
How Legends and Stories Were Told

Early visitors to the Bering Sea coast witnessed the strength and vitality of Yup'ik narrative traditions. Smithsonian naturalist Edward Nelson (1899:451) observed: "On lower Kuskokwim river and the adjacent district toward the Yukon mouth, some of the important tales are given by two men, who sit cross-legged near together and facing each other; one is the narrator and the other holds a bundle of small sticks in one hand. The tale proceeds and at certain points one of these sticks is placed on the floor between them, forming a sort of chapter mark. If the narrator is at fault he is prompted by his companion." Although no sticks were used as chapter marks while the stories in this book were told, narrators acknowledge distinct story sections by pauses, changes in tone, and sometimes by explicitly pointing out the end of one section and the beginning of the next, as when Dick Andrew said, "There's not much to say about this part of the story. Now it's time to go to the next part." Readers will also note the regular acknowledgment by listeners to the narrative flow in the following pages. These are often noted with a simple "Yes" or "I see," or with a word of sympathy, such as *"Nakleng* [Poor]."

Nelson (1899:451) also noted how vividly stories were told: "The voice is intoned to imitate the different characters in a more or less dramatic manner, and with the gestures makes a very effective recital. The listeners are quiet and attentive, and at certain incidents express by a word or two their feelings of surprise or satisfaction. These tales are heard with pleasure over and over again." Storytelling was then and is today an art never to be forgotten by those fortunate enough to hear it.

Lantis (1946:316) noted how much songs and conversation were parts of these stories, showing that direct quotation was not a literary device recently acquired. She also noted how enjoyable it was to listen to stories: "Of course the stories are not so good when read as when told. By acting out many parts of them very realistically, by singing, by lowering the voice almost to a whisper for the dramatic passages, the storyteller puts on a one-man show." Joe Ayagarak (December 1987:34) recalled how old men helping one another would burst out laughing while telling stories when he was a boy in Qissunaq: "When I used to see men who had stopped doing things, there were three of them who were the same age who helped one another fix their story. When they would speak, they faced one another. When this one made a mistake, one of them would take over [the story] and speak about what happened for a while. They would break into laughter from time to time. It was because they were really imagining what they were talking about."

Readers already familiar with Yup'ik storytelling will know this to be true. We encourage everyone, even those who do not speak the language, to listen to the stories while reading along at the "Story" section of our Yup'ik Atlas at http://eloka-arctic.org/communities/yupik/, where we have posted the original recordings of more than a dozen of the stories included in this book. There one can hear the rise and fall of the speaker's voice, how pauses and changes in tone are used for dramatic effect, as well as the songs and dialogue that are ubiquitous in these stories. There one can also hear bits of conversation between the storyteller and his or her audience. Some narrators told their stories in a quiet, understated way, using a tone of voice that encouraged quiet listening, as in Magdalene Sunny's sparrow story. Other storytelling sessions were less sedate, as when Frances Usugan gave her lively account of Raven traveling along, with my eight-month-old son, Nicky, chortling in the background. Other background noises include phones ringing, water running, men sawing, and children playing, as well as occasional bits of household conversation.

Titles for particular stories, such as those listed in our table of contents, were not a part of traditional storytelling. Narrators might refer to central characters by name or by a defining action, such as Raven, Qanikcaartuli, or the person who came upon wolf pups. No other designations were used.

Narrators of *qulirat* often employ formal opening phrases such as, "There was a grandmother and grandchild living by themselves," marking these narratives as old, often well-known tales. *Anuurluq* is a word for grandmother used in many stories, as well as the terms *anuurluqelriik* (lit., "grandmother related ones") and *maurluqelriik* (from *maurluq,* the everyday word for "grandmother") for a grandmother and her grandchild.

Narrators also often close their tales with phrases like "This is the length of my story," "That's where the story ends," or the more elegant "This is how long this legend is. And the parts that I missed have situated themselves in their proper places." Stylized endings differ from place to place and person to person, depending on who tells the story. For instance, narrators on the lower Kuskokwim sometimes end their stories "It is going forward on its path, getting better and better." Nick Lupie (March 1992:13) ended a long story with these words: "This is the extent of it. But when [stories] would end, they used to say this, that it has ended, that it is going on its way toward where it is heading, becoming more accurate while on its way." Such endings are used less frequently today, but they are far from extinct.

Narrators also often use repetition to signal the beginning and end of a story or story section, as when Nick Andrew follows his description of the experiences of Neryull'er in the wilderness declaring, "He had evidently become a shaman," words he repeats at the end of the story. Words or phrases may also be repeated within a story, as when Frances Usugan says repeatedly, "Ravens are naughty," or when Raphael Jimmy intones, "Going out, going out, going out," to emphasize the shaman's slow exit from the *qasgi* in his story, "One Who Stole Spirit Helpers." Stephanie Nayagniq uses both repetition and a shrill voice to dramatize the older sister's reaction to the beetle—"Throw it! Throw it!"—drawing appreciative laughter from her audience. Repetition is true of Yup'ik oratory generally, giving it a denser feel than casual conversation, and both Alice and Marie have carefully retained it in their translations.

Place names and the geographic locations of particular events are also important parts of many stories. In his introduction to the story "Sibling Brothers" told by Nunivak elder Andrew Noatak, Robert Drozda (2007:105) notes that the Nunivak stories he has heard or read in translation "are not only enriched by knowledge of Nunivak geography but have an actual physical component in the landscape." He continues: "There are many examples of this narrative/landscape bond within the corpus of Nuniwarmiut traditional stories. For instance, in the tale recounted below Andrew offers a number of place names that provide a geographic context to the story. This is not unusual in Yup'ik narratives, but in this Nunivak Island story we also have physical objects, both man-made and natural landforms, that have their locations as well as their origins explained to us. The final resting places of the story characters have been firmly and physically identified." The narrators of origin stories we have included in this volume also refer to particular places on Nelson Island, including the island itself, where Raven and his daughter left marks on the landscape recalling their activities in the distant past. Specific mountains, including Qasginguaq (a hilltop knob said to be the dwelling of *ircenrraat*) and Ing'errlugaat (the lava cones from which children lost underground were said to have reemerged), are also identified in a number of stories

In Yup'ik oral tradition, the spoken word was widely recognized as having the power to evoke that which it described. This power of speech was part of the reason people were admonished to be careful with their words, lest they injure another's mind. Conversely, compassionate speech could have real benefit to both the speaker and listener. In many tales, such as Magdalene Sunny's "Sparrow Story," the protagonist sings songs that produce hoped-for results, and the stories themselves had the potential to influence events. These stories were much more than recreation—they were indirect (and sometimes direct) instruction in proper living. In this sense they were important to hear repeatedly, regardless of how well-known they were.

These narratives remain powerful vehicles that promote a successful future as they recall the past. The men and women who told them were sharing their history, with their eyes firmly on the future. At the end of his story, Raphael Jimmy says rhetorically: "I wonder why I don't forget this one. I think it's because I tell it from time to time. . . . If we don't sing a song or we don't tell a story and a *quliraq*, we will lose it. But when we tell it like this, when we speak of it from time to time, we won't lose it." "The traditions of our ancestors," Raphael continued, "are something that one should be extremely sad to lose, as they can save a person who is feeling remorse or who is sorrowful. If listened to and followed, the *qaneryaraq* [words of advice, lit., 'that which is spoken'] has a good consequence, the *qaneryaraq* of our ancestors."

✌ *Ca Pitekluku Qanemcilallrat* ✊
Why Stories Were Told

The following pages provide background information on the stories, explaining ideas and expressions unfamiliar to non-Yup'ik and younger Yup'ik readers. I have also guided readers to similar stories other elders have told in previously published collections. I have not, however, attempted detailed interpretation or analysis. Within Yup'ik oral tradition, stories were not considered to have a single "moral." To understand a story, one must listen to it again and again. Each time one brings different experiences and takes away new meanings. This depth of meaning, many point out, is the mark of great literature worldwide.

Yup'ik scholar Elsie Mather compared analyzing oral literature to "opening up stories with a can opener," causing listeners to lose their sense of awe. Mather and others emphasize that much more is lost than gained by the scholarly tendency to overanalyze and explain. Elsie noted that she grew up listening to stories that she really did not understand. The value of the stories, she said, was in hearing them. That her parents and other village elders cared enough to tell her stories was more important than any particular moral or meaning the story might possess.

In part because of this reticence to analyze, we have presented these stories without interruption. Background material and information normally presented in footnotes or endnotes has been included in this introduction. The translated texts include some common Yup'ik words with complex meanings—such as *qasgi* (communal men's house) and *akutaq* (festive mixture of berries, fat, and boned fish)—which are defined on their first occurrence as well as included in a glossary at the book's end. Introductory remarks are intended to provide readers with a better understanding of the speakers' intentions without explaining their words away. Elders assumed their listeners possessed basic linguistic and cultural information, and this, rather than elaborate interpretation, is what this introduction provides.

Anthropologist Julie Cruikshank (1990:ix) observed that texts do not unambiguously speak for themselves. As noted, none are anonymous and all are shared with particular listeners in mind. To fully appreciate the stories that follow, readers will benefit from an understanding of the contexts in which they were told.

The stories that follow have much in common. Each was told in either Yup'ik or Cup'ig by a respected elder born in the early 1900s after change had come to southwest Alaska but while stories were still routinely told in *qasgit* and homes. All the stories were shared at the request of a younger community member (in most cases, men and women in their thirties or forties) so that they could be recorded. Nonetheless, each story was an intimate gift given to close friends and relatives.

Half of the stories that follow were recorded on Nelson Island in the 1980s as part of the Nelson Island Oral History Project. The Alaska Humanities Forum had given the Toksook Bay Traditional Council a small grant to pay for the project, including funds to pay elders and the men and women who worked with them. Interviewers for the project included Toksook Bay residents Ruth Jimmie, Cathy Moses, Marie Brite, and David Chanar (born and raised on Nelson Island but living in Anchorage). All are fluent speakers of the Yup'ik language and intensely interested in what the elders had to say. I was also part of the audience, manning the tape recorder. I had lived in Toksook in 1976 and 1977, trying to learn the Yup'ik language, and all of the elders knew me well. In 1985, I was back in Toksook for the summer with my three children.

During the Nelson Island project, all our conversations took place in the homes of particular elders. Along with visiting people we knew in Toksook, we traveled to nearby Nightmute and Chefornak to talk to elders, and we recorded dozens of hours of storytelling. No simultaneous translation took place. I could follow some of the conversation and asked some questions, but the elders' intended audience was people whom they knew fully understood what they were saying. Visits were usually an hour or so, and we visited some—Frances Usugan, Tim Agagtak, and Magdalene Sunny—again and again.

Four additional stories come from recordings that Eliza Orr made with women in Tununak—including her mother, Theresa Hooper—in 1976 as part of documentation work taking place in that community. Again, the women she worked with all knew her from childhood, and the recordings were eloquent, uninterrupted renditions of rarely heard stories. We are profoundly grateful for permission to include them.

Another half-dozen stories were recorded by Marie Meade and me, and more by Marie on her own, in preparation for the Yup'ik mask exhibit, *Agayuliyararput/ Our Way of Making Prayer,* which opened in Toksook Bay in January 1996. Again, we visited elders in their homes, where Marie prompted them to share what they knew. Marie had known some, like Dick Andrew of Bethel, all her life. She was meeting others, like Dick Anthony, for the first time. In all cases elders shared much more than we have included here.

Finally, six of the stories in this collection were recorded as part of elder gatherings and culture camps supported by the Calista Elders Council. In these cases, elders spoke among their peers, with young people listening as well. These include wonderful stories, both long, like the story of Atertayagaq told by John Phillip in the company of Roland Phillip and George Billy as well as CEC staff, and short, like the story of the caribou boy, told at the end of a June day to students gathered at CEC's Umkumiut Culture Camp. In the case of the story of Atertayagaq, we had invited John Phillip, Roland Phillip, and George Billy to Bethel specifically to share and discuss this story, which they had heard from Atertayagaq himself many years after his experiences. John Alirkar's story of caribou boy was one he chose to tell during one of the hour-long storytelling sessions that closed each day at Umkumiut.

I recorded the well-known story of the peopling of Nunivak Island from Jack Williams while he spoke to students at the newly opened Nelson Island High School in 1976. Although the first part of the story is well known, Jack Williams added several episodes that are rarely heard, which made us very much want to include his version of the story. When I made the recording, however, I was inexperienced and missed the beginning of Jack's story. Thanks to a recording Robert Drozda made with Jack telling the same story in his home in Mekoryuk in 1991, we have been able to share a fuller version. This is not an ideal solution, as in each case the audience was very different. Yet parts of the story that both Robert and I recorded are identical not always in phrasing but in content. Here, too, we are grateful to Robert for both his generosity and for his longtime interest in this story.

Although we cannot know beyond doubt, our experience tells us that when Yup'ik elders speak with a tape recorder running, they are aware that their stories will live beyond them and be shared with new audiences. Most view this as a good thing. Among Yup'ik people, sharing knowledge, like sharing food and friendship generally, is highly valued. Knowledge is not owned, and no one assumes proprietary rights over particular stories. On the contrary, elders like Raphael Jimmy express concern that stories are being forgotten.

Most of the stories that follow are old stories, rarely heard today. More than half—twenty of the thirty-six tales in this book—were told by women. Women's voices have always been strong, both in sharing and passing on Yup'ik oral traditions. CEC gatherings have always included women, especially in our early work concerning *qanruyutet* (oral instructions) (Fienup-Riordan 2005; Rearden, Meade, and Fienup-Riordan 2005). Since then, however, a number of topics we have documented have favored men's voices, including hunting, fishing, kayak building, traveling on the land and sea, and knowledge of sea ice and snow conditions (Andrew 2008; Fienup-Riordan 2007b; Fienup-Riordan and Rearden 2012). It is a great pleasure to present *qulirat* in which men's and women's voices can be heard side by side.

In what they said, both men and women were motivated by their desire to help Yup'ik young people live better lives. In speaking out, they were doing what their own elders had done for them. John Phillip (October 2010) noted, "This is what they used to tell me when I was young, 'You there, you dear boy, don't live without an elder. If you try to live without an elder, you won't live a good life.' . . . Our future generations, although we are gone, if they heard that instruction, we will help them. A person won't die although he passed on; if his instruction is there, that person is alive."

∼ *Ciuliaqatuut* ∽
First Ancestors

Southwest Alaska has never been rich in the commercial resources—sea otters, gold, whales—that have drawn non-Natives to other parts of the state. What the region lacks, however, is more than made up for in access to abundant food resources. The land and sea were in the past and continue today to be rich in animals and plants, including seals, walrus, fish, birds, and berries gathered during the annual harvesting cycle. Men hunt for bearded seals, spotted seals, ringed seals, and walrus from the shorefast ice, beginning in March or early April. By May, geese and ducks crowd the flyways, returning to their summer nesting grounds. In June, many families move to fish camps, where men set nets for herring, salmon, flounder, and whitefish that women dry for winter use. Even children fill baskets with the kelp laden with herring eggs and the tiny capelin that wash up during high tides. Women gather greens close to home, or they camp on the tundra with their families for days at a time to gather eggs and berries. Fishing and trapping continue into late fall, when people return to their winter villages where harvesting activities are more circumscribed. Before the 1800s, this abundance supported the densest regional population in Alaska, and some scholars have called the Bering Sea coast the "cradle of Eskimo civilization."

Yet animals in southwest Alaska are more than food for the table. The relationship between men and women and the animals they hunt and harvest is of central importance. Animals are not mere resources but co-inhabitants in a sentient universe viewed as responsive to human thought, word, and deed. This includes animals of every size and shape, from the tiny water beetle to formidable beluga whales and walrus. For thousands of years, relations between humans and animals of all kinds have been the stuff of stories, and the following pages are filled with tales of their interactions. Moreover, animals play many different roles in stories, sometimes acting with compassion and sometimes not.

One of the first animals children might have heard about was the clever trickster Raven, both the crafty beach scavenger and creator of their homeland. Dennis Panruk, Frances Usugan, and Magdalene Sunny relate a series of *qulingssaat* (short *qulirat*) about Tulukaruller (the mischievous Raven), traveling along the shore and sometimes, but not always, outsmarting those he meets. These stories are well known along the Bering Sea coast, and over the years versions have been recorded from a number of narrators, including Frank Andrew (2008:406–419) of Kwigillingok, Andy Charlie (Orr et al. 1997:258–271) and Theresa Hooper (Orr and Orr 1995:78–99) of Tununak, Mary Worm (1986:46–58) of Kongiganak, and Marie Wassilie (1978:99–101). Three versions were also recorded on Nunivak Island in the 1930s, one by Hans Himmelheber (Fienup-Riordan, ed. 2000:50–54) and two by Margaret Lantis (1946:297–300).

Both Frances Usugan and Dennis Panruk tell a sequence of five short raven stories, full of songs and lively dialogue. The first is the story of Raven's encounter with Sea Anemone, who grabs him by the foot as he is walking along the shore. Pleading for his release, Raven offers Sea Anemone various things belonging to his maternal uncle, including a kayak, a seal-gut parka, and his uncle's wife. When Sea Anemone finally releases him, Raven taunts him, saying he has no maternal uncle and grew from a pit in the ground. In some versions, such as Frank Andrew's (2008:409), Raven kills the gullible creature with a stick before continuing on his way.

Raven then meets Squirrel, blocking her path and preventing her from entering her den. Squirrel, however, sings a song, and while Raven dances, she quickly slips inside. In the third story, Raven taunts two small birds trying to start a fire—two redpolls in Frances Usugan's version and a redpoll and a chickadee in Dennis Panruk's. Raven next encounters a mother owl singing to her fledglings, who fly away when he sings to them in turn. Finally, Raven comes upon a whale—a beluga in some versions and a bowhead whale in others. When the whale opens its mouth, Raven flies inside where his actions cause the animal's death. Men find the beached whale and begin to butcher it, but once again, the wily Raven deceives them, stealing all the meat and keeping it for himself.

The order of these stories varies, although narrators usually begin with Raven's encounter with Sea Anemone and end with the story of Raven and the whale. Andy Charlie (Orr et al. 1997:258–271) told only this last story, adding the story of how Raven then married Mink, with whom he shared the meat. Andy Charlie's version is an interesting variation on the story "The Raven, the Whale, and the Mink," recorded by Edward Nelson (1899:464–467) more than one hundred years earlier, and Mary Worm's (1986:46–58) account, "The Crow and the Mink." In her version, "The Lying Raven," Theresa Hooper (Orr and Orr 1995:78–99), also of Tununak, omitted this last story of Raven and the whale but included another short story of Raven meeting men while they were cutting up caribou and tricking them into leaving him all their meat. In her version in this volume, Magdalene Sunny relates only the first two stories of the sequence, referring to Raven enigmatically as *yun'engqurraurluq* (a poor young lad). These stories are probably very old, and divergence through time is not surprising.

In their notes for Theresa Hooper's story, Eliza and Ben Orr (1995:364) point out that punning and word play are characteristic features of these short, memorable

Raven stories. Indeed, both Frances Usugan and Dennis Panruk chuckled throughout their narrations. Frances noted that Raven is mischievous and naughty, and stories about him are meant to be a bit naughty as well, playing on the names of various body parts and bodily functions. The name for Sea Anemone—*teq*—also translates as "anus." In Frank Andrew's version (2008:411) Squirrel offers Raven different berries, but instead he wants to eat *qallitek* (the fatty muscles on her chest, i.e. her breasts). In the story of the two little birds lighting a fire, the name for redpoll, *puyiiq* sounds like *puyir-* (to be or make smoky). And both the little birds and owl fledglings taunt Raven with the same words, telling him to eat *uqrun* or *uqrutaq,* which can mean either "butt wipes" or "shelter, windbreak" (from *uqeq,* "lee side") (Andrew 2008:410–411; Orr and Orr 1995:364).

Although these short stories were often told to children and are, as Frances noted, "like comics," they were not simple fairy tales but quite adult in both language and content. Both men and women knew and told these stories. In them, the gluttonous Raven lies repeatedly, sometimes gaining his object—a free meal— but sometimes being scolded in return. In Dennis Panruk's version, the two small birds conclude by taunting Raven, telling him to eat bits of feces. The exploits of Raven the trickster were always entertaining and often left both storyteller and listener smiling.

Stories about Ciuliaqatuk, Raven the creator, have also been recorded, although less frequently (Himmelheber in Fienup-Riordan, ed. 2000:29; Fienup-Riordan 1983:373; Lantis 1946:313; Nelson 1899:452–462, 483–485; Orr et al. 1997:213–257). We include stories told by Paul John, Michael John of Newtok, and Simeon Agnus of Nightmute (Rearden and Fienup-Riordan 2011:2–13) in which they describe how Raven created Nelson Island and the origin of *uiteraq* (red ocher) at Qilengpak, on the cliffs above Tununak, where Raven's daughter was said to have stayed during her first menstruation. Paul John also recalled how Raven broke his ice pick while chopping ice at Cikuliullret (lit., "those that one chopped with an ice pick"; from *ciku,* "ice"). A story fragment recorded by the Eskimo Language Workshop in the 1970s describes what might have happened had Raven succeeded: "Down the [coast from Qilengpak] was a place where the [Raven] father was picking on the ice above Englullugaq [Engelullugarmiut]. They look just exactly like chipped ice. The father, by ice picking, was attempting to make a hole in the earth. He almost did it except that his ice pick broke. If he had made a hole, even though people die, they would have come out of death through there and not die" (Fienup-Riordan 1983:248, note 22). These named places remain evidence of Raven's role in the creation of Nelson Island. The stories were told to a large audience, including other elders and young people as well as several non-Natives, sitting on a beach during a boat trip around the island. The purpose of the trip was to document Yup'ik history, of which the activities of Ciuliaqatuk are an important part.

In 1897, Moravian missionary John Henry Kilbuck, then living in Bethel, recorded the story of how Raven, identified as Ernerculria (lit., "one in search of daylight") created Nelson Island as well as a variety of animals (Fienup-Riordan 1983:373). After his father, identified as the *yuk* (person) Spider, destroys his first wife, Raven leaves home, plunges into the water, walks on the bottom, and emerges on dry land, naked and without another living thing around. First he creates an image of a fish, which swims away. Raven continues filling the sea with living creatures and then makes a deer, which runs away on land. Traveling farther along, he reaches a river that he wants to cross, but the tide is flooding. Sitting down to wait, he falls asleep, waking only when the tide is flooding again. After this happens several times, he makes a mosquito, which begins to sting and bite him around the ears. The mosquito thus keeps him awake, enabling him to cross to the other side.[2]

Nelson (1899:452–462) recorded a series of stories of the creator bird from an Unaliq man living at "Kigiktauik" (Qikertaruk, east of St. Michael), noting the wide distribution of these tales. In fact, raven stories are told by Yup'ik and Iñupiaq people on both sides of the Bering Strait, throughout southwest Alaska, and among the Tlingit, Haida, Tsimshian, Bella Bella, and Kwakiutl of southeast Alaska and British Columbia. According to the Unaliq account, in the beginning there were no people on the earth-plane until Man was born from the pod of a beach pea. Then Raven approached, raising one of his wings and pushing back his beak like a mask, changing into a human. To feed Man, Raven flew off and created salmonberries and heatherberries (crowberries), followed by the creation of mountain sheep, tame and wild reindeer, sticklebacks (needlefish), grayling, blackfish, a shrew-mouse, various birds, salmon, then insects, and finally bear to scare Man so that he would not destroy everything Raven had created. Raven then created a woman, as well as other men, then various trees—birch, spruce, and cottonwood—and walrus, whales, and grampus (killer whales).

Because men continued to kill so many animals, Raven took away the sun, but Raven boy brought back the light. Nelson (1899:461, 483–485) wrote down several versions of this story, which Quinhagak elder Charlie Pleasant also knew. According to Charlie Pleasant (Tennant and Bitar 1981:179–181), Raven boasted in the *qasgi* that he would bring daylight to his people. He then traveled through the air on snowshoes. Arriving at a sod home, he shrank and was ingested by a woman when she drank water. She became pregnant, and when Raven was born, he continually pestered his parents to let him play with the bright bladders that contained the light. When his parents finally consented and gave him the bladders, Raven stole them and took them home, where he gave them to his own people.

My favorite Raven creation story is the account Nelson (1899:462) recorded at Qikertaruk of the origin of ordinary ravens: "[Raven-boy] came to a village where lived the children of the other men last born from the pea-vine. There he took a wife and lived a long time, having many children, all of whom became Raven people like himself and were able to fly over the earth, but they gradually lost their magic powers until finally they became ordinary ravens like the birds we see now on the tundras." To anyone who enjoys watching ravens, they are still extraordinary. Raphael Jimmy (December 2015) thought so, too. He told the story of a hunter from Nunam Iqua who shared his food with a raven. Later, the bird led him to a bearded seal. Ravens, he said, like humans, remember generous acts and repay in kind.

୬୨ *Nuniwam Cung'eqarraarutii* ୬ୠ
How Nunivak Came to Be Inhabited

Like stories of the mischievous Raven, the story Jack Williams tells is well known in Bering Sea coastal communities. The story is sometimes referred to as "Dog Husband," and versions have been recorded from Paul John (Fienup-Riordan 1983:236–238; Shield and Fienup-Riordan 2003:598–609), Marie Augustine (Tennant and Bitar 1981:252–255) of Alakanuk, the Nunivak woman Nussalar (Lantis 1946:267–268; Himmelheber in Fienup-Riordan, ed. 2000:35–37), and Robert Kolerok (Fienup-Riordan, ed. 2000:197–200), also of Nunivak. Edward Curtis (1930:78–79) also recorded the story, although he does not name his narrator. Jack Williams told the story many times, and Robert Drozda, Bill Sheppard, and I are all fortunate that he shared it with us. My recording, made in 1976, was incomplete, and it is only thanks to Robert Drozda and Bill Sheppard, who recorded Jack Williams telling the story in his home in 1991, that we can provide the translation that follows.

Paul John's rendition, "How Nunivak First Got Its People" (Shield and Fienup-Riordan 2003:598–609), told to students at the Nelson Island High School in 1977, describes how the daughter of a *nukalpiaq* (great hunter) refuses to listen to her father and marry one of the eligible men in her comunity. Instead, she takes her dog as a husband. Shamed by her behavior, her father travels with her by kayak to Nunivak Island, where the dog follows and finds her. There she gives birth to five puppies. Her father loves his grandchildren and regularly crosses Etolin Strait to visit them. The dog also swims back and forth from the island to the mainland to acquire food for his wife. On one such trip, the girl's father fills the dog's backpack with rocks, causing the dog to drown. The girl tells her children to attack and kill their grandfather in retribution, which they do. The mother and her puppy-children continue to live alone until one day she spies the puppies nipping at their muzzles and pulling off their dog skins, becoming young men. These men then obtain wives from Nelson Island and so populate Nunivak. Marie Augustine (Tennant and Bitar 1981:252–255) tells an abbreviated version of the story, emphasizing the girl's unwillingness to listen to her parents as the character flaw that sets the drama in motion.

Both Lantis and Himmelheber recorded the story from the same woman, Nussalar, and their versions are similar. In Lantis's rendition, the girl is originally from Hooper Bay, and she settles with her dog husband at Qimugglugpagmiut (lit., "People of the big, bad *qimugta* [dog]"), later moving to Ellikarrmiut (lit., "People of the *ellikarer* [whetstone]") when her family grows larger. The people of Nash Harbor, Lantis noted, are all descended from them, and in fact both older sites are referred to as Nash Harbor today (Drozda 1994:114, 116). Lantis (1946:314) also noted the seriousness of the story, dealing as it does with broken taboos and antisocial acts.

In most versions, the girl's father is the one who burdens the dog with the heavy poke that causes his death. According to Nussalar, however, other community members load the poke with rocks and cause the dog to drown, and the girl's revenge on her father is thus unwarranted. Nussalar's version also includes details that both Paul John and Marie Augustine omit. She ends her account with the mother becoming an old dog, while her children transform into human beings. These young men find a young woman from the southern part of Nunivak whom they take as their wife. The men have many children themselves, and these in turn find spouses on Nelson Island. Their descendants are the original inhabitants of Nunivak.

Robert Kolerok's version of the story, recorded by Marie Meade in February 1995 during her visit to Nunivak, is the most recent recording (Fienup-Riordan, ed. 2000:197–200). He placed the events of the story in Nash Harbor without mention of Qimugglugpagmiut. Kolerok's version also retains direct evidence of the story's important communicative function. As he made clear, he told his guest this story to help her understand that the dog, said by many mainlanders to be from Nunivak, was actually from Hooper Bay. He assumed rightly that Marie already knew the story, and he wanted to correct her understanding.

At the end of the story, Robert Kolerok noted that many people on Nunivak feel uncomfortable when mainlanders say that Nunivakers evolved from a dog. In giving Marie Meade an accurate account, he was trusting her to correct misinformation. Just as some Nunivakers feel that their Cup'ig language is viewed not just as different but as "aberrant" by mainland speakers of Central Yup'ik, some feel their ancestry is also considered suspect. While some contemporary Nuniwarmiut emphasize the distinction between themselves and mainland Yupiit, some resist what they interpret as a disparaging attribution of non-human ancestry.

Jack Williams's version of this story is by far the most detailed. It is, in fact, a single epic account with several "chapters" that others have told as separate stories. In the 1976 version, Jack Williams—like Paul John—was speaking to students at the newly opened Nelson Island High School in Toksook Bay, and switching between Yup'ik and Cup'ig for their benefit. He first explained that what he was sharing was a real *quliraq*, a true story about the two first inhabitants of Nunivak Island. He then recounted in great detail the story of the willful daughter who lived with her parents at Aternermiut, on Nelson Island (not Hooper Bay as in Robert Kolerok's and Nussalar's versions). He also described her marriage to the dog, her father's journey to Nunivak where he left his daughter alone, and the dog swimming across Etolin Strait to find his wife. There she becomes pregnant and bears five puppies. After their grandfather causes the dog's death, the woman tells the puppies to go to him and kill him. When the puppies do, in fact, confront their grandfather and tear him apart, she scolds them for heeding her. Whereas the woman had not listened to her parents and so married her dog, her puppy-children listened to their mother, who then criticized them for doing what she asked. According to Jack Williams's version, after this event the puppy-children no longer want to stay with their mother and travel to other parts of the island, leaving her alone.

All other versions of the story that I have heard end at this point, but Jack Williams's 1976 account includes a second important episode. After her puppy-children leave, the woman survives the winter alone with difficulty. Two brothers then arrive by kayak, and the younger one takes her home as his wife. From their actions, it is clear that they are other than human, and in fact, they are *ircenrraat* inhabiting hills near present-day Mekoryuk. She fully realizes this one day after they have moved to the old village of Nuqariillermiut and the woman goes to pick berries far back from the coast. There she is found by a man who had drifted away from the mainland near modern Quinhagak. When she tries to show him the village where she lives, she finds only mounds. Together, the Nelson Island woman and Quinhagak man then travel south past Ing'errlag, becoming the first two inhabitants of Nunivak. They create a large family. Moreover, the woman teaches her offspring to speak the language of the *ircenrraat* among whom she had lived, accounting for the distinctive character of the Cup'ig language. According to this version, Nunivak people are not descended from dogs but from this first couple.

In Jack Williams's 1991 version, he went further and recounted how two drifters from Hooper Bay also land on Nunivak west of Nash Harbor. The two travel around the island and come to a village of the children of the initial inhabitants of Nunivak. There the men settle down and find wives. Jack Williams concluded that the first inhabitants of Nunivak came from three places: Nelson Island, Hooper Bay, and Quinhagak. Finally he stated: "The first form of life on Nunivak Island was a dog. The second was a woman from Nelson Island. The third were drifters from Hooper Bay. The fourth was a drifter from Quinhagak. The three humans and a dog never attempted to return to their homes but settled on Nunivak as their new home."[3]

In 1976, Jack Williams told this story to students on Nelson Island in part to thank them for the hospitality residents had shown his two daughters who were then living in Toksook Bay. Again, in 1991, he shared the story with Robert Drozda and Bill Sheppard, both of whom he trusted and knew had a great interest in Nunivak history. While Jack Williams adds to our understanding of the story, the similarity of his narrative to other accounts is also striking. The first part of the story includes essentially the same series of events as those related by Nussalar, Robert Kolerok, Paul John, and other narrators. The narrative sequence is the same for both early and late twentieth-century versions. This is not surprising. As Himmelheber (Fienup-Riordan, ed. 2000:20) noted, Nunivakers "have very exact ideas as to each happening reported in their poetry." Indeed, Yup'ik and Cup'ig orators pay close attention to detail, and their oral tradition is extremely conservative. Yet, although narrators do not have the freedom to change the sequence of events, they can embellish this sequence with considerable effect, as in both Robert Kolerok's and Jack Williams's framing of their accounts to correct perceived misunderstandings of Nunivak history and the original peopling of Nunivak Island.

≈ Yuut, Ungungssit, Imarpigmiutaat-llu ≈ Humans and Animals

Raven was not the only animal immortalized in *qulingssaat* or *qulingssaaraat* (short *qulirat*). These tales are remembered by many elders today, who fondly recall falling asleep while listening to their parents and grandparents telling them stories. *Qulingssaat* are indeed fun to listen to, including numerous songs and exclamations of annoyance or surprise. These little gems are sometimes labeled children's stories, but listeners of all ages did and still do enjoy them.

While animals appear as animals in many *qulingssaat*, they often interact as people, as when, in Magdalene Sunny's story, the sparrow mother follows her husband and mourns his death, rejects two suitors—raven and crane—and finally accepts longspur as her new husband. In Martha Mann's story, muskrat and grebe are described as *qatngutkellriik*—two who share everything they possess, including their wives—explaining why they are often found together in ponds and lakes today. According to Dick Andrew, "The area where there are grebes never lacks muskrats, because they are related in that way" (Meade and Fienup-Riordan 1996:220).

John Alirkar's story of red fox and the white-fronted goose is also both humanized and used to explain how the world has come to be the way it is. In the story, red fox repeatedly chases a white-fronted goose but foolishly lets it escape while waiting for its meat to cool. When the white-fronted goose reaches a lake and swims to safety, the fox turns red from regret. He then rubs black charcoal on the backs of his ears and forelegs, improving his appearance. Olga Mute of Kongiganak (Tennant and Bitar 1981:150–151) knew and told the same story. Stories also describe the creation of certain animal species as, for example, the story Lantis (1946:290–291) recorded on the origin of beluga and killer whales.

In other *qulirat,* animals do not merely act as humans but appear in human form. For example, in John Alirkar's story of the caribou boy, a mother singing to her hungry child is approached by a caribou who appears to her as a sweaty young man. She hides him under her sled, sealing the sides with saliva (an act creating a protective barrier). Five wolves arrive, take off their hoods, and ask if she has seen anyone. She lies to them, saying that their quarry is just ahead. Their father is the next to arrive, and she sends him after his sons. Finally an old wolf arrives, takes off her hood, and reveals herself as an elderly woman. She also leaves singing, asking the others to save her some fat from the caribou's buttocks. The grateful caribou boy then emerges and, removing his arm from his parka, gives her some of his fat, telling her to cut it into pieces and sprinkle them in her ice fishing hole. She follows his advice and is rewarded with an abundance of fish.

In "One Who Speared a Human," Dick Anthony told the story of a seal hunter who encounters a human emerging from the ocean. He tries to flee, but the person repeatedly blocks his path. Finally he throws his harpoon at its chest, and the person disappears. Years later, the man's son encounters the same sea person, who returns his father's harpoon, causing the son to capsize and disappear. A young, apparently powerless girl eventually travels to the ocean, retrieving both the harpoon point and the man's son, whom she revives and takes as a husband.

In "Our Father Was Saved by a Dog," Martha Mann told how her father encounters a ghost that, like the sea person, will not let him pass. Seeing a beam of light, he follows it and finds a woman with a nosepiece, surrounded by sleeping children. He crawls in beside her and in the morning awakens to find himself lying beside a dog with many puppies. A streak across the dog's nose was the nosepiece he had seen on the woman's face the night before.

Tim Agagtak's story of Ayugutarin is well known on Nelson Island, with versions recorded from Sipary Chukfak of Nightmute (Fienup-Riordan 1983:238–239) and Simeon Agnus (Rearden and Fienup-Riordan 2011:64–71). Ayugutarin's wife sees a wolf gnawing on her husband's kayak, and Ayugutarin scolds him. Tim noted that this was long ago when people talked to animals. The wolf then places his paw on his mouth and lifts up his skin, removing his hood and revealing his human side. Ayugutarin invites his guest to stay with him. But his guest continually crunches bones when he eats, revealing his animal nature and causing Ayugutarin to lose his luck in hunting. Finally Ayugutarin makes a new kayak, painting a mink design on its gunwales, while his visitor paints a wolf on his kayak. When Ayugutarin looks away, his guest becomes a wolf and then a man. When his visitor quickly looks away, Ayugutarin transforms into a mink and swims away, returning with two bearded seals. At the story's end, the visitor fails to arrive at his usual time and is later seen towing his kayak inland, up toward the small mountains behind Umkumiut. When he reaches the top, he rolls around and becomes a wolf again before disappearing from view. Tim concluded: "Later they would say that the aspiring hunter of Pamalirugmiut [the home of the dead] down there had come and tried to take away Ayugutarin's wife, but he had not succeeded."

Many stories describe humans encountering animals in human form and learning from them, being cared for by them, and sometimes marrying them (e.g., Curtis 1930:91–92; Orr and Orr 1995:101–125). For example, Curtis (1930:80–82) told the Cup'ig story of five brothers whose sister was stolen. A flounder spirit guides them to her, and they escape riding on the flounder's back. The flounder then marries the sister, but he is not happy. Finally he tells her, "You have always thought of me as a human. Now watch me!" Both he and his kayak become flatter and flatter and then flop in the water and become a flounder.

Paul John (Shield and Fienup-Riordan 2003:29–120) told a number of such stories, including the well-known tale of the boy who traveled with the bladders and spent a year living among seals in their underwater home. There he perceived the different species of seals as different kinds of humans. Moreover, his seal mentor instructed him in how humans who act in lazy or careless ways are perceived by the seals they hunt. Versions of this story have also been told by Frank Andrew (2008:420–437), Thomas Chikigak (Rearden and Fienup-Riordan 2014:202–227), and Edward Curtis (1930:79–80).

This story is one of my favorites, as it says so much about the relationship between humans and animals and the parallel but closely related worlds in which they live.[4] As other versions are already in print, we have not included it here. Instead, we are sharing the story of Atertayagaq, who spent time living with seals and other sea mammals in a different way.

As a young man from the Canineq area, Atertayagaq floated away on ice, traveling south for three months before he was rescued and brought back to land. This event took place in the early 1900s, and John Phillip heard Atertayagaq himself tell his story in the village church in Kwigillingok years after his return. Among other things, the story highlights how Atertayagaq, although he was young and lacked experience, had paid attention to the qanruyutet (oral instructions) concerning ocean hunting. He had kept these instructions stored in his mind and, as a result, when he came upon obstacles, was able to survive (Fienup-Riordan and Rearden 2012:21–26).[5]

After he had been on the ice for over a month, Atertayagaq said, he became akin to the sea mammals. Once a small walrus approached him and seemed to be telling him something, but he couldn't understand what it was saying. When the walrus swam away, he followed it in his small kayak. Soon he spotted three kayakers ahead of him and a group of people on the ice. Thinking they were seal hunters from Quinhagak, he paddled toward them. Just as he was about to reach them, he looked to one side, and when he looked back, the people had transformed into walrus. Atertayagaq told his audience how much he regretted looking away. He said that if he had kept looking forward, he would have reached the walrus in human form. While the story of the boy who lived with the seals is old, Atertayagaq's experiences are relatively recent. Martha Mann's father's experience with the dog who appeared to him as a woman with a nosepiece is another recent example of an animal appearing as a human. All three stories describe a world in which animals can and do take on human form to instruct and protect people trying to live and survive in difficult circumstances.

❧ *Anuurluqelriik* ❧
Grandmother and Grandchild

Many old and well-loved Yup'ik and Cup'ig *qulirat* begin with a grandmother and grandchild living by themselves along a river. These *anuurluqelriik* (lit., "grandmother-related ones") include either a grandmother and grandson or grandmother and granddaughter. The term *tutgara'urlurqellriik* (lit., "grandchild-related ones," from *tutgar,* "grandchild") is also sometimes used. While the two live quietly, harvesting what they need, the grandmother admonishes her grandchild to avoid a certain area—the mouth of their river, a patch of tundra, a headwater lake. The grandchild heeds her grandmother until one day curiosity wins out or until the grandchild simply wanders off and ends up in the forbidden area. In most cases the young person undergoes hardship and lives to regret his or her actions. In this sense, the stories can be seen as sending the message, "Follow the rules or reap the consequences!" Yet in some cases, such as that described in "One Who Transformed into a Water Beetle," the grandchild uses her wits and in the end lives happily. These stories are much more than didactic tales. Breaking an admonishment sets up dramatic tension at the beginning of the story, and the plots that follow can be quite complex and intriguing to listeners, involving flights into different worlds where the grandchild encounters both dangerous and protective beings.

Both Elsie Tommy's and Lucy Inakak's stories are well-known *qulirat* describing disobedient grandsons and the consequences of their misdeeds. In Elsie's story, the grandson wanders to the mouth of the river, from which he is unable to return, even when he calls for his grandmother to help him. In Lucy's story, the grandson asks his grandmother to use her drum to change the rainy weather. The grandmother tells him to let her know when the weather begins to clear, but being entertained by what he sees, he lies to her three times and she continues to sing. After the third song, he finds their elevated cache has already burned. His grandmother quickly gives him a weasel skin, telling him to put it on and to dig in the ground. The fire singes their tails as the pair disappears, and today the tips of weasel tails are still dark.

Wassillie Evan's short *quliraq,* "The Little Needlefish," tells of a grandmother and her grandchild who are scared when they hear singing and so pack up all their belongings, including the paths around their home. When they are just about to make their escape, they see a small needlefish heading upriver singing, "Two over there, I wish I could eat them raw, cutting them down their middle." The grandmother uses her dipper to catch the mischievous fish, cuts it in half, eats it raw, and returns home. Unbelievable activities, like packing up one's paths, make this story fun to listen to and to try to imagine.

Stephanie Nayagniq told two very different stories, both employing the same formulaic beginning, with a grandmother and granddaughter living alone. In "One Who Transformed into a Water Beetle," the granddaughter disobeys her grandmother's admonishment never to travel upriver. When she reaches the river and tries to cross, she sees a large water beetle watching her closely. Traveling along, she finds the home of a young man, who takes her as his wife. This happy outcome is threatened when a woman in a cormorant parka visits her while her husband is away and forces her to change parkas with her. The exchange transforms the granddaughter into a beetle, with the former beetle taking her place as the young man's wife. Stephanie increased the story's drama by raising the pitch of her voice and emphasizing the reaction of the man's sisters when they discover their sister-in-law in beetle form. All ends well, and the beetle woman is thrown away.

Although this is the only long version of the story I have ever heard, a "beetle mask" and abbreviated story were collected by Otto William Geist in 1934 from Old Hamilton (Nunapiggluugaq) at the mouth of the Yukon River and subsequently sold to the University of Alaska Museum of the North. A photograph of the mask is published in *The Living Tradition of Yup'ik Masks: Agayuliyararput/Our Way of Making Prayer* (Fienup-Riordan 1996:248) along with the mask's story:

A beetle turned into a human being and wished to have a parka. She went to a village and entered one of the houses. The woman of the house was seated on the floor. The beetle wished to exchange her old skin for the woman's parka in order to get a husband. After the woman and the beetle had changed parkas the woman tried to walk, but her parka was too stiff, so she crawled on the floor. After a while she found that she had turned into a beetle. In the evening the woman crawled under the dripping oil lamp. When the oil dripped on her, the beetle's skin sprang open and the woman stepped out. She grabbed her own parka from the beetle and pushed her out of the house.

In 1996, this brief story—written down by Geist in English—was a rare find, as so few nineteenth- and early twentieth-century Yup'ik masks in museum collections today include any trace of the stories they embodied during the dancing in which they played such an important role. Stephanie Nayagniq's detailed narrative—told forty years after Geist collected the mask and in the village of Tununak, 100 miles south of Old Hamilton—indicates that this story was probably both old and widespread.

Stephanie Nayagniq also told the story of "Long Nails," in which a grandmother admonishes her granddaughter never to travel to the headwaters of their river. When the granddaughter does so, she finds a sod house, which she enters. The woman living there has long, scary copper nails and says to her knowingly, "Because you got tired of being obedient, you have broken your admonishment." The girl soon realizes that this woman is dangerous, and she makes her escape, leaping back over the river. When the old woman tries to follow her, she lands in the water and drowns. On reaching home, the grandmother announces, "You are so disobedient. Now walk around as much as you like. You no longer have an enemy."

Marie Meade heard versions of this story when she was growing up in Nunapitchuk, and she used it as the basis for *Cetugpak* (lit., "long nails"), the first Yup'ik story published in the new orthography by the Eskimo Language Workshop in the early 1970s. Marie remembered reading the story out loud in Yup'ik to her young students at the Nunapitchuk school. Natalie White of Nunapitchuk told a slightly different version of the story, transcribed and translated by Elsie Mather and Phyllis Morrow and published as "Yaqutgiarcaq and Her Family" (White, Mather, and Morrow 2007:729). Elsie had never heard the story before listening to Natalie White's version, although she had heard another story in which a fat woman chased two children who escaped over a river by clinging to a crane's legs. In her introduction to "Yaqutgiarcaq," Phyllis Morrow (2007:9) notes how reminiscent this story is of storyknife tales generally: "Storyknife tales often centered around young females who disobeyed their elders to explore forbidden places, particularly hills, which commonly turned into sod houses inhabited by supernatural beings (sometimes, as in this story, old women) from whom they escape."

Finally, Margaret Lantis (1946:293–297) recorded a long Cup'ig story cycle, "Two Little Birds," one episode of which describes how a tricky woman tries to capture and cook the heroine, Little Bird. In the Cup'ig story, the tricky woman's daughters have human fingernails all over their parkas. In another story episode, Little Bird races with the tricky woman and causes her to drown. Both episodes echo the granddaughter's experiences in Stephanie Nayagniq's story. The central character, Little Bird, also recalls the granddaughter in Natalie White's story, as Yaqutgiarcaq comes from the word *yaqulek* ("bird").

In her discussion, Lantis (1946:315) noted that this story cycle is a string of stories, each complete in itself, tied together only by the two characters, Little Bird and her daughter. She adds that on Nunivak these stories were well known but that she knew of no similar story cycle from southwest Alaska. Such cycles did, in fact, exist but have since broken apart into some of the short stories that continue to be told. Not only does Lantis's rare story cycle include reference to "Long Nails," but another episode has much in common with Magdalene Sunny's sparrow story, in which a mother sparrow loses her husband and seeks a replacement, refusing several suitors, including both ptarmigan and crane in Lantis's version and raven, crane, and longspur in Magdalene Sunny's account. In 2001, Frank Andrew shared another story cycle consisting of five episodes, including a variation on the tale, "One Who Became What He Saw," that Theresa Hooper (p. 266, this volume) tells as a separate story (Andrew and Rearden 2007:79).

❧ *Cat Paivngallratni* ❧
When Extraordinary Beings Were Present

What has always been formidable about the Yup'ik view of the world is that it includes so much more than meets the eye. Many understand the world as inhabited by a variety of persons, including human persons, nonhuman persons (animals), and extraordinary or other-than-human persons, such as *ircenrraat, cingssiiget* (small persons with pointed heads), and *inglugpayugaat* (ones who have one of something, from *inglu-*, "other one of a pair"). Appearances are often deceiving. A man encountered on the tundra might be an *ircenrraq* in human form. Wolf cubs playing in the grass might be *ircenrraat* in animal incarnation.

In the past, when the earth was thin (*nuna mamkitellrani*, from *nuna*, "land," and *mamkite-*, "to be thin, of a flat object"), encounters with unusual persons were said to be more common. According to Brentina Chanar (February 1991) of Toksook Bay:

> Kegluneq said that her grandmother used to say that long ago when the land was thin, things like that used to appear. . . .
>
> When it was thin and when it freezes, you know things going on top of it become resonant. You could also easily hear people walking outside. At that particular time, apparitions became numerous, what they call *carayiit* [lit., "terrible, fearsome things"]. So when the soil was thin skinned, those footsteps would wake them up.

Although nonhuman persons often have special traits, they are not considered to be supernatural but rather part of the world that may or may not be experienced. Many accounts describe encounters with such persons. Yup'ik parents continue to tell these stories so that young people will know how to act if they have such an experience.

Ircenrraat are perhaps the most commonly encountered extraordinary beings, and they are believed to possess a mixture of traits requiring special treatment. Like human and animal persons, they possess both mind and awareness and so merit careful treatment and respect. *Ircenrraat* are said to live underground and are still sometimes encountered. Stories of those who have visited them describe a world both like and unlike its human counterpart, where a year is experienced as a single day. Although sightings of *ircenrraat* are not as common as in the past, their tracks and footprints are still found, along with an occasional tool or piece of clothing. People also sometimes hear the singing, stamping, and thumping of *ircenrraat,* proof that they are still present in the land.[6]

Brentina Chanar (February 1991) stated that *ircenrraat* can appear as ordinary people. Although she had not seen them herself, she had heard their songs—proof of their reality. Others say they are small people, two to three feet high, and as early as 1899, Edward Nelson (1899:480) described them as dwarves. Occasionally a person encounters *ircenrraat* as *yuut* (people) and later sees them as wolves or foxes or other small mammals. At other times, humans encounter wolves or foxes who later reveal themselves to be *ircenrraat.*

Although *ircenrraat* can appear anywhere, they generally prefer hilly areas, including specific places like the hilltop knob known as Qasginguaq, about five miles northeast of Toksook Bay, which Frances Usugan mentions in her story. The name *Qasginguaq* translates as "place that looks like a *qasgi* or communal men's house," referring to the belief that the knob is the semi-subterranean home of *ircenrraat.* Frances tells how her older brother, Cyril Chanar, heard the songs of the *ircenrraat* while they were celebrating in their *qasgi* within Qasginguaq. They say that when one hears *ircenrraat* singing, that person learns their songs right away. So it was with Cyril, who brought back the songs he heard and taught them to his relatives and friends on Nelson Island, where they are sung to this day.

A person might also visit *ircenrraat* in their homes, where the human visitor could see his hosts as people. The visitor's ability to return to the human world depended on his reception. Frances Usugan told the story of a poor man who was taken into the world of the *ircenrraat*. At the time, he was wearing a patchwork parka made of the skins of a variety of small birds. When the *ircenrraat* asked about them, he said that different relatives had caught each one. Worried that their guest had a large family that would seek revenge if he was harmed, they decided to release him. Three doors led out of their underground *qasgi*, and he was instructed to exit through the middle door back to the earth's surface. Had he gone through the lower door, he would have remained underground, while the upper door would have taken him into the sky.

Some people say that if a person brings something back from the *ircenrraat*, such as a tool or piece of clothing, it will bring good luck. Possession of the hunting tool of an *ircenrraq*, for example, will make that person a better hunter. People may also acquire good fortune by exchanging something with an *ircenrraq*. Eddie Alexie of Togiak told the story of a man who killed a caribou and then fell asleep. Two people (who were actually *ircenrraat*) appeared to him and said that they wanted to trade for his catch. When he awoke, his caribou was gone, but the following spring he was able to catch beluga whales, which had avoided him in the past.

Many accounts of encounters with *ircenrraat* contain the implicit moral that if animals are treated poorly, their "persons" will call the offender to account. In "The Person Who Came upon Wolf Pups," Dick Andrew told the well-known story of a man's encounter with wolves (actually *ircenrraat*), one of whom he injures while trying to defend himself.[7] That night, he camps on the tundra, where two young men appear, saying that they have been sent to bring him to their settlement. There he sees the wolf that he had struck as a human. He heals the man and is tested by his hosts. When they finally release him through the middle door, he finds that the seasons have already changed. Although he had only stayed a single night with the *ircenrraat*, many months had actually passed.

Ircenrraat might also take the form of killer whales, and rules forbid hunting or injuring killer whales for that reason. Anyone who did so doomed an immediate family member to die. Frances Usugan told how people sometimes hear the noises of kayaks being launched close to Nuuget, the capes on the west side of Nelson Island, and soon see killer whales heading out to sea.

Ircenrraat are also believed to reveal people's futures. For example, Brentina Chanar (February 1991) told how her husband, Cyril, once saw lights coming down the hills toward Nunakauyaq (the present site of Toksook Bay), and sometimes people would hear roaring noises coming from the same direction. Brentina concluded: "Now Ski-Doos make light going across there and coming down from Nialruq. I used to suspect that [*ircenrraat*] revealed what was to be and roaring Ski-Doos approaching! . . . It was probably them, revealing what people will do, the coming generation."

Ircenrraat are not the only extraordinary beings people might encounter. Frances Usugan told the story of the deep trench created just outside the old village of Cakcaarmiut by *agiirrnguat* (lit., "those pretending to arrive"). Their slow progress toward the village is the result of a grandchild who ignores the admonition not to continually search her surroundings, anxious for someone's arrival. The advancing *agiirrnguat,* taking the form of old-style coffins making creaking noises and moving toward the village, are deflected by the powerful mind of the child's grandmother. Frances stated this lesson at the beginning of her story, and she repeated it at the end: "When something happened to people and there was a story about it, they told us not to engage in it."

Mary Napoka of Tuluksak described her experience as a young girl when she and her companion happened upon an old house pit, outside of which they found many clay pots turned upside down, as well as lamps, urine containers, and large wooden bowls. The girls played with them all night, viewing them as toys, and when morning came turned them over again and left them, thinking that they would play with them again. When they recalled their experiences much later, the pots and bowls were nowhere to be found. It was believed that if they had left them upright or "traded" for them, leaving something in exchange, the bowls would not have disappeared. To this day, it is generally believed that *ircenrraat* and others make things available to some people. Such gifts can bring wealth or healing power if received.

Mary Napoka also briefly mentioned *kalngat* (grass storage bags) with two legs which, once filled, would stand up and walk away, carrying their own load: "They say those [storage bags] are visible to [people] who they find to be bright. They are visible to people they like when they want to be visible." These days, Mary noted, they no longer do that.

Theresa Hooper's story of the one who became what he saw evokes some experiences with *ircenrraat*. In the story, a young hunter happens upon something that looks like a window, and he peeks inside. There he sees a couple, one of whom lies down, grows to an enormous size while he sleeps, has a log grow from his side and a muskrat run in and out of his ear, and finally returns to his normal size. When the young man gets up, he finds that his bow and arrows are pale and weathered, as he has been there a long time. As in other such encounters, on his way home he is able to cross a large river in a single leap. When he arrives, his mother greets him as one who has returned from the dead. He lies down and replicates everything he has seen, growing and shrinking exactly like the one he had watched.[8]

❧ *Tuunrat* ❧
Spirit Helpers

In the past, those who encountered *ircenrraat* or who underwent other unusual experiences often obtained the power to see, hear, and do things that their fellows could not. Some became *angalkut* (shamans), active mediators between the visible, everyday world and the unseen worlds of *ircenrraat* and others. As such, they traveled up to the moon as well as under the sea, to procure good weather and abundant harvests in the coming season. They did so with the aid of their *tuunrat* (spirit helpers), which often took the form of specific animals, as in Nick Andrew's story of Neryull'er.

One winter while Neryull'er travels toward his hunting camp, he happens upon martin tracks. As he follows them, they change into human footprints. Climbing a hill, he sees the martin enter what appears to be the window of a *qasgi*. Like the boy who became what he saw, Neryull'er lies down and looks through the window. Inside are people with different animal heads in front of them, including a man sitting beside a martin head. Neryull'er circles the place with his eyes. When he gets up, he finds that his clothing has already rotted and that it is summer. He returns home, crossing the Yukon River in two steps. After that experience, Neryull'er becomes a shaman and all the animals he has seen become his *tuunrat*.

As a shaman, Neryull'er drums, searching for fish for the Yukon River. One day, he says he has found a fat fish in the Nushagak River. Using his shaman powers and with the help of his *tuunrat*, Neryull'er travels to the Nushagak River, where he steals the fish—a king salmon—from two powerful shamans and returns with it to the Yukon. Although the two shamans try to retrieve it, they are unsuccessful, and to this day the Yukon River is known for its king salmon.

Nick Andrew's story focuses on the results of Neryull'er's journey but says little about how exactly he traveled and used his *tuunrat* to help him. Raphael Jimmy's story, "One Who Stole Spirit Powers from a Powerful Shaman," focuses on the journey itself. In Raphael's story, a *qelatuli* (a shaman who practiced divination) travels south to confront a more powerful shaman living beyond the village of Qissunaq. As he travels, he wears out six pairs of waterproof skin boots, emphasizing the length of his journey. He worries that he has no *tuunrat* to help him. On his way, however, two hard-to-obtain animals—first a weasel and then a peregrine falcon—allow him to take them and put them inside him, where they are invisible. He also finds a huge log that tapers to a thin point, which he slowly pushes into his ear. When he arrives at his destination, the powerful shaman does not recognize him. His guest challenges him, first letting the weasel out and telling people to try to kill it, which they do. The *qelatuli* takes it and places it by his side, telling his host to do the same. His host takes out a weasel and lets it loose, telling them to kill it, but it runs around and disappears. The same thing happens with the peregrine falcon, and when the host lets his falcon fly, it also disappears. The *qelatuli* then leaves the *qasgi* moving sideways through the entranceway (indicating travel between worlds), which he blocks with the log. Taking three steps, he arrives home. Sometime later, the powerful shaman finds his *tuunrat* have disappeared, stolen by the *qelatuli*.

Many but not all *tuunrat* are perceived in the form of a particular animal or plant, which then bestows its power on a human, who may use it to benefit or harm others. Many shamans were considered healers in the past. Those who were sick or in need would receive an *iinruq*, an amulet, often either an image or actual part of that animal or plant. Theresa Moses (August 1987:7) of Toksook Bay said that a shaman had given her wild celery as an *iinruq*. She could not eat the plant, and she said that she grew thin each year when wild celery withered and fatter again each spring when plants started to grow. A recurring element in many *qulirat* is the power of the part to recall the whole, as when the grandmother and her grandson used a weasel skin to become weasels. These transformations were no different in kind from the power inherent in *iinrut*, consisting of a piece of skin or bone (Lantis 1946:314; Fienup-Riordan 1994:201–202).

❧ *Ellat Allat* ❧
Other Worlds

In stories of *ircenrraat* and *tuunrat,* we begin to see the world as inclusive of much more than is immediately apparent. Hills may conceal the underground homes of *ircenrraat,* with exit ways potentially leading deep underground or into the sky. *Qulirat* reveal a view of the universe as one with many layers, with paths alternately opening and closing between them. Elsie Tommy's story of Pamalirugmiut is one such tale, a story she has never forgotten. The story is old, and a number of versions have been recorded, in both English and Yup'ik (Fienup-Riordan 1994: 4–10; Mather 1985:108–115; Morrow and Mather 1994:37–56; Nelson 1899:488–490; Orr et al. 1997:432–453).

Elsie stated what many believed to be true: When people die, they travel a path to another place. Many things might block this path, including inappropriate actions by their living relatives. In those days, when the earth was thin, only a few steps were believed to separate the world of the living and the dead—four for a man and five for a woman. Indeed, the numbers four and five recur in many *qulirat*—five puppies, five brothers, five stone doors, five somersaults—as well as in Yup'ik cosmology generally, recalling, among other things, the four corners and the center of the men's house, skylight, and ice hole to which libations were offered during various ceremonies.

Elsie Tommy's story tells of a young girl who dies and goes to Pamalirugmiut, the place of the dead. When her living relatives hold a feast, she and other dead ones return to join them. Gifts given to namesakes during the feast were believed to feed and clothe the dead as well, and relatives who did not share food caused their dead relatives to suffer and starve. At the close of the feast, the girl forgets her bowl and returns to retrieve it; she then finds that her companions have already disappeared. She is discovered in the *qasgi* entryway and taken to her parents, who are overjoyed to see her. They wash her and clothe her, and she stays with them. While there, she misses the food she had once enjoyed at Pamalirugmiut, but her mother cleverly cuts whitefish to resemble what she desires.

In most versions of the story of Pamalirugmiut, the young girl is said to have returned with her dead companions during the annual Feast for the Dead (known in some areas as Merr'aq, from *meq*, "water"), the public occasion on which people invited the human dead into their community and presented them with the food, water, and clothing they required. Men placed stakes at the gravesides to initiate the feast, signaling the dead to enter the village. People ritually cleansed the community in preparation for the arrival of the dead, and throughout the ceremony they carefully limited activities (such as sewing or chopping wood) that might injure the dead or cut their path as they entered the village. Elriq (the Great Feast for the Dead) was also intended to supply the dead through gift-giving to their living namesakes. It was, however, much more elaborate, requiring years of preparation and attracting hundreds of guests from villages near and far.

At the beginning of her story, Elsie Tommy also spoke briefly about ceremonies she witnessed when she was young, including the Bladder Festival and feasting generally. In the past, Yup'ik people enjoyed an elaborate ceremonial round, during which communication as well as movement between worlds were important parts.[9] The Bladder Festival (Nakaciuryaraq, lit., "way of doing something with bladders") marked the opening of the winter ceremonial season. At the time of the winter solstice, men inflated the bladders of seals and other animals killed that year and brought them into the *qasgi*. The bladders, believed to contain the animals' souls, were hung across the back wall, where they were feasted and treated as honored guests. At the festival's close, the bladders were deflated and pushed through a hole in the ice with hopes that the animals would return the following season.

In many places ceremonies preceded the Bladder Festival proper, including both Qaariitaaq and Aaniryaraq, mentioned in Martha Mann's story "Ones Who Went Beneath." Qaariitaaq was held after freeze-up. Men painted the faces of village children with white clay and charcoal designs and then, on three successive nights, sent them house to house receiving food from the women. Through this ritual circuit, the children opened the community to the spirit world and may have represented the spirits' gradual approach. Parents advised children not to remove the paint from their faces and, when they awoke with the paint worn off, assured them that Qaariitaaq had come in the night and licked them clean. Some communities held Aaniryaraq (lit., "process of providing with a mother") directly after Qaariitaaq. During Aaniryaraq, two older men, dressed in gut parkas and referred to as "mothers," led a group of boys, whom they referred to as their dogs, around the village. The men collected newly made bowls filled with *akutaq* from women—a partial reversal of the usual pattern of women bringing food to their men in the *qasgi*.

Martha Mann's story is also well-known (Fienup-Riordan 1994:273). She told how young children going inside homes during Qaariitaaq miss their path and travel beneath the ground. The last in their group is a young boy. As he tries to follow the others, a woman—later identified as a dead person—sitting just inside the house he has entered tells him to slowly back out, which he does. Once outside again, he blacks out and becomes aware in another village. His companions, who have gone ahead of him through the corner of the house, remain underground, and their parents continue to hear them crying from beneath them. The children finally emerge from the side of Ing'errlugaat, a group of lava cones north of Nelson Island. The door they came out of can be seen to this day.

Although the dead have their own home, they are believed to often travel among the living, usually invisible to the human eye. Sometimes, however, they are seen, as in Martha Mann's brief account of how her father saw the dead going to and returning from a feast. Just as the living give gifts to the dead, so the dead give gifts to the living, as when the dead woman presents the young boy participating in Qaariitaaq with a bearded-seal rib bone before he leaves her, a gift that becomes covered with meat and allows him to survive many years later during a time of famine, as she has predicted.

Magdalene Sunny's story of the woman with long hair also portrays a human traveling into another dimension and acquiring a unique perspective on the world from which he came. In the story, the youngest of five brothers is being towed in his kayak when a woman with long hair and a red complexion comes up out of the water and breaks his tow line, taking the young man to a place he does not recognize. There she brings him into a home to meet her parents, who also have red complexions. He becomes the woman's husband and stays with them until one day he follows a caribou up a mountain that his father-in-law has warned him never to climb. From there, he recognizes his old home and instantly becomes homesick. When he returns to his in-laws, he says that he wants to visit his family and bring his new wife with him. His father-in-law warns him that he will not be able to return with his new wife, but the young man insists. As he and his wife approach the village, the people there perceive them as flames and send a man down to the shore to perform an incantation, blowing toward them and stopping their forward movement. The young man finally gives up and returns to his wife's family. Magdalene concluded: "Those with long hair are offspring of *itqiirpiit*, the reddish people. They say other people who see them for the first time see them as a flame with a dark thing along their center."

Others describe *itqiirpak* (lit., "big hand") as having mouths on each fingertip; it is said to rise from the ocean as a huge, red ball of light (John Phillip and Neva Rivers in Fienup-Riordan and Rearden 2012:71). In some stories, *itgiirpak* comes out of the ocean and enters a *qasgi*, devouring a group of rowdy children. The parents then lure it back into the *qasgi* and destroy it. Its mate, however, survives and is sometimes seen emerging from the ocean as a red ball of fire when someone is about to die.

While the activities of *ircenrraat* and other extraordinary beings often take place on the earth or just below its surface, much of the action in Dick Andrew's story of Qanikcaartuli takes place in an upper world. In his story, a grandmother admonishes her grandson not to go to a small tundra mound covered with berries. Eventually, however, he travels there. As he is picking berries, he sees the feet of a homely woman, wearing snowshoes in summer, who slides the unlucky young man inside her pike-skin garment, spins around, and lifts off the ground. First they arrive at the center of the universe and then at her small house, where she keeps him captive.

One day while she is gone, a woman with one eye peeks in, saying she will help him escape, which she does, pulling him up through the skylight using a harness. Once outside, she dusts him off and has him do five somersaults, acts intended to purify him. She then spins around and carries him off to her home. Five days later, the pair hear someone banging on the house, accusing Iingaqruaq (from *ii*, "eye" or *iingaq*, "eye-ball") of stealing her husband and calling for his return. Instead, Iingaqruaq goes out and turns her into a pile of bones.

The young man later returns to his grandmother by following a path that leads him past the homes of three sisters, each of whom he cares for following Iingaqruaq's instructions. Finally he reaches a huge spider sitting by a hole who descends with him to the world he once knew. There he finds his grandmother dead, and in despair, he dives into the river and becomes a grebe.

Michael John of Newtok (Tennant and Bitar 1981:190–213) told a version of this story in which the young man's rescuer, Kanikchar, cannot enter the house to save him, as he is in a tomb. Mike Angaiak of Tununak (Orr and Orr 1995:211) also told this story, in which the boy's rescuers are identified as Qanikcaarculi and her younger sister, who use a harness to remove him from the grave where he is held captive. Ben and Eliza Orr (1995:372) noted that the boy's captor is said to be a bear in other versions of the story, revealed as such by her bad temper and rough behavior. Dick Andrew identified the boy's captor, not rescuer, as Qanikcaartuli and gives no indication that she is actually a bear, yet in other respects the story's trajectory and movement between worlds remain the same.

A striking feature of this story is that, like the story of the woman who transformed into a water beetle, we have some evidence that at least one mask may have been made depicting Qanikcaartuli. In 1924, Knud Rasmussen commissioned a group of Nunivak men whom he had met in Nome during the last leg of the Fifth Thule Expedition to make masks for him, which they did. The following year, St. Michael trader Paul Ivanoff shipped twenty-eight masks to Copenhagen, where they remain today in the collection of the Danish National Museum. Among the masks is one designated the legendary creature "Husband Seeker." In descriptive notes regarding the mask, Ivanoff wrote: "After getting for her husband [she] kills them and uses them for mattresses. . . . This usually have men cautious about women" (Sonne 1988:144). This short, suggestive description recalls the human bones that the young man found under his sleeping mat, remnants of Qanikcaartuli's previous husbands.

We know from work with Yup'ik elders in the 1990s how masks were made and used in dances to tell stories. These stories often involved special events in people's lives, including extraordinary encounters with animals and other-than-human creatures (Fienup-Riordan 1996:101–122). What is becoming clear is that masks were also made and used in performances portraying older, well-known *qulirat,* like both the story of Qanikcaartuli and the story of the woman who was transformed into a water beetle.

Qulirat, as we know, include many songs. In the past, elders have described how some dance songs—especially the slow, old-style dances performed by women during the fall festival Ingula—were songs from *qulirat.* But masks were not used during the performance of Ingula dances. Until now, we have had nothing to indicate the connection between *qulirat* and dancing with masks. The fragments of information that help us connect particular *qulirat* and particular masks are precious indeed. Thousands of masks in museums today were collected without their stories, so that the connection between *qulirat* and masked dancing was almost lost. Thanks to storytellers like Dick Andrew and Stephanie Nayagniq, we have a hint at how important this connection may have been.

✌ *Ungungssit Imarpigmiutaat-llu Akinautullrat* ↜
Animals Reciprocate

What of the day-to-day understandings of relations between humans and animals that a Yup'ik listener would bring to the stories elders share? Along with listening to the stories themselves, it is important to consider how people were taught to interact with animals in their daily lives. In "Care of Fish and Food," Joshua Phillip stressed what is "first and most important"—to take good care of the fish and food that will provide strength in the future. Food should never be left laying around: *Uqlautevkenaku* (One should not make a mess of it). To do so will cause people to lose their ability to catch animals. Joshua Phillip emphasized that the availability of fish and food depends on the care it is given. A husband becomes poor at catching fish if his wife does not take care of them. Conversely, a woman who treats fish with care and respect will cause her husband's catch to increase. Joshua also noted the importance of a woman immediately processing her husband's catch. He was adamant: fish and food without anyone to work on it becomes scarce.

Joshua Phillip also underscored the importance of sharing food. He spoke of the instruction never to sell fish during a famine, when a desperate person would exchange his kayak for a single meal. Their subsequent bitterness would cause the greedy man to lose his luck, while one who gave without pay would start to catch more.

Elsie Tommy told the story of a woman who acts compassionately toward an animal, not a person, and in return is given the gift of everlasting life. While egg hunting on the tundra, she found the eggs of a common loon. The mother loon, however, landed in front of her and asked her to replace them, saying, "We do grieve for the loss of our children just like you do because we are aware and can feel no differently than you." In exchange, the mother loon offered her everlasting life for her and her offspring, which the woman gratefully accepted: "That person who was spoken to by a common loon had a long line of generations."

Just as compassion toward animals produces a positive response, injuring an animal can have disastrous consequences. Martha Mann told the story of the boy, Mancuaq, who strikes a swallow's nest, killing all the newly hatched chicks. Others tell him not to do so, as swallows are said to be sensitive. The boy responds that they are merely birds and not dangerous. Yet when he marries and has children of his own, they continually die: "One time he said that swallows were very powerful beings and should not be harmed." Esther Green (1976:45) of Bethel told the story of a poor boy transforming into a swallow so that he can find his own food, and she gave this as the origin of the admonition not to harm swallows, as they come from that little boy. Justina Mike (Meade and Fienup-Riordan 1996:45) of St. Marys reiterated the admonition never to bother swallows. She said that once a woman's son injured a swallow's wing, and the boy's mother talked to the bird, telling it that the boy wasn't aware of his actions and hadn't meant to hurt it, and asking it not to seek revenge. Justina concluded, "It appears they have ways of reciprocating." Every animal, they say, can reciprocate: If a person mistreats it, it will mistreat that person.

Elsie Tommy's account of those with healing hands describes another powerful and beneficial interaction between humans and animals that sometimes occurs when a person discovers insects during a tundra expedition looking for mouse food. Each fall, men and women scour the tundra for the well-stocked caches of tundra mice (actually voles) who are known to store the tasty and nutritious roots and tubers of a variety of plants. When uncovering a mouse cache, one may also find insects of various kinds. If one covers these insects with the hem of one's garment, then one's hands, palms up, the insects are said to enter the person's hands and bestow healing powers. Many know this to be true, both from stories they have heard as well as personal experiences.

Elsie described uncovering furry caterpillars in a mouse cache but finding them "creepy" and covering them back up, so missing the opportune moment. This happened to Elsie and her cousin twice, and their aunt remarked regretfully that had they accepted them, they would have had wonderful hands. Tiny as they are, insects are a fascinating example of how all animals are viewed as responsive to human thought and deed. Whereas maggots might consume food neglected by a lazy wife, with disastrous consequences for both the individual and the community, caterpillars can enter a pure body, bestowing extraordinary healing power.

Among the many *qanruyutet* that guide people's interactions with both humans and animals, the foremost admonition was for a person to act with compassion, sharing with and helping those in need. "Those who share," they say, "are given another day." Second, people were taught to control their own thoughts and feelings, avoiding private conflict and public confrontation. As they say, "Braid your anger in your hair so that it will not become loose." These two admonishments— to act with compassion and restraint—reflect neither selfless altruism nor passive acquiescence. Rather, both are a direct response to the Yup'ik understanding of the positive and negative powers of the human mind. To act with compassion elicits the gratitude of those one helps and brings the power of their minds to bear on one's future success. To act selfishly or in anger, as when a stingy man sells food during a famine, injures the minds of one's fellows and produces dangerous negative effects. This immediate and tangible reciprocity is at the core of Yup'ik social and emotional life (Fienup-Riordan 2005:43–77).

Andy Kinzy shared a personal story of how compassionate human relations impacted his relations with animals. Once, while traveling, he was weathered over in the village of Qissunaq. While there, he shared his provisions with an old man. Just before he left for home, the man asked him for three bullets, as he had none. Andy gave him a box-ful, and with tears in his eyes, the poor man said, "It's okay, it will be replaced." Indeed, as he traveled north, Andy killed a white fox sitting beside the trail and later found seven mink inside his fishtrap: "Then all during spring an animal would be available for me to catch every time I hunted. Perhaps the old man's mind was very strong when he said that the shells would be replaced."

In "The Mind's Power," Leo Moses (1999:81–88; Woodbury 1984b:65–69) reiterated the power of positive thinking. He told the story of an orphan who is walking along the shore, looking for meat and wishing that he could be like the Arctic loon, then finding meat by his mind's power: "Through the power of the mind, those who want to can wish to be like those who are successful. . . . But a person will only succeed in life if he lives correctly. . . . Only the mind will make a person continue on, only his will to follow those who are successful will bring him finally to his goal."

In southwest Alaska today, the admonition "Those who share are given another day" also applies to knowledge. Many tell old stories to provide tools for understanding the present, claiming legitimacy for Yup'ik views of the world as alternatives to Western interpretations. Paul John (April 2009) compared the effect of CEC's documentation efforts, including this book, to that of the election of President Obama. He said, "If white people see these books, they will think, 'These Yup'ik people evidently are knowledgeable and know how to take care of their own affairs through their traditional ways.' Like the African-American who has become president, our young people will be able to independently practice their way of living."

I have said before and I say again that in retelling these stories, both elders and translators are not just trying to say something but to *do* something. They know they possess a narrative tradition second to none, and they seek a future in which the Yup'ik view of the world will be both recognized and valued. Written words do not merely report the past but allow us to engage with it in the future. Ironically, sharing the stories, giving them away, enables us to keep them. This has always been true of oral traditions, and in this book, sharing continues in new ways.

Yugtun Igautellrit Kass'atun-llu Mumigtellrit

Yup'ik Transcription and Translation

The Central Alaskan Yup'ik language is spoken on the Bering Sea coast from Norton Sound to the Alaska Peninsula, as well as along the lower Yukon, Kuskokwim, and Nushagak rivers. It is one of four Yupik languages, all of which are closely related to the Inuit/Iñupiaq languages of the arctic coast of Alaska, northern Canada, and Greenland, although they are not mutually intelligible. Together, Inuit/Iñupiaq and Yupik constitute the Eskimo branch of the Eskimo-Aleut family of languages. No apostrophe is used when speaking of Yupik languages generally, but an apostrophe is used for Central Alaskan Yup'ik and its dialects.

There are five dialects of Central Yup'ik: Norton Sound, Hooper Bay/Chevak (Cup'ik), Nunivak Island (Cup'ig), Egegik, and General Central Yup'ik. All are mutually intelligible with some phonological and vocabulary differences (Jacobson 2012:35–46; Woodbury 1984a:49–63). With the exception of Cup'ig elder Jack Williams from Nunivak Island, all of the narrators in this book speak General Central Yup'ik. Cup'ig is considered the most divergent dialect of Central Yup'ik (Amos and Amos 2003).

The Central Yup'ik language remained unwritten until the end of the nineteenth century, when Russian Orthodox, Moravian, and Jesuit Catholic missionaries, working independently of one another but in consultation with Native converts, developed a variety of orthographies. The orthography used consistently throughout this book is the standard one developed between 1967 and 1972 at the University of Alaska Fairbanks and detailed in works published by the Alaska Native Language Center and others (Reed, Miyaoka, Jacobson, Afcan, and Krauss 1977; Miyaoka and Mather 1979; Jacobson 1995).

The standard orthography for Central Yup'ik represents the language with letters and letter combinations, each corresponding to a distinct sound as follows:

Consonants

	labials	apicals	front velars	back velars
stops	p	t c	k	q
voiced fricatives	v	l s/y	g (ug)	r (ur)
voiceless fricatives	vv	ll ss	gg (w)	rr
voiced nasals	m	n	ng	
voiceless nasals	m	n	ng	

Symbols in parentheses represent the sounds made with the lips rounded.

Vowels

	front		back
high	i		u
mid		e	
low		a	

The apostrophe indicates consonant gemination, or doubling (and serves several other less important functions). There are also conventions for undoubling the letters for voiceless fricatives under certain circumstances (Jacobson 1995:6–7). This standard orthography accurately represents the Yup'ik language in that a given word can be written in only one way and a given spelling can be pronounced in only one way. Note that certain predictable features of pronunciation, specifically automatic gemination and rhythmic length, are not explicitly shown in the spelling.

～ *Mumigtellrit* ～
Translation

As translators, Alice Rearden and Marie Meade offer distinctive strategies for bridging differences between Yup'ik and English without erasing them. For both, the goal has been a "natural-sounding," free translation, as opposed to either literal translation (at one extreme) or paraphrasing (at the other). Paraphrasing may communicate some of the sense of the original, but such interpretive translations modify the original to the point where the speaker's voice is alternately erased or transformed. Literal, word-for-word translation also falls short. At best, it is awkward, and at worst, it makes no sense. The narrator's choice of words is respected in this book, although translators may modify word order and sentence structure slightly to communicate original meaning. They do this in different ways.

Experienced translator Marie Meade, for example, is freer with English word choice, paragraphing, and paraphrasing in contrast to Alice Rearden, who retains a more literal word choice and style. This volume includes multiple versions of several well-known Raven stories, to help readers understand both variations in how these stories were told and the different ways in which the stories can be rendered into English.

Because their primary goal is communication, no translation in this book mechanically follows the structure of the original language. For example, Yup'ik word order is "English turned on its head," in which suffixes indicating tense, person, case, and other units of meaning are appended to verb and noun bases. Thus, the English phrase "my little boat" corresponds to the single Yup'ik word *angyacuarqa,* which consists of *angya-* "boat," plus *-cuar-* "little," plus *-qa* "my," so that the order of the parts within the Yup'ik word is "boat, little, my." In Yup'ik discourse, the object also typically precedes the verb. A literal translation might read "bucket/new one/to make/I." A more natural translation would employ typical English word order, that is, verb followed by object, and would read "I/ make/a new bucket." Thus translation involves a continuous process of reordering.

Other characteristics of Yup'ik oratory have been carefully retained. For example, redundancies and repetitions are important rhetorical devices in Yup'ik narrative. Narrators frequently restate important points, often phrased somewhat differently, at the beginning and end of a story, both to enhance memory and to add emphasis and depth. Use of repetition gives Yup'ik texts a denser texture than typical English phrasings, which careful attention in the translation can retain. Structured repetitions are characteristic of Yup'ik narrative art and vital to its structural integrity. To smooth them over or omit them would impoverish the translations.

Several grammatical features of the Yup'ik language pose potential problems for translators. First, relatively free word order characterizes the Yup'ik language. For example, the meaning of the English sentence "The man lost the dog" can only be conveyed by placing the words "man," "lost," and "dog" in this order. A Yup'ik speaker, however, can arrange the three words *angutem* ("man"), *tamallrua* ("s/he lost it"), and *qimugta* ("dog") in any of six possible word orders with no significant change in meaning. Nevertheless, word order is not totally irrelevant to interpreting Yup'ik sentences. Word order may be the only key to appropriate interpretation where the ending alone is insufficient. For example, the sentence *Arnam atra nallua* (literally, "woman//his/her name//s/he not knowing it") can mean either "The woman does not know his name" or "He does not know the woman's name." The same three words in a different word order, however, are less ambiguous. *Arnam nallua atra* is commonly taken to mean "The woman does not know his name." In contrast with other languages that have a free word order, the relative position of postbases inside a Yup'ik word is very rigid. Consequently, syntactic problems may occur in words that occur only in sentences in translation.

Translation is further complicated by the fact that the Yup'ik language does not specify gender in third-person endings. The listener is left to deduce gender from the context of the account. When a speaker describes women's tasks, we have translated the pronominal ending as "she," as that is the way an English speaker can best understand the speaker's intent. Conversely, pronominal endings are translated as "he" when the speaker is describing men's activities. In general discussions, we have used either "it" or "he," depending on the context. Readers should also know that Yup'ik orators sometimes mix singular and plural endings in a single oral "sentence," and we have retained these grammatical variations to reflect the complexity of the Yup'ik original.

Yup'ik verb tenses also differ from English tenses. Although some postbases place an action clearly in the future and others place action definitely in the past, a verb without one of these time-specific postbases may refer to an action that is happening in either the past or the present (Jacobson 1984:22). Accounts of events or customs that are no longer practiced in southwest Alaska have been translated in the past tense. Readers should also note that tense may vary within a paragraph, especially in discussions of *qanruyutet* (oral instructions) marked by the enclitic "-gguq," which can be translated "they said," "they say," or "it is said," depending on the context. Traditional *qanruyutet* that speakers indicate still apply are translated using the present tense.

Our narrators also frequently used nonspecific pronouns and phrases that are difficult for English readers to follow. For example, a storyteller may say "that one who told the story," rather than naming a specific person. Storytellers also often use phrases such as "he went down" or "he arrived" without specific places mentioned. Readers should note that the Yup'ik language has an elaborate set of demonstratives that situate listeners and that indicate relative placement of action and movement of people often very specifically without ever mentioning places directly. These include terms such as *pikavet* (toward the area up above), *piavet* (up the slope), and *kanavet* (down the slope, toward the area down below) as well as *uavet* (toward the mouth of a river, toward the door), to name but a few (Jacobson 2012:963–967). Demonstratives also distinguish between things upslope, downslope, etc., that require more than a single glance to be seen, things that can be seen fully in a single glance, and things that are obscured from view. Where necessary we have tried to clarify these phrases using brackets to indicate the narrator's intent. We have used parenthesis to designate passages where narrators themselves offer explanations important for the reader but not necessarily part of the story.

Many narrators attach the postbase "miut" (people of) to the name of a river or slough to designate the people living there, as in Kuigpagmiut (the people of the

Kuigpak [Yukon River]). The names of many villages also derive from the name of the river where they are located, for example, the village of Qissunamiut on the Qissunaq River. However, narrators may also use the name Qissunaq for the village itself, and in fact often do so. Other village names may be rendered with or without the "miut" ending. The maps that accompany this text show the most commonly used place name. The text, however, reflects what narrators actually said, designating the place with or without the "miut" ending.

Yup'ik oral rendering values close attention to detail and consistent retellings, and whatever their stylistic preferences, Alice and Marie continue to work in that tradition. As Yup'ik scholar Elsie Mather (1995:32) notes, "The most respected conveyers of Yup'ik knowledge are those who express things that listeners already know in artful or different ways, offering new expressions of the same."

✑ Igautellrit ✎
Transcription

As if translation from one language to another were not challenging enough, this book involves the movement from oral to written language. Our starting point is the verbal artistry of individual elders, but critical to understanding their words is the transfer of their voices onto the page. Through the 1970s, little attention was given to reflecting the dynamics and dramatic techniques of the performance, including the speakers' shifts in tone and rhythm. The oral origins of texts were all but hidden from view. Texts were routinely transcribed in paragraph form, as if the paragraph were the "natural" form of all speech.

Beginning in the 1980s, when so many basic tenets of anthropology were being scrutinized, the ubiquitous paragraph came under attack, especially in the work of Dell Hymes (1981) and fellow linguist Dennis Tedlock (1983). Together Tedlock and Hymes inspired a generation of linguists and anthropologists who have since adopted and adapted their insights in a variety of sociolinguistic transcription styles, igniting a veritable "renaissance" in the translation of Native American literature (Swann 1994:xxvii-i). Although neither Alice or Marie have chosen to employ the "short line" verse format favored by many translators, they use the prose format with a new sensitivity. In their work, paragraphs are no longer arbitrary groupings disconnected from the speaker's original oral performance but are distinguished by prominent line-initial particles like *tua-i-llu* ("so then"), by cohesion between contiguous lines, and by pauses between units. This is by no means a mechanical process, however, and different translators make different choices about what markers require a new paragraph.

As we think about both the limitations and power of translation to communicate meaning across cultural and linguistic boundaries, it is useful to recall that translation is not the endpoint of understanding, but the beginning (Becker 2000:18). Similarly the reader is invited to engage these translations and use them as starting points for understanding and respecting the profound differences between literary traditions that, in turn, make it possible for us to better understand ourselves.

FIRST ANCESTORS

❧ *There Are Many Stories* ❧

Dennis Panruk and David Chanar, Chefornak, December 1987

David Chanar: And we hear short *qulirat* [legends] about how ravens became black or how they got their designs and about how common loons got their designs. As you know, they have those kinds of stories.

Dennis Panruk: I do know various *qulirat* because long ago *qulirat* were the only things we heard in the evening.

They also used to tell stories about Raven; that's why they're smart today. [The story] about the time when he was walking around kicking sea anemones and one closed in on [his foot].

David Chanar: Yes.

Dennis Panruk: Long ago, those clever elderly men told *qulirat* to put people to sleep. When we would go to sleep, in the *qasgi* [communal men's house], we poor boys would pile our mittens on top of logs, on top of the floor boards since they had wooden headrests, and take our arms out of our shabby parkas and put our sleeves down and sleep. And we had no blankets.

And we never said that our sleeping mats were uncomfortable. It was an admonishment for us boys who were just starting out life not to sleep comfortably.

And we always tried to get up before our peers. [The ones being dragged out of their bedding] wouldn't get mad at all, they wouldn't do anything at all when we would get dragged in the morning. They even spilled elderly men's urine from containers on their heads. We wouldn't get mad at one another at all. All those people were given teachings.

One of [the boys] would cry. And when he was dragged, he would cry in front of the hole of the entrance passage.

The ones who could speak regarding their actions would say to them, "That poor one out there is once again [crying] like this since he is so disobedient."

CIULIAQATUUT

❧ *Qanemcit Amllertut* ❧

Panruk Cingurruk-llu, Cevv'arneq, December 1987

Cingurruk: Makunek-ll'-am quliraarnek niitelalriakut, qaillun makut iciw' tulukaruut waten tungurillratnek, wall' waten tua-i qaralingellratnek, makut-llu tunutellget qaill' qaralingellratnek. Iciw' qanemcingqelalriit tamakunek.

Panruk: Cat tua-i quliraat nallunricaaqanka ak'a avani kiingita atakumi niiskengaqellruamteki quliraat.

Tua-i tauna-ll'-am tua-i tulukaruk tua-i pitullrukiit; taumek maa-i usvitulriit. Terr'et kitengkaqluki ayagyaaqellermini quumkautellra.

Cingurruk: Ii-i.

Panruk: Akaar angulluarrallraat qavangcautekellruit quliraat. Waten tua-i inartaqamta, qasgimi wangkeurlumta maani tan'gaurlurni muragat qaingatnun, nacitet qaingatnun, akitengqelaata, aliumatput elliqerluki qalliqarrluki, atkull-raput-llu aliiqerluki, aliput elliqerluki inarrluta. Tua-i camek-llu uligmek caunata.

Camek asqialliqniluta-ll' acimtenek qanyuunata. Inerquutaqellruarput aya-kata'arni tan'gaurlurni asqigcaarluta inarcesqevkenata.

Ilamta call' ciungatni tupangnaqerrlainarluta. Qenqerrucugnaunateng, ca-yugnaunateng qamu'urtautaqamta unuakumi. Angullualleraat qurrutaitnek, teq'urritnek qamiqurritgun tuaten kuvuurluki. Qenqerrucugnaunata. Aler-quutengqerrluteng-am tamakut tamalkurmeng.

Iliit taugken tua-i qiaqtara'arluni. Qamurciuquni-ll', amiigem uani, kalvagyaram ciuqerrani qiaqtara'arluni.

Ukut pistekaita qanrulluki, "Ugnaurluq-am tua-i waten piuq ugaani niicugnaitem."

And sometimes we wouldn't remove our boots when we were about to go to bed. They told us that if we got dragged and they let us go, to quickly stand and run outside. And when we went outside, since they used to get up before the sun came up, and when we went outside, they told us to immediately look toward the ocean first thing.

And again, if we were woken up with [urine] being spilled on our heads, immediately when we woke, they told us to quickly get ready and go outside. We wouldn't do anything at all to the person who did that to us, and we wouldn't immediately start to loathe him either. But we had the desire, "I wish I could repay him now." That's the only thing we thought. And eventually we would repay him, we would repay them.

People didn't hate one another. They only wanted their fellow people to live righteously. They lived following a wonderful way of living. They didn't want their fellow person to head in the wrong direction but wanted him to live righteously.

The life that our forbearers lived was very joyful. It's because they really lived by having great love for one another and having close family ties. They encouraged their fellow people, not wanting them to head in the wrong direction.

But when some people didn't follow their instruction, [they would say,] "Be that way as you will come upon what you want to come upon as you are living."

It's because they saw everything that was in the future. And the following, and here there were few white people around at the time, some people would say, "These poor future generations will start to travel through the sky." I would think, "How will they travel through the sky without wings?" It so happens that we would come upon that today.

That's why that one named Puyulkuk, when he first saw an airplane, although he was an elderly man, he cried. He saw a person inside the airplane that was flying in the sky. That's the very first time he saw one; and he had become an elderly man. When he saw it outside, he apparently sat and cried.

Then one of them asked him why he cried. He said [he cried] with the thought of the time when they couldn't do that [fly] at all. That [airplane] brought his past to his mind, their instructions, the instructions they were given. And they didn't see these [airplanes]. He said when it suddenly came to mind, and he was overwhelmed, he let it out [cried].

David Chanar: So those people would say that they would eventually [travel through the sky]?

Dennis Panruk: They would say the younger generations would travel through the sky one day. When they'd say that and I heard it with my very own ears, I would think, "How will they travel through the sky not having wings?"

It so happens that they used to talk about the time they would indeed start traveling with airplanes. Those things that were not even fathomable in my mind, I

Kamilartevkenata-ll' iliini qavaqataamta. Qamu'urciuqumta, pegeskakut egmian nang'errluta anqercesqelluta. Ankumta-llu, erpailgan tupatullruameng, ankumta-llu imarpiim tungii egmian' takuyaasqelluku ciukluku.

Tuamtallu cali tuaten tupagcesciuqumta, qamiquput kuvluku, egmian call' mak'arutemcetun, egmian up'arrluta anesqelluta. Tauna pistevvut qaill' piyugnaunaku, uumikngarcugnaunaku-llu. Taugaam tua-i piyuumirluta, waten, "Akiyaqerlaku-tuq waniwa." Tuaten taugaam tua-i umyuarteqluta. Tua-i pivakarluku akiluku, akiaqluki.

Uumikutengssaarallrunritut. Ilateng taugaam elluarrluku ayaasqumaluku pillruit. Yuucirkaqegtaar aturluku pillruut. Ilateng iqlutun ayaasqumavkenak' elluarrluku taugaam ayaasqumaluku.

Augna kingunemta atullrat tua-i nunanirquq cakneq. Tua-i imna kenkuyutqapiar aturluku, ilakuyun aturluku pillruameng. Ilateng cingumaluk' iqlutun ayaasqumavkenaki.

Tua-i taugken tamana pisqutseng ilaita-am atunritaqatki-llu, "Tua-i tuaten ayuqi ayainanerpeni tekicukngan tekiciiqan."

Tangvatullruamegteggu augna ciunerkaq tamalkuan. Waten-ll'-am, kass'at-wa nauwa nurnalriit, ilait-am qanernaurtut, "Aa kinguliaurluut makut ellakun-am, ellakun ayalangarkaugut." Wiinga tua-i umyuarteqnaurtua, "Qaillun-mi-gguq yaqrunateng ellakun ayagaciqat?" Cunawa-m maa-i tekilluku tua-i.

Taumeg' imna Puyulkugmek at'lek tengssuutmek tangerqerraallermini angutngurteng'ermi qiallinilria. Iluani yuk tangerrluku ellakun ayalria tengssuun. Tua-i tangerqerraakacagarluni; angutngurrluni-llu. Ellami tua-i tangrrami aqumluni qiallinilria.

Tua-ll' iliita aptellinia ciin qiacianek. Tua-i-wa-gguq waten piyugnaitellrat umyuaqluku pill'. Augna kinguneni cayugarceskii aug'um, imna qaneryaraat, qaneryarallrat. Makunek-llu tangssuunateng. Wanteqaan-gguq tua-i arenqiapakaami antuq.

Cingurruk: Tuaten-qaa tua-i tamakut qanraqluteng tua-i pilarciqniluki?

Panruk: Kinguliat ellakun ayalangciqniluki. Wiinga tua-i ciutqapiaramkun piaqata umyuarteqnaurtua, "Qaillun-mi yaqrunateng ellakun ayagangciqat?"

Cunaw' maa-i tengssuutetgun-am ayagangllerkaat ilumun ellakun qanrutektullrullinikait. Wii umyuaqsugnaitkacagallrenka, qaill' yaqrunaki taugaam

would only wonder how they would start to travel through the sky without wings, thinking of birds.

Those [people] were amazing. When I would come upon a situation [they predicted], I would recognize it, when I would come upon this particular thing, I would recognize what I used to hear. And even today, I don't think I'll stop recognizing [the things they predicted].

I do know different kinds of short *qulirat*. I enjoyed some. The ones I enjoyed, I tried not to fall asleep listening to them. [*chuckles*]

I really enjoyed listening to those two. There is also [the story] of sisters, all females, that is also pretty long. And [the story] about Qayarrlugaq who was traveling along the ocean shore isn't very long. These are ones that I enjoyed.

And there is also [a story about] a village with a poor orphan. That one that I used to have fun listening to, but it's pretty long. Uilingiatarciqaq [One who searched for an older unmarried woman], about how a young *nukalpiaq* [great hunter] searched for a wife, one who the people of that village didn't know, an older unmarried woman; since these dear orphans knew things.

And [a story] about grandchildren who weren't weak when it was time to catch animals. These [stories] that gave me the desire to be strong, I still haven't forgotten them today. People didn't know that some people were capable.

And long ago that's apparently how they used to perceive people who had come to hunt in their area. Some people would [look at what he was wearing and] consider him worthless. But their *nukalpiat* [great hunters] wouldn't think he looked worthless because they understood what he was like by the clothes he was wearing. They could do nothing to him.

There are many stories [to tell], there are actually many, including *qulirat*.

✍ *Short Raven Legends* ✍

Dennis Panruk and David Chanar, Chefornak, December 1987

Dennis Panruk: I should tell the *quliraq* [legend]. It's a *quliraq*.
David Chanar: Yes.
Dennis Panruk: I'm going to tell an old *qulingssaaq* [short *quliraq*], a short *quliraq*.
Raven was walking along the ocean shore kicking sea anemones. When he would kick them, and they'd suddenly close, when they'd squirt water, he would watch them, amused.

Over along their end, he came upon a very small sea anemone smaller than those others there.

qaillun ellakun ayagayaurtellerkaat kiingan umyuaqurnaurqa, yaqulget um-yuaqluki.

Iillanarqellruliittangtua-i. Tua-iunatekitaqamkuelitaqaqluku, unatekitaqamku elitaqaqluku niitelalqa. Tua-i maa-i-ll' tua-i elitaqiunrirngaicugnarqelrianga.

Tua-i-w' piciatun qulingssaaraat nallunricaaqekenka. Ilait anglakluki. Angla-kek'nganka qavanrilkurrluki pitullrukenka. [ngelaq'ertuq]

Wiinga tua-i anglakek'acagallrukegka. Cali-ll' ukut alqaqelriit arnarrlainaat cali tua-i taukut takrarluteng-am cali. Cali-ll' taksiyaagpek'nani Qayarrlugaq imarpiim ceniikun cenirtellria. Anglakek'nganka maa-i makut.

Tuamtallu cali nunat elliraaraurlurmek ilalget. Tauna tua-i anglak'lalqa tua-i takrarluni taugaam tua-i. Uilingiatarciqaq, nukalpiartayagaq nulirkarcullra, nunat taukut nallukiitnek, uilingiatarmek; nallutaitelaameng makut elliraaraurluut.

Cali-ll' tutgara'urluut pinariaqateng cirliqvakayuunateng pitamek mat'umek. Tua-i makut maa-i piniryuumiutekluki pitullrenka, cali tua-i maa-i avauqsaunaki. Waten yuut taugaam nalluaqluki ilait piyugngallrat.

Akaar-llu cali tuaten pitullrulliniut makunek pissuryanek. Ilaita tangnerr-lukluku. Makut-am taugken nukalpiarita tangnerrluksugnaunaku akluikun taringluku. Qaillun pisciiganaku.

Qanengssiit amllertut, amllerrsaaqut, quliraat tuaten.

✍ *Tulukaruum Qulingssaari* ✎

Panruk Cingurruk-llu, Cevv'arneq, December 1987

Panruk: Quli'irqekumku. Qulirauguq.
Cingurruk: Ii-i.
Panruk: Qulingssaarmek tua-i akaartarrarmek, qulingssaarqatartua.

Tulukarug' una terr'et kitengkaqluki ayalria imarpiim ceniini. Tua-i-llu kitngi-gaqateng, tua-i quuqertaqameng, mermek agtallagaqata tua-i tangssugaqluki anglaniluni.

Ingna-wa iquatni, tekicartulliniuq, anarcuuksuayaaq taukuni mikelqurrauluni, tamakuni.

Then when he came upon it, when he kicked it, his leg suddenly entered and [Sea Anemone] closed in on it.

When it enclosed [his leg], he was pulling and straining but it couldn't come out.

My, oh my! As he was pulling and straining, beware, the water down there started to head up to shore.

When it started heading to shore, if the water came upon him and [Sea Anemone] didn't let him go, since he wouldn't be able to do anything, Raven had an idea.

When he had an idea, he sang. He said to [Sea Anemone], "Sea Anemone, Sea Anemone, let go of me, let go of me! And I will pay you with my maternal uncle's, my maternal uncle's other kayak."

Then Sea Anemone down there answered him, "Those, those, I don't want those, *narraan-ii!*" When he would name the kayak's equipment, [Sea Anemone] would decline them. Eventually, the water reached him.

Then when [the water] began to reach him, the water reached his legs. Right when [the water] reached them, he said to it, "Sea Anemone, Sea Anemone, let go of me, let go of me *raa-i!* And I will pay you with my dear uncle's, my uncle's other wife."

Then the one below him said, "Really?"

Since wily Raven is smart, [he said,] "Indeed, I'm not lying to you. If you let me go, I will go and get her now." And here he didn't know of a maternal uncle that he had.

It said to him, "Are you indeed not lying?"

"I'm not lying. If you let go of me, I will go and get her right now."

After a while when [Sea Anemone] suddenly opened up, he pulled his leg out. And just when his old parka's bottom edge had gotten wet, when the water just started reaching it, he headed up. When he went up [to the land] above [Sea Anemone] he saw a small pit in the ground that was old.

When he stood along its edge, he looked down [toward the water] at [Sea Anemone and said], "You poor Sea Anemone down there, I don't have a maternal uncle. I don't have anything. I have nothing. I grew from a pit in the ground. Here's where I grew." That one who said he had a maternal uncle [said that]. Then that Sea Anemone really started to spew water.

After watching for a while, he got tired and turned and left.

As he was going along, when he started to come upon something that was smoking a little up ahead, he saw Chickadee and Redpoll trying to start a fire with a fire drill.

He then crawled toward them. When he got to the other side of a clump of grass, while they were overwhelmed with smoke over there . . . although they would start a fire, it would go out.

Tua-i-llu tekicamiu kitngikii, kitngikiini irua itqerrluni quumkaulluku.

Quumkaucani angaqlaayaaqluni, cayaaqluni aug'arciiganani.

Aren, arenqia! Tua-i-am angaqlaanginanrani tuallitua mer' un'a tagyar-tunga'artuq.

Tagyartunga'arcan, mer'em tua-i tekiskani, pegtenrilkani, aren qaill' piscii-gaciiqngami, tulukaruk-am umyuangelliniluni.

Umyuangami atulliniuq. Pillinia, "Tiiq, Tiiq, pegesnga, pegesnga raa-i! Angama, angacarama, qayaan aipaanek nunulirniamken."

Tua-llu-gguq cam'um terr'em kiugaa, "Tamakut, tamakut qessakanka-aa, narraan-ii!" Tua-i aklui[nek] qayam piyaaqaqani, qessakaqluki. Kiituani tua-i mer'em tekitaa.

Tua-i-llu tekitenga'arcani, irug' imkuk mer'em engeleksagullukek. Engelek-saguteqertellukek pillinia, "Tiiq, Tiiq, pegesnga, pegesnga raa-i! Angama, anga-carama nulirran aipaanek nunulirniamken."

Tua-ll' camna nutaan atlia, "Ilumun-qaa?"
Aa, tulukarulkuk-am usvituami-llu [kiugaa], "Tua-i-w' ilumun iqluvkenak pikemken. Pegeskuvgnga waniwa aqvaciqaqa." Camek-wa tuaten nallulria angaminek.
Tua-i pilliniluku, "Tua-i-q' ilumun iqluvkenak?"
"Iqluvkenii-w' tua-i pilrianga. Pegeskuvnga aqvaciqaqa wanirpak."
Piuraqerluni cill'aqercan iruni amugluku. Atkullrain-llu tua-i man'a akuat mecungtengqanrakun, mer'em tekitengqanrakun, tagluni. Keluanun taggliniuq, teq'acillruar una ak'allauluni tua-i.

Ayumian ceniinun-am nang'ercami ketmun takuyalliniluku, "Teurluuq kacuuq, angaitua. Caitua. Piitua. Teq'ermek naullruunga. Waniwa tang nauvilqa." Imna-am angangqelleq. Mermek nutaan puy'illagalliniluni taun' teq.

Tua-i pilnguami ulurluku ayalliniluni, ayagturalliniluni.
Ayainanermini puyiksuaralriamek ing'umek tekicartuami pillinia, Cekpiipii-raankuk Puyitaaq-llu nucungnaqelriik keningnaqlutek.

Ayumian aurrlukek [aurrluni ullagak]. Tua-i can'guaraat amatiitnun elliami, yaa-i tua-i puyiukacagarlutek pillragni . . . ken'ngilaryaaqelriamek nipiaqlutek.

He said to them over there, *"Cek-pii-pii-pii-puyi!!* [sound chickadees and redpolls make]" Then he quickly hid. It would look around for him. It said to its partner, "Listen. Someone is taunting us."

After looking around, they would get to work again.

Then after a while, the other said, "Okay then." Their eyes were closed. It was because they were looking at that [firepit] down there. It said to its partner, "You should open your eyes and look around for a while."

While they were [starting the fire], on the other side of a clump of grass, Raven lifted his head. He taunted them over there and said to them, *"Cek-pii-pii-pii-pii!"*

Before he went out of view, the other said to him, "My, so it is you who have been taunting us, even though we haven't asked for it. Okay then, let's answer you, so don't suddenly hide and stay where you are."

Right then, his wily partner said to him over there, "Alongside a path, go and eat bits of feces!" When he attacked them, they flew off!

When they flew, when they flew, after looking at them for a while as they went, he left.

As he was going along, he heard something singing.

He became watchful and saw in the midst of grass a shorteared owl singing to her fledglings.

She had them stand alongside her, in front of her. [singing] *"Ayagumaar-ayagumaa. Ayagumaar-ayagumaa.* Flap your wings! Flap your wings! Your father, when he arrives, you will eat five parboiled [pieces of] blubber. *Ayagumaa. Ayagumaar-ayagumaa.* Flap your wings! Flap your wings!"

They started to flap their wings a little. When they started to flap their wings, wily Raven, letting them know he was there, approached them and said, "My goodness! You are singing to them in the wrong way!"

[She said,] "How?" She had five fledglings. "How?"

"Sing to them like this, '*Ayagum.*'" He had already learned her song. *"Ayagumaar-ayagumaa. Ayagumaar-ayagumaa.* Flap your wings! Flap your wings! Your father, when he arrives, you will eat five large mice. *Ayagumaa. Ayagumaar-ayagumaa.* Flap your wings! Flap your wings!"

Short-eared owl said to her fledglings quietly, "You here, now watch me. He's thinking of eating you. When I suddenly fly off, fly off after me."

[Raven said,] "Yes, okay now, sing to them like I did, like I just did." She sang, *"Ayagumaar-ayagumaa. Ayagumaar-ayagumaa.* Flap your wings! Flap your wings! Your father, when he arrives, you will eat five parboiled blubber [pieces]." When he quickly came over, they suddenly flew off. When she flew off, her fledglings quickly followed her and flew away.

Tua-i yaa-i yaaviaralliniag'-am, "Cek-pii-pii-pii-puyi!" Ip'arrluni-llu. Tua-i kiarcaaqnauraa. Aipani pillinia, "Kaaka. Cam imum piakuk."

Kiarcaaqerraarlutek allamek tua-i yagtaqlutek.

Tua-ll' tua-i pivakarluni aipaan pillinia, "Kitak." Qelemngalutek-am tua-i. Kan'a-w' tua-i tangviimegen'gu. Aipani pillinia, "Uilluten kiarqurluten piqaqina."

Piinanragni, can'guaraat amatiitgun tua-i tulukaruk qamiqulkucimauralliniuq. Yaavet nakuteklukek pilliniak, "Cek-pii-pii-pii-pii!"

Ip'arpailgan aipaan pillinia, "Aling elpet-am cunaw' picetaarutenrilengra-megnuk pilaqevkuk. Kitak' akiyaqernaamegten ip'artevkenak tuanteqaa."

Ayumian-am aipallriin taum yaaviallinia, "Tumyarat caniqerratnek ananek pukuviluvii!" Curukaryaaqngatek-llu tengvallaglutek!

Tengengamek tua-i, tengengagnek avavet tangvauraqarraarlukek ayalliniluni.

Ayainanermini cameg' imumek niitelliniluni atulriamek.

Maaten tua-i cumikluni pilliniuq can'get akuliitni keneqpatag' una irniaminek atuucilria.

Avavet tua-i mengleminun, ciuqerminun nangertevkarluki. [aturluni] "Aya-gumaar-ayagumaa. Ayagumaar-ayagumaa. Yaqiurci! Yaqiuklagci! Atasi ima-qaa, tekiskan imaq, aa-nerniartuci uullanek talliman-aak. Ayagumaa. Ayagumaar-aya-gumaa. Yaqiurci! Yaqiuklagci!"

Yaqiuksuaranga'artelliniluteng. Yaqiuksuaranga'arcata tulukarulkuum, elpe-kevkarluni ullagluki pillinii, "Arenqiapaa! Iqlutun atuutaten!"

[Piuq,] "Qaillun?" Tallimauluteng taukut irniari. "Qaillun?"

"Atam waten atuuski, 'Ayagum'" Ak'a-am tua-i yuarutii elitelliniluku. "Aya-gumaar-ayagumaa. Ayagumaar-ayagumaa. Yaqiurci! Yaqiuklagci! Atasi imaqaa tekiskan ima aa-nerniartuci ugenvagnek talliman-aak. Ayagumaa. Ayagumaar-ayagumaa. Yaqiurci! Yaqiuklagci!"

Keneqpatiim irniani pivguarallinii, "Ukuut, kitak' tua-i murilkellua pikici. Nernaluci piaci. Tengvallakuma maligarrlua tengkici."

"Yaa. Kitak' atuuski wangtun, aug'utun." Pillinia. Tua-i atulliniluni, "Aya-gumaar-ayagumaa. Ayagumaar-ayagumaa. Yaqiurci! Yaqiuklagci! Atasi ima-qaa tekiskan imaq' aanerniartuci uullanek tallimanaak." Taigarcaaqell', teng-vallalliniluteng. Tengvalliin irniarin maligarrluk' tenglliniluteng.

He watched them as they went since Raven had nothing to do. When he got tired of looking at them, Raven pulled away his neck but it got stiff. And his whiskers here suddenly started to face forward. When he had nothing to do, he left.

As he was going along, he came upon Squirrel's den. It was new.

[Squirrel's] den was new. Then he stood outside it and stayed there. His stomach became extremely hungry.

As he was there, Squirrel came into view, holding a bucket. It seemed she had large chest muscles [breasts]. Although he really wanted to eat her, he wanted to eat her since he was hungry.

When she suddenly came upon him, she said to him, "Hello, Caruata Piruata, move out of my way." Then wily Raven said to her, "I will not move out of your way!"

"Move out of my way and I will give you some blueberries from the corner of my bucket."

"I don't eat those kind!"

"Aa, move out of my way and I'll give you some nagoonberries from the corner of my bucket."

"I don't eat that kind!"

Although she offered those, he told her that he didn't eat that kind.

Then, since she knew his intentions, since he was coveting her, since he would eat her, she said to him, "Yes, okay, dance flamboyantly, moving from side to side, singing to yourself. You can eat me when I fall asleep."

When she said something about eating her, since he was starving, he immediately started to lean from side to side in front of her den, singing to himself. Gee how he had many songs to sing. "'*Lliken-ta-aa-aa-aa. 'Lliken-ta-aa-aa-aa. 'Lliken, 'lliken, 'liken. Cetek-aa-aa.*"

And Squirrel moved slightly forward [attempting to run inside her den].

Then Raven said to her, "What were you just about to do?"

"Thinking that you might trip and fall on that small thing there, I almost removed it. Aa, if you really lean sideways, if you really go from side to side, I will fall asleep."

He got more invigorated. Gee, since he coveted eating her, too.

"'*Lliken-ta-aa.*" He went faster! "'*Lliken-ta-aa. 'Lliken-ta-aa. 'Lliken, 'lliken, lliken. Cetek-aa-a.*" And that [Squirrel] suddenly ran inside.

When she ran inside, he quickly followed her, but only his head suddenly entered. He got caught on his shoulders. After digging the opening [of the den] for a while [Raven] . . .

When wily Squirrel entered, she removed her clothing until she was completely without clothes. She looked at Raven out there. And here [Raven] really wanted to eat her.

Tua-i avavet tangssulliniluk' caarkaiculliimi-am tulukaruk. Tangssulnguamiki uyaquni cayugyaaqaa eyuqautellinikii tulukaruum. Ukut-llu tua-i ungai ciutmuruariqerrluteng. Aren tua-i caarkaiculliimi ayalliniluni.

Ayainanermini Qanganaarrluaraam igtiinun tekitelliniluni. Nutarauluni tua-i. Nutarauluni taun' igtii. Ayumian tua-i elatiinun nang'errluni uitaqalliniluni. Tua-i anrutaraa-w' kaikacagangell'.

Uitainanrani tua-llu tua-i igvaryartulliniuq Qanganaarrluar, qaltaq-wa tegumiara. Tuarpiaq-gguq qallicitacia. Aren tua-i neryung'ermiu tua-i arenqianani, neryugyaaqluku kaigami.

Tekiarcamiu-am pillinia, "Waqaa, Caruata Piruata, aviteqernga." Tua-ll' tulukarulkuum-am pillinia, "Avicaalqarrngaitamken!"

"Aa tua-i aviteqernga qaltama waken kangiraanek curanek cikirniamken."

"Tamakutuussuitua!"
"Aa, kitak' aviteqernga waken qaltama kangiraanek puyuraarnek cikirniamken."
"Tamakutuussuitua!"
Aren tua-i-am piyaaqekiini tua-i tamakutussuitniluni pilliniluku.

Tua-i-ll', aren tua-i waniw' tua-i nallunrilamiu, aglumaluni piani, nerciqngani, tua-i pillinia, "Yaa. Kitak' tua-i kassengtaagaqaa, aviqumceta'arluten elpenek atuulluten. Qavaqaquma nerniarpenga."

Aren tuaten tua-i nerkunaqaan, kaigami-llu, ayumian imumek qav'iqtaarluni igtiin ciuqerrani pilliniluni, ellminek atuulluni. Yuarutkaminek-llut'anem paivngalilallinivaa. "'Lliken-ta-aa-aa-aa. 'Lliken-ta-aa-aa-aa. 'Lliken, 'lliken, 'lliken. Cetek-aa-aa."

Qanganaarrluar-llu taun' angayaaqerluni.

Tua-ll' Tulukaruum pillinia, "Waqaa cayarpiarcit?"

"Tamana-wa cayuggluyagaq paallauteknayukluku aug'aryarpiaqeka. Aa, qav'iqtaapassiyaagluten, qer'aqtaapassiyaagluten cakneq pikuvet, tua-i qava-qerciqua."

Tua-i ilungkanirtuq. Aren tua-i nernaluku-ll' aglumiimiu.

"'Lliken-ta-aa." Cukarikanirluni! "'Lliken-ta-aa. 'Lliken-ta-aa. 'Lliken, 'lliken, 'lliken. Cetek-aa-a." Itqerrluni-ll' augna.

Itqercan tua-i maligarcaaqekni qamiqurra taugaam una nallmikun itqerrluni. Tusgegminun naggluni. Painga tauna wani elagaqeryaaqerraarluku . . .

Qanganaarrluaralkuk im' itrami matareskili tua-i matkacagarluni. Tulukaruk uavet tangssugluku. Aa neryugyaaqluku-w' tua-i elliin arenqiacaaqekii.

He said to her back there, since she wouldn't head down [to him,] "You in there, you in there, give me your chest muscles, so that I can eat them!"

Clever Squirrel said to him out there, "Come inside now and come and eat them." [Raven] really would move around aggressively [to try to get in]. When he could do nothing, and since she wouldn't come out, he left her and went on his way.

As he was going along, he came upon a river. Beluga whales were down there breaching inside it. One of them was a very large beluga whale, a large one.

He immediately sat along the land above it, he sat along the edge of the water and said to all of them down there, "How incredible! Now breach with great force! And turn this way and open your mouths very wide so that you may look magnificent!"

The ones breaching started to [breach] with more force. He said to that very large beluga whale, "You down there, open your mouth very wide and breach with great might in front of me so that you may look magnificent!"

Then when it opened its mouth wide and breached forcefully, he aimed and went right inside its mouth. [*chuckles*]

When he quickly went inside, when he got inside there, he quickly went inside and there was an elderly woman back there who was working [sewing]. The roof boards of her home were curved, they were all curved. She was working.

When he ran inside, that one said to him, "Hello, Caruata Piruata, you've entered. How did you ever enter?"

"Trying to go inside, I have come inside now."

That one [said] to him, "Okay, then eat."

After a while, she gave him some small tomcod to eat. She gave him all small tomcod to eat.

He stayed there. She warned him, "Okay, I'm going to warn you now. Don't ever touch that one out there that is bright. If you touch it, you will [kill] us."

That wily Raven, when he got tired of being there, when she slept, he went to it and saw that her light was round. He took it and popped it.

And right when it popped, they were suddenly in the dark.

He stayed there. Then while he was there, that [thing he was inside of] started to move. When it started to move, the end of a semilunar knife appeared between its roof boards. There were people out there doing something, and even talking.

Then when he could fit through, when the semilunar knife was pulled out, when there was a large gap, he quickly went out through there and flew off. One of them spotted him for just a second. He landed beyond them, out of their view. While the people down there were butchering, he went to them.

Aa tua-i kiaviaraa, anelrarngailan-llu, "Qamyumaa-aa, qamyumaa-aa, qalliteg-ken taiyarkaak, nerniagkaa-aa!"

Aren qanganaarrluarallraam tua-i uavet pia, "Iterluten waniw' neryarturkek." Tua-i calekcagayaaqnaurtuq tua-i. Tua-i caarkaunringami, anngailan-llu unilluku tua-i ayalliniluni.

Ayainanermini kuigmeg' mat'umek tekitelliniluni. Cetuat-wa unkut iluani qaktaalriit. Iliit-wa taun' ceturpakayall'er, tua-i angtuaq tua-i.

Ayumian-am tua-i keluanun aqumluni, mer'em ceniinun aqumluni unaviallinii, "Alingnaq'! Cakneq at' qakervagaqluci! Ukatmun-llu cauluci aitarrluci cakneq ucurnaqvallaarnaurtuci!"

Qaktaallrit atam makut pikanilriit. Tamana tamaa-i ceturpall'er angtuaq pillinia, "Unsuuq aitarrluten cakneq qakervakaa wavet ciuqamnun, ucurnaq-vallaarniartuten!"

Tua-i-ll'-am tua-i imumek tua-i aitarrluni cakneq qakervallrani, uqliq'erluni-am qanranun itqertelliniluni. [ngelaq'ertuq]

Itqercami, iluanun qamavet tekiarcami, itqertelliniuq arnassagaq kiugna caliu-ralria. Enii-wa tang tua-i man'a qanai tua-i perluteng, perelriarrlainaat. Caliura-ll'.

Tua-ll'-am taum wani tua-i itqercan pillinia, "Waqaa, Caruata Piruata, iterpagcit. Qaillun-tam' itercit?"

"Tua-i-w' itengnaqlua-am waniw' itellrianga."

Aren tua-i taum wani [pia], "Kitak' neri."

Piuraqerluni imkunek iqalluayaarnek neqkitliniluku. Iqalluayaarrlainarnek tua-i neqkitliniluku.

Tua-i tamaantelliniluni. Inerqulliniluku, "Kitaki waniw' inerquqataramken. Angurrlugmek ugna tanqigcelnguq ugna agtuq'eryaqunaku. Tua-i agtuq'aquvgu wangkugnek piciqerpekuk."

Tua-i-am tulukarulkuk pilnguami, tamaantelnguungami, qavallrani ullagluku pillinia tua-i akagenqeggluni kenurraa. Teguluku-am qagertelliniluku.

Tua-i-ll' qagruciatun tua-i tayima tua-i, tan'germetqerlutek.

Tua-i uitaaqell' tayima. Tua-i-ll' piinanrani pektaagutenglliniluni tamana. Pektaagutengqertelluku uluam iqua tua-ll', tamakut qanain akuliitgun, tua-ll' puggliniluni. Qakemkut-wa qakma cauralriit, qanelkitarluteng tuaten.

Tua-i-ll' engelqayagucamiu, uluaq tauna amullrani, man'a callarpanga'arcan, tuaggun anqerrluni tengluni ayalliniluni. Taukut tua-i iliita tangssukarluku. Yaatiitnun mill'uni ipluki. Kana-i tua-i yuut kankut pilallratni ullalliniluki.

When he went to them, he said to them, "Hello, this here isn't something for you to [eat]. Didn't you just happen to see something while you were [butchering]?"

They said something, something quickly took off through its ribs. "My, I also just saw it. Don't try to [butcher it] and leave it. I won't ask for a share." He left them and went on his way. And when they went out of view, he stopped and would peek at them.

Then after a while, when they started to leave, since wily Raven is smart, when they left, he went down to that one they were butchering and ate until he was very full since he was hungry. [*chuckles*]

Since he was hungry, he ate until he was full and went behind it and lay in the sun with his mouth gaped open since he was very full.

It so happened, that wily Raven, when he got hungry, would immediately go down. He was the only one to eat that beluga whale alone. Being tricky, his intention was to eat it.

Then when it was finished, he left it. There is nothing else to say. Those who tell the story end it here.

❧ *Raven Legends* ☙

Frances Usugan and Cathy Moses, Toksook Bay, July 1985

Cathy Moses: Those black birds, do you call them something? *Tulukarut* [ravens]? *Tulukarutet?* Are there also stories about those?

Frances Usugan: I don't know. These ravens are naughty. Ravens are mischievous.

Cathy Moses: Are they *qulirat* [traditional tales]?

Frances Usugan: A *quliraq,* there is also a *quliraq* about Raven.

Cathy Moses: There is a story about it?

Frances Usugan: There is a real *quliraq* about Raven. Since I've forgotten the *qulirat,* this is how this raven story starts. I probably won't tell some of it.

A raven was walking along kicking sea anemones.

You know those *terr'et* [sea anemones, lit., "ass holes"], you've probably seen them down the coast, and they are quick to close up. They are along the ocean shore. I want to eat sea anemones. I want some. I want to eat sea anemones by cooking them.

During very low tide, Raven evidently walked along kicking sea anemones as he went. Then as he went along kicking sea anemones, a sea anemone closed in on his poor leg and wouldn't let go of it.

After the tide had been out, the tide came up.

These ravens are naughty.

Ulliimiki pillinii, "Waqaa, man'a tang tua-i elpeciingulriani piyunaicaaqell'. Waniwa-qaa camek tangerqanrituci piinanerpeceni?"

Augna-gguq, ca augna, tulimain ukut akuliitgun, ca augna ayagartuq. "Aren wiinga-ll' tangssugaqa. Pingnaqevkenaku uniciu. Wiinga tua-i aruqucetarngaitua." Unilluk' ayagluni. Ipcata-llu arulairluni tua-i paq'atararaqluki.

Tua-ll' piuraqerluteng ayangarcata, Tulukarulkuk usvituami, tayima tua-i ayiita ayumian atrarluni tamaavet amiillratnun tua-i nerrliniluni aqeskacagarluni, kaigami. [ngelaq'ertuq]

Kaigami tua-i, aqsingami keluanun tagluni macilliniluni, aitamyaggluni arenqialan aqsiami.

Cunawa-gguq im' Tulukarulkuk kaingaqami, tua-i egmianun atraraqluni. Neq-kautekluku taman' cetuaq elliin taugaam. Usvituluniami tua-i neqauteknaluku pilallinikii.

Tua-i-llu nangeng'an tua-i unitelliniluku. Tua-i qaneryararkartairullun'. Waken tua-i quli'irqestaita taq'laraat.

⤳ *Tulukaruum Qulirai* ⤴

Piyuuk Keggutailnguq-llu, Nunakauyaq, July 1985

Keggutailnguq: Tungulriit-qaa *bird*-at canek pituaci? Tulukarut? Tulukarutet? Tamakunek-llu-qaa qanemcitangqertuq?

Piyuuk: Naam. Tulukaruut-wa makut asriulriit. Asriugut tulukaruut.

Keggutailnguq: Qulirauluteng-qaa?

Piyuuk: Quli'irmek cali tulukarugmek quli'irtangqertuq.

Keggutailnguq: There is a story about it?

Piyuuk: Qulirapiaruluku taugaam tulukarugtangqertuq. Wiinga-wa tua-i qulirat nalluyagucamki waten man'a tulukaruk ayagnilalria. Ilii tayima pingaitellikeka.

Tulukaruk una terr'et kitengkaqluki ayaagalria.

Iciw' terr'et, un'gani tanglallilriaten-qaa quuqercukaarluteng. Cenami. Teryu-gyaaqua. Piyugyaaqua. Kenirluki teturyugyaaqua.

Waten envallrani Tulukaruk ayaagallinilria terr'et kitengkaqluki. Tua-i-ll' terr'et kitengkarpiirluki, terr'em imum quuqerrulluku, iru'urlua imna peggngaunaku.

Tua-i eningayaaqvigminek ulel'uni.
Asriugut makut tulukaruut.

After the tide had been out, when the tide came in, when he started to wade in water, when Raven started to become desperate when the water started to reach him, Raven sang, he went, "Sea Anemone, Sea Anemone, let go of me, let go of me. I will pay you with my maternal uncle's, my maternal uncle's other curved carving knife. Let go of me."

Then they pretended to have Sea Anemone reply to him. "Sea anemone, Sea Anemone, I won't let go of you."

Then he said again, "Sea Anemone, Sea Anemone, let go of me, let go of me. I'll pay you with my maternal uncle's, my dear maternal uncle's other kayak. Let go of me."

Then he would answer him in that way time and again, "Sea Anemone, Sea Anemone, I won't let go of you."

Then he named all of them, "Sea Anemone, Sea Anemone, let go of me."

It is said [the water] started to come up to a certain part of Raven. "Let go of me, let go of me. I will pay you with my maternal uncle's, my dear maternal uncle's other paddle. Let go of me."

Sea Anemone replied to him in the same way, "Sea Anemone, Sea Anemone, I will not let go of you." [chuckles]

Then he finished [naming] all his things. Since he was so desperate, he said again, "Sea Anemone, Sea Anemone, let go of me, let go of me. I will pay you with the other seal-gut rain garment of my maternal uncle, my dear maternal uncle. Let go of me."

Then the one down there said, "Will you not lie?"

Even though they are insignificant, they would have [animals and living things in] qulirat speak like people.

Then he was extremely happy [to be offered] his other seal-gut garment. That darn Raven would say that his maternal uncle had two of each belonging. These ravens are naughty.

Sea Anemone let him go, and he headed up and wrung out his clothes. What kind of clothing did he have? He wrung out his clothing and said to him down there, "You poor Sea Anemone down there, I don't have things, I don't have anything, I don't have a maternal uncle. I grew from a pit!" [laughter]

Ravens are naughty.

Proudly, [Raven] would say those things [to Sea Anemone]. What [Raven] was saying about his maternal uncle, he wasn't referring to him as one who was not respectable, but he would always refer to him as his dear uncle because he was a great hunter, a real person, and not someone who was needy.

Wringing his clothes, and being extremely annoying, he would say to it, "You poor Sea Anemone down there, I don't have things, I don't have anything, I don't have a maternal uncle. I grew from a pit in the ground." He pretended to have

Eningayaaqvigminek ulngan, ivrumangarcami, tua-ll' Tulukaruk nani-kuangarcami mer'em tekitenga'arcani, Tulukaruk tua-i atulliniuq, tua-i waten pilliniuq, "Tiiq, Tiiq, pegesnga, pegesnga. Angama, angama mellgaraan aipaanek nunulirniamken. Pegesnga."

Tua-llu termun-am kiunguartelluku. "Terr'em, Terr'em, pegcalqaarrngai-tamken."

Tua-i tuamtell' piuq, "Tiiq, Tiiq, pegesnga, pegesnga. Angama, angacarama qayaan aipaanek nunulirniamken. Pegesnga."

Tua-i-ll' tuaten kiugaqluku, "Terr'em, Terr'em pegcalqaarrngaitamken."

Tua-i-ll' qaqilluki tua-i, "Tiiq, Tiiq pegesnga."
Kiituani-gguq Tulukaruk natkiinguq. "Pegesnga, pegesnga. Angama, angaca-rama anguarutiin aipaanek nunulirniamken. Pegesnga."

Terr'em-am tuaten call' kiulliniluku, "Terr'em, Terr'em pegcalqaarrngaitam-ken." [*ngelaq'ertuq*]
Tua-i cakluarai qaqilluki. Arenqialami tua-i, tuamtell' tua-i, "Tiiq, Tiiq, pegesnga, pegesnga. Angama, angacarama imarnitegken aipaigkenek nunulirniamken. Pegesnga."

Tua-llu-gguq camna, "Tua-llu-qaa tua-i iqlungaituten?"
Tua-i caunrilengraata-ll' waten makucetun qannguavkaraqluki qulirat.

Tua-i-ll' qatngurluni imarnitegken aipaigkenek. Angani-am taun' cangqel-kugcequ'urluku malruinek tulukaruum. Tulukaruut makut asriugut.

Tua-i Terr'em peggluku tua-i tagluni ciuqcaarluki aturallrani. Tua-i camek aturangqerta? Aturallrani ciuqcaarluki-am kanavet [pia], "Teurluuq kacuuq, caitua, piitua, angaitua. Teq'ermek naullruunga!" [*ngel'artut*]

Tulukaruut asriugut.
Tua-i-am picuggluni tua-i tuaten piaqluku. Imna-am angani, angakeggne-ruvkenaku-ll', tua-i-w' nukalpiarullra, yupiarullra, kinguqsinritellra pitekluku angacaraminek piuralallrua.

Tuaten-am tua-i ciurturturluni tua-i, nekanarquq, pilallinikii, "Teurluuq ka-cuuq caitua, piitua, angaitua. Teq'ermek naullruunga." Caitkacaganguarluni. [*ngelaq'ertuq*] Tua-i ciurturraarluni ayagluni.

nothing at all. [*chuckles*] After wringing out his clothes, he left.

I'll probably mix up some of the parts [of the story].

✌ *Raven and Squirrel* ℘

[Raven] evidently came upon Squirrel's den.

I'll probably be mixing up some parts of the story.

When he came upon her den, while he was sitting outside of it, Squirrel evidently came into view.

What, she was probably human.

She was extremely sweaty. Her bucket, she had a bucket. Her bucket was a traditional bucket made of driftwood.

It is said that her bucket was filled with all kinds [of berries]. [In it were] blueberries, crowberries, cranberries, bunchberries, salmonberries. That awful Raven blocked her entrance, he stood over her den.

When he blocked her den, [she said], "My goodness, don't block me out, I'm tired. I'm tired, move out of my way."

The wily Raven answered her, "I won't get out of your way."

"Gee, this one is so infuriating. Now hurry up, I want to go in, I'm very anxious." It is said the poor thing was extremely sweaty because she had picked berries.

"Now you don't want to get out of my way." Squirrel started to sit down. She would say to him, "Now hurry up and get out of my way, and I will pay you with some salmonberries from my bucket."

Raven would respond to her, "In this place, I don't eat those." [*chuckles*]

"Hurry up and get out of my way, and I'll pay you some blueberries that are along the corner of my bucket." That awful one constantly said, "In this place, I don't eat those." It's because he is one who eats feces.

Then she offered him all the berries she had picked one by one, but he would say that at this place, he didn't eat those.

[In the story] this is how they would let [Raven] answer, "*Maanirmiuni tamakutussuitua* [At this place, I don't eat those]."

Squirrel said to him, "Now since you're too adamant, close your eyes and dance and entertain me."

Although Raven is usually not compliant, he evidently danced, closing his eyes like she told him to. He evidently sang, dancing a little, "'*Lliken-ta-aa-aa-aa. 'Lliken-ta-aa-aa. 'Lliken, 'lliken, cetek-aa-ap.*"

Squirrel said to him, "Gee you aren't dancing very much. Dance by really trying to look nice, by going side to side."

Tayima tua-i mumigurqelluki-ll' piciqellikeka.

❧ *Tulukaruk Qanganaarrluar-llu* ❧

[Tulukaruk] Qanganaarrluaraam igtiinek tekiartelliniluni.
Mumigurqeciqellikeka-w'.
Igtiinek tekiarcami elatiinun aqumluni piinanrani Qanganaarrluar igvalliniluni.

Qaillun-tam', tua-i yuuyaaqellilria-w'.
Kiryuk'acagarluni. Tua-i-w' qaltaa-wa-gguq, qaltarluni. Qaltaa-wa-gguq una imna muragaaraat akaartaat qaltaq.
Qaltaa-wa-gguq una tamanek imarluni. Curanek, tan'gerpagnek, tumaglinek, cingqullektarnek, naunrarnek. Taulkuum-am Tulukaruum amiingirluku, igtii capluku.
Tua-i aren igtii capluku pillrani, "Arenqiapaa-ll' capevkenii tang taqsuqelrianga. Taqsuqelrianga, avisnga."
Tulukarulkuum-am kiulliniluku, "Aren aviciiqenritamken."
"Aling eqnarquq una. Tang amci, iteryugtua, nerilegtellrianga tang." Kireckacagaurlurmiluni-gguq tua-i tauna unatallruami.
"Kitek' tua-i avicunritarpenga." Aqumengluni Qanganaarrluar. Waten piaqluku, "Amci avisnga waken-llu nunulirniamken qaltama iluanek naunrarnek."

Tulukaruum-am kiullininauraa, "Maanirmiuni tamakutussuitua." [*ngelaq'ertuq*]
"Amci avisnga waken-llu qaltama kangiraanek nunulirniamken curanek." Tuaten-am piuralkugluni tua-i, "Maanirmiuni tamakutussuitua." Tua-i-w' anarturtenguami.
Tua-i-llu qaqilluki tua-i makut unatani qaqilluki piuryaaqluku, tua-i maanirmiuni tamakutussuitniluni.
Waten-am tua-i kiunguarcetaqekiit, "Maanirmiuni tamakutussuitua."

Qanganaarrluaraam pia, "Kitek tua-i arenqiatuten, yuraaraqaa qelmurluten tangssiiquraqernga."
Tua-i Tulukaruk imna niicuitetungermi tua-llu yuralliniuq, qelmurluni pisquciatun. Atulliniuq yuraksuarluni, "'Lliken-ta-aa-aa-aa. 'Lliken-ta-aa-aa. 'Lliken, 'lliken, cetek-aa-ap."
Tua-i imumek Qanganaarrluaraam piluku, "Aling yuramyassiyaagpagcit. Cakneq tangningnaqluten yuraa cuqiagurluten."

Then he [danced] even livelier. *"'Lliken-ta-aa-aa-aa. 'Lliken-ta-aa-aa. 'Lliken, ''liken, cetek-aa-ap."*

When he began to make arm movements, when he began to dance in a very lively way, when she was thinking of quickly going inside, when he opened his eyes, he said, "What were you about to do?"

Squirrel replied to him, "I thought you might trip on that, get caught on that, so I was just about to remove it." It was something small.

Then she told him to [dance] livelier. As he was moving his arms, Squirrel, when he did something, quickly ran inside.

My, when she ran inside, Raven there said, "My goodness, what has that one done?"

When she entered, she removed her clothes and watched him out there since he couldn't enter, and since she was hot and sweaty, she cooled off.

When that poor Raven would suddenly [try to] run inside, he would get caught on his shoulders. After Raven tried hard to get her, since he had nowhere to dig, Raven evidently left.

✌ *Raven and Two Redpolls* ☙

As he was going along, [Raven] came upon *puyitaaraak* [two redpolls] that were trying to light a fire. (What are these *qulirat*?)

It is said those two redpolls were trying to light a fire, and they were probably using a fire starter. They were trying to light [a fire in] their fire pit outside, and because they were overwhelmed with too much smoke, their eyes were shedding tears.

That awful Raven watched them from beyond them without their knowing, and Raven said, "*Aluvi-luvii* [Tears], their eyes are shedding tears!" [*chuckles*] He would quickly go out of view.

Then they said, "Where is that one talking from?"

When they resumed, just as before, since these ravens are naughty, when they would resume, he would peek at them over there and say to them, "*Aluvi-luvii*, their eyes are shedding tears!" [*chuckles*] He would quickly go out of view.

Those two poor redpolls really looked around. As they were there, when he did that, they happened to see him. They said they saw him. After going over and laughing at them and poking fun at them, he left again.

Tua-i pikanirluni pilliniluni. "'Lliken-ta-aa-aa-aa. 'Lliken-ta-aa-aa. 'Lliken, 'lliken, cetek-aa-ap."

Imumek tua-i yagirqingellrani, imumek waten cakneq *dance*-assiyaangellrani itqerrnaluni piyaaqelriim, uigarcami, "Waq' cayarpiarcit?"

Qanganaarrluaraam kiulliniluku, "Tamana-wa paallauteknayukluku, nagu-teknayukluku aug'aryarpiaryaaqekeka." Tayima tua-i calqurraq.

Tua-i-llu pikaniisqaqluku. Piinanrani tua-i yagirqingellrani, Qanganaarrluar imna caqallran itqertelliniluni.

Aren itqercan Tulukaruk tauna, "Areqiapaa-ll' qaillun augna pia?"

Aren itrami tua-i ugayarluni matarrluni, uavet tangssugluku iterngailan, kiiryuami nengllacilliniluni.

Tulukarugeurluq im' itqercaaqaqami tusgegminun nagtaqluni. Tua-i cakneq tua-i Tulukaruum taum pingnatukaryaaqerraarluku qaillun lakcarviitelliami-ll' ayalliniluni Tulukaruk.

❧ *Tulukaruk Puyitaaraak-llu* ❧

Tua-i-am piinanermini [Tulukaruk] puyitaaraagnek tekitelliniuq kenissaal-riignek. (Tua-i qulirat makut caugat?)

Puyitaaraak-gguq imkuk kumartengnatulriik, tayima tua-i nucukcarlutek-llu-am pillilriik. Kenillertek kumartengnatukiik ellami, puyium ugaan' iigekek maqlutek.

Tulukarulkuum-am yaatiignek tangssuarlukek nalluagnegun pilliniuq-am Tulukaruk, "Aluvi-luvii, iikek maqlutek!" [*ngelaq'ertuq*] Ip'artaqluni.

Tua-llu pilliniuk, "Qaill' naken imna?"

Ataam piaqagnek, tuaten-am tua-i, tulukaruut makut asriungameng, tuaten piaqagnek, igvaqussaaglukek-am yaavet pilliniaqlukek, "Aluvi-luvii, iikek maqlutek!" [*ngelaq'ertuq*] Ip'artaqluni.

Tua-i taukuk puyitaaraurluuk taukuk tua-i cakneq kiarrlutek. Piinanermegni tuatnallrani-am, tua-i cunaw', tangerqerluku. Tangerrniluku tua-i. Tua-i-am tailuni engelaratekengssaggaarlukek, tuamtell' tua-i ayagluni.

✺   *Raven and Snowy Owl*   ✺

Along the ocean shore, it seemed to me that he was traveling along the ocean shore.

Then after a while, he came upon a snowy owl taking care of her fledglings. When he arrived, he came upon a snowy owl who was cooing to her fledglings. This is what they would have [the snowy owl] say, that one cooing, [singing] "*Ayaguumaar ayaguumaa, ayagumaar ayaguum.* When your father arrives, you will eat five large mice. *Aayaguumaa ayagumaar aayaguum.* Flap your wings, fly."

It is said when she would tell her fledglings to flap their wings, they would flap their wings, extremely happy [*chuckles*] about what their mother promised. You know how these snowy owls eat mice.

She would [sing to] them again, "*Aayagumaar aayaguumaa, ayagumaar aayaguum.* When your father arrives you will eat five large mice. *Aayaguma aayaguumar, aayaguum,* flap your wings, fly." When she would [sing] to them, her small fledglings would flap their small wings. [*chuckles*]

When he got tired of watching them, [Raven] left again.

✺   *Raven and Bowhead Whale*   ✺

After a while, was it an *arveq* [bowhead or other large whale] that was continually surfacing and diving that he saw, one of the large animals.

Once again that darn Raven started to want to catch it down there. He would tell [the whale] to [swim] close to shore, he would tell it to open its mouth. When it surfaced with its mouth open, when it surfaced with its mouth open, he evidently quickly entered through its mouth. [*chuckles*]

(These *qulirat* do things, they are like these comics. And although these [stories] aren't true.)

[Raven] quickly entered [the whale], and it was a home. [Raven] saw its ribs, some roof boards. That's what [Raven] did. Now as they say, there are no other words [to the story]. It has ended as they say.

[The story] has ended.

❧ *Tulukaruk Anipaq-llu* ❧

Cenakun, wangrramni tua-i tuartang imarpiim ceniikun ayaagarqelria.

Tuamtall'-am tua-i piuraqerluni anipamek irnialriamek tekilluni. Tekicami, tua-i anipamek irniaminek inqilriamek tua-i-am waten pivkaraqluku inqilria-gguq-am tauna, "Aayaguumaar-ayaguumaa, ayagumaar-ayaguum. Atasi-ima-qaa tekisan imaq' aa-nerniartuci ugenvagnek tallimaaneg. Aayaguumaa ayaguumaar aayaguum. Yaqiuklagci, tengauklagci-ii."

Tuaten-gguq yaqiuklaasqaqateng irniari imkut yaqiuraluteng quyak'aca-garluteng [*ngelaq'ertuq*] aanameng taum akqutiinek. Iciw' makut anipat uugnarnek neqengqellriit.

Ataam piaqluki, "Aayagumaar aayagumaa, ayagumaar aayaguum. Ata-si-ima-qaa tekiskan-imaq' aa-nerniartuci ugenvagnek tallimaneg. Aayaguma aayaguumar, aayaguum, yaqiuklagci tengauklagci-ii." Tuaten piaqateng tua-i irniari unkut yaqiuklayagarluteng pinaurtut. [*ngelaq'ertuq*]

Tua-i tangssulnguamiki [Tulukaruk] ayalliniluni-am tua-i.

❧ *Tulukaruk Arveq-llu* ❧

Piuraqerluni tua-i camek arvermek-qaa puguralriamek qaktaalriamek, naliatnek ungungssirpiit, tangerrluni.

Tua-i-am Tulukarulkuum taum unavet tua-i cucungluku. Cenaqvaarkun pis-qevviaqluni, aitarrluku pisqevviaqluni. Qaktaalria-am imna tua-i aitarmi, pugluni aitarmi pillrani qanrakun itqertelliniluni. [*ngelaq'ertuq*]

(Tua-i qulirat makut cangssaaq, makucetun tua-i *comic*-aatun. Piciunrilnger-meng-llu makut maa-i.)

Itqertelliniuq-am, ena man'a. Tulimainek-am tua-i, qanagnek. Tuatnaluni. Tua-i-llu tua-i apqiitnek qaneryararkairulluniam tua-i. Tayima-gguq tua-i iquklilluni.

Tua-i iquklituq.

ᴁ *A Poor Young Lad* ᴔ

Magdalene Sunny and Ruth Jimmie, Nightmute, July 1985

Magdalene Sunny: One day a poor young lad was going along the ocean. As he was going he began to see these things he didn't recognize. Soon he started to kick them with his feet as he went along.

And as he came upon another one of those things and kicked it, it suddenly snapped shut [on his foot]. When it snapped shut on his foot, he tried to pull it out, but it couldn't come out, he couldn't pull it out.

After attempting to pull his foot out, and realizing that the tide might be coming soon, he started to cry and began pleading with the thing and said, "*Tii-iq* [Sea Anemone]. Sea Anemone. Let go of [my foot]. Release [my foot]. And I will grant you one of my maternal uncle's kayaks."

[Sea Anemone quickly replied,] "I don't use that kind."

The poor boy begged again, "Sea Anemone. Sea Anemone. Let go of [my foot]. Release [my foot]. And I will grant you one of my maternal uncle's pronged bird spears."

[Sea Anemone replied,] "I don't use that kind."

After trying to pull out [his foot]; soon the water started coming up. The tide was coming in and getting close to him.

After trying and trying [to pull his leg out], once again he cried, "Sea Anemone. Sea Anemone. Let go of [my foot]. Release [my foot]. If you do, I will grant you one of my uncle's fish-skin mittens."

[Sea Anemone answered,] "I don't use that kind."

[The lad got irritated and blurted out], "What is it that you want that you don't release [my foot]? Sea Anemone. Sea Anemone. Please release me. Please release me."

By then the incoming tide had reached [him], and he was standing in water up to his waist. He begged, "Sea Anemone. Sea Anemone. Let go of [my foot]. Please release me. And I will grant you one of my uncle's seal-gut garments."

[Sea Anemone quickly answered,] "*Cii!* Now, that is what I'll take."

When he released him, he went up and stopped just behind [Sea Anemone] and removed his clothes and wrung them out and looked at the thing below and said, "You poor Sea Anemone down there, I don't have things. I don't own anything. I have no uncle. I grew up from a pit."

[Sea Anemone yelled,] "How infuriating! Why has the darn thing lied to me?" [The lad] continued wringing out his clothes and continued on his way.

Ruth Jimmie: Who is that?

Magdalene Sunny: A young lad.

∝ *Yun'engqurraurluq* ∽

Missan Angalgaq-llu, Negtemiut, July 1985

Missan: Yun'engqurraurluq una imarpiim ceniikun ayalria. Ayainanermi canek makunek tekitenguq. Ayumian tua-i kitengkaqluki ayalliniluni.

Tua-i-ll' kitengkarpiinret iliitni quuqerruskiliu. Quuqerrucani tua-i iruni cayussaagyaaqekni, tua-i pisciiganani, cayugciiganaku.

Aren ulnayukluku pingengami, tua-i nucugngairucan, qiaqcaaralliniluni, "Tii-iq. Tii-iq. Pegesnga. Pegesnga. Angama, angacarama qayaan aipaanek nunu-lirniaramke-en."

"Tamakunek pissuitua."
Allamek tua-i piaqluni. "Tii-iq. Tii-iq. Pegesnga. Pegesnga. Angama, anga-carama nuusaarpain aipaanek nunulirniaramke-en."

"Tamakunek pissuitua."
Tua-i nucussaagyaaqerraarluku; kiituan' tua-i ulnguq. Ulem tua-i tekitnia-rarluku.
Cayaaqvigminek tua-i tuamtell'-am tua-i qiaqcaaraurlurluni, "Tii-iq. Tii-iq. Pegesnga. Pegesnga. Angama, angacarama arilluan aipaanek nunulirniamke-en."

"Tamakunek pissuitua."
"Camek pinaluten pegtenrilkurpakarcia? Tii-iq. Tii-iq. Pegesnga. Pegesnga."

Kiituan' tua-i ulem mat'um tekitengaa tua-i naqugnekaarangluni. "Tii-iq. Tii-iq. Pegesnga. Pegesnga. Angama, angacarama imarnitegken aipaigketnek nunulirniaramken-en."
"Cii! Nutaan atam."
Tua-i pegcani, ayumian tua-i tagluni keluanun matarqelluni ciuqcaaralliniuq, kanavet tuaten qanrulluku, "Teurluuq kacuuq, caitua. Piitua. Angaitua. Teq'ermek naullruunga."

"Eqnarivakar! Ciiqtaq iqluqua?" Tua-i piluku. Tua-i aturallrani tamakut ciuq-caararraarluki ayagluni.
Angalgaq: Kina-gguq tauna?
Missan: Yun'engqurraq.

Ruth Jimmie: What is a *yun'engqurraq*?

Magdalene Sunny: Well, a young lad. A young lad, a young boy.

As he was going along he came to Squirrel's den. He stopped and sat along its opening and reclined, putting his head right over the den hole.

Then without warning Squirrel suddenly appeared looking quite worn and exhausted. She was holding a bucket.

[Gasping for breath she said], "My goodness, you there, I'm sweating and about to suffocate, get out of my way! I'm so sweaty, please move out of my way."

Then [the young lad] said to her, "Would you please dance."

[The lad] began to sing, *"'Llikentaa-aa-aa. 'Llikentaa-aa-aa. 'Lliken. 'Lliken. Cetek-aa-a!"*

[The lad said,] "What were you about to do?"

[Squirrel said,] "Thinking you may trip on that there, I was thinking to remove it."

As soon as [the lad] started singing, Squirrel began to dance with gusto, moving and swinging her body back and forth.

Soon the lad stood up and started dancing following her movements.

The lad said, "Dance again and give more emphasis in your motions."

Then he sang for her, *"'Llikentaa-aa-aa. 'Llikentaa-aa-aa. 'Lliken. 'Lliken. Cetek-aa-a!"* When [the lad] intensified his motions and moved farther to the side, when her den hole appeared, [Squirrel] jumped inside. [*chuckles*]

As soon as [Squirrel] got inside, she lay on her mattress and just laid on her back.

Gee, [the lad] quickly followed her, but he got caught on his shoulders [and couldn't enter].

Ruth Jimmie: That boy?

Magdalene Sunny: Yes, that lad.

After attempting to [go through the hole] again and again, when he'd try to enter with as much force as he could, he would get caught at his shoulders.

❧ *First Ancestor* ❧

Paul John, Michael John, and Simeon Agnus, Umkumiut,
Nelson Island, July 2007

Paul John: They say that Nelson Island was once *evunret* [piled ice]; they were ice. And after they were ice, they turned into land.

Angalgaq: Ca-tam' tauna yun'engqurraq?

Missan: Tua-i-wa, yun'engqucitaar. Yun'engqucitaar, tanekcitagglugaq.

Ayainanermini piqertuq Qanganaarrluaraam una igtii. Painganun wavet aqumqerluni amiiga akitekqerluku taklauyaarluni.

Piqainanrani Qanganaarrluar una igvaartuq tua-i arenqianani tua-i. Qaltaq-wa tegumiara.

"Arenqiapaa usuuq, kiiryugtua, epqatartua aviteqernga! Tua-i kiryuk'acagartua aviarteqernga."

Tua-ll' [Yun'engqucitaaraam] pia, "Kitak' yuraqaa."

Atuutengaartaa-am, "'Llikentaa-aa-aa. 'Llikentaa-aa-aa. 'Lliken. 'Lliken. Cetek-aa-a!"

"Waq' cayarpiarcit?"

"Tamana-wa pallauteknayukluku aug'arnaluk' piyaaqekeka."

Qanganaarrluar tauna cakneq tua-i cuqiuqetaassiyaagluni yuralria atuucani.

Taun' tua-i yun'engqucitaar tauna nangertengluni maligtaqungaa.

Yun'engqucitaaraam pia, "Cakneqvaar aviqequ'urluten."

Taum atuucani, "'Llikentaa-aa-aa. 'Llikentaa-aa-aa. 'Lliken. 'Lliken. Cetek-aa-a!" Imumek tua-i [Yun'engqucitaar] cakneq cuqiuqetaarluni pillermini, yaa-i tua-i igteni alaircan itqertelliniluni. [*ngelaq'ertuq*]

Itqercami tua-i aciminun taklarrluni taklauyaarqili.

Aren, maligarrluku [Yun'engqucitaar] itqercaaqelriim tusgegminun nageskili.

Angalgaq: Tauna-q' tan'gurraq?

Missan: Ii-i yun'engqucitaar tauna.

Allamek tua-i pirraarluni, pinertutacirmitun itqercaaqaqami, tusgegminun nagtaqluni.

❧ *Ciuliaqatuk* ❧

Kangrilnguq, Qukailnguk, Unangik-llu, Umkumiut, Qaluyaat, July 2007

Kangrilnguq: Ukut waniwa Qaluyaat evunrullrunilarait; cikuuluki. Tua-i-llu cikuurraarluteng nunaurrluteng.

Along the other side, the place where that [Raven] chopped with his ice pick, the rocks on the [north] side look like ice that was chopped with an ice pick. I think [the rocks there] were indeed once ice.

And the one who was chopping with his ice pick, when he broke his ice pick, when he placed the broken section of his ice pick along the upper part of a stream called Iqallugtuli, this is what they say he said: "In the distant future, when one of the descendants finds the piece that broke from my ice pick, they won't lack anything anymore." It is probably some form of wealth. That's all I can say about it.

They say that this place was once water before it turned into land. When I heard the story, the inland village of Kalskag [is located] along the very end the mountains. The village of Kalskag is located between the mountains of the Yukon and Kuskokwim rivers; as you know there are no mountains below that village.

I heard that Ciuliaqatuk [First Ancestor, Raven] tossed his small amount of ashes and said, "So that in the distant future, the descendents will live on it." They say this area turned into land starting from the time that he tossed his few ashes. I know the story to that extent.

Michael John: They'd tell us those things. And when I used to hear of [Nelson Island] in stories, the person who spoke of them would say that they were once *evunret*. He said that these mountains [on Nelson Island] were once *evunret*.

You've seen *evunret* down on the ocean. They are ice piles that grow on sandbars, and they grow large. They called those *evunret*.

And they'd say that those *evunret* grow in their usual places every year.

And this place here [the mountains of Nelson Island], when I first started to hear stories about them in the past, they would say that they were once *evunret*. And Raven also, I heard them talking about it, but they didn't mention where his village was down there.

Their daughter, in winter when it came time, she was fishing for tomcod there on a piece of ice; on that ice there that had stuck to that place where she was jigging for tomcod with a hook. These days you do that here, too, you jig for tomcod, you fish with hooks. One day they told him that the ice had detached and his daughter had floated away.

When they said the ice had broken off and floated away while she was on it, and he saw her, he filled the bottom of his garment with land from the surrounding ground, and he splashed it on these *evunret* here.

He took some [dirt] from the tundra around here since he probably had a hooded garment; he filled [the skirt along] his hooded garment or his parka. He filled that. He filled the bottom of his garment and when he splashed it, this place turned into land.

That's how I heard the story. It turned into land.

Tamaa-i akmalirnermi taum cikuliullri, tua-i cikuliurutem tumellritun cikumi teggalqut akmalirnermi uitaut. Cikuupigtellrungatut.

Tua-i tauna-llu tuglleq, tugminek ayimciami, kuiggaam kangranun, Iqallugtulim-gguq mat'um, tugmi ayimnera elliamiu, waten qanellrunilaraat: "Akwaku kinguliat iliita nalaqekuniu una tugma ayimnera, camek kepqutairuciiquq." Akiuguq tayima. Tuaten taugaam tua-i wiinga qanruteksugngaaqa.

Taugaam man'a maani tua-i mer'ullrunilaryaaqaat nunaurpailgan. Wiinga qanemciuluku niitellemni, qamkut qama-i Kalskag-armiut ingrit nuukait. Ukuk wani Kuigpiinkuk Kusquqviim-llu akiqliin, ingrikenka akuliitni Kalskag-armiut [uitaut]; tua-i uatiit man' ingritailnguq.

Niitellruunga taum-gguq Ciuliaqatuum qamllerkuani ciqruskii qanerluni, "Akwaku kinguliat nunakniaraat." Tua-i-gguq nunaurtellruuq maa-i man'a, taum qamllerkuaminek ciqrucillra ayagneqluku. Tuaten wii qanemciuluku nallunritetaaqa.

Qukailnguq: Tamakunek tamaa-i. Ukut cali waniwa wii niitelallemni qanemciuluki, tamaa-i evunrullruniluki qanrutkelallruit qanrutkestaita. Evunrullruut-gguq ukut ingrit.

Iciw' unani imarpigmi tanglalriaci evunernek. Cikunek qalliqluteng marayami naucilrianek, angturriluteng-llu. Tamakut tamaa-i evunernek pitullruit.

Tamakut-llu evunret allamiaqan enemeggni tua-i nauyarameggni nautuniaqluki.

Tua-ll' ukut waniwa, ukut cali niiteqarraalallemni avani qanemcikevkarluki, evunrullruut-gguq. Tauna-llu Tulukaruk tauna, nani tua-i uani nunii aperturpek'naku, nani uitallra tuaten niitelallruaqa.

Paniak tauna, waten uksumi tua-i pinarinrakun pillermini, iqalluarcurluni tamaani, cikurrami; cikumi-w' tua-i tamaani, taukunun, ukunun, neptellermun, iqalluarcurluni manallinilria. Maani-ll' maa-i pilalriaci, iqalluanek iqsagluci, caluci, manarluci. Piinanrani pilliniat pania augna qecuutniluku.

Tua-i-ll' taum qecuutniluku piaku, qecuutellinian, tangrramiu, nunamek maaken kenirmigluni ukunun tua-i evunernun ciqrutliniluku.

Nunapigmek maaken tua-i tegulluni qaspengqelliami; qaspemi wall'u atkumi pianun imirluku. Imirluku tauna. Imirluku tua-i kenirmigluni ciqruskii, ukut waniw' nunaurtelliniluteng.

Tuaten tua-i qanemciuluku niitelallruaqa. Tua-i nunaurrluteng.

And when [Raven's] daughter had her first menstruation, they say at that place up there, he built a house at Qilengpak, he build her a house. These two just mentioned that her menstrual blood became *uiteraq* [red ocher].

At that time, Qilengpak up there, I think it was along the upper side, they used to say that it had a doorway.

And Caaciquq's deceased father, he said that when he was a boy, when he was up there hunting with his bow and arrow, when he would travel on foot, he would hold his arm along its doorway up there and hold his bow along the end of his hand to measure the width of [the doorway], he'd extend his arms out and add the bow to measure the size of that, to see how large it was.

He said when those who weren't going to live long kept going in and out of that place, it caused [the doorway] to shrink fast. That's what they used to say about it.

They used to say that Raven was our ancestor, too.

And down below Engelullugarmiut, there is a large boulder. It used to be a certain height when I saw it. I used to see some etchings along the top like this, some etchings. They would say that those are Raven's tracks, his tracks on top of the boulder. I used to see those when our village first formed.

Simeon Agnus: Yes, Qilengpak up there isn't visible from here, from this place [Umkumiut]. But we know of Qilengpak up there. Qilengpak is where people who are getting *uiteraq* go.

Although people go there, [red ocher] isn't visible to some. They say it isn't visible to them, they disappear for them. It isn't put out for some people. It isn't available to them. The red ocher isn't displayed to some people.

But they say it's displayed to some people. Their surrounding area is probably very red. That's how it is.

That one up there isn't a person; although it isn't human, it presents [red ochre] to some people, and it's absent for some people. That's how that place is up there.

It is said when some people go and get red ocher, they go directly to the place and return home without having obtained any. One of these days you will see it up there.

That's what Qilengpak up there is like; that's what they say about it. It displays it for some people, and for others it's absent. I'm not sure why that place up there is like that.

Now I want to briefly add another thing, about my *iluraq* [male cross-cousin] Angutekayak. You will hear it when I tell it.

He evidently stopped up beyond Arutaaq [from *aru-*, "to ripen or rot"]. Was it he and his wife? He got out, and he said that he saw some red things along Nanvaruk [Baird Inlet], beyond Arutaaq [River]. They saw that they were [pieces of] red ocher. He picked them as he walked along, picking the ones that were visible.

Panini-ll' tauna aglerngan, pik'umi-gguq, Qilengpagkun nel'illiniluni, nel'iluku. Ava-i qanrutkaa ukuk taman' aunrallra uitrurtellruniluku.

Tuani tua-i, pikna Qilengpak, kialirnerakun piyugnarquq, amingqerrnilallruat.

Aug'um-llu Caaciquum atallran, tamaa-i-gguq tan'gurraullermini-llu amii- gakun urluvminek, piteggniarqami pagaani, pektaqami, yaggluni-llu tallini us- gulirluku waten piqtaarqami, taum neqututacia, tua-i neqututassiirluku yaggluni urluvminek inglulirluni taum angtacia, tuaten angtallra nallunriraqluku.

Tamaa-i-gguq yuugarkaunrilnguut itqetaarluku quullra cukavkallruat. Tuaten tua-i tuaten qanrutketullruat.

Tua-i tauna Tulukaruk ciuliaqniluku-llu qanrutketullruat.
Ava-i-llu cali yaani Engelullugarmiut ketiitni teggalquq tauna ang'uq. Qaill' tayim' qertutalallruuq tanglallemni. Kangrani tua-i waten ceternek tanglallruunga, ceternek. Tua-i-gguq Tulukaruum tumellri, tumellri taum teggalqum qaingani. Taukut tua-i tanglallruanka tua-i tamaani nunaurcugarallemteni.
Unangik: Yaa, pikna pika-i Qilengpak alaicuituq waken, maaken. Taugaam tua-i nallunritarput pikna Qilengpak. Qilengpak tua-i uiterartellriit ullatuat.

Taugken ullangermegteggu ilait alailucuitait. Alailucuitait-gguq tua-i, ta- maumalluki. Ilait paivucuitait. Paivngacuitait. Tua-i manimatevkenaki tamatum uiteram.
Ilii-gguq taugken paivngalluku tua-i. Avatii man'a kavirpaugaqluni pillilria. Tuaten tua-i.
Pikna pikani tuaten yuunginaraunrituq; yuunrilngermi, yuum ilii paivngalluku, ilii-ll' tamaumalluku. Tuaten tua-i ayuquq pikna.
Ilaita-gguq tua-i uiterarcaaqaqameng ullakapigtetuat tua-i camek unangev- kenateng tua-i utertaqluteng. Tangerciqaci pikani tayima cam iliini.

Waten tua-i ayuquq pikna Qilengpak; tuaten tua-i qanrutketukiit. Ilii paivngalluku, ilii-ll' tamaumalluku. Tua-i caulriim tuaten ayuqa pikna.

Tua-i-ll' aug'umek cali ilaqerluku, iluramnek Angutekayagmek. Tua-i-w' tayim' qanrutkekumku niiciiqan.
Kiavet Arutaam yaalirneranun arulailliniuq. Aipani-llu-qaa piuk? Yuuluni pilliniuq makut-gguq maani kavircenateng tua-i, Nanvaruum, Arutaam yaalirne- rani. Maaten-gguq tang piuk uiteraullinilriit. Avurturluni cenirtelliniuq, alailnguut teguurluki.

When he returned, when he turned back, once again, larger ones appeared. Then he picked them up on his way back. And again, when he looked back, he saw that they appeared even larger than before. He picked them up without thinking anything.

And when he returned from the place where he went by walking along the shore, they became even larger again. He picked them up and placed them inside his boat. Since they started to become alarmed, they left.

And when he arrived in his village and brought them inside his home, he stored the red ocher in a good place. When they wanted to use them, they checked and saw that the pieces of red ocher that he had brought home were gone. What happened to those?

Paul John: Yes, starting with that story, that elder, my deceased *ataataruk* [big paternal uncle] Uqamailnguq, the one who they called Caucicqum Atii, I wanted to tell the story he told about Qilengpak across there.

He said Qilengpak across there was the place where the daughter of Ciuliaqatuk [Raven] stayed when she had her first menstrual period.

When his daughter had her first menstrual period, they say Ciuliaqatuk had her go across to Qilengpak and sit there [in isolation]. And it is said the area that her blood soaked is red ocher.

That's what that elder briefly said about Qilengpak over there, that it was the place where Ciuliaqatuk's daughter sat [in seclusion] during her first menstrual period. He said that the area that her blood soaked is red ocher.

Now, what this person mentioned about ones that disappeared; since they originate with *ircenrraat* [other-than-human persons], they disappeared, the ones that my younger sibling had picked.

And in recent days, some people would find mammoth tusks out there once in a while. Sometimes people would leave them, planning to get them at a later time. When they'd go and get them, they'd see that they had disappeared.

They mention that these things that come from *ircenrraat* disappear, the things that became visible through *ircenrraat*. But the things that didn't become visible to people through *ircenrraat,* they don't disappear although they leave them behind. All things that God provided to a person don't disappear. That's what it's like.

And since that's what it's like, if a person placed an item somewhere, even for a number of years, and after not having gone to get that item, when they go to it, if a person hadn't taken it, it will still be where he left it; although some things start to sink into the land. But from long ago they mention that these things that came from *ircenrraat* disappear.

These *ircenrraat* don't live in [the world] that we see. They live in their own world, and I think that they view the underground as a world to live in. When they tell stories about them, why is it that *ircenrraat* go into the land and disappear?

Utercami cali, kingutmun caungami pilliniuq, anglirikanirluteng cali tamakut alaillinilriit. Tuamtell' avurluki tua-i uterrluni. Tuamtell' kingyaami pilliniuq, anglirikanirluteng cali alairluteng. Avurluk' tua-i camek pivkenani.

Yaaken cali tua-i cenirtellminek cenakun utertuq, anglirikanirluteng cali. Tua-i avurluki angyaminun ekluki. Alingengaarcamek ayalliniuk.

Tua-i-llu kingunicami, nem'inun it'rucamiki taukut nek'eggluki tua-i piyaa-qellinii. Aturyuamegenki piyaaqelliniuk, uiterat tua-i tayima taukut utrutellri tua-i tamaumaluteng. Qaill' taukut pillruat?

Kangrilnguq: Ii-i, augna ciukarrluku, aug'um tegganrem ataatairutma Uqa-mailnguum, Cauciqum Atiinek pitullrata, ikna ika-i Qilengpak qanemcikellra qanemcikqernaluku.
Ikai-gguq ikna Qilengpak Ciuliaqatuum panian aglenrarauvikelqaa.

Tua-i-gguq taum Ciuliaqatuum panini aglenraraan ikavet ika-i Qilengpagmun pivkarluku aqumgavkallrua. Tamaa-i-llu-gguq augan mecillra uiterauluni.

Tuaten tua-i aug'um tegganrulriim qanrutkeqallrua ikna Qilengpak, Ciu-liaqatuum panianun aqumgavilqeniluku. Augna tua-i mecillra tamaa-i uite-raularniluku.
Tua-i-ll' augna uum tamallernek qanellra augna; tua-i ircen'ertaungameng ava-i tamalriit, uyu'urma am'um avuryaaqellri.

Cali-llu maa-i augkut quugaarpiit cirunritnek ilait nalaqut'laryaaqellrullinilriit caqalriit avani. Tua-i aqvaarkauluku ilii uniciyaaqelalliniuq. Aqvayaaqnaurait-gguq tayim' tamallinilriit.
Makut maa-i avanirpak ircen'ernek kingunelget waten tamatuniluki qan-rutkelarait, ircen'erteggun alaitellret. Taugken ircen'erteggun alaitenrilnguut tua-i uniteng'ermeng tamayuunateng. Agayutem tua-i tuanlluku yugmun pikiu-tekumak'ngaa tamayuunani, ca man' tamarmi. Tuaten tua-i ayuqluni.
Tuaten-llu ayuqngami, allrakuni-ll' qavcini yuum ellillni ullaksaicimarraarluku ullagluku pikani, yuum tegunrilkani, tuantarkauluni tua-i ellivillrani; ilait imumek apqiitnek tevgutengllliningermeng nunamun qap'itengluteng. Makut taugaam maa-i ircen'ernek kingunelget tuaten tua-i tamaraqluki pituniaqekait ukanirpak.

Makut ircenrraat wangkuta tangerkengamteni uitavkenateng. Ellarrameg-teggun tayima, nunam-ll' acia ellaulluku tayim' ellakelaryugnarqaat. Qanem-ciugaqameng, ciin nunamun iterluteng tamatuat tamakut ircenrraat?

And again, I think this occurred before we were born. One man was evidently walking along the shore looking for dead beached sea mammals. When he looked ahead toward the ocean, he saw a man towing a seal coming up on the shore.

When that person noticed him, the one towing a seal started to quicken his pace. And since [the man] understood that he wasn't human, when he was trying to catch up to him, when he came upon an eroded bank along the ocean, that person went inside [the ground]. And just as the seal that he was towing was going inside the land, he tripped and fell forward on top of it, and it was left behind. But the person who was towing it went into the ground and disappeared because he was an *ircenrraq* [other-than-human person].

✑ *How Nunivak Came to Be Inhabited* ✎

Jack Williams, Toksook Bay, November 1976, and Mekoryuk, July 1991

Jack Williams: Let me have you [students at the Nelson Island High School] hear a *qaneryaraq* [word of advice, lit., "that which is spoken"] that they told long ago, this *quliraq* as they called it, a *quliraq* that was told by our ancestors long ago. It isn't exactly a *quliraq*, it is a true story. These real *qulirat*, those real *qulirat* that were told in the early days, the real *qulirat* from ancient times that they told. The first thing that I'm going to talk about now, I'm going to talk about the two first inhabitants of Nunivak Island, the very first two original inhabitants long ago, long ago after the time the world came to exist, after it came to exist, long after it came to exist.
     And then, before Nunivak Island became an island, it was apparently once all land including Nelson Island, reaching the Aleutian Islands. It apparently existed like that before these lands became islands; before these islands became islands long ago, it was all land. And during that time there was apparently a great earthquake on the land.

Those early ancestors, the people of the Aleutian Islands, the people of Unalaska used to talk about that, I heard them talk about that. They apparently learned that from their ancestors and talked about it. They say long, long ago, and when the Aleutian Islands were all land, back when there was a great earthquake on the land, during the time when those Aleutian Islands over there became islands, the area to the north reaching Nome was once land, but it apparently sunk.

Nelson Island became an island. And Nunivak Island evidently became an island during that time up to now. No wonder those elephant-like animals

Tua-ll'-am cali, tua-i wangkuta tayim' yuurpailemta pillrungatuq. Angutet iliit waten apeqmeggnek cenakun mallussurluni cenirqurallinilria. Maaten tua-i ciuneni, un'a imarpim tunglirnera tangllinia angun un'a taqukamek qamurluni tag'uralria.

Taum tua-i cumikarcamiu, cukangnaqngartelliniuq augna qamulek taqukamek. Tua-i elliin-llu yuunrilucia taringamiu tua-i angungnaqsaaqellrani waten uss'aryugmun imarpiim ceniinun tekicami, tauna imna yug' itliniuq. Una-llu tua-i qamuqengaa taqukaq nunamun itqatarturtelluk', paallagvikekiini tua-i uitallliniluni. Imna taugaam tayima qamurtii yuk nunamun iterluni tua-i tamarluni tua-i ircenrraungami.

ও *Nuniwam Cungeqarraarutii* ও

Uyuruciar, Nunakauyaq, November 1976, Mikuryaq, July 1991-llu

Uyuruciar: Ak'a tamaani qaneryaraqtullratneg qaneryarameg niitevkaqerrnaumci, uumek kwani apqiitneg quliramog, quliraqtukngaatneg ak'a awani ciuliamta. Quliraqapiarauvkenani, piciuluni. Qulirapiat makut, qulirapiat-wa tawa-i augkut ciuqvani, ciuqvaqapiarni qulirapiat qaneryarraullratnek, tawa-i qanrutketullrat. Ciuqliuluni una qanrutkengaqa kwanirpag, Nuniwam uum ciuqlikacagarmeg cung'eqarraaruteg taukuk kwani qanrutekqataragka, cung'eqarrarpiarauteg ukuk kwani ak'a, ak'a tamaani ella man'a ellaurcugaryugnaatartellran kinguani, ellaurtellran kinguani, kingurpaagaani.

Tawa-lli-wa, man'a una Nuniwaq kwani qikertaurpaalgan tamaa-i ayuqluni nunaullrullinilria tamana Qaluyaat ilakluki, amawet ngelkarrluni Aleutian Island-anun tekisngaluni, elgaringaluni. Tawaten taqumallrullinilria ak'a awani qikertaurqevvailgata makut nunat; qikertat-wa makut qikertaurqevvailgata ak'a awani ayuqluni nunaullrulliniami tamana. Nut'an-llu tamatum nalliini tayima nuna uulegterpallrullinilluni ak'a tayima.

Ciuliaqvat augkut, awani kwani augkut, Aleutian Island-armiut ingkut, Unalaska-rmiut tamana qanrutektullruat, qanrutkevkarluku niitellruaqa. Ak'a ciuliameggneg tamaa-i elisseklngaqluku, eliskengaqluku tamana qanrutkellrulliniat. Ak'aqapig-ggur tayima augkut-llu Aleutian Island-at ingkut ayuqluteng nunaullratni tamaa-i nuna uulegterpallrani tamaatum nalliini, ingkut yaa-i-llu Aleutian Island-aat qikertaurcata, qagna Nome-ar engelkarrluku nunaullrulliniyaaqellriim kit'ellrullinilria.

Qaluyaat qikertaurrluteng. Una-llu-w' Nuniwar qikertaurtellrulliniur tamaa-i tamatum nalliini. Anirtima imkut cat augkut *elephant*-allraat, tamakut imkut cat

[mammoths], those ancient animals, their bones are seen along the bay of the village they call Mikuryarmiut [Mekoryuk]. Their bones used to be visible when the tide went out. Some people still find some of their bones today.

And back when the land first came to be, after the time it first became an island, long after that time, and you probably know this, your Nelson Island ancestors probably told you, your elders probably told you what your ancestors experienced and did.

The person who spoke of this *qaneryaraq* died; inside the *qasgi*, the person they call Lurtussiikaq, he told about the woman who first inhabited our land [Nunivak Island] here.

He said there in that place [on Nelson Island] that they used to call Aternermiut, before they started calling it Up'nerkillermiut, they apparently called Up'nerkillermiut Aternermiut. That was apparently the main village that existed back then. And that village across inside Kangirrluar [Toksook Bay], what do you call it again? I think you call it Englullugmiut [Engel'umiut]. That was also a village.

And before the village of Tununak was fully established, during that time, during those times, they say a *nukalpiar* [rich person], a man who didn't lack anything, that village up there that we used to call Aternermiut, the one you call Up'nerkillermiut up there, that evidently started there. And your ancestors probably mentioned this [story], or maybe you all know about it. . . .[10]

A place called Aternermiut. That's what their village was called. And there was, they say that village had a *nukalpiar*. Using this person as an example; this person is rich. He is a rich person, he is a *nukalpiar*. He is rich. He doesn't lack anything, he isn't deprived of anything. The only thing he lacks is a child. A child is the only thing he lacks. They say everything he did was actually easy for him. Since this person doesn't have a child, the only thing he lacks is a child.

(Since there is no one to hear me [who understands Cup'ig] I'm using this person [one of the men listening to the story] as a counterpoint, comparing him to that *nukalpiar*.[11] Since this person is a *nukalpiar*, he actually doesn't lack anything. And he has a camera.) But he lacks a child, a child. He lacks a child; the only thing that he lacks is a child-to-be.

Then one day, after a long time had passed, a long time after they began calling that village by its name after it was established, the *nukalpiar* there, the *nukalpiar* of the people of Aternermiut, when he arrived after being gone, his wife went to him and told him, "I feel something inside my belly down there." His wife told him that.

"Since I'm starting to feel something I'm letting you know since you are my husband." She wanted him to know. Then her husband searched for an *angalkuq*

pitarkallraat ak'allat tamakut nenrit maani kwani tangrruulartut, ukut nunat Mikuryarmiuneg pitukaita unani taciata illuani. Kenutaqluki illait tamaa-i tangerr-narqetullruut. Maa-i cali illait calriit alaqut'larluteng tamakuneg tamaa-i nenrita ilaitneg.

Cali-llu tamaa-i nunaurcugallrani tawaten qikertaurterraallran kinguakun, kingurpiikun, amtallu tayima nallunritliksi elpeci tamakut ciuliavci, ciuqlirpeci-wa Qaluyaarmiuni tawani qanrut'lallrullikaiceci augkut ciulirnerpeci-wa, ciuliaci-w' augkut qaallun pilallratneg tamaa-i qanrutek'lallrulliit.

Uum kwani qaneryaram qanrutkestellra tayima yuunrillruuq tamaani; uum kwani Lurtussiikameg pitukiita qanrutkurallrukii qasgimi tauna kwani uum nunamta cung'eqarraarutellra arnar.

Tawani-ggur tawani taukut kwani Aternermiuneg pitullratni, Up'nerki-llermiuneg, Up'nerkillermiuneg piturivvailgatki tamaa-i Aternermiuneg pi-tullrullinikait taukut wan' Up'nerkillermiut. Taukut kiimeng nunaurpallull-rulliniameng. Ik'ut-llu Kangirrluarmi imkut kiugkut camiuneg pilarceciki? Englu-llugmiunek-llu pilalliaci. Taukut nunauluteng.

Amkut-llu cali Tununermiut nunaussiyaagpailgata, tamatum nuniini, ta-matum ellaullrani tamaani, tauna-ggur kwani nukalpiar tauna, tawa-i cameg nuuqitenrilngur angun tauna taukut kwani Aternermiuneg pitukengallemta pingkut, Up'nerkillermiuneg qakma-i pilaqengaci, tamaa-i tamana, man'a kwani ayagnengellrulliniur ak'a tamaani. Tayimani-llu ciuliarpeci tayim' qan-rutek'lallrullia man'a, kwall'u elpeci nallunricaaqelliarci. . . .

Aternermiut-ggur taukut. Atengqerrluteng nunait. Nut'an-llu pitangqelliniluni, nunat taukut nukalpiangqertut-ggur. Una ayuqekuciarutekluku; una kwai tukur-liugur. Tukurliuluni cuugulliniur, nukalpiaruluni. Tukurliuluni tawa-i. Cameg nuuqitevkenani, nuuqevkenani cameg. Nuuqutengqerrluni taugg'am tan'gurr-meg. Nuuqutii tauna tan'gurrer kiimi nuuqutnguluni. Callri-ggur tamarmeng qacignaqsaaqut. Una qetunraalami qetunrermeg taugg'am nuuqilluni.

(Waten niicestaalama una inglukureluku, inglukureluku qanaatekaqa, ayuqe-kuciarutekluku tautun nukalpiatun. Nukalpiarungami una cameg nuuqen-ricaaqur. Tarenraarissuuterluni-llu.) Taugg'am nuuqitur tan'gurrmeg qetun'er-kamineg kessiin nuuqutekluk'u. Nuuqutekluku qetunrani tauna; qetun'erkani nuuqutekluku kiingan.

Tawa-llu erenret illiitni, akaurrnerakun erner tamana apertuqtaarallrat, nunat taukut nunauluteng apertuqtaarallrat, tauna nukalpiar, nukalpiarat Aternermiut taukut ayallraneg tekitellrani nulirran ullagluku una qanrutaa, "Alangruunga camani cameg cam'umeg aqsiigma illuani." Nulirran qanrulluku.

"Alangrungama nallunritevkaramken wikngamken." Nallunricesqelluku. Tawa-llu taum angutiin yugarluni angalkumeg. Kass'at makut apertaaqengaitneg

[shaman]. The ones these white people call magician doctor; that man, the *nukalpiar* searched for one of those.

That rich man, paying him with his material things, paying him and asking that shaman to check on his wife, he asked him to find out why she was feeling something in her body.

The shaman went to her and put her on her back like this, letting her lie down flat, placing her on a flat surface. He lifted his arms, he opened up her parka and started to push down on her belly with his right hand, he pushed down on her, and [his hand] would go up and go down.

They say he told her when he was done, "This is evidently a small child. She is not going to be strong. She is a girl." He said she was a female. He was happy since he was a father, he was extremely grateful. He finally paid him with his material possessions, he paid him because he was grateful that he had let him understand [that he would have a daughter].

After sometime, after a number of months of being in the womb, a female was born. They saw she was a female when she was born. She was a child. She was their only child. Since he wanted her and she was his child, he brought material things to the *qasgi* to give away. They filled the *akirtat* [wooden serving dishes] with *akutaq* [festive mixture of berries, fat, and boned fish] and brought them to the *qasgi*. He gave half of his wealth to the old people, to elderly men. He gave the gifts away; [the custom] was called *all'artelluku* for that child although she was a female.

During that time, from being small, that child grew. When she began walking, her mother and her father said, "Let's find a companion for her from somewhere. That companion of hers will be her playmate and will keep her from getting lonely."

When both parents of that female child agreed, when they were in agreement, they got her a puppy to have as a playmate. It was about so big. They got her a puppy that wasn't so large. That dog, that puppy, small puppy was white and had designs on it.

(Unfortunately, even though I wish you two could understand what I'm saying, you are looking at me not understanding what I'm saying. But it's okay, this is how you two [Robert Drozda and Bill Sheppard who I'm speaking to] wanted it.)

Constantly playing with that puppy, that child grew older. Eventually, after a number of years passed, and ten years probably passed, probably after ten years, that girl became of age to get married, to get a husband.

Her very big dog down there, a very huge dog down on the floor, and there was no other dog larger than that dog in that village. They didn't give a name for that dog. They didn't give a name for that dog, but they would just call that dog *qimugta* [dog].

magician doctor; tamatumek yugarluni tauna angun nukalpiar.

Nukalpiam taum nunulirluku aklumineg, nunulirluku taumun angalkumun cuvrisqelluku tauna nulini ellimerulluku caluku alangrullraneg temiini uumi.

Taum angalkum ullagluku taklarrluku kwaten, nalqiggluku, *flat*-allriamun, manilriamun elliluku. Talligni kangiwarlukeg, atkua man'a ikirrluku ukuminegggur tallirpimineg kenegtarturaraa aqsii, kenegtarturluku qussigiaqluku, atraraqluku.
Qanrutaa-ggur taqlerminiu, "Una tan'gurracuaraulliniuq. Nukiarkaunrilnguuluni. Arnaulun'i." Arnauniluku qanruteklinia. Quyaluni una ataungami, quyaluni cakner. Nut'an akilirluku tamakuneg aklumineg akililluku, nunulirluku taringevkallni quyaluku.

Ak'anuiqerluni tayima qayutun tanqit aturluki qumiuluni, arnar tauna an'ur. Arnaullinilluni cuurtur maaten. Qetunrauluni. Kiimi tawa kiingan qetunraqluku. Uum piyukengaqluku qetunraqngamiu akluneg qasgimun payugqelluni. Akirtat akutameg imirluki qasgimun qasgitaqluki. Tawa-i tukuutmi avgit cikiutekluki ak'allanun angutngurtelrianun. Cikiutekluki; tawa-ggur atengqerrluni all'artelluku tauna tan'gurrer arnaungraan.

Tamatum nalliini tan'gurrer tauna miktellermineg angliluni. Piyuaturiqerluku, piuturiqerluku aanag taukug, atii-llu qanlliniug, "Aaparkaaneg-tur kwangkug katurrlug naken alaqullunug pilug. Aapaa tauna aapaqerkaqniaraa alliayuutekevkenaku."
Nut'an-llu nakingameg tamarmeg angayuqaag taum tan'guraraam arnam, nakingameg tamarmeg qimugkauyara'armeg alegniirutliniluku. Qayutun tayim' angtaurciq'ur. Mikelqurpaarmeg qimugkauyara'armeg alegniirulluku. Qaralingqerrluni qaterpauluni qimugta tauna qimugkauyarer, qimukcuarer.
(Arenqiatur taringumasqumayaaqamteg, taringeksaunateg tawa-i tangssugarpetegnga. Taugg'am canritur elpeteg piyulleqerteg.)

Tauna qimukcuarer aapaqu'urluku taum tan'gurram naugurallinilria angliluni. Ki'-ima tauna allrakut qayuturrluki, tayimaa-llu allrakut qulngurtelliut, qulen naatellii allrakut tawa-i aapangyaqlegurrluni, wingyaqlegurrluni arnar tauna.
Qimugkugpallraa-wa kan'a, natermi qimugterpall'er angqapiareluni, angtataunani-llu tawani nunani qimugta tauna. Qimugta tauna aterpagteksaataat kitumeg. Acirluku qanrutek'lanritaat taugg'am qimugtemeg aterpagtaqluku qimugta tauna.

(Although I want you to understand this [story], you two haven't been able to understand it since you wanted me to speak in Cup'ig like I am doing now.)

They say that dog was smart. This was up at Aternermiut on Nelson Island. And its companion grew and became a young woman. And she was the only child of that married couple. She was their only child.

And finally during that time, when it was time, the father of that girl told her, her father told his daughter that she should hurry and accept the proposal of one who wanted to marry her, to take him as a husband if he wanted her. His daughter agreed and said she would [marry him].

After that, not long after, when one of the men chose her, because he liked that woman, he asked her to be his wife, he asked to have her as his wife. He would take her for a spouse, she would become his wife. That woman accepted him, she accepted him because she liked him.

The next morning she put on her parka and searched for him in the *qasgi* taking along a bowl, and she handed the bowl to him since he was her husband-to-be.

Then she went out. When he took that bowl from her, she went out. Her mother told her to hurry up and go get his bowl. For some reason the girl didn't want to get it, they say she didn't want to get it. And he had given her a new parka. He had her put one on. She took off that parka and threw it over there. She said she didn't want the man who wanted her for a wife as a husband. And she didn't go and get his bowl.

It so happened that he was the first, one [man], the one she would start with. She threw that man away and didn't want him for a husband. Another, after that, again another went to go and see that woman. Just like the other, he gave her a really nice parka to use so that she would be his wife.

That woman accepted him [as her husband]. Her mother told her to go and give food to him by filling his bowl in the morning. In the morning, she went and gave him food. She gave him the bowl. When he took it, she went out. When it was time, when it was time for him to finish, she went and got his bowl and brought it inside. And then she tossed it toward the back, she just tossed it like this toward the back. After tossing it, she removed her parka and threw it toward the exit. She said she was done [being married to him] since she was tired of him.

They say that woman, the husbands that she liked, after going and giving them food, she used to go and get their bowls. And one she didn't like, she would go and give him food and not go and get his bowl. That's what she was like. This was up at Nelson Island in a village called Aternermiut.

The people of Nelson Island, when their men would climb to the top above Aternermiut and look for ice [on the ocean], they would see this island. They knew of it and would call it Nuniwar. The men knew it. And some women who walked, who were picking crowberries, and those getting mouse food and searching their

(Man'a maa-i taringesqumangramku taringeksaatarteg tayima elpeteg piyugluteg qanresqengavtegnga waten Cugtun.)

Tauna-ggur qimugta uswituluni qimugtenguur. Piani pia-i Aternermiuni pingkuni Qaluyaani. Tauna-llu angturiluni neviarcaurrluni aapaa. Kiingan-llu qetunraqluku taukug nulirqelriik. Kiingan tawa-i qetunraqluk'u.

Nut'an-llu tamatum nalliini pinaringan, arnar tauna uum atiin, uum atiin qanrutaa panini piyugtengqerkan angutmeg amci ciuniuresqelluku, wikesqelluku piyukagu. Anglliniluni tauna pania piciqniluku.

Kinguakun tamatum ak'anuivkenaku illiita angutet cucukngamiu, piniqngamiu tauna arnar nulirrnialliniluku, nulirrniarluku tawa-i. Aapaqsagutarkauluku, nuliqsagutarkauluku. Arnam taum ciuniurluku, ciuniqerluku piniqngamiu.

Unuakungan atkullaareluni qasgimi yugarluku payugtellinia qantameg ang'arrluni, qantar-llu tauna tunluku elliinun wikaqngamiu.

Tawa-i-llu anluni. Ciuniurngagu qantar tauna, anluni. Aaniin pissaaqluku amci qantaa aqvasqelluku. Caluni-ggur uum arnam piyunritaa, aqvayunritaaggur. Atkugkitellruluku-llu nutaraneg atkugneg. At'evkallruluku. Taukut atkut yuuluki yaawet egtelliniluki. Tauna nuliqsugteni wiksuuminritniluku. Qantaa-llu aqvavkenaku.

Cuna-ggur tawa-i ciuqlir, ataucir, ayagniqautii. Eggluku angun tauna wiksuumirpek'nak'u. Allam, allam kinguakun amtallu-am paqluku arnar tauna. Ayuqluku cikirluku atkukegtaarneg atu'urkaineg nuliqnaluku.

Ciuniurluku arnam taum. Aaniin qanrulluku payugcesqelluku qantaa imirluku unuakum'i. Unuakumi payuggluku. Qantar tunluku. Teguagu anluni. Pinaringan, nangucugnaringan qantaa aqvaluku itrulluku. Kiatmun-llu nalugluku, waten tawa nalugluku kiatmun. Naluggaarluku atkuni yuuluki egtelliniluki-am yaawet uatmun. Tawa-i taqsuqucamiu taqniluku.

Tawa-ggur arnam taum piniqluki wikekngani, payugqaarluki qantait aqvatulqai. Piniqenrilkeni-llu payuggluku qantaa aqvavkenaku. Tawaten ayuqlun'i. Piani pia-i Qaluyaani Aternermiuneg at'legni nunani pingkun'i.

Ukut Qaluyaarmiut cikussurluteng mayuraqameng angutait pikawet qulliinun, Aternerem qulliinun, qikertar una tangrraqluk'u. Nalluvkenaku Nuniwaameg aperturaqluku. Angutet nalluvkenaku. Arnat-llu illaita pekelriit paunerrsuralriit makut-llu uugnarraat neqaitnek aqvatelriit kiartelriit Qaluyaaneg piaken, Nuniwar

surroundings knew of Nuniwar and would see it. But they didn't know if Nuniwar was inhabited; they never heard of anyone coming up to shore from there.

During that time, the father became tired of his daughter. Eventually, the father stopped going inside the *qasgi*. Because all the people of the *qasgi* had become his sons-in-law; although they had wives, they would ask her to be their wife since that woman was attractive.

After they tried to take her for a wife [and failed], her father became ashamed and stopped going to the *qasgi*.

(I'm telling this story in a hurry because our time will go fast. But I won't leave anything out when I tell it.)

Then her father, her father, being ashamed told his daughter in the morning, her father asked her, "Why is it that although a man wants you, you have been disregarding them? And I find myself unable to enter the *qasgi* since the men inside the *qasgi* have all become my sons-in-law. Why is it that you keep refusing to get a husband? Don't you keep in mind that I may not have someone to help me, don't you keep in mind that getting old like this, I may not have someone to help me?"

They say before he said that, her father would leave and not be seen, he would leave and be gone for many days. Before he said that to her, before he asked her why she hadn't gotten a husband, he would leave and be gone for many days.

Then one day, her father asked her the following, why it was that she continually refused to get a husband. They say her father, feeling sorrow in his heart, had stopped going to the *qasgi* since they all had become his sons-in-law, when [she had married] all the people of the *qasgi*. He finally said to his daughter like he was scolding her, he said the following, "Are you refusing to get a husband so that you would marry your dog there?"

They say that dog pricked up his ears up there when the father spoke to the dog. After pricking up his ears for a long time, ?whining, after making noise, when he stood, he went outside.

[The dog] went out and after being gone for a short while, he came back inside and was biting on an old boot sole. That old boot sole that he was biting on, while his owner, the girl was just sitting there, the dog gave it to her by setting that old boot sole on her lap, that dog was ?whining.

And then he pushed her with his snout here and pushed her onto her back. Then [the dog] copulated with her for the first time there.

(Although these things were shameful, those old people let us hear them. Although something is shameful, I will speak of it not wanting you to experience it or wanting you to experience it. Since these are supposed to be taught to our young people, to the young people, since they are supposed to be taught to them, even though they were shameful, those *ciuliaqatuut* [first ancestors] used to talk about them. These *ciuliaqatuut* are ancient.)

nalluvkenaku tangrraqluk'u. Taugg'am cungqerruciinak'u Nuniwar; cugmeg tamaaken atelriameg, tagelriameg niicuunateng kwatqapig tayima.

Tamatum nalliini atiin taum uum kwani panini taqsuqutengllinia. Kiitawani tauna atauluni una qasgimun iternanrirtur. Tamakut qasgim yui, cui qaqilluteng nengaulleqsagucamegteggu, nengaulleqsagucamiki; nulingqeng'ermeng nulirr-niaquluku tangyunarqengan arnar tauna.

Nulirrniaqussaqerraarluku, atii tauna kasnguyungluni qasginanrirluni-llu.

(Una cukanraareluku piaqa cass'aput makut cukan'erciqngata. Tawa-i amin-kiruarpek'naku taugg'am qanrutkurciqaqa.)

Tawa-llu atiin taum, uum kwani atiin, uum kwa-i, unuakumi kasnguyugluni panini tauna arnar qanrutlinia apluku atiin uum, "Caluten angutem piyungraaten ilangcissuiterpakarcit? Qasgimun-llu itlerkaqa kwaniwa kalivyagulluku uggaani nengauksagucamki, nengaulleqsagucamki qaqilluki angutet qasgim illuani. Carpakarluten wingenrilkurterpakarcit? Ukisqaatellerkaqa-qaa umyugaqenritan, ak'allaurrlua kwaten ukisqaatellerkaqa umyugaqenritan?"

Mat'umek-ggur qanerpaalegmi atii tauna tayima ayagluni tangrrunrirluni, ayagluni erenret qavcin aturluki nultaratullruur una atii. Tamatumeg qanru-paalegmiu, caluku wingeksaatellraneg apepaalegmiu ayagluni-ggur nultarer-tallruur.

Tawa-llu pinginanermini, picit illiitni atiin taum mat'umeg maa-i aptellinia caluku wingenrilkurterpakaucianek. Atii-ggur, iluteqluni qamaggun ircaqumikun qasginanrillni pitekluku uggaani nengaulleqsagucamiki tamakut, qasgim cui qaqicat'a. Nut'an-llu panini tauna nunulriatun piluku, nunuyakelriatun piluku qanrutlinia, ukatmun qanerluni, "Angu-qaa taumeg qimugtevneg wingnaluten wingenrilkurterpakartuten?"

Taum-ggur qimugtem ciutegegni pakemkug nikiagurarak, tauna ata qanellrani taumun qimugtem'un. Nikiagurraumaarraarlukeg, ?nimluarluni, neplirturluni pirraarluni, nangercami, nekevngami anlliniluni tayima.

Anluni tayimnguqerluni akaurtenrilngurmeg itertur atungallraarmeg keggmiarlun'i. Atungallraar tauna keggmiani itrautellinia taum cum'i arnam kwaten aqumgaurallran'i, qimugtem taum tunlliniluku kuwet manuanun atungallruar tauna, ?nimluareluni qimugta.

Nut'an-llu ukugneg cugg'egmineg cingqerluku kugg'un nev'ertevkalliniluku. Nut'an-llu tawa-i ciuqlirmeg atarrluku tawani.

(Makut maa-i kasngunarqengraata niitevkartaarait augkut ak'allat. Ca imna cayarar kasngunarqengraan qanrutekciqaqa elpenun atuusqevkenaku, kwall'u atusqelluku. Makut maa-i tawaten alerquutnguarkaungata makunun ayag-yuaramtenun, ayagyuarenun alerquutnguarkaungata kasngunarqengraata qanaa-tektulqait augkut ciuliaqatuut. Ciuliaqatuut makut ak'allaugut.)

So it was that the dog copulated with that girl for the first time there. After copulating with her, he dragged her outside. Finally he dragged her around outside trying to drop that woman.

Then before [the dog] went inside the home, he dropped her outside. It so happened that was the first time he did that to her. Every day and even at night, he would continually drag her around like that. When he wanted her, that dog would copulate with his owner and drag her outside.

While the people of the *qasgi* were outside, the young people who had asked her to be their wife, when they saw her being dragged around by that dog, they would laugh at her. [They would laugh] about how that woman had really gotten a man who was capable now for a husband.

(This is what you wanted to hear, how [Nelson Island] across there came to be inhabited and how Nunivak here came to be inhabited. My intention is to progress toward how Nunivak came to be inhabited. . . .)

(I'm gradually heading toward where [Nunivak Island] becomes inhabited by people, following what my grandfather told me about it.)

When that dog would drag her around while copulating with her, the ones who asked to marry her would make fun of that woman and laugh at her. They would poke fun at her and laugh at her for marrying a rich person who didn't lack anything. (We Cup'ig people are instructed not to laugh at our fellow people.)

(Since our young people haven't learned the things they should hear, in my understanding, this *quli'ir* [legend], this true saying that is like a *quliraq*, this is the reason why you two want me to speak of it. I believe in the responsibility to pass it on to school students. [I'm telling the story] thinking that my grandchild will learn more about it.)

And after [the dog] dragged her around like that, her father became distressed by it after having encouraged it, since the dog heeded [his words], since he did heed, listening with both ears. The dog became like a real live person, but he couldn't speak. Although he could understand when hearing something, that dog couldn't speak; he couldn't communicate and speak.

Her father, the woman's father told the dog, "At this time out there, those with sons-in-law. . . ." This is what he told that dog, "Those who have sons-in-law, their sons-in-law will go caribou hunting. This evening, I wish I could have fresh caribou meat that was newly caught by my son-in-law."

They say that dog's ears started to prick up while he was below lying on his belly facing that woman, his owner, on the floor. When the dog suddenly stood, they say he sniffed his owner, that woman, here for a short while. After sniffing her, the dog suddenly spun around and went out.

Cuna-wa-ggur tawa-i ciuqlirmeg tawani atartelliniluku tauna arnar qimugtem taum. Atarqaarluku qamurluku anutelliniluku ellamun. Nut'an ellami qiini qamuraluku cangualuni katangnaqluku arnar tauna.

Tawa-llu enmun iterpaalegmi katagturraanalliniluku ellamun. Cunawa-ggur tawa-i ciuqliliriluku. Erner tamalkuan unugtuuman qamuraurnaaluku tawaten. Piyungaqamiu qimugtem taum cun'i atarrluku qamuraqluku anulluku.

Imkut an'gillratni qasgimi witalriit ayagyuarat nulirrniartekqullri, qamuravkarluku qimugtemun taumun tangrraqamegteggu, englacitekurenauraat. Nut'an piyumanarqelriameg angutmeg wingellinillraneg arnar tauna.

(Man'a maa-i niicumiqngaqertek ik'um qikertam cung'eqarraarutii, uum-llu Nuniwam cungeqarraarutii. Tamana piluku tungiinun ayagturtua cung'ellerkaan uum Nuniwam ayuqucian. . . .)

(Maa-i cung'ellerkaan ayuqucianeg, ayuqucian tungiinun agg'urtua aparrlugama qanruyutellra aturluku tawacet'un.)

Ellami qamuraaqagu qimugtem taum atangqaluku, nulirrniartellrin tamakut englacitekurenauraat temcikluku arnar tauna. Tukurlimeg nuuqitenrilngurmeg wingellraneg temcikluku englaqutekureraqluku. (Kwangkuta-wa alerquumamilriakut Cugni ilamteneg temciyugaqluta pisqevkenata.)

(Makut maa-i ayagyuaramta niitarkateng elicimanrilaiteki, taringellemni man'a quli'ir, qaneryarar una piciulria, quliratun ayuqelria qanrutkesqelliniateg. Man'a ukvekaqa elitnauranun *school*-aranun ukunun cikiutekarkaullra. Tawaggun elitekanirnayukluku elturaqa.)

Tawacetun-llu qamurarraartelluku, amtallu-am qakyutkengluku taum atiin kiikirnginarraarluku, qimugta tauna niitetulliningami, ciutelirluni inglugtun, niitetulliningam'i. Qimugta anerteqelriatun cugtun ayuqsagullun'i, taugg'am qanyuunan'i. Tawa-i taringturingermi niitaqami qimugta tauna taugg'am qanssuituq; qanerluni neplirluni pissuitur.

Taum-am atiin, atiin arnam taum uum qanrutaa tauna qimugta, "Qakma-i-am tawa nengaulget. . . ." Tauna tawa-i qimugta piluku, "Nengaulget nengaungit tuntussurciqelriit. Atakurpag-tur kwiinga tuntuturliinga nutarameg pitnerraarmeg, nengauma pitaanek."

Qimugtem-ggur ciutek imkug nikiagurraungartug-am kanani caumaluku arnar tauna cun'i palungqaurallermini natermi. Nang'ercami qimugta, nekevngami, maaggun-ggur ukugnegun narqetaaqerraa tauna cun'i, arnar tauna. Narqetaaqerrerluku wivqerrluni an'uq tayima qimugta.

When [the dog] went out, the mother of that woman followed him and went out, and he was running outside up there on all fours climbing above Aterneq. He disappeared over the hill. After he disappeared over the hill, when she went inside, she told her husband, she told that person, "The dog just left running on all fours up there." The man told his daughter, "I will travel tomorrow. When I arrive, you will come." His daughter became happy and agreed.

The midday sun up there, before the sun went down and had stopped rising, during the afternoon, one of the people entered and said that their dog was coming down from up there with a caribou on his back.

When that man went out and looked, he saw their dog coming down with a caribou on his back. And here was the above-ground cache, the above-ground cache here. He dropped the caribou next to the above-ground cache; the dog carried the bull caribou on his back and brought it home.

(These are things young men must learn. They must understand them.)

Finally this person, after sharpening his small knife he went to that caribou and butchered it. When he was done butchering it, he removed its skin and dried it since he would use it.

And part of its meat, the man over there who had become elderly and the small woman across there with no provider and the orphan with no provider, he gave part of it to them to eat. (A person who isn't jealous is like that. He will give away his catch. He will prepare food for one who is hungry, he will give water to a person who is thirsty, even if it's just a drink of water. Using his tongue, he will give good instructions to a person about how it is to live a good life, having the person who he is speaking to hear what he has to say.)

(The elderly men, when they spoke and gave advice, they would speak using their arms here inside the *qasgi*. They would say this is what that is like.)

When the next morning came, this person apparently went somewhere with a kayak. His daughter didn't know where he went. And although he told his wife where he was going, she didn't tell their daughter.

Toward evening, below Aternermiut, her father appeared paddling slowly. When the woman recognized him, she followed him and went down toward shore when he got out and towed his kayak. When he got out, his daughter went and checked on him, and there was a bowl in the back of the kayak that was filled to the brim with salmonberries. He had picked salmonberries, filling his bowl to the brim.

His daughter asked her father, "Where did you pick these, my father?" Her father told his daughter, "When you are able, you will go and pick them." She got happy and listened to her father. And she agreed and brought her father's kayak up [to shore].

Anellrani arnam taum aaniin maligarrluku an'ur pangalegluni piini Aternerem qulliini mayulria qimugta tauna. Tayima talurtelliniluni. Talurtellran kinguani itrami wini qanrulluku, una qanrulluku, "Imna qimugta pangalegluni ayagtur piiwet tayima." Taum angutem uum panini qanrutaa, "Unuaqu ayagciqua. Tekiskuma taaciquten." Pania quyaqerluni ang'lliniluni.

Ernequr' pikna, puqlaner una atrevvailgan, cali-llu mayunriqerluni ernequrtellrani, cuuget illiit itqerluni qanertuq qimugtiit-ggur at'ertuq pagna tuntumeg atmagluni pamaggun.

Maaten imna angun una anqerluni kiartur, qimugtiit man'a atralria tuntuwa atmii tunuani. Ukut-wa mayurrviit, mayurrviit ukut kwani witalriit. Taukut mayurrviit caniatnun katakalliniluku cirunelek; cirunelegpag angutvag qimugtem atmagluku ut'rulluku.

(Makut maa-i tan'gurraat elitarkait. Taringluki piarkaugait.)

Nut'an uum caviggacuarani anguluku cingiggarluku tauna tuntu ullagluku pilagluku nutaan. Pilanermeg taqngamiu qecia agarrluku kinracirluku aturkaqngamiu.

Illiineg-llu kemgem makut taqnerurtelria ingna angullugaralria, arnalqucungiir-llu ikna pistaalngur elliqcunguniir-llu una pistaalngur, taum illiineg nerr'erkaaraaneg cikirluku. (Tawaten cug ciknanrilngur ayuquq. Cikiqengarkauluni pitamineg. Neqliurkauluku cugkalria, meqsulria miitarkauluku, meq'ernginaartelluku pingremiu. Cuuyaram ayuqucianeg elluarrluku cug qanrutarkauluku uluni aturluk'u niitevkarluku tauna qanruskengani.)

(Makut maa-i imkut angullugaraat qanruciaqameng talligteng ukug aturlukeg qanrucitullruut qasgim illuani. Tawacetun-ggur tauna una ayuqur tamakucetun.)

Unuaqullrani una qayarluni tayima ayalliniluni natmun. Nalluluku natmun assaucia panian taum. Tauna-llu nulini qanrutellruciqengraani, nulirran taum panigteg qanrutevkenaku.

Atakuyarturluku Aternermiut aciatgun igwaaralliniuq cukassaagarpek'nani anguarturluni atii tauna. Elitaqngamiu arnam taum maligarrluku ketvarluni pillrani qayani qamurluku yuuluni tawa. Yuullrani panian curtuqaraa qantar kinguani, qayaan kinguani atsameg ellmaumaluni. Atsaneg unatallrulliuq qantani ellmarluku.

Panian taum atani una aptellinia, "Naken makuneg unatallruyit atama?" Atiin uum panini qanrutaa, "Piyunarikuwet unataryarturciqaten." Quyaqerluni tawa niicugniureluku atani. Atami-llu qassaa mayurrluku niicugniureluni.

That dog would bring his woman out and drag her around outside when she became his wife. After some time, this part of her no longer had hair from the dog constantly putting her on her back and dragging her around. Eventually she no longer had hair along the back of her head.

Although she was alone, she was apparently the very first inhabitant of Nunivak Island.

Then after some time passed, when the dog was calm, her father said to the dog, "I wish I could eat caribou tonight. Other sons-in-law will be feeding their fathers-in-law from the caribou they caught. I wish I had many sons-in-law and was also one of those people." The dog's ears twitched for a long time, [and he was] ?whining.

When he suddenly stood, he smelled his owner's [legs], that woman's legs, her knees here. [The dog] spun around and ran out.

His woman, the owner of that dog, followed him and saw that he was running up over the hill on all fours and went out of sight.

When she entered, she told her father, "That one went up there and disappeared over the hill and left." "Yes." Her father said to her, "If you want to pick salmonberries, I will bring you to those berries." She got happy and got a grass pack ready and filled it with waterproof gear, a container, and a bucket, and they went down to the shore.

Her father put his kayak down in the water, and when they embarked, he had her get inside the kayak. When she went inside, he placed her bag along the lower part. When she got inside and was out of view, he seemed to be traveling up following the Tuqsuk River; his kayak was facing that way. He took off and she was inside there listening to the lapping of the water. He seemed to be going [east] up [the bay].

As he was traveling along, that woman slept. When she woke from her long sleep, she heard Arctic terns outside making noise, they were making noise making the outdoors sound nice.

He called to her, "Daughter, it's time for you to wake up." He told her to wake up. She replied and told him that she was awake. He headed up toward the side and slowed down and stopped. When he stopped, she took her pack sack out. He said to her, "You've arrived at the place where you will pick berries. You will pick berries."

The woman got out of the kayak. When she got out, she looked around and her surroundings appeared strange. It had many rocks. There were many rocks. When she got out of the kayak, her father pushed away from the shore and quickly went down to the water. He said to her, "Since this is to be your home, I have left you at your home-to-be. If I am able to, I will come and see you from time to time. The salmonberries you will pick are up there."

Niicugniinanrani taum tawani qimugtem qamurnauraa ellami anulluku arnani tauna nuliqsagucamiu. Ki'-ima ukua qiuqlaarutur newerrluku qamurturallran qimugtem taum. Una talirnera qiuqlai nangluteng melqurriulluni.

Tawaten taw ellrung'ermi Nuniwar una cul'iqaarrarpiarallrullinia.

Tawa-lli-wa qakukuurrnerakun utumallrani, uum-am atiin tauna qimugta qanrutlinia, "Tawatur-tam kwaniwa tunturliinga ataku. Allat-wa nengaulget caki-teng tuntutameggneg neqliuruarciqiaqait. Kwiinga-llu-tur nengaulirlua kwaten ilagaulliinga tamakunun." Qimugtem-ggur-am im' ciutek qipiagurraumalliniug ?nimluareluni.

Nekwarcami-am narqetaaqallinilukeg ukug cum'i taum arnam irug, ukug ciisquuk. Qip'arrluni anlliniluni tayima.

Nut'an taum arniin, cuan qimugtem, maligarrluku pia pangalegluni-am mayullinilria tayim' piiwet tayima talurrluni-llu.

Iterngami atani qanrutaa, "Pagaawet tayima talurtur ayagluni augna." "Aa-ang." Atiin uum qanrulluku, "Unataryukuwet assauciiqamken imkucinun atsa-nun tamakunun." Quyaqerluni upluni issratmeg kalngagmeg piluni mecungniurr-suutmineg imirluku akirtarkamineg, qaltaurmeg-llu, atralliniluteg cenamun.

Atiin taum qayani at'errluku ekciqiarngameg kinguminun pulavkallinia qayam illuanun. Pulangan kalngii tauna uatiinun ellilliniluku. Pulamangami qawawet Tuqsug aturluku ayagciqiarnganani; qassaa caumaluni tamaawet. Ayagartelliniur qakmani lurliureluni. Qawawet tayima ayagnganani.

Ayagngaqu'urngiinanrani qavalliniur tayima arnar tauna. Qavarturallermineg ak'anun tupagyarturtuq teqiyaaret qakemkut qalrialuteng, qalriurluteng, nii-cunariluku ellam illua.

Pillrani tuqlullinia, "Panii tupagnarriaten." Tupaasqelluku. Kiullinia kwani tupagniluni. Mengelmun tagluni cukaarulluni arulaalliniur. Arulaarngami *pack sack*-aara, kalngii yuuluku antelliniluku. Qanrutlinia, "Unatallerkarpenun tekituten kwaniwa. Unatarciquten."

Arnar tauna qayameg anluni. Anngami kiartur man'a tangellra allakauluni. Siimalilliluni. Siimat amllerrluteng. Ellii-llu tauna qayameg yuuluni piqallrani, atiin taum keluni ayalliniluku mermun ketvaqertelliniluni. Pillinia, "Nunakaqngavgu nunakarpenun uniciiqiaramken. Piyunarqellinikuma cam illiini paqtaqluten piciqelrianga. Unatarkaten pika-i pikani witaut."

He paddled going around the bend. When she turned this way, she looked around and there were mountains up there. There were mountains up there somewhere, and she didn't know where they were located. She didn't recognize them since she had never left her home before. She circled and searched her surroundings up there toward the land and saw land up there, the land up there. She climbed up on top of a high spot and looked over it, and there were a great many salmonberries. Two homes were over there situated one beyond the other.

It turns out she was across at that island called Triangle Island in English, on Qikertar across there. Your daughter [speaking figuratively] had ended up there since her father left her there, since you left her there. (I am pretending that you are the father of that woman at this time.)

Then when he left her, she got excited and went around those berries to be picked and went toward that place that looked like a home, and when she arrived upon it, she saw that it was a home. And along its side was something that looked like a small, partially underground storage cache.

She removed her pack sack and put it down, and since the doorway of the house was closed, she opened it and entered and saw that it was the inside of a home. It was a really nice home. One side had a mattress, the other side had no mattress. There were three containers in the back that were filled to the brim with seal oil. She saw that she was not lacking seal oil. (It's because seal oil was essential for people and something they couldn't be without. Sometimes the *qaneryarar* [oral instruction] is like a true thing.)

Then since she realized that was meant to be her home, she went out, and since that one was a small, partially underground storage cache, she opened it and looked inside and there were five sealskin containers. They were tied securely and behind them were dried fish. Looking at those fish and the three sealskin containers, she knew that some of them were half-dried [Dolly Varden] fish stored in seal oil, some were smoked fish in seal oil, and some had seal oil, and some were filled with other edible foods. She looked at those sealskin containers, and they were from Nelson Island. She recalled the foods that she had seen at her father's [home].

She felt guilty over her man, the dog, "I wonder what he will do. . . ."

And now going back to Nelson Island up there, before dark, toward evening, the people announced that the dog up there was heading down with a caribou on its back. And her father who had brought her had returned [from taking his daughter to the island] during that time.

The dog went down with a caribou on its back. Once again, he dropped it next to the aboveground storage cache down there and headed inside the house right away. They say when he entered that home, when he appeared, thinking he would see that woman right away, the dog looked for her but didn't know where she was.

Qipluni, anguarturluni wivluni, una cingig qipluku. Ukatmun caungan kiartur ingrit pingkut. Ingrit nani pingkut nani tayima nalluluki nani witallrat. Elitaqenritlinii witavini unilluki ayayuilam'i. Wivluni kelutmun kiartelliniur nuna paugna, nuna paugna. Mayurluni qaanganun qertulriim uyangtur ak'akika atsat. Enek-wa ingkug yaaqliqelriik.

Cuna-wa ikani ika-i qikertam'i Kass'atun at'legmi Triangle Island, Qikertami ikani. Paniin tauna tut'elliniluni tawawet atiin unicani, elpet unicavni. (Ataknguarcetamken taumun arnamun kwanirpag.)

Tawa-llu unicani quyaqerluni tamakut unatarkat atsat negurtarturluki ingna enngungalngur ullagluku tekitaa enngupiallinilria. Una-wa cali mengliini ayuqii ciqluggaunganani.

Kalngani yuuluku ellingamiu, ena amiiga tauna patumallininga, ikirrluku itertur enem illua. Enekegtaar. Inglua man'a cururluni, inglua agna curruinani. Akirtat kiugkut pingayun uqumeg qaqilluteng imarluteng. Uquryugyugnaatelliniluni. (Cuunginat makut uqur piutekngamegteggu piicalqaunani. Una kwa qaneryarar illiini piciulriatun ayuqur.)

Tawa-llu tamana enkaqliningamiu taringengamiu anluni tauna ciqluggaullininga ikirrluku qinertaa talliman caqutet. Qillengqakacagarluteng neqet-wa qaugkut kiatiini kinercimalriit. Neqet tamakut tangerrluki, cali-llu ukut caqutet pingayun nallunritai illait pingciutngululuteng illait uqumelnguuluteng, illait uquuluteng, illait tayima caneg neryunarqellrianeg imangqerrluteng pilriaruluteng. Tangraa-i taukut caqutet Qaluyaarmiutauluteng taqumaluteng. Enqarraa imum uum atami tangertukngai tamakut, tamakut neqet witallinilriit.

Imumeg umyugarniurtur angutmineg qimugtemeg, "Tayimaa-kir cacetun piurciq'a. . . ."

Nut'an-llu utermun uterrluta Qaluyaanun piawet, unugniareluku atakuyarturluku cuut qanertut qimugta-ggur pagna at'ertuq tuntumeg atmagluni pagaa-i. Tauna-llu atii tekitellrurrluni assaucestii.

Qimugta tauna at'erluni tuntumeg atmagluni. Imumun-am kanawet mayurrviit caniatnun katagluku egmianun-llu itqerluni enmun. Enmun-ggur tawawet itlermini, pugglermini egmianun tangerkengaqnaluku arnar tauna kiarcaaqaa qimugtem tamariluku.

When he went up, he headed inside, and after sniffing for a while, he suddenly turned around, and sniffing the area underneath his mattress, he ran outside. When he ran out, he quickly went down to the shore, down along the water's edge. And when he arrived, he went back and forth smelling the ground below, and then he looked back to where he had come from.

When he ran up on all fours, when he ran inside the house, he examined the inside of that house. They say that dog was scary when he did that. When he couldn't find his woman, they say he was scary.

[The dog] was extremely scary. Eventually he started to go in and out of other homes. After going to the *qasgi* first and smelling the ground underneath, when he didn't find her inside the *qasgi,* when going out, he would enter another home and after searching the inside of the home . . . they say that dog was scary when he opened up all the places and all the storage places when he searched.

Not finding her, after going to the very last place, when he went out, [the dog] quickly went to their home and ran inside. After going inside their home, continually sniffing the place where she had been sitting, he went out and went down to the shore, and after going back and forth down there, the dog sat down leaning on his front [legs] sitting on his haunches, and after looking at the area above, he would look back at that area over there and look there again. After looking back at it a number of times and looking around, when he stood, he took off to his right and went around the bend; he traveled along the shore.

They say [the dog] was gone for a long time, [the dog] was gone. For three days, he wasn't seen. Then on the fourth day in the evening, he arrived along the left side. They say the dog looked like he was extremely exhausted, like he was really exhausted. . . .[12]

When he arrived, he once again entered their home. When he reached her bed back there, after smelling that, he went outside and went back and forth along the shore down there. When he climbed up, he immediately climbed up above Aternermiut.

He continued to climb up there, and after getting to a high point, he went down again. He went down. When he arrived, he immediately went down. Running down slowly, when he went down toward the shore passing alongside their home, he immediately jumped into the water. It was during very calm weather, it was calm. He left swimming down toward the ocean.

Then the woman who came to be [the dog's] wife, since she had nothing to do, when the weather was calm, as she sat on top of her home looking around up toward Nelson Island, as she was searching the area toward that mountain, something whitish appeared down there. A polar bear came to her mind, [she was] thinking it was probably one of those. When it became distinguishable, it looked

Nugqercami itreluni naruraqarraarluku, qip'arrluni acini narr'urluku anqertelliniluni ellatmun. Anqercami egmianun cenamun atralliniluni, kanawet
mermun uum ceniinun. Tekicami-llu utqetaaqerluni naryaniurluku acini pirraarluku, kinguneni pagna kingyarluku tangssulliniluku.

Pangalegluni tagngami, enmun itqercami ena tamana cuvrilliniluku illua.
Alingnarqellruuq-ggur qimugta tauna tawaten pillermini. Arnamineg tamari-
llermini alingnarqellruuq-ggur.

Tawa-i alingnaqluni cakner. Kiitawani allanun en'un itertaanguq. Qasgi ciumeg
paqterraarluku acini naryaniurluku, qasgimi alaqenrilamiu anngami allamun
enmun iterluni, enem illua kiarqaarluku . . . tamalkuita-ggur ennguyaqleggat,
qemaggviuyaqleggat ikirqelluki kiartellermini, qimugta tauna alingnarqellruur.

Alaqevkenaku, iquklikacagaq pirraarluku anngami egmianun agluni enmeggnun itqertelliniluni. Enmeggnun itqerraarluni, tawaken-am eniinek, aqum-
gallranek narr'urluku anluni cenamun ketvarluni uterteqtaaqerraarluni kanani,
nutaan tauna qimugta aqumlliniur, aren ukug ciuqligni nekumalutek ma-
tertegminun aqumqerluni augna kialirneni tangssuggaarluku, augna kingyarluku
tangssugaqluku. Qayuturquni kingyarluku kiarteqtaarraarluku, tallirpimi tungiinun nek'wercami qipluni ayalliniur; cenar aturluku tayima tawa-i ayagluni.

Tayimaa-ggur tayima. Ukuni ernerni pingayuni tangrruksaunani tayima.
Tawa-llu-ggur una cetamiit atakuyarturluku ukaggun iqsulirnerem tungiikun te-
kitelliniur. Merenqapiarnganani-ggur qimugta tauna, mernuqapiarnganani. . . .

Tawa-i tekicami, tamta-llu-am enmeggnun iterluni. Tawaten-am tawa-i acia
kiugna tekicamiu naruraqarraarluku anluni atrarluni kanani cenami utqetaaqerluni. Mayurngami tawa-i egmianun mayurturalliniluni piiwet Aternermiut
qulliitnun.

Mayurturluni pika-i ak'akika quyigiqerrluni pirraarluni ataam atralliniluni.
Atrarluni tawa-i. Tekicami egmianun atrarluni. Tawa-i pangalkucigturluni atraami,
enmeng ellatiikun ketviimi egmianun tawa-i mermun qecliniluni. Quunkacagarmi,
kayukunani. Tayima tawa-i camawet imarpigmun kuimarluni ayalliniluni.

Tauna-llu tawa-i nuliqsaguskengaa tawa-i caarkailami-llu kayukitellrani,
enmi taum qaanganun aqumluni paugna Qaluyaat tungiit kiarqurainanerminiu,
ingrim tamatum tungii kiarqurainanrani, ca un'a alarucartullinilria qaterrlugl*uni.
Imna tawa-i nanuar umyugaqellinikii, tamakuuyuklukuarluku aapaagni.
Tawa-i nallunaarutur una-i tamakuunganani, tamakuciunganani-wa pillinilria.

like one of those, it apparently looked like one of those. Since they spoke of them, she thought it was one of those.

After some time, he reached land when there was low tide, at extreme low tide. And when he landed on the rocks down there, when he went up a ways and shook the water [from his fur], when she saw him shaking off the water, she apparently recognized that it was that one. [The dog] looked up at her, and after looking at her for a while, he slowly headed up.

She was anxious for him [to arrive], and she climbed and looked over. Since he was taking a trail that wasn't far away, he went down on his belly and watched her. He stood again and continued to approach her. When he wasn't too far away anymore, he went on his belly and watched her. Then he stood for the third time and approached her. When he was just about to reach her, that dog went on his belly in front of her.

When [the dog] did that, his owner, the one who became his wife said to him, "No one made you, but you have put yourself through suffering. If you hadn't handled me roughly in the village with many residents, and if you hadn't also dragged me around, you would not be missing me that much. Because you [dragged me] here and there outside, it made you miss me that much. And you even crossed the ocean that is impossible to cross. Evidently, you have found me because you were meant to find me. If you do that to me again, I will flee from you again and go somewhere where you will not find me."

[The dog] continually moved his ears up and down as she was speaking. Then as soon as she was done talking, when he went to her, he [copulated with her] as usual since that was what he usually did. Although he [copulated with] her, he didn't [drag] her here and there like before and [had sex with] her right there.

They say he began to do that to her and not bring [drag] her here and there. As time passed, his wife's stomach started to grow. She apparently became pregnant.

It is said that dog started to hunt a lot in winter. He continually caught seals. When he arrived after traveling somewhere, she'd see that he had caught a seal or he would arrive having caught a caribou from inland when he would leave *?kenwarluni*.

Then finally, one day that woman complained, "I wish we could eat some of my mother's *nin'amayuut* [herring aged in seal oil] up there, or I wish I could eat *nin'amayuk* that I customarily eat and not eat so many sea mammals."

He lifted his ears up and down like before. At the time, it was calm outside, and it was springtime. Once again, he ran *?tuwaqiimi* and jumped. When he jumped, he swam up toward the land. He swam and disappeared.

Qantullruata tawa-i tamakuuyukluku.

Tawa-i caqerluni maa-i tuc'artullinilria keningaluku, kenvaumaluku. Kana-i-llu tegalqunun kankunun tuc'ami mayuqerluni evcugarqullrani, evcullrani-wa tawa-i tangrramiu tawa-i elitaqliniluku tawa-i imungullinillraneg tauna. Tawa-i tangerrluku pikawet, tangwagturarraarluku tagg'urralliniluni cukavkenani.

Tayima tawa-i nerinilluni pirraarluni, mayurluni uyanglluni. Yaa-i yaaqsinrilngurkun piami, palu'urteqerluni tangwagturalliniluku. Nangerrluni ataam ullagturluku. Tamaa-i yaaqsinrirluku palurrluni tangwagturaraqluku. Tawall'am pingayiriluni nekevluni maa-i taagurluni. Tekitarkaurteqerluku kwani ciunranun tawa-i palurcimaalliniluni qimugta tauna.

Pillrani-am qanrutlinia yuan taum, nuliqsaguskengaan taum, "Cam tawa-i pinrilkiiten, elpet tawa-i taugg'am elpeneg-wa tawa-i makugtellriaten. Waten tawa-i nunarrlugugarni ilalkellanrilkuvnga qamuralua tawaten tawa-i pitalriameg yuganricararpenga. Tawa-i tawaten ayagallua ellami pilallerpet tawa-i yugaravkaqiiten tawaten pitalriameg. Cali ekruamayugnailngur man'a imarpig arviraqluku. Tawa-i kiitawani tawa-i nataqerkaullinilua tawa-i nataqerpenga. Uumiku cali tawaten pilaquvnga cali qimagciqkemken natmun tayima nutaan nataqsugnairullua elpenun."
Tawa-i-ggur-am ciutegni elivtaarturlukeg yaa qanerturallrani. Tawa-llu tawa-i qanenriuciatun ulliimiu-am tawa-i piciryaraqngamiu pilliniluku. Tawa-i piyaaqekniu imutun ayagatevkenaku tawani tawa-i piuralliniluku.

Tawa-i-ggur nutaan tawaten piyuriluku natmun-llu tariyucuirulluku tamaa-i. Piinanrani tawa-i aqsalingelliniluni tauna nulirra. Qingangelliniluni.
Tawa-i-ggur taun' qimugta tauna tawa-i pissunqeggilria uksumi. Taquka-qu'urluni. Naken ayaggaarluni tekiskuni taqukatliniluni kwall'u tuntutliniluni tekitnaurtuq pawaken ?kenwarluni/kenvarluni ayagaqami.

Tawa-i-llu nutaan tauna kwani caqerluni, caqerluni-am qaktelliur arnar tauna, "Pama-itur-tanem nin'amayuggautaitneg aanamegnug pamkut nin'amayagturlug, nin'amayagturli-wa kwaniwa tawa-i nertukngamnek makuneg caneg imarpig-miutassiyaagnek nerurassiyaagpeg'nii."
Ciutegni-ggur-am tawaten qikiaqerlukeg. Atam tawa-i kayukinani qakemna, kiapauruluni-llu cali. Ataam tawa-i pangalegluni ?tuwaqiimi qecliniluni tawa-i. Qecgami tawa-i kelutmun pawa-i kuimelliniluni. Kuimluni tayima tawa-i tama-lliniluni.

As her parents were staying up there, they announced that that dog had appeared down there, that he was approaching land. He got to land. They say when he got to shore and went up, he immediately opened their small elevated cache.

When he opened it and entered, he got a *kuusqun* [bag], some kind of small container, a container filled with *nin'amayuut* and dragged it outside. When he brought it outside, his father-in-law suddenly understood that he had come to get that, and he thought that perhaps because his daughter liked to eat *nin'amayuk,* [the dog] had gotten it.

He then fixed something for him, he made him a harness, a dog harness using some sealskin rope. Just as he finished, wearing it on his back, [the dog] apparently jumped in the water. When he left, he drifted away with it.

The men there felt a little upset by him, but since the dog belonged to their *nukalpiar,* the many men who had married that girl refrained from doing anything to him.

As that woman was sitting there, [the dog] appeared down there. When he arrived, she saw that he had that small container on his back. Her father had apparently made him straps for holding things on his back using pieces of sealskin rope.

When he brought it up, she apparently ate the foods she usually ate. From then on, that dog started to periodically swim up [to the mainland].

When he went up and arrived, the one who came to be his father-in-law would get containers filled with *nin'amayuut* and [dried] herring ready for him to take along.

One day toward fall he prepared [a container] for the dog, since he had made him a harness to carry things on his back. He filled that container with gravel and he stuffed the opening with some herring. When the dog was about to carry them, he would always check only the [container's] opening.

When [the dog] arrived, he was just about to place the container he had prepared for him on his back. When [the dog] was going to carry it on his back, he parted its opening and looked at its contents.

Then after checking its contents, when he bound it onto [the dog's] back, it was a little too heavy, but [the dog] just carried it on his back as it was.

When he jumped with it [into the water], he didn't look high out of the water down there as he left with it. Only a very small part of the top of [the dog] was peeking out [of the water].

It is said that when [the dog] went up [to the mainland] for the last time, he was gone for days, he didn't arrive. And not long after he failed to arrive, that woman

Tawa-i-am taukug angayuqag piani witainanragni qanlliniut-am tawa-i qimugta tamana alarucarturniluku una-i, tuc'arturyaaqniluku. Tawa-i tut'elliniluni. Tuc'ami -ggur tawa-i mayuami egmianun mayurrvicuarakeg taukut tawa-i ikirtellinii.

Ikircamikeg tawa-i iterngami kuusqutmeg tamatumek, cameg caquksuarmek-wa, caqutmeg tawa-i nin'amayuutmeg taumeg qamurluku anutelliniluni. Anucan tawa-i nutaan cakian taum taringarrluku aqvatlinian tamatumek, tauna-llu panini-llu nin'amayugyunqeggngan tamaa-i pillikii.

Tawa-i kitugutqerluku, nutaan anuqerluku, anuliqerluku caneg taprarrarneg. Tawa-i taquciatun-am tawa-i atmaku'urluku mermun qecliniluni. Ayima-i-am tawa-i atrulluku ayautelliniluku.

Tamakut tamaa-i angutet umyuarata navguurutkerrlugyaaqluku, taugg'am tawa-i nukalpiameng taumeng pikngatgu, pikngatgu tauna tawa-i qimugta tawa-i qaallukuanriquralliniyaaqekiit tamakut angutet nulirkalinrulriit nevviarcameg taumek.

Tawa-lli-g' tawa-i witainarani-am tauna arnaq, alarucartulliniluni una-i. Maaten tawa-i tekitur caquksuarmeg tamatumeg atmakulliniluni tamaa-i. Taprallruarneg atmaucilliniluku atiin taum.

Pilliniagu tawa-i, mayuulluku piagu tawa nertukngamineg nerurallliniluni. Tawa-i imna-am tawakenirneg ayagnirluni tawa-i tagqaqungllinluni qimugta tauna kuimarluni.

Tawa-i tagluni tekiskan, caqutneg tawa-i makuneg imkuneg nin'amayagneg iqalluarpagneg tawaten imalegneg caqutneg ang'aqitnauraa taum cakiksagus-kengaan.

Tawa-i-ll'-am cat illiitni uksuarkami upyutliniluku, anulillruamiu-llu tauna qimugta. Tuwapaggarneg, tuwapagmeg caqun tauna imillinluku iqalluarpagnek-llu paanga una kevirluku. Tawa-lli-ggur tamaa-i piqatarqamiki tamakut paangit taugg'am yuvrirrlainaqai qimugtem taum.

Tawa-i-ll'-am tawa-i tekilluni pian, tauna tawa-i upyuskengani nutaan tawa-i ang'aqliuteqatalliniluku. Tawa-i-ggur ang'aquqatallerminiu tawa-i paanga ikirarr-luku imai yuvrilliniluku.

Tawa-i-llu yuvrirraarluki nemragu nutaan tawa-i tunuminun pamawet piqallerminiu artulqiuteksaaqluku tawa-i, cavkenaku tawa-i tunumillliniluku.

Tawa-i-gg-ur tang tawa-i qecgucaqniu tawa-i qertuvkenani tawa-i unani tawa-i ayautellliniluku. Tawa-i caraquinermeg-ggur taugg'am tawa-i qalirnera man'a uyangssuakcuarturtelluku tayima tawa-i tamaaken.

Kinguqlirmeg-ggur tayima tawa-i tagngami tayima tawa-i kenglaunani, tayima tekitevkenani. Tekitenrilucian-llu tawa-i ak'anuivailgan, tauna tawa-i

gave birth to five puppies. She apparently gave birth to five pups.

Since they were her children, she took care of them. And they were such that they didn't make an effort to eat for themselves, but they only ate when she urged them to eat, being like humans.

Then as they were there, a kayak appeared down there inside Akuluraq [Etolin Strait] toward falltime. It approached slowly. When she became curious, when he became recognizeable, she saw that it was her father.

As he was approaching, those pups scattered along the brow of the cliff and sat and waited for him. Their mother told them that he was their grandfather, that they should show him great love.

That one down there *?kin'garluni* called to his *alungyarat* [lit., "lappers," from *alunge-*, "to lap with the tongue"] there. He apparently gave his grandchildren there kinship names, calling them his *alungyarat*.

When he came to call them by a special name, they got used to it, they would run down when he arrived and lick his face, happy to see him.

Realizing what happened to [her husband], that woman asked about whether he had arrived. He told her yes, that he had sent him away. She realized that he had drowned. After being there, [her father] left her and headed up [to the mainland].

When the times her father arrived began to get closer together, one day when those pups had grown, she said to them, "See your grandfather down there, after killing your father, look at him down there, he is continually having his fun with you." Just for the heck of it she said, "Don't leave him alone, but go to him right away and kill him." (Gee, even though her husband was a dog, she really was sad about losing him.)

Their grandfather arrived down there, *?kin'garluni*. Right when he called them his *alungyarat*, they immediately ran down. They went down, and when they came upon him and licked his face, eventually they cut open his nose, and eventually they *?anguktarluku* his face and fought him and killed him.

When they did that to him, when their mother approached them and scolded them, she scolded them harshly. She told them that she had said that just for the heck of it, that she hadn't said that to them so that they would heed her. She scolded them because they had listened right away when she merely told them something that wasn't true for the heck of it. She scolded them.

When she did that to them, those pups suddenly kept at a distance. After that, they began to want to stay at a distance. They say two of them would come closer inside, but they would once again stay at a distance. Although she would tell them to come, they wouldn't come to her any longer.

arnar irnilliniluni qimugkauyara'arneg tallimaneg. Qimugkara'arneg tallimaneg irnilliniluni.

Tawa-i qetunraqngamiki tukangcarturalliniluki. Tawa ellmeggnek-llu neryugluteng pinrilata tawa-i neresqumaaqateng taugg'am tawa-i nerlaata, yugcetun ayuqluteng tamaa-i.

Tawa-llu piinanratni tawa-ll' qayartarungairalliniluni un'a uksuarkaklagmi Akuluram illua. Agiirqurluni. Maaten tawa-i paqnayungelliami tayim' elitaqnariur imna tawa-i ataklinikii.

Tawaten tawa-i tekicartullrani taukut kwani qimugkauyaraat qauqaarmun kanawet caggluteng aqumluteng utaqallinikiit. Aaniita taum qanrut'lallii ap'aqniluku tawa-i cakner kenekluku tawa-i pilaasqelluku.

Imna tawa-i kanani kin'garluni tuqlullinilria alungyaramineg taukuneg. Tutgarani taukut tuqluucillinikai alungyaraminek.

Tuqluuciateng tawa-i eliyulluku, pangarvagluteng atraqerrluteng tekiskan tawaten, kegginaa man'a tawa-i alungnauraat angniutekluku.

Tawa-i taringluku tauna tawa-i, apyuteksaaqluku taum arnam kwani tayima tekitellrucianeg. Anglliniluku tawa-i ayagcitellruyaaqluku-ggur tayima. Tayima tawa-i eplinillraneg tawa-i taringluku. Tawa-i-am pirraarluni tayima-i unilluku tawa-i taggliniluni.

Tawaten tawa-i tekiteqtaangellra-am atiin taum akulkelliluni pillrani-am cat illiitni, taukut qimugkauyaraat angliriluteng pillratni, cat illiitni pillinii, "Tangerrluku tawa-i ap'arpeci un'um atayi tawa-i pitaqerraarluku una-i anglaniteku'urqekiici." Ellmikun tawa-i qannguayautekluku pillinikii, "Witatevkenaku tawa-i ciuniurluk' egmianun tuquskiciu." (Aling, qimugtengungraan-llu cakner qunukellinivaa tauna wini.)

Tawa-i un'a-am apaarat kanai tekilluni ?kin'garluni. Alungyamineg tuqluuciatun egmianun pangalegluteng atralliniluteng. Atreluteng tawa-i tekicamegteggu alungeqerluku kiitawani qengaa makerqelluku, kiitawani tawa-i kegginaa ?anguktarluku callugluku imna wirrluku tuqutelliniluku.

Tawaten piatgu aaniita taum ulliimiki tawa-i nunullinikai nutaan tawa-i cakner nunurluki ellmini tawa-i. Tawa-i pissaaqelliniluki picimeg niicesqumaluni qanrutenricaaqniluki. Ellmikun tawa-i qannguayaulluki qanrucaaqellratni niiteqtauciitneg tamaa-i nunuryaaqluki. Tawa-i nunurluki.

Tawaten tawa-i pikiiteng imkut qimugkauyaraat tawa-i ellaqvaqertelliniluteng. Cunawa-ggur tawa-i ellaqvatmun kessianeg tawa-i piyugnaaluteng pilliut. Malruk-ggur ukug tawa-i tumeqsigluteg pilaryaaqellriameg, taugg'am tawa-i tamtallu-am tamaa-i ellaqsigturluteg. Tamaa-i tawa-i taisqengraateng taisciigaliluteng tamaa-i pilliut.

Then they say when it froze, when winter came and right after freeze-up, when they split up and went their own ways, some of [the pups] seemed to head down the coast, and the others traveled toward the area out there. Three of them went toward the area out there. It is said after they left from there, they were no longer seen.

It is said that when they stopped, they would howl repeatedly, but it wasn't known what happened to them.

And again, after those [left], it got quiet. She had nothing to expect and look forward to any longer. And she stopped expecting her father to come since her sons had killed him.

In winter, when winter came, she eventually started to lack food. And since that place didn't have a lot of food, since there weren't any fish to be seen there at that small island. It was apparently that small island over there inside Akuluraq. That person apparently stayed there.

She started to lack food. Eventually she started to starve. One winter, she completely ran out of food. When she had nothing to eat, she started to eat her skin boots. She ate the edges of her skin boots. Since they were the only food she had left, she ate them.

And she didn't pay attention to her father's kayak; she was supposed to have learned how to paddle so that she could use it to go places.

(Since one cannot do something unless one has been taught and learned how, even though one is a woman, she probably would have been able to paddle. Those I saw in the past, including women, were good at [paddling] here; in the ocean and around here in summer, when they'd move to places and their husbands had two kayaks, women would paddle. That's how she could have learned if she had paid attention to her father's kayak. If she had observed him, she probably could have used it to travel somewhere, she probably would have used it to help herself survive.)

That one across there they call Qaneryartaleg [Qaneryartalegmiut] is not far from that island across there. And that place has fish and isn't completely without food.

The poor thing starved there in winter, running out of food. Eventually when she had [eaten] her boot down to her boot sole, but here those were the second pair of skin boots that she had eaten all winter. She started [eating] the other [boot], and when she started passing her knee, with great effort she tried to go outside, almost not making it in wonderful spring weather. When she went out she saw that it was foggy. The sun was actually shining above the fog, but fog was below it.

Remembering the place where her father used to arrive, although it was foggy, as she sat and watched the area below, from somewhere, she started to hear two

Imumek-llu-ggur tawa-i cikuluni man'a, uksurluni cikuqerluku tawa-i avegluteng ayalriit, aapait unatmurrnganateng aapait-llu awawet kwani yaalirnerem tungiinun. Pingayun taukut yaalirnerem tungiinun piluteng. Tawakenirneg-ggur tayima tawa-i ayiimeng tayima tawa-i tangrruunrir[tut].

Arulairaqameng-ggur taukut tawa-i marurpagalaryaaqellriit taugg'am tayim' qaallun pillratneg nataqumavkenateng.

Amta-llu tawa-i kinguatni nutaan tawa-i nepairulluni. Cameg-llu kwani tayima tawa-i neryuniugaarulluni. Tauna-llu atani tawa-i tayima neryuniurutkenrirluku taukut qetun'ermi tuqutellruatgu.

Tamaa-i uksumi uksurqan tawa-i kiitawani neqaaturangluni. Tamana-llu neqyanrilan, neqnek kwaten tangerrnauyuilan tauna kwani qikertarraq. Cunaw' ikna ika-i qikertacuar ikna Akuluram illuani. Tawani tawa-i tauna witallrulliniuq tauna.

Tamaa-i neqaiturangluni. Kiitawani tawa-i paluniqenglliniluni. Tawa-i uksut illiitni neqkairutkacagarluni. Tawa-i qaallun nervigkairucami pilugumineg tamakuneg neruranglliniluni. Piluguni tamakut ceniurluki. Kiingita tawa-i neqkaqsagucamiki nerr'uralliniaqekai.

Tamana-llu-am aatami qayaa cumikellruvkenaku; natmun ayakarrsuutekani anguanermeg elitnauquni elitarkauyaaqluni.

(Ca man'a elitnaurumavkenaku elicimaksaatellaami, tamaa-i arnaungermi anguaryugngassaaqeciqelliur tayim'. Makut-wa tangtullrenka anguanermeg arnat tawa-i elisngalalriit maani; imarpigmi maani tawa-i kiagmi-llu upagaaqameng, witeng kwani malrugneg qayangqerraqata, angualalriit arnat. Tawaten elitarkauyaaqsaaqluni tawa-i qayar tamana aatami taum qassaa cumikellrukuniu. Murilkellrukuniu-wa tamaa-i aapaagni natmun ayagssuutekaqsaaqekniu, angumqatugarcuutekaqsaaqellikii-wa.)

Ikna-wa yaaqsinricaaqellria Qaneryartalegmeg pilaqiit tawaken qikertameg ikaken. Neqyagluni-llu neqaitevkenani pilalria.

Tawa-lli-wa uksumi tawani paluurallrallinilria tawa-i neqkairulluni. Kiitawani tawa-i pilugumi inglua tauna kanawet nat'raminun tawa-i engelkessagucamiu, amtallu tawa-i kinguqliuluteg taukug tawa-i pilugug nerkengaag uksurpak. Aapaanun ayagnirluni, amtallu tawa-i neru'urluku, ciisquni tauna acitmun kitungenrakun, pegnem tawa-i anengnatugangnaqluni ellamun up'nerkaqegtaarmi. Taicirluni an'ur maaten. Pagna qullii akerciryaaqluni, acia man'a taicirluni.

Imna tawa-i aatami agiirtellernaaraa umyuaqluku, un'a tawa-i taicingraan aqumluni tangwagturainanrani, naken imkug yuug qanerturalriig tayim' niit-

people speaking. [The voices] sounded like they were coming from the water down below her.

When they became visible in the fog, two kayaks were down there. They had kayaks that were entirely white. They had apparently docked down below her.

Then when they got out down there, just when they brought up their kayaks, she could hear the other telling his partner down there, "My goodness, you are going to present yourself for nothing. Although men wanted to [marry her] before, she used to ignore them. I wonder what that one up there who your mind is set on will do with you?"

She thought, "My, I probably know that one down there, I probably know who he is."

After a while, the person he spoke to down there, the one who seemed younger answered him, "If she isn't going to [heed], she will say she won't. If she explains [why], it will be okay if we don't [take her]."

Using his paddle as a walking stick, he climbed up before him. And behind him, the one who seemed like an older brother stayed behind down there. He just watched him as he headed up away from shore.

While he was heading up, he followed behind him, he followed him. They climbed up. As he was coming toward her, she saw that it was a nice looking young person using his paddle as a walking stick.

He came upon her, but she couldn't speak, and she couldn't look up. Her clothes were ragged, and one of her boot soles was down there, the other boot sole down there.

While he was there, his older brother came upon her, one who appeared to be the older brother. He appeared older than the one who first came upon her.

When he reached her he asked, "So just like I told you she would, did she just ignore you even though you've asked her?" The one who seemed to be his younger brother told him that he wanted to ask her now, but he had not asked her. That's what he told him of his plan.

The one who looked like the older brother said to him, "Now hurry up, it's going to get dark on us. It's going to get dark on us." Then he said to her, "Will you just ignore us, even though we have come to get you?" Although she almost said yes, she stayed ?[t]alikupiggluni.

Because she hesitated, he said to him, "Just as expected, she's not going to pay attention to us. It would be best if we just hurried up and returned home."

When he said that, the young person asked her, "So is it indeed true?" She ignored his question once again. Closing her eyes that woman told him that although she wanted to go with him, being shy because her body was in that condition, although she wanted to agree right away, that she could not agree right

narilliniluteg. Tuar unaken-ggur tayima tuar ketiineg piaqelriik.

Maaten tawa-i tangerrnariug taitugmi qayag unkug. Qatellriarrlainarneg qayarluteg. Tawa-i kana-i ketiinun culurtelliniluteg.

Tawa-i-llu kana-i yuungamek, qayateg tamakut mayurteqerluki, aapaan camani niitnaqluni qanrutlinia, "Alingnaqvaat-lli tawa-i takuqatalriaten ellmikun. Tawa-i-w' civuani angutet piyungraatni ilangcissuitellrulria. Nut'an-kir tawa-i caksartaten umyugarpet tawa-i ciuneqek'ngaan pik'um?"

Umyugarteqliniur, "Aling tawa-i nallunricaaqellinikek'a tang kan'a aapaagni tayim', nallunritlikek'a-wa."

Tawa-lli-wa piqerluni ciunran cama-i kiullinia, ayaniilqengalkiin kiullinia, "Tawa-i kwani piarkaunrilkuni tawa-i piarkaunritniciqellria. Tawa-i nalqigeskan pinrilengramegni tawa-i cangailnguq."

Maa-i anguarutmineg ayarirluni mayurturalliniluni civuani. Kinguani-wa kan'a amaqliungalngur kana-i witauralria. Tawa-i tangwagturaqii kelutmun pawa-i tangerrluku.

Tawa-i maani tagg'urluni pillrani, amtall' kinguakun maliggluku, maligqurluku. Mayurluteg maa-i. Tekicarturturaraa ayagyuaqegtaarar una anguarutmineg ayarirluni.

Tawa-i tekicaaqluku qanerciiganani, ellii-llu kwaniw' ciugcesciiganani. qaalleraa-wa man'a, atungiin-wa inglua kan'a, atungiin-wa inglua kan'a kana-i.

Maaten tawa-i pillrani taum amaqlian tekilluku amaqliullinilriim. Ak'allarrartenrulliniluni taumi kwani tekiteqarraartiini.

Tekicamiu aptaa, "Tawa-lli-mamta-qaa tawa-i qanruyucimtun tawa-i apcaaqekevni tawa-i ilangcinrilkiiten?" Taum kwani kinguqliqngalkiin pillia kwaniwa tawa-i apcugyaaqluku apteksaatniluku. Tawaten tawa-i pillerkani piluku.

Imna tawa-i taum amaqliungalnguum pillia, "Amci tawa-i unungeciqaakug. Unungeciqekiikug tayima." Tawa-i-llu pillinia, "Tawa-lli-ma-qaa aqvayaaqmegten tawa-i ilangcingaituten?" Tawa-i angeryarpiangermi ?[t]alikupiggluni witaqalliniluni.

Witaqauciatun, witaqauciatun pillia, "Qayumi tang kwaniwa ilangciarkaunritlinikiikug. Amci tawa-i uterquraqumegnug kwani ataggauyalriakug."

Pillrani taum nut'an ayagyuam aptelliniluku, "Tawa-qaa tawa-i ilumun?" Tawa-iam apyutii augna tawa-i ilangciyugnaunag tawa-i apyutii. Tawa-i qelemqerluni arnam taum pilliniluku tawa-i maligcugyaaqeng'ermiu kwaniwa tawa-i takaryugluni piami kwaten-llu man'a qaallerani ayuqevkarluku angqeryung'ermi

away. And she also told him that she didn't say yes right away since she knew that she wasn't going to live well now.

Then he said to her, "Okay then, if you are to [go], if you are to go, you will. We will certainly come and get you tomorrow. Be ready tomorrow as we will come and get you then." She agreed, and she said that she would certainly go.

Then they said, "Hurry up now, it's going to get dark on us. We'll come tomorrow." They told her not to feel regret, not to feel regretful and to just wait.

He said to her, and his older brother, his older brother, the one who seemed to be his older brother went down. When he went down, that man said to her that if someone wanted [to get her] after them, to ignore him. He admonished her to ignore him completely. He said he had come to get her having great love for her. He told her that he would obtain her the next day, even though [she declined]. He told her that they would be visible again. She agreed with him when he told her that.

When they went down they got in [their kayaks] down there and left. When they got pretty far down, when they were about to disappear into the fog, they disappeared on the other side of a high piece of ice. After going out of view, as she was waiting for them to appear again, *aangikviik* [two eider ducks] appeared down there, and they immediately flew away.

The woman thought, "My, have those two who aren't human transformed into human form and spoken to me just now?" She was disappointed; although she tried to keep her mind positive, it couldn't stay positive. And although she wanted to quickly become a woman again, she couldn't.

Since she couldn't, she was overwhelmed. Since she couldn't, she couldn't. Then they were gone for a long while. And although the next day came, they didn't come around.

Then after being gone for a while, the sun came up again. Another morning came. When the sun came up again, toward evening when it started to get foggy, toward evening, from behind her, they apparently started making noise from behind her. And they approached back there speaking once again.

She had made up her mind to go with them for certain. Not long after, they appeared from the area behind her.

When they went up, when they got out [of their kayaks] down there, the one who seemed to be the older brother appeared to be holding something down there. He was holding something. They went up, and when they arrived, he was holding some sort of bag. He told her to go inside and quickly put on those clothes.

And the younger brother, the one who had gone to get her went inside with her. When he entered, he changed her garments. He put a really nice parka on her. After having her put it on, he apparently brought her outside.

patagmeg angqerciigatniluni. Kwaten cali elluarrluni tawa-i yuugarkaunrillni kwaniwa piluku angqanritniluni cukameg.

Tawa-i-llu pilliniluku, "Kitaki tawa-i piarkaukuwet, piarkaukuwet-wa tawa-i piciqellriaten. Unuaqu nutaan tawa-i aqvapigluten aqvaciqekmegten. Tawa-i unuaqu taugg'am upingakina-w' tawa-i nut'an aqvaciqamegten tawani." Tawa-i anglliniluni tawa-i pinrilngaitniluni piciqniluni.

Tawa-i-llu tawa-i pilliug, "Ampi tawa-i unukataraakug. Unuaqu tawa-i tai-ciqellriakug." Tawa-i umyugarniurpek'naku pisqelluku, umyugarniurpek'naku utaqalgiaraasqelluku ellmikun.

Pillia, anngaa-llu awa-i, amaqlia augna, amaqlia tawa-i, amaqliqngalkii awa-i atrarluni. Atrallrani taum kwani angutem pillia, kitak' tawa-i ampi cam piyungraagu ilangcisqevkenaku kingumegni. Ilangciqaasqevkenaku angurrluk inerqulliniluku tawa-i. Kwaniwa taugg'am kenekluku cakner aqvayaaqniluku elliin. Pingraan unuaqu tayima-i aapaagni unakeciqniluku. Aling-wa tangerrnariciqniluteg cali tawa qanrutlinikii. Angerluku tawa-i qanrucani.

Nut'an tayima tawa-i atraameg ekluteg una-i ayalliniluteg. Imumek kwani ketvaaraqerluteg taatugmun una-i tamarniaranga'arteqerluteg, cikumun tawa-i aug'umun qertuuralriamun iptelliniluteg. Ipterraarluteg tayima igwanercir-turainanrani aangikviik unkug igvalliniluteg una-i, egmianun-llu tenglutek tayima ayalliniluteg.

Arnar tauna umyuarteqliur, "Aling-qaa kwaniwa yuunrilnguuk augkuk yuugurullua kwaniwa awa-i qanrutaagnga?" Arenqiatelliniyaaqellria tawa-i; umyugani quyingnaqsaaqekniu quyigciiganani. Cali-llu cukameg kwani piyu-manarqelluni arnauyugyaaqeng'ermi nutaan tawa-i pisciiganani.

Tawa-i pisciigalami arenqianani tawa-i. Pisciigalami tawa-i pisciiganani. Nut'an tawa-i tayima, tayimngumaqalliniluteg ak'arrarmun. Unuaquurcaaqellria-llu tayima tawa-i alarutenritliniluteg tayima.

Tawa-i-ll' tayima tayimnguqerluteg ertenqiggluni. Unuaquq tamana erten-qiggluni allamek. Ertenqigteqerluku maaten-am tawa piug atakuyarturluku taitunga'arrnerakun, atakuyartullrani kelulirneran tungiineg pama-i neplirtu-rangartelliniluteg kelulirnerem tungiineg. Pama-i-am qanerturluteg agiirte-lliniluteg.

Nut'an tawa-i pinritevkenani maligtarkaulukeg tawa-i umyugamikun pill-ruluni. Tawa-i ak'anuivkenaku maa-i alarutliniluteg awa-i kelulirneran tungiineg.

Nut'an tawa-i mayuameg, yuuluteg kanani pillermegni, tauna tawa-i amaqliungalnguq, anngaqliungalngur tauna cameg un'umeg tawa-i tegumiar-turluni pilliniluni. Tegumiarluteg piluni. Mayurluteg tekitug cameg uumeg kwani kuusqutmeg. Pillia ampi tawa-i iterluku ukut aturat at'elaagesqelluki.

Taum-llu tawa-i uyuqlim, aqvastiin taum maliggluku tawa-i itliniluni. Itrami tawa-i, anui tamakut cimirturalliniluki. Atkukegtaarneg nutaraneg ac'equralliniluku. Ac'equrerraarluku tawa-i anutelliniluku.

The older brother told them to hurry, that someone would arrive upon them, he would tell them to hurry and go toward the edge of the cliff outside of where they were.

Then when she went out, situated across from one another, they brought her down [to the shore]. They brought her down, and when they got to their kayaks, the older brother had her get inside his kayak. He told her that one day she would be able to get inside his younger brother's kayak, that this time, she should get inside his kayak.

When they got inside, outside there, he quickly took her away. Apparently, he would travel with her for a long time.

As they were traveling for a while, after a while, when she woke from her sleep, and she had fallen asleep since they had served her some food. She could feel the kayak being lifted on top of a piece of ice out there.

After a while, he told her to hurry up and get out [of the kayak]. She looked and saw four people in the dark. There was a man and a woman who had become elderly. They told them, "You have apparently finally obtained her. You apparently brought her with you because she wanted to come with you." They got her and brought her up. And they brought her up and brought her inside the house in the dark.

That woman had apparently fixed a place for her beyond where she was. Immediately after having her go inside the place she had prepared for her, she put up some mats for a cover down below her.

Not long after putting up a partition, there was a loud rustling noise out there of someone entering and asking, "So did your two family members who seemed to be gone so late into the night arrive?" That woman told him yes, that they had arrived just now, that they had just arrived.

He told her that he was worried about them, afraid that they wouldn't arrive. She told him that she doesn't worry about them although they leave, that they travel using their *?nall'arartek*.

She was confined there. That woman tried to take care of her. At night she would give her a container to urinate in, have her urinate, take her urine outside, dish her food, feed her. And although that woman was starting to get embarrassed, she couldn't do anything.

One day seeing how she was, that woman said to her, "Okay then, tomorrow morning you will go out from there. You have a place across there ready for you. You will go across there. Although we want you to go out now, thinking someone might see you, we haven't let you out."

That woman apparently wasn't sleepy. Then when morning was about to come, that woman who had been occupied by her told her to hurry up and go across there. After being confined for a long time, she finally went out. They had

Amci tawa-i agiircetengqerturainarciqniluku, amci cukangnaqurelukeg pis-
qaqlukeg qauqatmun ellatiignun, anngaqlim taum amaqlim.

Tawa-i-llu tawa-i an'urainaan akiqliqluteg atraulluku. Atraulluku tekica-
megneki qayateg anngaqlim taum qayaminun tawa-i ekevkalliniluku. Cam illiini
qayaanun taum uyu'urmi ekenrurciiqniluku, maa-i ekenritqangraan qayaminun
ekesqelluku.

Nut'an tawa-i ekngameg qakmai ayagarutelliniluku. Cunawa-m' tawa-i
ak'anun cali assaucimanaluku tawa-i tayima.

Ayagaqnginanermegni tawa-i ak'anun piinanermini qavallermineg tawa-i
tupakallrani, neqmeg-llu neqliullruagni tawa-i qavaqalliniluni. Qakma-i qayar
man'a mayurtelliniluni cikum qainganun.

Piqerluku pilliniluku kiiki amci tawa-i yuuluku pisqelluku. Maaten piur
unugmi yuut ukut cetaman. Angun una arnaq-wa una arnaurtellria. Pilliag,
"Tawa-i unakurainapacilliarteg. Tawa-i, tawa-i piyugngateg, maligcugngateg,
malikelliarteg." Tawa-i unakluku mayuutelliniluku. Mayuulluku-ll' enmun
itrulluku tan'germi.

Enkiullrulliniluku yaawet yaatminun arnam taum. Egmianun tawa-i tawawet
kwani enkiuraminun itqercetraarluku uatii una kangciliqalliniluku curunek.

Kangciliqerraartelluku ak'anuirpailgan yug niugpallaggluni cakmani iterluni
aptelliur, "Tayimaa-qaa imkug ilagci unuksigiqerngatellreg tayim' tekitug?" Ang-
llinia arnam taum, kwanirpak kwani nutaan tekitnilukeg, awa-i tekitnera'arni-
lukeg kwanirpak.

Pilliur peng'garcaaqlukeg-ggur tawa-i tekitenriqurainarnayuklukeg aapaagni.
Pilliur tawa-i pengegnarqessuitnilukeg kwani ayangraagneg ?nall'ararteg atur-
turluku ayatunilukeg.

Nut'an tawa-i itertaulliniluni tawani. Tawa-i arnam taum tukangnaqutellinikii.
Unugmi qurrucirluku qurrmartelluku, qurrutii anlluku, neqliurluku nerqelluku.
Tawa-i tauna-llu-g' arnar tunringyaaqellriim arenqialngur tawa-i qaallun piviilami.

Imna tawa-i cat illiitni naspertuyagulluku taum kwani arnam pillia, "Kitak'
tawa-i unuaqu unuakumi tawaken anciquten. Ika-i ikawet enkangqertuten.
Ikawet piciquten. Kwanirpak kwani anesqumayaaqengramegten tangerteng-
qeqerrnayukluten pilunug kwani anevkanritamegten."

Tawa-i qavarninritlinilria arnar tauna. Tawa-llu unuakurtarkaurtenga'arrluku
arnam taum, uamqestiin taum pillia tawa-i ampi ikawirrluku pisqelluku. Imna
tawa-i qemagtauyaqviminek anyaqlirluni an'ur. Allanek-am tamtallu atkugneg

prepared another parka, other garments for her. When they gave them to her, she put them on.

They told her, "When you enter the *qasgi,* I will show you where tomorrow, you will give the bowl to a person who is along the back wall, on the right side of the wooden bowl-shaped lamp. If you had recognized him when he arrived the first or the second time, if you recognize him [bring him food]." She told her that she knew that person, that she had recognized that person.

The next day came; it was just about to get bright, and it was apparently spring there. When they were getting ready to eat breakfast, she brought food to him. She went to the *qasgi,* she went inside the *qasgi* and looked in, and when she looked closely there was someone along the back wall.

A woman down there popped her head in to look, a woman down there who hadn't been seen in that village before had arrived from somewhere. They were asking where that one down there came from.

Many young people there were eagerly expecting [her to give them food], and here they didn't know who she was, "I wonder which one of us she will give the bowl down there to?" When that one pulled herself up, she went inside and went to the back wall and gave that bowl to the youngest son of the *nukalpiartar* [rich man]. [They said], "My goodness, where have they found that beautiful girl?" They didn't know where that girl had come from who those two men had arrived with.

And then in the springtime, the place where the spring campers stayed was apparently a point. The area up from it was cut off. And it had two sand dunes. And there were other sand dunes far back that *?atliniluteng.* And there was another village upriver, another spring camp upstream. They went to the one downstream. The place where they arrived was apparently a very large village.

I said earlier that that woman was the first inhabitant of Nunivak Island, that she was the first inhabitant. This woman came from Nelson Island. And the village where she arrived, they mention it as being an *ircenrraq* [village]. That [woman] apparently married someone and moved to that village there as a daughter-in-law.

And then again, there again in summer, when summer came, the people around started talking about a fishing place. When they were talking about it, once again her husband put her in the sled and brought her up. Those sand dunes up there, and he also brought her inside this long bay. Apparently he brought her inside the bay of Mikuryarmiut [the village of Mekoryuk].

And then they apparently went to that old village that was upriver from our village, the old village that they used to call Nuqariillermiut. They mention that the people of Nuqariiller over there are *ircenrraat,* they mention that they are *ircenrraat.*

And then again, it is indeed a sign, that place up there they call Iqiucirwigmiut used to make rumbling noises [from kicking feet], they used to make rumbling noises there. I used to hear them, too, when those *ircenrraat* made rumbling noises.

aturaneg taukunek allaneg tamta-llu-am upyutliniluku, upyutellrulliniluku. Tawa-i pilliniatni all'uki.

Qanrutliag, "Qasgimun itquwet apertuuciiqekemken unuaqu, kiani egkumi nanilram tallirpilirnerani witalriamun qantar tauna tunciqken. Tayima kwani elitaqellrukuvgu tawani tekitellrani ciuqlirmeg kwall'u kinguqlirmeg tekitellrani elitaqellrukuvgu." Pillia nallunricaaqniluku tawa-i tauna elitaqellrussaaqniluku.

Tawa-i unuaqurrluni; imumeg kwani tawa-i tanqeggiqataarluni up'nerkaulliniluni tamana. Makyutartuqatangellratni tawa-i payugtelliniluku. Qasgiluni tawa-i qasgimun iterluni uyanglluni maaten cumikur kia-i egkumi kiugna.

Arnar kan'a uyangtelliur, tekitelliur-am naken kan'a arnar tangrrumayuilngur ukuni nunani tangerrnauyuilngur. Naken-lli-wa-ggur kan'a pillrullinia.

Cunrat makut tawa-i ak'akika neryuniulriit amlleqallinilriit ellaita-gg' nallukiit, "Nalimtenun-kir-kir kana-i kan'a qantar tuneniartau?" Imna tawa-i nugngami itreluni egkumun nukalpiartam avaqutaan uyuqlianun qantar tauna tunlliniluku. "Aling naken-kir-tanem tawa-i nalkutarturraanalliniag neviarcaqegtaarmeg aug'umeg?" Imna tawa-i naken piciinaku arnar tauna tawa-i tekiutellinikiig taukug anguteg.

Tamtallu-am up'nerkami tawa-i up'nerkiyalriit tauna kwani witaviat cinginrulliniluni. Kiatii kiugna kepumaluni. Pengurtalirluni-llu malrugnek. Amtalluwa pengut qaugkut kiaqvani tawaten ?atliniluteng. Allat-wa cali nunat kiugkut up'nerkillret kiugkut. Taukunun tawa-i uaqlirnun ciunilliniluteng. Ik'ikika nunarpakayaullinilriit taukut kwani tekisviit.

Awa-i qanellrulrianga Nuniwaamun tauna kwani arnar yuk'eqarraarniluku ciuqliuluku, yung'eqarraarutnguniluku. Una kwani arnar tawaken Qaluyaaneg pilriaruur. Cali-llu ukug kwani, taukut kwani ukut nunat taukut tekisvii imkut apqengaqait ircenrraneg pitukengait. Taukunun tawa-i ukurritliniluni tauna.

Amta-llu-am tamta-llu, amta-llu-am kwaten kwani kiagmi, kiagurrluku qanngellinilriit ukut tawa-i neqsurnermeg, neqsuryarameg tamatumeg. Pillermeggni-am amta-llu-am taum nutaan tawa-i wingan uciluku, amta-llu-am itrautelliniluku. Paugkut pengut, nutaan cali mat'umun tacimun taktuamun itrulluku. Cunawa mat'umun maa-i Mikuryarmiut taciatnun pillrullinikii tamaa-i, itrutliniluku.

Ingkunun-llu yaa-i kiugkunun kiaqlillemtenun nunallernun Nuqariillermiuneg pilaqaitnun, taukunun tawa-i ciunilliniluki. Taukut tawa-i kiugkut Nuqariillermiut ingkut ircenrraunilarait, ircenrrauniluki pituit.

Amta-llu-am tawa-i nallunailkutaugur ilumun, tukarratullrulria man'a kiugna Iqiucirwigmeg pitukiit tamaa-i tukarraqutullruut. Kwiinga-llu niitaqluki tukarratullratni tamaa-i ircenrraat tamakut.

And then again, one day that woman apparently left to pick berries from Nuqariiller over there, from the one they call Nuqariillermiut. As she was traveling far back there, when a man was following her from behind, she continually fled from him.

As she was fleeing from him, since that man was faster than she was, he followed her. He caught up to her, and she saw that the man was someone she hadn't seen before. But his way of speaking was similar to her way of speaking. He spoke in the same way as her parents spoke when she lived with them, but it was just a little bit different.

That person told her that although that place had been occupied, he didn't know about it all year. He said that finally from that mountain up there, that high mountain up there, when he climbed up and looked at his surroundings, he saw the smoke, and went to it, and he saw her.

That woman said to him, "You there, that village down there is occupied. There are people in that village down there. I have a husband there. If he sees you, he will confront you."

"My goodness, I've been walking around looking closely at the coast, but I never saw a place that could be a village. Since I haven't seen one, curious to see where smoke was coming from, and checking on it, I saw you and followed you. I came from Kuinerraq [Quinhagak]. This past spring, this past spring, when the weather suddenly got bad while I was [on the ocean], I apparently beached on this shore here, I apparently got beached on what appears to be this island here. They used to speak of Nuniwar. Maybe this is Nuniwar. My ancestors used to speak of that place. I thought that maybe it was that place. Since they told us this is the place that we must land on when we are in a desperate situation if it's visible, since they told us to land here, two of us landed here. My companion got into a mishap and died."

"Okay then." That woman said to him, "Okay then, since you don't believe me, I will bring you home. When the village becomes visible, I will let you know. Follow me. My husband will certainly confront you when he sees you. He really loves me, so he will confront you. Okay now, let's return home."

She brought that one home. She brought him home, they headed down through that route up there. As she approached her village, she looked and saw that the place where she lived was just mounds. She said her village here, she said it was once a village. That man said to her, "You there, you apparently went to a place where there weren't humans if you came from somewhere." She apparently pointed to her home, looking at those mountains up there, those Qaluyaat [Nelson Island mountains]. . . .

Amtalluam tawa-i waten kwani caqerluniam tamtallu arnar tauna amta-llu-am iqvarluni ayallrullinilria yaaken tawa-i Nuqariillerneg ingkuneg, Nuqariillermiuneg pitukaitneg. Qawawet kiaqvanun ayainanrani kinguaneg angutem maligqurraani qimagturalliniyaaqekii.

Maaten tawa-i qimagturainanrani angun tauna uqilanruami elliini maliggluku. Anguluku maaten piur tawa-i angun una tangnerraullinilria. Amta-llu-am cali qaneryarraa ayuqsaaqluni elliin qallayucirnaaratun. Imkugtun aanagmitun, aanagni nayutullermegni qallayucirnaaratun ayuqsaaqluni, taugg'am allayuggauluni carraquinermeg.

Pillia, cunawa-ggur-qaa man'a yungqengraan nallulliniaqekii allragnirpag. Nut'an-ggur kwaniwa tawa-i piaken ping'umeg ingrimeg ing'erpagmeg ping'umeg mayurluni nut'an nascami aruvillra kwaniw' tangerrluku tawa-i paqeskii, kwaniwa tawa-i tangerturainaqii.

Pillia arnam taum, "Atam ussuuq nunat kankut yungqertut. Nunat kankut yungqertut. Tawani wingqertua. Tayima tawa-i tangerkuniten piciqekiiten."

"Alingnaqvat-lli kwaniwa tawa-i unani cenaqvani canguyaaqellrianga nunauyugnalrianeg tangellrunrilngua. Tangenripakarlua tawa-i pilrianga naken aruvillraneg paqnayuglua, tawa-i tangrramken kwaniwa maligeskemken. Kwaniwa kingunengqertua Kuinerrarmek. Up'nerkar, up'nerkar ak'a ellam kwani cayukautellerminia maawet maa-i tepellrullinianga uumun camun, uumun qikertaungalngurmun tepellrullinianga. Tawa-i qanraqelriit Nuniwaameg. Nuniwaaruciqelliuq una. Tamatumeg tamaa-i qantullrulriit augkut ciulianka. Tamakuuyukluku. Tuswigkarput, tamaa-i nanikuakumta, tut'elqesqelluku alailkan pisqellruatgu megwiksaaqekpug malruulunug. Aapaqa tawa-i picurlalria pingnaqa'artevkenani."

"Ataki tawa-i." Arnam taum pillia, "Kitak' tawa-i ukvekenripakararpenga, ut'ruciiqekemken. Nunat tangerrnarikata qanruciiqamken. Tua maligqurqia. Pinritevkenii tawa-i wima piciqekiiten tayima tangerkuniten. Arenqialngur-wa kenekiinga cakner piciqekiiten tayim'. Kitaki uterrnaurtukug."

Imna tawa-i ut'rutliniluku. Ut'rulluku, anelrarluteg qawaggun. Imkut taukut nunani tekicarturluki maaten pii englullugnginaaraullinilriit taukut witavini. Kwaniwa-ggur ukut kwa nunai, nunaungatellruyaaqut-ggur ukut. Imna taum angutem pillia, "Ussuuq yuunrilngurnun tang ciunillrullinilriaten kwani naken pillrukuwet." Kinguneni kenirtullinia tangerrluki ingrit pingkut, pingkut pia-i Qaluyaat pingkut. . . .

"[My father] sent me here, he brought me here and has since died. Then although people were living here, just like I suspected, they apparently really are *ircenrraat*." He said, "Okay then, if you came from somewhere, let's leave."

Since she didn't see her village, that old village back there they call Nuqariillermiut, those *ircenrraat* there, they apparently called them Nuqariillermiut [those from Nuqariiller], something that is not the name of a village.

Finally, they cut across with Ing'errlag [Mountain] back there in mind. He brought her up to the top back when the weather was hardly ever cloudy.

But after bringing her up, he brought her a ways down from the one they call Tacirrlag to the shore, the sandy beach. Then they traveled along those sand dunes where he had originally landed on shore; along the end of them was a place they called Amyagmiut. That man apparently established that village. It apparently became a village during that time.

Those two, being the very first inhabitants, when they married, they apparently were the first to live here, were the first to land here.

From then on, that woman taught others; the people of Nunivak Island here evidently speak the language of those *ircenrraat*. From then on, they taught others. Those two were evidently the first two inhabitants of this island here.

When they had children, they multiplied. And again, when two people from up north who had drifted out into the ocean beached there again, there came to be more men. They continued to have children. Eventually there came to be many people.

This is a story they used to tell many years ago, and a story that my grandfather also used to tell.

And Ellikarrmiullret [the old village of Ellikarrmiut] down the coast, the story of those people also includes that place. And again that place Ellikarrmiullret down the coast was where they found that dog. The story is supposed to include that also. I'm telling this story up to this point.

You know who I am since you've seen me before. When I started becoming observant and started to observe things, I never forgot the stories they told. I am starting to forget some of them now though. And you, too, probably haven't forgotten the things that those older than you spoke of like me.

Okay, let me end [the story] there. This tape has been filled. [I'm telling] an old story that you wanted to hear. Since my daughter here said that you wanted to hear an old [story], I'm telling it now. I thank you very much. I'm ever so grateful that you have been hospitable to my daughters and haven't treated them differently as you've been with them. I am very grateful that they have been helped. I'm telling this story up to this point and have ended it like that.

"Maawet kwani tuyuqellrukiinga, ayautellrukiinga yuunrirluni-ll' tayim'. Tawa-i-llu maani maa-i yungqerrsaaqellriim man'a umyuama tawa-i kamakuciatun ircenrraungatpialliniut." Pilliur, "Kitak' tawa-i naken pillrukuwet, ayagnaurtukug."

Imna tawa-i nunani taukut tawa-i tangenrilamiki, kiugkut piani imkut nunallret Nuqariillermiuneg pitukengait, taukut tayim' ircenrraat taukut, Nuqarillermiuneg apertutullinikait taukut, nunam atqenrilkaineg.

Nut'an-am ayemqalliniluteg pingna pia-i Ing'errlag urenkelluku. qaanganun amtall' mayuutelliniluku amirlirpakayuitellrani tamaa-i ella man'a.

Amta-llu-am mayuuterraarluku, Tacirrlagmeg pitukiit kan'a uatrulluku kanautelliniluku cenamun qaugyamun. Nut'an-llu pengut tamakut cenirrluki tamaa-i tepviklerni taukut cenirrluki; uani iquatni Amyagmiut-ggur ukut. Taum tawa-i nunaliaqellinikai angutem. Tawani tawa-i nunaurtellrulliniluteng.

Taukug tawa-i, ciuqlikacagauluteg, aapaqsagucameg nutaan maani makurmiunguluteg yuurtellrulliniluteg, maawet tut'ellrulliniluteg.

Tayima tawa-i tamaaken eliciluni kwani tauna arnar; ircenrraat tamakut qalliyuciatnek ukut ukut Nuniwaarmiut qaneryarangqerrlalliniut. Tamaaken eliciluteg. Tamaa-i mat'um yuum kwani qikertam yuk'eqarrarpiaraqellrulliniag taukuk.

Irniangengameg nut'an yugyagiluteg. Tamtallu-am qagaaken amta-llu atertag taukug malrug tepngagneg, amta-llu-am tawa-i angutet-am amlleringluteng. Nut'an irniangurluteg. Kiitawani tawa-i yugyagingelliniur.

Man'a maa-i ak'a ak'arraq awa-i qanemcitukngallrat, ap'ama-llu tamatum qanemciktukngallra.

Ingna-llu cali ugna Ellikarrmiullret augkut cali tekisngayaaqekait. Amta-lluam cali qimugtemeg taumek kwani nalkutarvillrat ugkut kwani Ellikarrmiut. Tauna tekitarkauyaaqluku. Man'a kwani tawa-i tawaten pitaqerluku qanrutkaqa.

Kituuciqa-ll' tawa-i nallunritarci tanglaavcia-wa. Waten murilkessurilua murilkellemni qanemcitullrat nalluyagutellrunritaqa. Ilait qakma-i taugg'am nalluyagutenganka. Elpeci-llu-wa tayima ilavci qang'a ciuqlirrarpeci-wa qanrutkellrit tayima nalluyaguteksaatellikeci wangtun.

Kitak' tawa-i tawaten pitaqerluku. Man'a una *tape*-aq kwani imirtur. Aug'umegwa piyukengarpecenek qanemcimek ak'allarrarmek. Uum wani panima tawa-i ak'allarrarmek piyugniluten piaten qanrutekeka maa-i. Quyavikluci cakner. Tawa-i allaunritniteklukeg ukug paniigka murilkurallerci tawa-i quyakaqa tawa-i cakner palartevkenaku. Cakneqvaarneg quyaunga tawa-i ikayuumaciagneg. Tawaten pitaluku man'a tawa-i qanemcir man'a tawaten taqrerarput.

HUMANS AND ANIMALS

❧ *Sparrow Story* ❧

Magdalene Sunny and Ruth Jimmie, Nightmute, July 1985

Magdalene Sunny: These short *qulirat* [like the one I just told you].

There's another [story] about sparrows; their mother was pregnant. They were going up the mountain. Their tired pregnant mother called to their father up ahead and sang, "The sparrow family here going up. The sparrow family here going up. Their mother going slowly behind. *Ciuliuliuliu,* should we make our nest here?" The father looked back at her and said, "No, no, over yonder."

As they continued [up the mountain], she called again, "The sparrow family here going up. Their mother going slowly behind. *Ciuliuliuliu,* should we make our nest here?" [The father replied], "Okay, let's make our nest here."

My, as soon as they stopped mother sparrow laid her eggs.

Their father began to hunt food for them. (Gee, what a father they had.) He'd find maggots from underneath food racks [to feed his sparrow chicks].

One day one of the boys looked in. One of the men threw an object at the father of the sparrows and severed his head.

Then he disappeared.

[Mother sparrow] just left the one she was feeding and went out and started looking for him. She found [her husband] underneath the fish rack with his head next to his body, dead.

Struck with sorrow and desperation she squatted down and burst out crying, "My husband *taiyaayaa.* My husband *taiyaayaa.* One of the boys threw something and hit him and severed his head. *Ngaiggngaiggngaa.*"

Then a raven suddenly came and landed beside her. "I'll be your husband." She quickly looked at him and said, "Aa, you are too black." He quickly flew away.

YUUT, UNGUNGSSIT, IMARPIGMIUTAAT-LLU

Tekciugglugaat ∾

Missan Angalgaq-llu, Negtemiut, July 1985

Missan: Makut maa-i qulingssaaraat.

Cali-wam imkut tekciugglugaat; aaniit qingarluni. Ingrikun mayulriit. Tua-i aanaurluat aqsingami, ataseng avaviangellinia, "Taakciugglugaat ukut mayualriit. Taakciugglugaat ukut mayualriit. Aanayuat kiimi cukaunani-ii. Ciuliuliuliu, wavet-qaa?" Atiita-am takuyaraa, "Qang'a, qang'a, yaave-et."

Tua-i mayullratni tua-i-am piluku, "Taakciugglugaat ukut mayualriit. Aanayuat kiimi cukaunani-ii. Ciuliuliuliu, wavet-qaa?" "Aa tua-i wavet pilta."

Aren, arulairutmeggni tua-i irniqaurluqili aaniit.

Tua-i atiita taum angussaagaqiliki. (Atangqellinivaa-tam.) Paraluayaarnek angussaagalliniluni initat aciatnek.

Tua-i piinanrani tan'gurraat iliit qinertuq. Tekciugaat-gguq aatiit angutet iliita milqeraa qamiqurra qecengqertelluku.

Tua-i-ll' tayima.

Aamarkengani peggluku anluni kiartelliniluku. Piuq-gguq maaten initat waniw' aciani qamiquminek yaaqlirluni, tuqumall'.

Aren tua-i nanikuayallageurluami uyungqerluni qalrillageurlulliniluni. "Uika taiyaayaa. Uika taiyaayaa. Tan'gurraat iliita milqeraa qamiqurra qecengqertelluku. Ngaiggngaiggngaa."

Tua-i-ll' tulukaruk mip'allalliniuq canianun. "Wiinga uilirnauramke-en." Tangleraa, "Aa tungussiyaagpakalriaten." Tua-i-ll' tayim' tengvallagluni.

119

She cried again, "My husband *taiyaayaa*. One of the boys threw something and hit him and severed his head. *Ngaiggngaiggngaa!*"

Then a crane suddenly landed beside her. [He said,] "I'll be your husband." [She quickly replied], "Your legs are too long."

She [cried] again, "My husband *taiyaayaa*. My husband *taiyaayaa*. One of the boys threw something and hit him and severed his head. *Ngaiggngaiggngaa!*"

Then a longspur suddenly landed beside her making his bird call. [She said,] "Great! I'll accept that." He immediately became their father and they continued on living there.

❧ *Muskrat and Grebe* ☙

Martha Mann with Julia Azean and Marie Meade, Kongiganak, July 1994

Marie Meade: One person I talked to told me about those who referred to each other as *qatngun* [spouse exchange partner]. He told me about those who referred to each other as *qatngun*.

Julia Azean: Qatngutkellria [Being a spouse exchange partner] is not a good thing. With just anyone . . . it would be like two [men] swapping their wives.

Marie Meade: He said muskrat and red-throated loon were *qatngutek* [two who share everything they possess, including their wives].

He said that was why there are always muskrats around where there are red-throated loons.

Julia Azean: But they say that if there is a grebe in a lake, there is always a muskrat there, too.

Marie Meade: Or maybe he was talking about a grebe. Yes, I think he was talking about a grebe. He said it's because those two, muskrat and grebe, were *qatngutek*.

Julia Azean: They say where there's a grebe there's always a muskrat.

Martha Mann: They would share their wives. A husband would let his *qatngun* [spouse-exchange partner] sleep with his wife.

Marie Meade: The two men who were spouse-exchange partners?

Martha Mann: The two men would exchange and share their wives.

They say long ago that was the way of the *qatngutkellriit*.

Marie Meade: Yes. It was normal and accepted by society?

Martha Mann: Yes.

Allamek tua-i qiaqcaaraur[lurluni], "Uika taiyaayaa. Tan'gurraat iliita milqeraa qamiqurra qecengqertelluku. Ngaiggngaiggngaa!"

Qucillgaq mip'allagtuq. "Wiinga uilirnauramke-en." "Aa kanagagken tamakuk taksiyaagpakalriik."

Allamek-am tua-i [qialuni], "Uika taiyaayaa. Uika taiyaayaa. Tan'gurraat iliita milqeraa qamiqurra qecengqertelluku. Ngaiggngaiggngaa!"

Nacaqupagaq qalriurluni tuaten mip'allalliniluni. "Waqaa! Nutaan atam." Tua-i aatakqaurlurluku tua-i tuani uitaluteng.

൙ *Kanaqliinkuk Qaleqcuuk-llu* ൙

Mass'aluq, Anglluralria, Arnaq-llu, Kangirnaq, July 1994

Arnaq: Aug'um-ll'-am apqaullma iliita qanengssautengaanga qatngutkellrianek. Qatngutkellrianek.

Anglluralria: Qatngutkellria tamana assiitellriaruuq. Waten picimitun . . . ukuk tuaten, tua-i-w' akuyutellriatun pilutek nuliamegen'gun.
Arnaq: Kanaqliinkuk-gguq qaqatak-llu qatngutkuk.

Taumek-gguq qaqatiim nuniini kanaqlagtaicuilnguq.

Anglluralria: Taugaam imkut, iciw' qaleqcuuget-gguq tuani-gguq nanvami uitaaqata, tauna-gguq uitaviat kanaqlagtaicuituq.
Arnaq: Wall'u-q' qaleqcuugnek piuq. Ii-i qaleqcuuk piyugnarqaa. Tua-i-gguq qatngutekngamek taukuk, kanaqliinkuk qaleqcuuk-llu.
Anglluralria: Taum-gguq qaleqcuugem uitavia kanaqlagtaicuituq.
Mass'aluq: Nuliateng-gguq tua-i navrucituit. Aiparmeggnun qatngutmeggnun pivkaraqlug' pitullruut.
Arnaq: Taukuk-q' angutek qatngutkellriik?
Mass'aluq: Angutek nuliatek navrucitaaqlukek.
Ak'a-gguq tuaten qatngutkellriit piciryarangqellruut.
Arnaq: Ii-i. Cangalkevkenaku?
Mass'aluq: Ii-i.

◈ *Red Fox and White-fronted Goose* ◈

John Alirkar and Simeon Agnus, Umkumiut Culture Camp, June 2002

John Alirkar: One day in the summer there was a red fox going along, a red fox. He went along the land and kept going.

As he was going, he saw a molting white-fronted goose. You know, when they molt their mothers and fathers can't fly anymore. But their fledglings, they'd be with them [though they couldn't fly] and they'd grow.

When they became the same size as [their parents], these [wing feathers] on their mothers would come off by themselves. When their wing feathers come off, they call it *inglluteng* [molting]. They cannot fly anymore.

When [the red fox] saw [the molting goose] he ran after it. The red fox bounded off on all fours. He sang, "*Aa-yunaa yunaa, yunaa yunaa. Aa-yunaa yunaa, yunaa yunaa. Sami-ssaraa. Sami-ssaraa. Sami sami ua-ua. Sami sami ua-ua.*"

When he caught up to it, he suddenly bit it, he bit the white-fronted goose that couldn't fly. He was happy for his food.

Since [the bird] was warm, he put it beside him to cool it off. He closed his eyes and sang, "I wonder what I will eat *anga-ya-ya*. I may eat a large breast *anga-ya-ya*. With a lot of meat on it *anga-ya-ya-rra*."

The goose that he had placed beside him to cool off, he looked at it and it was gone. He saw that it had already gotten far away from him. [*laughter*] The one he thought he had bitten and killed.

Then he ran after it again [singing], "*Aa-yunaa yunaa, yunaa yunaa. Aa-yunaa yunaa, yunaa yunaa. Sami-ssaraa. Sami-ssaraa. Sami sami ua-ua. Sami sami ua-ua.*"

Then he bit it again. Since it was so warm, he didn't learn his lesson, he put it beside himself once again and he closed his eyes. Closing his eyes tightly he sang thinking about what he would eat. "I wonder what I will eat *anga-ya-ya*. I may eat a large leg."

Thinking about its legs and anticipating a delicious meal when he ate the goose [he sang], "I may eat a large leg *anga-ya-ya*. With a lot of meat on it *anga-ya-ya-rra*."

He suddenly opened his eyes, and it had already gotten far away. [*laughter*] He chased it running fast on four legs.

Simeon Agnus: Have you mentioned the large lake?

John Alirkar: I'm going to talk about it now.

Simeon Agnus: I see.

John Alirkar: He bounded really fast on four legs. "*Aa-yunaa.*" Again he sang, "*Aa-yunaa.*"

❧ *Kaviaq Neqleq-llu* ❧

Allirkar Unangik-llu, Umkumiut, June 2002

Allirkar: Tua-lli-wa-gguq una kaviar un' ayalria, *red fox*-aq, kiagmi. Nunam qaingakun tua ayagluni, ayagturluni.

Tua-i-ll' piinanermini, ayainanermini yaqulegmek neqlermek tanglliniluni, ingtamek. Waten iciw' ingtelalriit tengesciigalliluteng, aanait, aatait-llu. Taugken irniarit, irniateng malikluk' angliluteng.

Ellaicetun-ll'-am tua-i angtarikata, aanaita [yaqurrita melqurrit] makuit ellmeggnek qecuktarluteng. Tua-i-gguq inglluteng. Tengausciigalliluteng.

Tua-i tangrramiu, tangrramiu malirqalliniluku. Ava-i pangalegluni kaviaq. Waten aturluni, "Aa-yunaa yunaa, yunaa yunaa. Aa-yunaa yunaa, yunaa yunaa. Sami-ssaraa. Sami-ssaraa. Sami sami ua-ua. Sami sami ua-ua."

Anguamiu-ll' keglerluku, keggluku neqleq tauna tengesciigalnguq. Quyaluni neqkaminek.

Tua-llu puqlanian caniminun wavet elliluku nengllacirluku. Qelemluni aturtuq, "Caturniarcia-kiq anga-ya-ya. Qategpagturnayalliunga anga-ya-ya. Kemiilriigneg-naag anga-ya-ya-rra."

Imna tauna caniminun ellillni nengllaciarallni yaqulek tangerrsaaqaa cataunani. Maten piuq ava-i-am ak'a yaaqsigillinilria. [*ngel'artut*] Tuqucukellra keglerluku.

Tuamtall'-am malirqerluku [aturluni], "Aa-yunaa yunaa, yunaa yunaa. Aa-yunaa yunaa, yunaa yunaa. Sami-ssaraa. Sami-ssaraa. Sami sami ua-ua. Sami sami ua-ua."

Tuamtall' keglerluku. Tua-i-am puqelviin, anuciilnguq, caniminun-am wavet elliluku qelemluni. Qelemkacagarluni aturtuq nerrlerkaminek umyuarteqluni, "Caturniarcia-kiq anga-ya-ya. Irurpagturnayalliunga."

Irug' umyuaqlukek neqniliqatarluni yaqulegtuquni, "Irurpagturnayalliunga anga-ya-ya. Kemiilriigneg anga-ya-ya-rra."

Maaten-am uigartuq ak'a-am aug' yaaqsigillinilria. [*ngel'artut*] Ayumian-am tua malirqerluku pangalkacagarluni.

Unangik: Augna-mi nanevpall'er-qaa pinritan?

Allirkar: Waniw' piqataraqa.

Unangik: Aa-a.

Allirkar: Pangalkacagarluni ayagluni tua-i. "Aa-yunaa." Tua-i-am aturpagluni, "Aa-yunaa."

He sang with extreme enthusiasm. There was a large lake ahead of him, a large lake, a lake. He ran as fast as he could toward it, closing his eyes running fast on four legs.

"*Aa-yunaa yunaa, yunaa yunaa. Aa-yunaa yunaa, yunaa yunaa. Sami-ssaraa. Sami-ssaraa. Sami sami ua-ua. Sami sami ua.*"

He bit it again, but he fell face down into the lake. [*laughter*]

The white-fronted goose he was chasing was swimming away. He didn't go after it because it was in the water.

Gee whiz, he suddenly blushed, feeling great regret for his loss. [*laughter*]

You know red foxes are red. His body was very red. When he blushed his whole body got red except for the tip of his tail.

Gee, he felt doomed and had nothing to eat.

He went along the edge of the lake. As he was going along, he saw a firepit; it had wood in it. Someone had cooked at that spot.

When he took a piece of charcoal, the back of his ears up there, he rubbed the back of both of his ears.

You know how red foxes' ears are black on the tips. He also rubbed a little on the front of his forelegs here, and these two here. You know how their legs are slightly black.

He looked himself over, and gee, he looked better because he had rubbed these two spots [with charcoal], and these [ears] here. His appearance was better. The red fox looked good. He had rubbed black charcoal on the back of his ears.

And his belly hadn't gotten too red. It was a little white. You know how red fox [bellies] are a little red.

To him, he looked better now. He started to like the way he looked. And now it has ended, [the story] suddenly ended.

⮜ *Caribou Boy* ⮞

John Alirkar, Umkumiut Culture Camp, June 2003

John Alirkar: Yes, I am going to end this with a *quliraq* even if it's short. *Qulirat* used to be fun [to listen to]. I used to enjoy them. In the evenings when we went to bed, when he started telling a *quliraq*, I would listen very closely. Sometimes I would fall asleep because I'd have so much fun. I would scold myself for falling asleep wishing I had listened to the whole story.

When continually telling a *quli'ir,* one doesn't forget it. I am forgetting some stories because I don't tell them anymore, since I no longer tell *qulirat.* I just know a few of them, mostly the endings.

Ilungkacagarluni aturluni. Nanvaq-w' ingna ciunrani nanevpall'er, nanvaq. Tungiinun pitarvamitun qelemquulluni pangalegluni tauna.

"Aa-yunaa yunaa, yunaa yunaa. Aa-yunaa yunaa, yunaa yunaa. Sami-ssaraa. Sami-ssaraa. Sami sami ua-ua. Sami sami ua."

Kegleryaaqekni-ll' nanvamun kanaqerluni. [*ngel'artut*]

Neqleq malirqaq'ngaa tauna kuimarluni ava-i ayangarrluni. Elliin-llu pivkenaku mermun pian.

Arenqiapaa-ll', kavingallagluni tua' qessanayugluni. [*ngel'artut*]

Iciw' kavircelnguut *red fox*-at. Kavirpak tua' qainga. Pamyuan taugaam nuuga pinritqalliniluni kavingallallermini.

Aren tua qessanayugluni neqkaunani-llu.

Ceniikun nanvam ayalliniluni. Ayainanermini waten kenillermek; waten muragnek muragluni. Kenillrulliniluni kina tayim' pia.

Kangiplugmek tegucami, ciutegmi tunukek paugkuk, iciw' tunukek minguglukek inglugtun.

Iciw' *red fox*-at ciutaita kangiit tungulalriit. Makuk-llu talliigmi ciulirnerak call' minguvguayaarlukek ukuk, makuk-llu. Iciw' tunguksuaratulriit iruit.

Maaten yaatiirluni tangertuq, aren, assiriqertellinill' mingullruamikek ukugni, makut-llu. Tangniriqerrluni. Tangvallra assirluni kaviarem. Elliin kangiplugmek mingullrulukek ciutegmi kelukek.

Man'a-llu aqsii kavingallaumavkenani. Qaterrlugluni. Carrarmek iciw' kaviragcecarpialalriit kaviaret [aqsait].

Ellminek tangnikngarrluni. Tangellni assikenga'arrluku. Tua-i-ll' iquklilluni, iqukliarrluni.

๛ *Tan'gurraq Tuntuq* ๖

Allirkar, Umkumiut, June 2003

Allirkar: Yaa, kitak' tua-i quliramek nanilengraan iquqliliqata'arqa. Quliraat-llu makut anglanarqetullruut. Wii anglaktullruanka. Atakumi inartaqamta, tua-i-ll' quliramek ayagniqan niicugniurluku tua-i. Iliini qavaqallininaurtua ugaan' anglanim. Qavallemneg' nunuryaaqaqlua tamalkuan niicugyaaqluku.

Qanrutkuralriani quli'ir atam nalluyagutnaituq. Wiinga tua-i nalluyagurqanka tayim' qanemciksuirucamki, quliriyuirucama. Carraat taugaam qavcin tua-i nallunri[tanka], iqupkugpalluit.

The story I am going to tell now; a mother and her child were along a river. The child's mother, since they had no food, was fishing with a hookless lure.

The smelt, the people of Chefornak fish with hookless lures. The people of Chefornak [here at camp] know about it, and they also fish with hooks for smelt; they know about it.

That's how they were fishing. Her child began to cry because of hunger, but they had no food to eat. Although they fished with hookless lures, even though the child's mother fished with a hookless lure, she couldn't catch any fish. She never caught anything.

And although his mother sang to him and tried to put him to sleep, he couldn't go to sleep because he was hungry.

Her song went like this: "*Aa-nga-nga-i, ii-ngi-ngi-i. Aa-nga-nga-i, ii-ngi-ngi-i. Anga-rra-nga-i yi-gga. Aa-nga-nga-i, ii-ngi-ngi-i. Aya-rri-ya rra-nga-i.*"

The chorus goes like this: "We are hoping for something as we stay here. You are crying, *anga-i,* I am warning you, *anga.* Look at the things up there, those up there are moving, *anga-rra-ngaa-i yi-gga.*"

Referring to his crying [she sang], "You are crying, *anga.*" Because he was crying [she sang], "You are crying *anga,* look up there at the birds." Wanting him to look at the ones above, she sang. She was singing to her hungry child.

While she was singing that song, a young man suddenly arrived. He was sweaty; he was running. He said to her, "Can you not hide me now?" He kept looking back at where he came from.

He took his hood off and she saw that he was a young man who was hot and sweaty. He evidently was being chased. The person [she saw as a young man] evidently was a caribou. He apparently was a young caribou.

She let him get inside underneath her small sled. After she let him inside, she sealed the sides with her saliva. He sat in the middle [under the sled]. It was a kayak [seal hunting] sled.

Even if I call it *qamigautek* [kayak sled], you will not know what it is. You've never see one. They are sleds for kayaks. Maybe some of you have seen one.

[The woman] was using a kayak sled to sit on.

Soon five wolves arrived. They asked her, "That one we are chasing . . . ?" They asked if she had seen him.

"He just passed . . . " She lied to them, "He just passed. You will soon catch him."

They took off their hoods and they were wolves. The five boys she saw were wolves.

Then when they put on their hoods again, they became wolves. Then they left. She had lied to them that they were about to catch him.

Quli'irqeqataq'ngaqa waniw'; irniaquralriik kuigem iluani. Aanii-wa neq-kailamek uqtarluni.

Qusuuret maa-i, Cevv'arnermiut uqtatuut. Nallunritaat maa-i Cevv'arnermiut, manarluteng-llu qusuurnek; nalluvkenaki.

Tuaten tua-i iqsaglutek. Irniara tauna qiangluni tua-i neryugyaaqluni, neq-kaunatek taugken. Uqtang'ermek-llu, aanii uqtang'ermi picuunani. Tua-i piteng-ssaarayuunani.

Taum tua-i aaniin atuutengraani-llu qavangcarluni qavasciiganani, kaignga-meng.

Waten yuarutii ayuqluni: "Aa-nga-nga-i, ii-ngi-ngi-i. Aa-nga-nga-i, ii-ngi-ngi-i. Anga-rra-nga-i yi-gga. Aa-nga-nga-i, ii-ngi-ngi-i. Aya-rri-ya rra-nga-i."

Tua-ll' apallua: "Neryuniurlunu-uk uitauralriakuuk. Qiyauten anga-i iner-tamken anga. Pagkut tangerkii-i, arulartut pagkuut, anga-rra-ngaa-i yi-gga."

Qiallra ava-i, "Qiyauten anga." Waten qiangan [aturluni], "Qiyauten anga pagkut tangerki yaqulget." Pava-i pagkut tangrresqelluki aturpagluni. Irniani atuulluku kailria.

Tuaten tua-i atuinanrani man'a yun'erra'ar tekiartelliniuq. Tua' kiiryugluni; aqvaqurturluni. Tua-ll' pillinia, "Waniwa-qaa iiqerciigatarpenga?" Kinguneni tangerrsugpagluku augna.

Maaten tua-i nacairtelliniuq yun'errar una kiiryugluni cemlliurluni. Malir-qerciulliniluni. Tuntuullliniluni tauna. Tuntucuaraullliniluni.

Ayumian tua-i ikamracuaraagmi aciagnun qerrcetlin[iluku], itercetliniluku waten. Iterceqaarluku-ll', nuaminek man'a capluku avatii. Qukaani waniw' aqum-galuni. Qamigautngulutek tamakuk.

Qamigautegnek apengramkek nalluaci. Tangeqsaitaci. Qayat qamigautait ikamrat, Nalici tayim' tangerrsaaqellrullilria.

Qamigautegnek cururluni.

Tuamtall' piinanrani keglunret ukut tallimauluteng tekiartelliniut. Apluku, "Augna-qaa malirqaq'ngarput . . . ?" Tangeqsaitaarluku.

"Ava-i kitu . . ." Iqluluki, "Ava-i kitunerrartuq. Anguniarararci."

Maaten nacairtelliniut keglunret. Tan'gurraat talliman keglunruluteng.

Tuamtall'-am tua-i waten nacaqerngameng keglunrurrluteng. Tuamtall' tayim' ayallliniluteng tamaa-i. Iqlullruluki anguniararniluku.

While she was there, later on when she heard someone singing from a distance, she looked and saw one wolf approaching.

When he arrived; he evidently was the father of the five wolves. He asked her, "Those poor ones. . . ." He referred to his sons as those poor ones. "Are those poor ones still far from catching up to the one they are chasing?"

"Gee, they just went by, and they were so close to catching him."

Soon he left and began to sing. How did the beginning of the song go? Maybe I won't remember it. He sang this.

"You mighty ones, you mighty ones, leave me some intestines *aug-uu,* of the animal with fat at the tip of its ears. *Aa-rra-yi-rri-am aug-uu.*"

Continually singing that song, he disappeared.

Then she began to sing to her poor child, the song she sang earlier.

"*Aa-nga-nga-i, ii-ngi-ngi-i. Aa-nga-nga-i, ii-ngi-ngii. Ii-rri-yaa-rra-nga.* Look at those up there. Those up there are moving. *Anga-rra-ngaa-yi-ggaa.* We are hoping for something as we stay here. You are crying *anga-i,* I am warning you, *angaa.* Look at those up there. Those up there are moving. *Anga-rra-ngaa-yi-ggaa.*"

Right when she was done singing that song, one wolf arrived. When it took off its hood it was an old woman, it was an elderly woman.

Then she asked, "Have those poor ones, the one they were chasing, are they still far from catching him?" [She asked] if they were far from catching up to him.

"Gee, they are so close to catching up to him."

Soon that wily one heard his heart beating, that elderly woman [heard it]. His heart was beating very hard as he was underneath the kayak sled fearful that she might see him.

That elderly woman said, "Seems like I hear a heart beating."

She said to her, referring to her child, "This poor thing who has been crying, since he's been crying so much, his heart is starting to beat."

"Oh, I see. Is that poor one's heart beating?" She left. As she left she sang: "You poor ones, you poor ones, leave me some intestines *auguu, auguu.* The buttocks of the caribou . . ." [*laughing*]

Its buttocks, its buttocks. [*laughs*]

You know caribou have fat on their buttocks, along here. [*laughing*]

When [the old woman] stopped singing the woman said, "Yes, let her think she is about to eat caribou fat."

The wily one heard her say that. She quickly looked back at her. "What, will I not eat any caribou fat?" [*laughs*]

She answered her, "I'm just expressing the fact that you are going to eat caribou fat and wishing I had some, too."

"I see!" She sang again.

Then she left. The old woman went away limping slightly.

Piinanrani tua-i, tua-ll' tuamtall'-am atulriamek avaken niicami pilliniuq, ataucirraq kegluneq man'a tekicartulria.

Tekiarcami; taukut aatakliniluku keglunret talliman. Aptaa-am, "Augkurluut-qaa. . . ." Augkurluurnek aperluku qetunrani. "Augkurluut-qaa maligeskengarteng cali anguyugnaitaat?"

"Aren ava-i anguqatak'acagallruat."

Ayumian aug' ayagluni aturluni-am tua-i. Qaillun imat'am ayagnengqellria atullra? Neq'akqatanricugnarqaqa. Waten aturluni.

"Augkuruut, augkuruut qilumllugkuiqaqicia-am aug-uu, ciutiin kangia tunuurralaak. Aa-rra-yi-rri-am aug-uu."

Tuaten tua-i aturturluni tayima pellaluni.

Tuamtall'-am tua-i irniani tauna atuuteurlurluku watua aug'umek atullminek.

"Aa-nga-nga-i, ii-ngi-ngi-i. Aa-nga-nga-i, ii-ngi-ngii. Ii-rri-yaa-rra-nga. Pagkut tangerki-ii. Arulartut pagku-ut. Anga-rra-ngaa-yi-ggaa. Neryuniurlunuuk uitau-ralriakuuk. Qiyauten anga-i, inertamken angaa. Pagkut tangerki-ii. Arulartut pagkuut. Anga-rra-ngaa-yi-ggaa."

Tuaten-am tua-i atunermek taqeqanrakun kegluneq amna ataucirraq tekiartelliniuq. Maaten nacairtelliniuq arnassaagar' una, arnassagauluni.

Ayumian-am una aptuq, "Augkurluut-qaa tayima mali'irqaq'ngarteng cali anguyugnaite[llruat]?" Anguyugnaitellranek [apluni].

"Aren, ava-i anguqatak'acagarluku."

Ayumian tua-i tauqtam ircaqurran nutngallra niilluku, taum tua-i arnassaa-gaam. Ircaqruak'acagarluni qamigauteg' aciagni uitaluni tangerrnayukluni.

Ayumian tauna, tauna arnassaagaq pilliniuq, "Tuartang ircaqum nutngallranek niitelalrianga."

Taum piqallinia, irniani piluku, "Uurlum-wa wani qiavakalriim, qiavakaami ircaqurra nutngangelria."

"Aa-aa. Taurluum-qaa ircaqurra nutngartuq?" Ava-i tua-i ayagluni. Ayagarcami-am aturluni tuaten ayagtuq, "Augkuruut, augkuruut, qilumllugkuiqaqicia-am auguu, auguu. Nulluuk tun . . ." [*ngel'artuq*]

Nulluuk, nulluuk. [*ngel'artuq*]

Tuntut iciw' nullumegteggun tunungqellriit maaggun. [*ngel'artuq*]

Tuaten tua-i atunermek taq'ercan taum arnam pillinia, "Ii-i, tunurturciqlilria tayim'."

Niiteqtallinia. Takuyaartaa. "Ai, tunurturngaitua-qaa?" [*ngel'artuq*]

Taum-am tua-i kiugaa, "Tunurturnguucirkarpenek ayuqniarluten piam-ken."

"Aa-aa!" Tua-i-am aturluni.

Tuamtall' ava-i ayagluni. Tussivlerrluni arnassagaq tauna ayagluni ava-i.

Then when she left, he came out. When she told him to come out, he came out when [the old woman] disappeared, when she quickly vanished.

That caribou was grateful.

He started to try to take his arms out of his sleeves. He was trying to pull his arms inside his parka. He was having a hard time. Finally [his arms] came out [of the sleeves].

When [his arms] came out [of his sleeves], he once again had a hard time trying to get some fat from here. He was trying to take some to give to those two, to give some to her small son. He tried to remove some and eventually got some.

When he handed her [the fat], he said to them, "Okay now, cut it into small pieces and sprinkle some inside your ice fishing hole when I leave."

Then like he had told them to, she cut those pieces of fat into tiny pieces and dropped them inside the ice fishing hole. They were floating.

My, right when she sprinkled them, many fish came and filled up that ice fishing hole. She pulled up many fish!

His mother pulled up fish after fish. He had told her to do that whenever [fish] became scarce.

My, in an instant they had food and weren't going to go hungry. They pulled up many fish! They suddenly had an abundance of food! His mother started to catch lots.

They went up to the village and gave some food to people. And she didn't show them the caribou fat bait that she used to catch the fish.

When they weren't paying attention, they would quickly pull up fish, his mother would [do that].

From there, I have forgotten the rest [of the story]. From there, I have forgotten the rest and can't tell it.

But another [story].

✑ *One Who Speared a Human* ✎

Dick Anthony and Marie Meade, Nightmute, January 1996

Dick Anthony: Let me tell you the story that was told to me by a man from Nunivak Island. I know the story from beginning to end. That man from Nunivak liked telling stories. Unfortunately he has already died.

Long ago, their ancestors . . . that person [in the story] was probably one of their ancestors.

That man, in the fall he would go down to the ocean, because that village [Mekoryuk] is along the ocean shore, they used to pursue bearded seals in water,

Ayiin-llu tua-i anluni. Anesqengani anluni tayim' pelliin, pell'aqercan.

Quyaluni tauna tuntuq.
Waniwa tua-i aliingnaqluni. Talligni-w' makuk atkumi iluanun pingnaqlukek. Pisciigalliqluni. Cayaqlirlutek anlutek.

Anngagnek maaken tunurrlugnek pisciigalliqluni-am augaucessaagluni. Augaucessaagluni taukugnun tun'arkaminek, taumun tua-i qetunrarriinun. Augautengnaqluni augaulluni.
Tungamiu piak, "Kitak' tua-i ciqumqurayaarluku anluarpetegnun tuavet kanveskitgu ayakuma."
Tua-i-ll' pisqellratun tua-i tunurrluyagaat tamakut ciqumlluki anluamun peggluki. Pugtaqraqluki.
Aren kanvuciatun, uqtaqngarugaat neviqerluku tauna anluaq tamana. Mayurqurriluni neqnek!
Aanii tua-i nugerqiluni. Mikuirutaqata tuaten pilaasqelluku.

Aren kaigyugnaiteqertuk. Uqtaqnganek mayurqurrilutek! Cir'iqerrlutek! Aanii-w' tua-i picuriqerrluni.

Nunanun taglutek tamakut ilait neqkilluki tuaken. Apertuutevkenaki-ll' taukunek neqcaminek tununek.
Tuaten tua-i cumikenritaqata neqnek tua-i mayurqurrilaakaraqlutek, aanii.

Tuaken uunguciiruskeka. Tuaken tua-i uunguciirutaqa, qaillun qanrutkesciigataqa.
Allamek taugaam.

✑ *Narulkaqenglleq Yugmek* ✐

Minegtuli Arnaq-llu, Negtemiut, January 1996

Minegtuli: Aug'umek Nunivaarmium qanemcillranek qanemcillaken. Tua-i nallunritaqa iquklitellranun. Qanemciuryunqeggami augna Nunivaarmiu. Tuqu'urlullrulria-w' taugaam ak'a.
Ak'a avani ciuliaqatuteng . . . ciuliaqatuulallilria-w' tauna.

Tauna angun tauna, waten uksuarmi kanavet kana-i imarpigmun, imarpiim ceniinlameng kankut, waten maklaarnek maliqniaraluteng pitullruameng,

since the weather was always calm long ago, since it wasn't windy all the time like it is now.

They say he didn't catch something every time he went hunting, but he was good at catching easily. He caught more often than his fellow hunters, though he sometimes went home without catching anything.

He had a child, he had a son, too.

This [story] comes from the ancient times.

So when his son there came to be of an age to have a kayak, his father built him a kayak. And his father there didn't go hunting quite as much anymore.

One day his father went down to Akuluraq [Etolin Strait] to pursue seals. In the days when they hunted with spears when pursuing seals, they called it *maliqniarluteng*.

So all day long, he didn't see a seal down there in the ocean.

So he spent all day in calm weather.

When night was beginning to fall, right away, he went home.

On his way home, up ahead he finally spotted his first seal of that entire day.

He approached it. It would surface, getting closer and closer to him. It would get closer to him every time it surfaced.

After a while, it got closer to him. After it had been underwater for a while, he knew that when it emerged again it was going to come up next to him.

When it surfaced where one could recognize its exact nature, it was a human.

When he realized it was human, he began to go toward his village down there in a hurry.

As he was going along, that one surfaced much closer in front of him.

My, and when he'd turn his back to it and start [paddling], even if it wasn't toward his village, it would surface in front of him closer than before.

Then pretty soon, it surfaced right in front of him as a human.

It was [out of the water] up to here, and its shoulders were exposed as it surfaced.

Marie Meade: It was up to its waist?

Dick Anthony: It wasn't up to its waist.

Grabbing his harpoon, he speared it, and it suddenly went underwater.

Marie Meade: Right in the middle of its chest?

Dick Anthony: Exactly.

Since it never surfaced again, he went home.

He was thinking that when he reached home he was going to have an *angalkuq* [shaman] look into him to ascertain what he had just seen.

And because he seldom came home empty-handed, as he was approaching and was about to reach his village, because it was his wife's custom, he noticed her going down toward the place where he usually stopped.

quunilgullruami ak'a, waten anuqlirturayuitellruami.

Tua-i kesianek ayallni tamalkuan pitenricaaquq-gguq, taugaam-gguq tua-i pitqayuluni. Ilamini-w' tua-i unangqayunruaqluni iliini ut'rinalang'ermi.

Irniarluni, qetunrarluni call' angutmek.
Ciulaqatugtaulria man'a.
Tua-i qetunraa tauna qayangyugngarian atiin qayiluku. Ellii-ll' tua-i cali atii ayagallni taman' piluanringluku.
Tua-i caqerluni taun' atii ayalliniluni-am tua-i unavet Akuluramun ayagluni maliqniarluni. Apqiitnek maliqniarluteng pitulriit narulkaquluteng pitullermeggni.

Tua-i ernerpak im' tua-i taqukamek tangyuunani unani imarpigmi.
Quuniurumallinilria tua-i ernerpak.
Tua-i unuksigiarkaurcan ayumian utertelliniluni.
Uterrnginanermini tua-ll' am'umek ciunermini, taqukamek am'umek nutaan tua-i ernekutagpall'er tangerpaalulliniluni.
Tua-i ullagluk'. Pug'aqluni ukaqvaqanirluni. Malkanirluku-w' tua-i pug'aqluni pugyungaqami.
Tua-i caqerluni ukaqsigiluni. Tua-i tayim' anglluumarraarluni pugkuni tua-i nuniikun maaggun pug'arkauluni.
Maaten tua-i elitaqnaqluni puggliniuq yuulallinilria.
Tua-i yuurciamiu, nunami taum kat'um tungiinun ayagluni cumiggluni.

Piinanrani-am imna ukaqvaqanirluni ciunrakun puggliniuq.
Aren tunutqapiarluku-ll' tua-i nunami tungkenrilengraaku ayagyaaqaqan, pugglininaurtuq canimellikanirlun' ciunrakun.
Tua-i pivakarluni 'gguun tua-i ciuqerrakun puggliniuq yuuluni.
Imumek tua-i maatekaarluni, ukuk-llu tusgegni alairlukek, pugumaluni.

Arnaq: Qukakaarluni?
Minegtuli: Tua-i qukakaarpek'nani.
Nanerpani teguluku narulkaqiini tua-i murucillalliniluni.
Arnaq: Qat'giin qukaakun?
Mingegtuli: Ii-i.
Tua-i pugenqigtenrilan, utertelliniluni.
Tua-i umyuarteqliniluni waniw' tekiskuni angalkumun tua-i qaillun tuunri-tevkararkauluni tangellminek angalkumun.
Tua-i ut'rinarpakayuilami, tua-i nunameggnun tekicarturluni pilliniuq, tua-i-am ayuquciqngamiu nulirran, ayumian ketvaumaaralliniuq ava-i arulairviktuk'-ngaan tungiinun.

His thoughts were suddenly interrupted by the fact that he had arrived without catching anything, not even a bird.

He was suddenly concerned about her impending disappointment.

He completely forgot about the matter that he was going to have an *angalkuq* look into when he arrived.

It so happened that he wouldn't remember it again after that. That matter of him spearing a human would never come to his mind again.

The only thing that he was concerned about was his wife's impending disappointment because he hadn't caught anything, not even a bird.

Then after he arrived he never remembered anything about that incident [of spearing a human].

When his son started hunting, the father stopped hunting. When he stopped hunting, his son in turn started to go hunting.

Just like his father, even when his fellow hunters didn't catch anything, he would come home with a catch.

Then one day, just like his father's experience, all day long he [hunted] in calm weather.

Then when it was going to get dark on him, he returned home before seeing anything. He was still a young man.

Then soon, just like his father, he saw a seal up ahead of him.

So being eager to catch it and thinking that it might get too dark for him . . . when it was close enough to recognize, he saw it was a human! Since he was a young man, being scared, he paddled as fast as he could toward his village!

While he was [paddling home], it surfaced in front of him!

And he would turn his back to it and [paddle] on. It would surface up ahead of him closer than before.

Then soon, when it emerged right in front of him, he stopped paddling.

[It surfaced] up to its shoulders.

It continued to come up; when it was up to a certain point, he saw that it started to lift its arms out of the water, holding a harpoon.

It said to him, "This one here that your father gave me, I am going to give it to you."

After saying it was going to give it to him, it aimed that harpoon at him.

Because he was terrified, he sat still.

"Your father gave his harpoon to me. And now I am going to give it to you."

Then it harpooned him at close range.

When it harpooned him, his kayak tipped over!

Then he never arrived home.

Umyugaa qanengssakalliniuq pitevkenani tekitellminek, yaquleggaungraan-llu.

Qacuvallallerkaanek umyuangartelliniuq.

Imna umyuaqurallni angalkumun tekiskuni pivkararkaullni tua-i avaurluku tua-i.

Cunawa-gguq tua-i taqluku tua-i umyuaqenqiggngairulluku. Umyugaani ui-tanqiggngairulluni tauna narulkengellni yugmek.

Tauna taugaam nuliami tua-i qacuvallallerkaa yaquleggaungraan pitenrit-lerminek piluni.

Tua-i uitalliniluni tekitelliniluni natii neq'aksuunaku taum.

Tua-i taun' qetunraa ayagayaurcan, ellii-ll' atii ayagananrirluni. Ayagananringan qeturaan kipulleggluku ayagalangluni.

Tua-i-am tautun atamitun, ilamini makuni, ilani pitenrilengraata iliini pill'uni tekitaqluni.

Tua-i-am piuraqerluni, tua-i-am atamitun tua-i ernerpak quuniurumalliniluni.

Tua-i unugarkaurcani-am tua-i utertelliniluni camek tua-i tangerqerpailegmi. Tan'gurrauluni.

Tua-am piuraqerluni, tuaten tua-i atamitun, taqukamek am'umek ciuneminek tangerrluni.

Tua-i-am pitangyuutekngamiu tua-i unuksigilengssiyaallerkaminek piluni . . . tua-i-am elitaqnarilliniuq yuullinilria! Tua-i tan'gurraungami, alingami tua-i, nunami tungiinun piurqautelliniluni!

Piinanrani-am puggliniuq ciunrakun!

Tua-i tunutqapiarluku-ll' ayagyaaqaqluni. Ciunrakun canimellikanirluni pug'aqluni.

Tua-i pivakarlun'-am uuggun ciuqerrakun pugngan, tua-i anguanriqertelli-niluni.

[Pug'uq] tuskaarluni.

Nugngiinaqerluni; qaill' tua-i pitariqerluku pillinia, mermek maaken naluu-maaralliniak talligni, nanerpak-wa tegumiara.

Pillinia, "Man'a maa-i atavet, atavet man'a taitellra, elpenun tunqata'arqa."

Tua-i tunqatarnirraarluku tungiinun tua-i cautellinia taman' nanerpak.

Tua-i alingami tua-i uitaluni.

"Aatavet man'a nanerpani wangnun taitellrukii. Tua-i-ll' waniw' elpenun tunqatarluku."

Tua-i narulkalliniluku wavet.

Narulkaani tua-i kitnguluni!

Tua-i-ll' tayim' tekitevkenani.

This was in the fall.

They [searched] for him, they tried to see if they could find him drifted on shore.

So his father became frantic, both his parents did.

They visited each and every shaman.

They went to every [shaman].

So among their residents, they had this old woman with a granddaughter to help her.

When she, the granddaughter of that old woman, whenever she went to fetch water, her peers would spill her bucket. Or they would make her cry and also hurt her. They probably despised her, I don't know what they did.

When he had gone to all the shamans, he had given them his valuable material possessions. He was giving away his belongings as compensation when asking [the shamans to help him].

When he ran out of alternatives, he told his wife to go and see if the old woman could do anything. This was in the evening.

When she went [and entered the old woman's home] the old woman asked her, "I wonder why you have briefly dropped in?"

That person she asked said to her, "Since my husband across there told me to come see you, I've come to see you. We want very much to see the body of our son."

That old woman told her that she didn't know a thing, she said she didn't have power [to inquire]. She told her instead to tell her granddaughter across there, the young girl.

When [the woman] told [the girl], [the girl] said to her, "Okay then, go across [to your home] and make a seal-gut rain parka for an adult. But do not dare put any adornments on it. Just make it plain." And she told her not to put fringes or anything hanging from it. She told her to sew them without putting any kind of adornment on them.

And when they were finished, she should finish them just the way they were.

And when she finished it, she told her to make an adult-size parka. She told her not to adorn it either.

And if she made waterproof wading boots, she also told her to make plain wading boots.

When she was finished with them, she told her to wrap them in a woven grass mat and bring them to the *qasgi*.

And after bringing them to the *qasgi*, she told her to come and tell her.

When she went across [to their house], she told her husband.

So her husband said to her, "Okay, we have plenty of time to sleep, let's try to finish them!"

So getting a ringed seal, her man scraped it to make it pliant. And his poor mother worked on the seal-gut parka and the fur parka.

Uksuarmi.

Tua-i cayaaqluku, tua-i mallussuquyaaqluku.

Tua-i kapiangenglliniuq im' atii, angayuqaak.

Angalkuaraat ceniluki.

Tua-i ceniyaaqluki.

Ukugnek-gguq ilangqertut, arnassagaurlurmek uumek ilangqertut tutgarminek arnamek kevgarrarluni.

Tamaa-i mertarqan-gguq tauna tutgara'urlua taum arnassagaam, makut pitatain qaltaanek kuviaqluku. Wall'u tua-i qiarqelluku akngiraluku piaqluku. Tangnerrlukluku-w' pilallrullikiit, qaill' piatgu.

Tua-i angalkut qaqicamiki tua-i, akluiruyutekluki tua-i nangengluki tamakut tukuuterugani. Cat-wa tua-i akluni waten ellimerruteku'urluki.

Tua-i callerkairucami pillinia nuliani arnarkar paqnguaqaasqelluku. Atakumi.

Tua-i-ll' tua-i agngami elkegnun [itran] arnassagaam-am pillinia, "Cassuqerluten-kiq-tam tua-i itqercit?"

Tua-i-ll' taum ciunran pillinia, "Tua-i-wam ik'um aiparma paqcesqengaten waniw' paqcaaqekemken. Tua-i kemga tangerqeryuumiryaaqluku qetunramnuk."

Taum tua-i anrnassagallraam pillinia ellii nallumaniluni tua-i, camek piitniluni. Ikna taugaam tutgarani qanrutesqelluku, nasaurlurraq.

Qanrucani pillinia, "Kitak' arvirluten imarnici temircitegnek. Taugaam kenuguciqeryaqunakek. Tua-i taqkikek tua-i taq'ercenarraulukek." Imkunek-llu agauciqaasqevkenak'. Tua-i mingqesqellukek camek elliiqaqsaunakek kenuguka'armek.

Tua-ll' taqkagnek tua-i taqesqelluku.

Cali-llu taq'urainaqakek cali atkulisqelluku temircitegnek atkugnek. Cali tua-i kenugarcesqevkenakek.

Cali-llu ivrucilikan, tua-i cali taq'ercenarraagnek ivrucilisqelluku.

Taqkakek, tupiganek caquqerluk' qasgicesqelluki.

Qasgiqaarluki qanrucartuusqelluni.

Tua-i arviami uini qanrulluku.

Tua-i uingan pillinia, "Kitak' tua-i qavallerkarpuk amllertuq, taqengnaqnaupuk!"

Tua-i nayirmek piluni angutii calugciluni. Aanaurlua-ll' tua-i taukunek tua-i imarnitnek, atkugnek-llu caliluni.

So when they finally finished . . . they had worked even at night.

Just as she had instructed them, they wrapped them inside the grass kayak mat and took them to the *qasgi*.

While they were at the *qasgi,* [the man's wife] came in holding the woven grass mat.

When she put them down on the *qasgi* floor, the people started to comment, "What is that person down there about to do? What is she doing?"

After she put them down, she went out.

When she went out, she went to tell that old woman's granddaughter. When she told her, she got ready and then went out.

So while they were at the [*qasgi*], that old woman's granddaughter came up through the entrance hole. And when she pulled herself up through the hole, when she sat down just past those garments, she began to undress. She took off her parka and took off her boots.

The people in the *qasgi* had no clue what was going on because she had never done anything in their presence. And some would ask what she was going to do, "What is that one down there going to do?"

And then she said after she undressed, "I wish one of the people who used to mistreat me would put these boots on me! I hope that they put them on me!"

So because they knew that they used to mistreat her, two boys put those wading boots on her.

When they went up [and sat], again she said, "Oh my, I wish the two who used to mistreat me would come and put this parka on me!"

Two boys went down and put [the parka] on her.

When they went up, she said, "Oh my! Those two who harmed me, I wish they would put a seal-gut parka on me!"

Then two of them put the seal-gut parka on her. Although they were too large for her [they put them on her].

She commented, after they were finished with her, that she did not have a belt. She told them to get a skin line for her to use as a belt. So they went and got it for her and came in with skin line.

She said, "I wish the two who used to beat me would put the belt on me!"

When two young men came down to put the belt on her, she told them to tie a knot on her back. She also told them to tie it extremely tight.

So she lay face down and had them put a belt on her; she went down on her knees and hunched over when they were about to tie it on her back.

She told them to use all their strength when they put the belt on her, not to go easy on her.

They tied it tightly and made a real knot on it when they tied it.

When they were finished with her, instead of getting up right away, she began to stretch and get up ever so slowly, and she grunted and said that it was loose.

Tua-i taququrainaryaqliamek . . . unugtuumaan caliaqlutek.

Tua-i alerquuciatun ikaraliitnek pequnqaulluki qasgilluki.

Qasgimiut uitainanratni, tauna imna [angutem nuliara] itliniuq tupiganek tegumiarluni.

Kanavet-llu qasgim natranun elliaki, ukut wani qanqetaangartelliniut, "Qaill' kan'a, caqatall'erta kan'a? Qaillun pilun' pia?"

Ellirraarluki tayim' anlliniluni.

Anngami tua-i tauna arnassagaam tutgarii qanrucarturluku. Qanrucani tua tayima upluni anlliniluni.

Piinanratni tauna tua-i arnassagaam tutgarii nuggliniuq. Nugngami-ll' taukut tua-i aturat kiatiitnun aqumngami, ayumian ugayangartelliuq. Atkuni yuuluki piluguugni-ll' yuulukek.

Tua-i uunguciinateng ukut qasgimiut takumeggni qaill' piyuilan. Caqatallranek-llu tua-i qanaagaqluteng, "Caqatarta kan'a?"

Tua-i qanlliniuq matangqariqercami, "Imkuk-llu ilalkestek'lallma iliita piluguuk ukuk ac'etqaqsaunakek! Ac'ellitkek!"

Tua-i nallunrilameng ilacuk'lallruamegteggu, malruulutek tan'gurraak tua-i taukuk ivrucik acetlinilukek.

Tua-i tagngagnek pilliniuq cali, "Aling imkuk, tayima-tuq imkuk ilalkuurlua pistek'lallma atkukarlignga!"

Tua-i malruulluku tan'gurraak atrarlutek aturarluku.

Tagngagnek tuamtell' pilliuq, "Aling imkuk-llu, imkuk-llu akngiralua ilalkestekvakalallma imarniteryuagnga!"

Tuamtell' tua-i malruulluku imarnitek at'ellukek. Tua-i angkengraaki.

Pilliniuq taq'ercagni, naqugutkaitniluni. Taprarmek naqugutkaminek aqvatesqelluki. Tua-i aqvalluku itrutliniat taprarmek.

Pilliniuq, "Imkuk-tuq nangetruyilua pisteklallma tayim' naqugteqerlignga!"

Tua-i-am atrarlutek yun'errak naqugteqataagni pilliniuq pamaggun qillerniisqelluku. Qilqapiarluku cali qillercesqelluku cagniluku cakneq.

Tua-i palu'urrluni naqugcetliniluni; ciisqumigarrluni palu'urrluni pamaggun qillerteqataagni.

Pilliniak tua-i piniag' aturluku naqugcesqelluni aaqesqevkenani.

Tua-i cagniqu'urluku tua-i qillertelliniluku, qilpiarluku-ll' qillerrluku.

Tua-i taqngagni imumek mak'artevkenani-ll', makqataraqerluni nengvailegmi, engaaqerluni qanlliniuq, qacngatuq-gguq.

"I thought I told you to use all your strength to tie me tightly. Put your feet here. Step on my thighs and use them to reinforce your strength. Using my thighs as leverage, never mind about hurting me, tie it tightly!"

So using her thighs as leverage, they pulled using all their strength, and pressing down there, they really tied a knot guaranteed to stay. And they tied it extremely tight.

When they told her that they were finished, she slowly got up, and when she stood up straight, she said that was good this time.

When she was about to go out, she told them to drum all night.

When she went out, she went down through the entrance hole and disappeared.

[The drummers] began to drum and drummed all night long.

Later on that night, that one out there entered.

When she came up through the entrance hole, she had a person on her back inside her seal-gut rain parka.

She said, "I wish those two who hurt me when they beat me would pull me up!"

They went to her and pulled her up.

They pulled her up; here she [still] had on that tight belt. Yet behind her were two legs dangling, and up on top was a head.

Then she said, "Let those who used to mistreat me remove my garments!"

They removed her garments and took him out.

Everyone wondered how she had managed to pull the body up under the tightly fastened belt.

When they laid him down, they saw that he hadn't lost any of his clothing including his cap.

He looked like he was sleeping down there.

Then before she put on her clothes, she went to his father.

When she went to his father, she squatted down in front of him and said, "I am now going to ask you a question! Now, as you've been living, you have caught everything. You have caught every kind of animal. Have you ever caught anything that you thought was unusual?"

After he had his head down, he said that while he was coming along in life, he had not caught anything that he thought was unusual.

She said to him, "Now down in the ocean, you have caught every creature. So now, are you sure that you have not killed anything that was unusual?"

So after he sat for a moment he said that he had never killed anything strange down in the ocean.

"Okay! You have not killed one! Now on land, you have also killed every kind of animal that could be hunted! Have you ever caught any animal that was unusual?"

"Pinirtek-ggem aturluku cagnitesqua. Ukugnun tukerlutek. Mecangqagka tukruteklukek. Mecangqagka tukruteklukek, akngirtellerkaqa umyuaqevkenaku cagnilluku qillertegu!"

Tua-i mecangqaak aturlukek, tua-i nuqluku pinirteg aturluku, kan'a call' tua-i neg'arrluku, nutaan tua-i qilpiarluku qillertelliniluku. Cagniqu'urluku-ll' call' tua-i qillerrluku.

Tua-i taqniagni makluni, makqata'arluni, nengumariqercami pilliniuq, nutaan-gguq assirtuq.

Tua-i pillinii anqataami tua-i unugpak cauyarturaasqelluki.

Anngami tua-i uavet kalvaggluni tua-i tayima.

Unugpak tua-i cauyanglliniut.

Tua-i unuumainanrani tua-ll' ugna.

Nuggliniuq amarluni yugmek imarnitegmi iluani.

Pilliuq, "Imkug-tuq tayim' akngirassiyaaglua nangetruyitestek'lallma nuggli-gnga!"

Tua-i ullagluku nugtelliniluku.

Nugtelliniak; naqugutertulria-gguq-wa tamatumek cagnik'ayalriamek. Kingu-lirneregni-wa irug aqevlalriik, qamiquq-wa pikna.

Pilliniuq, "Imkut tua-i pistek'lallma ugayarlitnga!"

Tua-i ugayarluku yuulliniat.

Qaillun-gguq waniw' naqugutminun-llu itertellruagu.

Taklartelliniat natminek-llu nacarraminek-llu katagiqallrunritlinilria.

Tuar-gguq kanani qavalria.

Tua-i atii ullalliniluku aturarpailegmi.

Atii ulliimiu, ketiinun uyungqerluni pillinia, "Waniw' apteqataramken! Waniwa-qaa uka-i agiiqurallerpeni, ca tamalkuan pitaqeken. Ungungssiq ta-malkuan pitaqeken. Tua-lli-wa-qaa tua-i allayukek'ngarpenek waniw' tua-i pit-qaqsailnguten?"

Tua-i kananglluggluni uitaurarraarluni pilliuq, tua-i-gguq waniw' uka-i agiirqurallermini tua-i waniw' elliin allakek'ngaminek pitqaqsaituq.

Pillinia, "Tua-i tayima unani imarpigmi cat ungungssilqurraat tamalkuita pitaqsaaqaten. Tua-lli-wa-qaa tua-i ilumun cangalngurmek tua-i waniw' tuquci-qaqsailnguten?"

Tua-i uitarraarluni piuq tua-i-gguq-wa waniw' cangalngurmek tua-i tuquci-qaqsailnguq tua-i unani imarpigmi.

"Ii-i! Tuquciqaqsaitelliniuten! Tua-lli-wa-qaa cali maani nunam qaingani pitarkauyugnat tamalkuita pitaqelriarukten! Tua-lli-wa-qaa cali allayuk'ngarpenek waniw' pitqaqsailnguten?"

After he waited a while, he told her that without having killed anything unusual, he had reached this age.

"Yes! You apparently have not killed one! Down on the ocean, you have not killed one! And also on land, you have not killed an unusual one!"

She slowly extended her right arm [and unfolded her hand], "Here is your harpoon."

It was the spearhead of the harpoon!

"Here is your harpoon! This is the spear point that hit the one that you caught! It apparently gave this to your son!"

Then and there, he suddenly remembered that one he had harpooned!

Marie Meade: He had forgotten all about it?

Dick Anthony: The one he had forgotten, only when she showed [the harpoon point], he suddenly remembered it.

After she put her clothes on, when she was done getting dressed, she said to his parents, "Okay, take your son home and treat him the same way you cared for him when he was a child. And put a lamp next to him, and do not let its flame go out during day and night. And every time you wake, always check his wound. If you notice a little change, if any part of him is a little different. . . ." She told them to go to her and inform her immediately.

So they did exactly as told. When one of them was tending to him, they would fold over the cover and check his wound.

Then one day when his wife uncovered it, she saw that the end of his wound was beginning to heal.

After dozing off, when she woke, she watched his body down there.

She observed, while she was looking at him, it seemed that his belly would move slowly down there.

Seeing that it indeed moved, she woke her husband.

After she woke him, she said to him, "What is that one down there doing? If my eyes are not fooling me, it seems that his belly is moving."

So when his father checked it, he saw that both [ends] were healing.

He told [his wife] to go and tell that girl.

As soon as [the wife] entered [their house] at night, when that girl rushed out as soon as she came in, she quickly followed her, but that one she quickly followed was nowhere to be seen!

Rushing over to their house, she saw that that girl was already tending to him.

Marie Meade: What [was she tending to]?

Dick Anthony: The [girl who the mother] had fetched, she was bending the joints in his arms and his legs.

She said to them, "For heaven sakes! I thought I told you that in the event that something was different, to come and tell me right away."

Tua-i uitaurarraarluni pillia tua-i-gguq-wa allayuk'ngaminek waniw' tua-i tuquciqerpailegmi tua-i waten ellilria.

"Ii-i! Tuquciqaqsaitelliniuten! Unani imarpigmi tuquciqaqsaitelliniuten! Cali-llu nunam qaingani cali tuquciqaqsaitelliniuten allayugnarqelriamek!"

Tallirpimi tungiinun yaggluku nengcimaarallinia, "Waniwa tang un' nanerpiin."

Cingilga!

"Waniwa tang un' nanerpiin! Pitallerpet waniw' caskutallra! Qetunrarpenun tunellrullinikii una!"

Nutaan im' narulkaq'ngellni neq'aqalliniluku!

Arnaq: Nalluyagutelliniluku?

Mingigtuli: Nalluyagutellni tua-i nutaan tua-i maniaku neq'aqerluku.

Tuan' tua-i aturarluni piami, aturanermek taqngami angayuqaak pilliniak, "Kitak' kan'a qetunrartek mikelnguullratun pitaluku agulluku aulukitegu. Kenurrirluku cali kenurraa nipevkanrilkurrluku erenrungraan, unuungraan. Cali tupakallertek tamalkuan ekia yuvrirrlainarluku. Qaillun ayuqluku tangerquvtegnegu, nat'arii im' qaillurraq ayuquciatun. . . ." Egmian qanrucartuusqelluni.

Cunawa-gguq tua-i. Aipaagnek piaqamiu, qakeggluku tangrraqluku ekia.

Tua-i-ll' caqerluni-am nulirran pakillinia, ekian un' iqua mamnengcuarallinilria.

Tua-i qavaqerraarluni tupiimi qayuw' tua-i tangvauralliniluku kan' qainga. Pilliniuq, tangvaurainanrani tuar-gguq tang pekcimaaralalriik kankuk aqsiik.

Tua-i pekcimaaralalliniagnek uini tupaggluku.

Tupagqaarluku pillinia, "Qaill' kan' pia? Tuartang kana-i, iigma iqlunrilkagnia, aqsiik pektelalriik."

Tua-i atiin pillinia, paqnaklinia, tua-i tamarmek mamngellinilriik.

Qanrucartuusqelluku taun' nasaurluq.

Tauna tua-i itruciatun unugmi, itruciatun tua-i taun' nasaurluq kipulkarluk' tayim' anqercan, elliin maligarcaaqellinia, nauwa imna maligartellra!

Nem'egnun agqerrluni pilliniuq, ak'a caumangellrullinikii taum nasaurlurraam.

Arnaq: Ca taman'?

Mingigtuli: Tua-i-w' tauna aqvallni, makut arivniaskai tallig iruk-llu makut arivniaskai.

Pilliak, "Aling! Qanrutellruamtek-ggem kia una qaillun allayutmun pikan, egmian qanrucartuusqellruunga-ggem."

Then soon that one started to open his eyes. And his legs, his joints were beginning to move from her bending them.

He opened his eyes and started to blink.

Helping him up, when she let him try inside the house, he walked.

When his walking improved, she said to him, "Go on and go outside and scan the ocean. If you see anything, come in."

When he went out, as he was scanning the ocean, he saw the one who had harpooned him down there!

When he saw it, he went inside.

When he came in that girl asked him, "So did you see anything?"

Marie Meade: Was it a person?

Dick Anthony: Yes, he saw it as a human in the ocean. He saw it as he had seen it before.

[She] asked him, "So, did you see anything?"

He told her that he saw the person who had speared him last fall down there.

[She said] it was the one who [harpooned him].

[The boy's parents] had promised her that if she allowed them to see his body, if that girl allowed them to see his body, if she allowed them to see his body alive, they would make him her husband.

Just as they promised, they had their son take the one who brought him back to life as a wife.

That was how long that person who told me that story told it.

Marie Meade: Yes. That Jack Williams?

Dick Anthony: Because that person never forgot [stories], when he told stories, he even mentioned the names of those people.

That Jack, now what did they call him in Yup'ik? They called him Uyuruciaq. I see his younger sister up at Bethel.

❧ *Our Father Was Saved by a Dog* ❧

Martha Mann with Julia Azean and Marie Meade, Kongiganak, July 1994

Martha Mann: Our father was saved by a dog one time. When our father went out from their home as a young man in the middle of the night to drink some water, a ghost came to him. When he was going in their doorway. he bumped into a person.

When he went back out he tried to go into the other houses, but they all had that same person along their doorways. He began to panic. And soon that person

Tua-i pivakarluni uiteng!liniluni tauna. Iruk-llu ipii makut arivniangluteng arivniurqurallranek.

Tua-i uilluni qelemyaqtaangengluni-llu.

Tua-i makluku maani enem iluani naspaavkaqiini, kangarluni.

Tua-i pektellra una assirian pillia, "Kitek' anluten imarpik kiarcarturru. Camek tangerquvet iterniartuten."

Anngami tua-i un'a imarpik kiarrnginanerminiu pilliniuq, imna kana-i narulkartellra!

Tua-i tangrramiu itliniluni.

Itran tua-i taum nasaurluum pillinia, "Tua-llu-q' camek tangertuten?"

Arnaq: Yug'uluni?

Mingigtuli: Ii-i, yug'uluku tua-i tangerrluku imarpigmi. Tangkucillmitun tua-i tangerrluku.

Pillinia, "Tua-llu-q' camek tangenrrituten?"

Imna-gguq-wa uksuaq narulkartellni kana-i tangerqii.

Tua-i-gguq-wa tauna pistellra.

Tua-i akqellruamegen'gu kemga tangerceskaku, taum nasaurluum kemga tangerceskaku, cavkenaku-w' tua-i tangerceskaku, aipaqliutevkarciqniluku.

Tua-i qanllertek tua-i aturluku tauna tua-i qetunrarmegnun aipaqevkarluku unguirtellra.

Tuaten tua-i aug'um qanemcitestema taktaluku qanemcikellrukii.

Arnaq: Ii-i. Taum-qaa Jack Williams-aam?

Mingigtuli: Avaurtaitelliniami augna tua-i qanemcikuni, arivqurluki-ll' tamakut yuut atrit.

Jack-aq-wa tua-i tauna, Yugtun kiturrarmek imat'am pilaqiit? Uyuruciamek piaqluku. Nayagaa-w' tua-i kiani tanglaqka Mamterillermi.

ᴂ *Atavut Qimugtem Anirtullrua* ᴔ

Mass'aluq, Anglluralria, Arnaq-llu, Kangirnaq, July 1994

Mass'aluq: Tauna-gguq-am im' atavut qimugtem anirtullrukii. Alangruluni-gguq tauna atavut meqsarturyaaqluni yun'errauluni unugmi nem'eggnek meq-suami. Itellriim-gguq amimeggnek puukpakili yugmun.

Tua-i anngami nunat imkut ceniyaaqellinii amiingit tamarmeng pitarluteng taumek. Tua-i-gguq nanikuangluni. Tauna-llu-gguq imna amigmecaaqvigminek

came up through the doorway. At that time a young girl had died across [the Kuskokwim River] in Eek.

They say when people died, their inner selves became the outer layer. During that time he was a young man and wasn't married yet. Our father was a shaman, too. At that time they say people didn't know it yet.

Oh my, he began to panic. When that person got to the outer entrance he began to lift his arms beckoning to receive him.

And since [the ghost] was hovering above the ground and the ground beneath it was twirling, he began to think of escaping through that spot. When he would come upon [the ghost] he would turn his back to it and leave. It would be standing in front of him once again. It felt as though the ground suddenly tilted and sloped toward the side [of the ghost].

And though he was trying to pull himself back, he would find himself running toward it, and he would run right through its chest. While he attempted to escape from it, he suddenly noticed something. It looked like a streak of light coming out of something ahead.

After he started going away from it, he turned and crawled slowly toward it. He reached the place where the light was coming from. He kept moving toward it.

As he was moving, he noticed a woven grass flap in front of him. He opened it and saw a woman inside. And on the side there were many children sleeping. The woman back there was sewing many little boots. She had a nosepiece. She looked like she had a nosepiece.

Julia Azean: Do you know what a *kakitaq* is?

Marie Meade: Yes, I don't know what it is.

Julia Azean: A hole [in the nose], and you'd put something [through it].

Martha Mann: Then the woman said, without even looking at him, "What, are you in such distress?" Then he told her that he was in dire straits with nowhere to escape. She said, "Then come inside and lie down behind us back there." When he went inside, the only thing he remembered was laying down.

Julia Azean: There were many children sleeping next to the woman. And their mother was working on many little boots.

Martha Mann: He slept. When he woke up the next morning he found that he had slept inside a dugout of a dog raising puppies. [The dog] had saved him. He looked at the dog and saw a mark across her snout. It was the nosepiece he saw [on the woman the night before]. There were many little puppies [next to the dog]. He went out. The dog was sitting in the hole in the ground with her puppies. He said that the dog saved him.

nugluni. Takuani-gguq tuan' neviarcar tuqullruluni Iigmi ikani.

Makut-gguq tang tuqullret iluqlilteng elaqliqsagutetullinikait. Tamaani tamaa-i nulirtuqsaunani-ll' yun'errauluni. Cali-llu angalkuullruuq tauna atavut. Alaiqsaunani-gguq tamatum nalliini.

Aren nanikuallinilria tua-i. Kiituani-gguq tang ellayaramun elliami talligni-ll' ellavrusnganrirluk' akurturyuguangaa.

Tua-i-gguq acini qerratiiku, kan'a aciani uivelria, tuavet tua-i anagturnaluni umyuarteqengyaaqluni. Tua-i-gguq tekitaqamiu tunulluku ayagyaaqnaurtuq. Pinaurtuq-gguq ciunrani ingna. Aren tuar-gguq nuna uvqertelal' tungiinek.

Tua-i-gguq tang pinritsaangermi aqvaqurlun' ullagluk' qat'gaikun-ll' aya-karluni. Caqerluni-am tua-i ayallermini piqalliniuq, ca man'a. Tuar-gguq avan' kenurram anqertellra.

Unicaaqerraarluku aurrurluni unatni piluki ayagturalliniuq. Pilliniuq-gguq waniwa kenurram anqertellra. Ayallinilria tua-i akirturluku.

Ayainanermini pilliniuq ikirtuqat ukut tupigat. Ikirtellinia arnaq kiugna. Ukut-wa-gguq tang mikelngurugaat qavalriit. Arnaq-gguq kiug' piluguyagarnek calilria. Kakitarluni-gguq. Kakitangqerrnganani qengagmikun.

Anglluralria: Kakitaq-qaa nalluan?

Arnaq: Ii-i, nalluaqa.

Anglluralria: Ukineq [qengami], waten camek-llu . . .

Mass'aluq: Tua-llu-gguq tangerpek'naku taum arnam pia, "Waq' tua-i arenqialiuten?" Tua-llu-gguq pia tua-i waniw' arenqialuniluni natmun anagvig-kairutniluni. "Kitak' kelumtenun pavavet iterluten inarten." Itrami tua keluatnun inararucini taugaam elpekqerluku.

Anglluralria: Taum-gguq arnam yaatiini mikelngurugaat qavalriit. Aaniit-gguq piluguyagarugarnek caliluni.

Mass'aluq: Tua-i qavalliniluni. Maaten-gguq tang unuaquan tupagtuq qimugtem irniayaalriim irniayaarviani qavallinilria. Taum-am tua-i anirtuqallinikii. Maaten-gguq tang imna tauna qimugta pia cugg'ucillengqellinilria. Kakitaqsukellra imna. Ukut-wa-gguq tang qimugkauyararugaat. Anllinilun' tua-i. Elanerem iluani irnia-yaallinilun' taun' qimugta. Tua-i-gguq taum anirtullrua qimugtem.

↜ *Ayugutarin* ↝

Tim Agagtak with Ruth Jimmie and Ann Fienup-Riordan, Nightmute, July 1985

Tim Agagtak: His name was Ayugutarin.

A grandmother and her grandchild. This is how the story first starts. A grandchild and his grandmother lived alone. Where were those two born? They lived down on the coast somewhere.

When her grandchild would get ready to hunt his grandmother would get his things ready, filling his pack with food.

They lived along the seashore. I don't know where exactly they resided, but along the seashore.

At the time of this story, they weren't sure where Qaluyaat [Nelson Island] was. But the [story] starts on the coast.

In the spring [when it was time to hunt], she would fill up his pack with a lot of food when things were plentiful. She would do that again and again [before he went out].

Then one day she was preparing [food] for him back when there were no extreme storms and high winds. Her grandson asked her, "Why is it that [you pack food] even though my destination is close?" He asked her why she packed a lot of provisions for him.

His grandmother said to him . . . (They always said this to them, "*Eng-ng!* What is the matter?" They would say *"eng"* to them. When people say *"eng"* in their speech, it is an expression of empathy toward that person, knowing that person's future held circumstances and unfortunate predicaments.)

[His grandmother said,] *"Eng-ng!* Why are you questioning what I do for you? You see, one day [while you are out there] you could get totally lost and be unable to find your way home."

(Down on the ocean when it's foggy and one is on the water, back when they didn't have compasses, it gets difficult to see where you are going. And you won't even know where the sun is up there. Because it's so foggy it's hard to tell where you came from.)

(But by observing the immediate surroundings [one would know where he was]. These birds never get lost. When they migrate, they only fly north when they are starting to arrive, and they don't go toward other directions. Especially the loons, they are like compasses. And walrus too, they always head in the direction they are going. And here there is no visibility at all.)

(Those were their indicators. I, too, when weather got bad out, I used to watch [those animals] and use them [to tell direction] when I participated [in hunting] down there [on the ocean.])

✺ *Ayugutarin* ✺

Akagtaq, Angalgaq, Ellaq'am Arnaan-llu, Negtemiut, July 1985

Akagtaq: Ayugutarimek aterluni tauna.

Taukuk tutgarquralriik. Maa-i man' ayagniqarraallra. Tutgarquralriik maur-luni-llu kiimek tua-i yuulliniaqelriik. Naken taukuk yuurtellruak? Nani tua-i unani cenami.

Tua-i waten uptaqan tutgarii maurlullriin taum uptelliniaqekii tua-i issratii imirluku taquirluku.

Unani cenami taugaam. Naniqapiar-llu uitaciitagka taukuk, taugaam imarpiim ceniini.

Qaluyaat-llu uunguciinaki. Taum ayagniqarraallra tua-i cenami.

Waten up'nerkarqan taquilliniaqekii tua-i issratii imirluku neqnek tua-i am-llernek ca paivngallrani. Tua-i pulengtaq tua-i piuralliniaqekii.

Tua-i-ll'am pivakartelluni, tuaten-am tua-i uptellrani akaar anuqliyuitellrani tamaa-i cakneq. Pillinikii taum tua-i tutgariin, "Ciin waniwa canimelengraan-llu [taquilarcia]?" Taquilaucirminek amllernek.

Taum tua-i maurluan pillinia . . . (Qanruciiratullruit waten, "Eng-ng! Caaqsit waniw'?" Eng'aluggluki. Tua-i-wa naklekutngulria tauna tua-i engaalleq. Augna ciunerkaa umyuaqluku.)

"Eng-ng! Caaqsit waniwa? Atam cam iliini kingunitlerkan nalluniaran uunguciitkacagarluten."

(Unani atam imarpigmi taicirqami tua-i mer'em qaingani uitalriani, kam-paassaangqessuitellratni, tua-i uunguciinani. Pakemna-llu akerta uunguciinani. Tua-i ugaan taicim kinguneq uunguciinani.)

(Maaggun taugaam. Yaqulget makut pellaaneq nalluat. Negetmun ayag-tura'arqelriit waten tekicuga'arqameng, piciatun-llu piyuunateng. Imkut tunu-tellget arcaqerluteng kampaassatun ayuqluteng. Imkut-llu kaugpiit cali, tua-i cali ciunerteng tua-i caumaurluku. Wall'u tang tua-i camek tangerrnaitqapiartuq.)

(Tamaa-i tua-i nallunailkutaqluki. Wiinga-ll' assiirarutaqaanga atutullruanka unani ilagautetullemni.)

As usual, [when he was ready to hunt] she filled his pack with quite a bit of food in spring.

So, he went down to the ocean. Just when he got where land wasn't visible, visibility became low. Fog started coming. And he couldn't figure out where he had come from.

Since he couldn't tell the direction that he came from, he stopped and stayed where he was. (When fog comes, it gets very calm. Fog only comes in calm weather. The fog can get very thick when it isn't windy.)

He just stayed on the ice and never moved. He stayed and stayed on that ice all spring long. Soon the provisions that the old woman had prepared for him. . . . (Probably [she prepared] because she knew what would happen. Because those people in the past were somehow [exceptional]. This story that is told is actually a *quliraq*.)

He was there all spring. After sleeping all night. . . . It never got windy while he was there. He would get up and the weather was the same. There was a very thick fog. And it never got windy.

Ruth Jimmie: The sun wouldn't come out either?

Tim Agagtak: It didn't come out. And it didn't appear.

Ruth Jimmie: So did that person spend the spring there?

Tim Agagtak: Yes. He stayed down there on floating [ice]. Eventually his food dwindled. He started eating very little to save what was left. He started to conserve them. He was unable to eat lots.

Oh how pitiful. They told the story like that. He was there like that all spring.

One day, the sun came up, and it was like that once again. And back when visibility was good, he had not seen any mountains either.

He just stayed on the water for a long time.

At daybreak when the weather is calm, noises can be heard from a great distance away, various noises. He heard two women talking from over yonder. He heard two people making sounds now and then. They weren't birds, but people.

Soon when they talked, he started to understand what they were saying. . . . (The ocean down there, Akuluraq [Etolin Strait], when there is a northward current flow, the water rushes north for two days. And when the current flows outward, the rush of water lasts for two days again. That used to happen when I hunted down there.)

Soon, as they spoke, he understood what they were saying, "Be careful, he may miss the way!" There were two people talking. [They spoke] in the fog, and he couldn't see where they were.

Then soon he saw a line [of ice] where two ocean currents met right there in front of him. He was there next to it. And that there . . . the ice, what they called

Tua-i tuaten tua-i taquillinia-am tua-i amllerrarnek tua-i up'nerkami.

Tua-i-ll' unavet atralria-am, unavet imarpigmun. Tua-i nunatailqumun elli-qerluku, kiarnairutliniluni. Taitungluni tua-i. Kinguneni-llu nalluyagulluku.

Tua-i aren nalluamiu tua-i kinguneni uitauralliniuq. (Man'a taituk quunruuq. Quunirqami taugaam tua-i taicilartuq. Tua-i tairvagluni cakneq anuqlinritaqan.)

Tua-i cikum qaingani waten uitauralliniuq tua-i. Cunawa-gguq tua-i waniw' iquiriluni up'nerkarpak taum qaingani ugingaaqellria. Kiituani taukut imkut ta-quiyutkellri taum tua-i arnassagaam. . . . (Tua-i nallunritliami-w'. Qaillun-wa tamakut pillruameng avani tua-i yullret. Qulirauyaaquq man'a qanemciutuli.)

Tua-i up'nerkilliniaquq. Unugpak qavarraarluni. . . . Anuqliucuilani-llu. Mak-tellininaurtuq imutun ayuqluni. Tua-i tairvagluni. Anuqliyuunani-llu.

Angalgaq: Akerta-llu-q' anyuunani?
Akagtaq: Anyuunani. Alaicuunani-llu.
Angalgaq: Up'nerkiluni-qaa tua-i tauna?
Akagtaq: Ii-i. Unani tua-i pugtalriami uitalliniaquq. Kiituani taquari taukut tua-i carraurtelliniluteng. Aninqurangluki-llu. Aninqurangluki tua-i. Amllermek pisciigaliluni, neresciigaliluni amllermek.
     Aling nakleng. Tua-i tuaten qanemciku'urluku tua-i. Up'nerkarpak pilli-niaqelria.
     Tua-i pivakarluni, tua-i-am ertelliniuq tua-i tuaten tua-i. Tamaa-i-llu kiarnar-qetullrani ingrinek-llu tangyuunani.
     Uitalliniaqelria mer'em qaingani.
     Tanqigiartelluku quunirqan avaken yaaqvanek alaitelartut cat-wa tua-i neplilriit, nepliqaquuralriit. Yuug' amkuk arnaulutek pilriik. Tua-i nepuaqaqulriik. Yaqulguvkenatek yuulutek taugaam.
     Tua-i-ll' taringnarilliniuk maaten. . . . (Un'a atam imarpik Akuluraq negetmur-niqan erenregni malrugni [pituuq]. Tuamtell' ancarniquni erenregni malrugni. Tua-i wiinga-llu aturaqluku unani.)>

Maaten tua-i qanaallrak, nepuallrak taringnarilliniuq, "Aulluvaa-llu uniuru-ciiqellria!" Tua-i yuulutek qanellrak. Taitugmi tua-i, naken-llu piciinakek.

Tua-i-ll' piqerluni qisnermek mat'umek tanglliniluni. Maa-i aturluku. Tamana-ll' . . . cikut ilayugaqameng-gguq, ilacarnermek pilallrat taman' ilakluku tua-i qisen-

ilacarneq, it was a line of ice where two currents meet. It was a thin [line of ice] that wasn't wide.

He apparently was next to that kind of ice. He noticed that water was rising. Kangirrluar [Toksook Bay] was sucking in [ocean water]. The tide was coming up. (The one that sucks [in ocean water], you know that place that has a current. You've seen it down there. At that time Umkumiut was not yet a village. There was no village.)

He started to understand what they were saying, and they were saying, "Careful, he may miss the way." (How did those people know things?)

When he recognized [they were women] and where their voices were coming from, he realized that they were [speaking] from out there. Knowing which way to go, he headed straight toward them.

As he got closer to them, he felt physically transformed and his vision began to change. Then he began to go out [of the fog], and he entered into a space where he could see his surroundings, and he found himself next to huge ice piles on the shore. He viewed [the ice piles] from close up and recognized that they were the ones down the coast. He wasn't too far down [the coast]. You know how Umkumiut isn't too far down the coast, right over there along Kangirrluar.

There were two people walking up there who were both women. Since it was calm, they could be heard while talking, "Careful, he might miss the way." This is what they would say. (How did they know he was there?)

One of the [women] spotted him. The younger sister saw him first, just when that one down there was reaching land. The area behind [Umkumiut camp], that area down below was the water's edge. And down where their village [Umkumiut] is, there was water there.

The little river down the coast, the little river down there, one flowing below Umkuuk, it was their river. That was their source of water. Their old village down the coast is that place up there. . . . . .

Ruth Jimmie: The one on top of Umkuuk?

Tim Agagtak: Yes. (I never saw [that large rock] before it broke off and fell. When I first started seeing it, the piece that broke off used to be huge, the piece that cracked and fell sideways.)

Ruth Jimmie: (And now has that [rock] down the coast gotten smaller?)

Tim Agagtak: (It has gotten small, it has sunk. Beneath it, it's all stone. One person from Nunivak Island, when people from Nunivak were landed there, when one of them slept, when travelers slept in their kayaks; there are [human] remains beneath [that rock] now. We used to see his old kayak mat back when there was a current there. They didn't rot since they were grass. How did these grasses [not rot]? I saw [the grass mat] before.)

ruluni waten. Cikurraq iqtuvkenani.

Tamatumi uitanglliniluni. Ulyugluni. Kangirrluaraam melugluku. Ulyullini-luni. (Im' melutuli, iciw' carvanituli. Tanglaqen tayim' unegna. Umkumiut-llu nu-nauvkenateng tamatum tua-i nalliini. Nunataunani.)

Tua-i-ll' taringnarilliniuk taumek tua-i qanlallinilriik, "Aulluvaa-llu uniuru-ciiqelria." (Qaillun tamakut nallunrit'lartat?)

Tua-i-ll' taungurciamikek, tauna-llu nepualallrak tunglirnera, avaken pila-llinilutek. Tua-i nallunrilami tungiignun ilalqerluni ayalliniluni.

Canimellillrak maliggluku qaillun man'a elliriinalliniluni allayuurrluni kiar-tellra. Piqerluni kiarnarqellriamun anyartuqalliniuq evunpallraat ukut. Maaten tua-i wavet pillinii unegkut. Uaqsigpek'nani. Iciw' Umkumiut uaqsinrilnguut yaa-i Kangirrluaraam ceniini.

Paugkuk-wa tang yuuk malruk kangalriik arnarrlainaak. Tua-i quunian, ne-pualkek taugaam alaunatek, "Aulluvaall' uniuruciiqelria." Waniwa qaneryaraak. (Qaillun-tam' nallunrirtan'gu tauna?)

Tua-i aipaagnek tangerqalliniluku. Uyuraan taum tangerqerluku, tut'eqataan tua-i kan'a. Man'a imna keluatni, unegna mer'em ngelekluku. Unegna-llu nunat uitallrat imna, mer'uluni.

Tauna imna kuicuar unegna un'gaa-i, kuicuar imna unegna, Umkuuk aciak, kuikluku. Meqluku tua-i taukuk. Ua-i ugna nunallrak, pikani imna. . . .

Angalgaq: Umkuuk qaingagni?
Akagtaq: Ii-i. (Wii tauna tangellrunritaqa uspailgan. Ugna ua-i ussnera angell-ruyaaquq tua-i tanglallemni, kep'arrluni ayaluqertellra.)

Angalgaq: (Ua-i-llu-qaa mikliriinarluni?)
Akagtaq: (Mikliluni, muruggluni. Teggalqurrulria-wa acia. Nunivaarmiumek ataucimek, Nunivaarmiut kankut tusngallratni, iliit qavallrani, qayameggni qavaqutullratni; atlingertuq atam ua-i. Ikaraliitellri imkut cat tupigarraat qayaan carvanilallrani alaitellruut. Aruyuitut can'guameng-wa. Qaillun makut can'get pilartat? Tangerqall[ruanka].)

When he came up on land, that one ran down to meet him. They say she was a girl. The younger sister hadn't yet reached puberty. There were two females. There were two of them, and he didn't know if they had parents, the two he came upon.

He didn't know anything. That's what is said about them.

Ruth Jimmie: Did they have a home up there?

Tim Agagtak: Up there on Umkuuk, I'm sure you've see it, that one up there. . . .

Ruth Jimmie: I've seen the old house pit.

Tim Agagtak: There's the other, there are two small old house pits. There is another one also. There are just two. They say that was his *qasgi*.

And back there along the shores of the little river, on the ocean side down there, I used to see them, the two logs stuck in the ground not too far apart. They say that was where they had their skin boat [stored] on crossed pole supports. They looked like soil [when I saw them]. They were actually wood, but they [had rotted and] looked like soil. When I would touch them, they were like the surrounding soil. They say those were the poles from his boat support.

So, since he didn't know where else to go he stayed with them and built a *qasgi*. The younger girl became his spouse back when they didn't have church weddings. [*laughs*] He got a wife.

(In my lifetime when I was younger they never used to have church weddings. They just became a couple without any formalities. But I caught those who used to do that in the past.)

Then they lived there. And he made a skin boat. The area up the coast from the little river up to Cingigarrluar [lit., "Small point"] had no driftwood. It was behind them. Driftwood apparently drifted on shore up the coast. This was when there was a lack of current [or wind] along Umkuuk. This was back when things were plentiful.

They say when this would occur, when there was a current, beluga whales would be [swimming] along the point when they were feeding along shore. Along where the eddy was the strongest, belugas would be tucked underneath below Umkuuk. Since [the land] jutted out a little, the shoreline was farther back.

(That [rock] must have collapsed recently. The [rock] that fell over used to be big when I first started seeing it. It didn't fall to the side, but it fell straight down toward the water. You've seen it down there. And it was not easy to climb on top of [the fallen rock] when I first started seeing it.)

The top of Umkuuk. He joined [the girls there]. (And his grandmother, they used to have them call them *anuurlut* [grandmothers]. And they would call [their grandchildren] *tutgarrlugaat*. That's what they used to have them call them.)

Though he thought of [his grandmother], he couldn't do anything because he didn't know where she was. He had not seen mountains in that area before. He

Tua-i tagngan tauna im' atraqerrluni. Nasaurluuluni-gguq tauna. Arnaur-teluaqsaunani uyuraa. Arnarrlainaak. Malruulutek tua-i, angayuqangqerru-ciinatek-llu taukuk tua-i tekitellrek.

Tua-i camek nalluluni. Tuaten taugaam qanrutkumauk.

Angalgaq: Nengqerrlutek-qaa pikani?

Akagtaq: Pikaggun pika-i Umkuuk qaingagen'gun, tanglaqen tayima, pikani imna. . . .

Angalgaq: Elanelleq tangtuaqa.

Akagtaq: Aipaa-wa, elanecuarallrek. Cali-w' aipaa. Malrurraulutek. Qasgillra-gguq.

Piani-wa kuigaaraam ceniini, imarpiim tunglirnerani unani, tanglallruyaaqag-ka, imkuk muragak kapusngalriik akultuvkenatek. Tamaa-i-gguq angyaata mayu-rutellri. Nevutun ayuqluteng. Amtall' tua-i murauyaaqlutek, amtall' nevutun ayuqlutek. Waten tua-i tegulaqa'arqamtek mat'umun tua-i ilaklutek nevutun ayuqlutek pisciigatevkenatek. Tamaa-i-gguq angyaata mayurutellra.

Tua-i natetmurrvigkailami ilaganga'artellinilukek qasgililuni tua-i. Taumek tua-i uyuraanek aipangluni kassuucuitellermeggni. [*ngel'artuq*] Aipangluni tua-i.

(Kassuucuitellruut avani. Tua-i aipaqsagutaqluteng camek pivkenateng. Taug-ken angullruanka tamakut tuaten pitullret.)

Tua-i-ll' uitaluteng tua-i. Angyiluni-llu tauna. Man'a tua-i kuigaaraam kialirnera kiavet Cingigarrluarmun muraunani tua-i. Maanlluni keluatni. Tep'aryat teptulliniluki qavavet. Qamanrullrani tauna Umkuuk piak. Cat amllellratni.

Waten-gguq tua-i piaqan, tua-i-w' carvani'irqan imkut cetuat, wani tua-i nuugegni neraniurarqameng cenami [pituut]. Imum' tua-i cagniriqertellrani qa-manrani, cetuat camavet tua-i Umkuuk aciagnun qercuguaraluteng piaqluteng. Waten tekarrlugluni pimallrulliniami, un'a acia keluqsinruluni.

Ukaqvaggun pillrulliuq tauna ustellermini. Tua-i tanglaqarraallemni angell-ruyaaquq ugna ayaluqertelleq. Maavet-llu taquminun pivkenani. Tua-i ketmuqapik tua-i. Ua-i tanglaqen. Mayuqayunaunani-llu tanglaqarraallemni.

Umkuuk qaingak. Tua-i ilagarlukek. (Tauna-llu, tauna-w' tua-i maurluni, anuurluitnek pivkatullruit. Tamakut-llu tutgarrlugaitnek. Tuaten tua-i tuqlura'ar-turcet'lallruit.)

Nanluciilamiu tua-i umyuaqeng'ermiu-ll' qaill' pisciiganaku tua-i. Ingrinek-llu tamaani tangyuitellruami. Tua-i unaken, pavaken tuaten kelumeggnek tuntunek,

[hunted and brought home his catch] from down there [in the ocean] as well as caribou from the land back there, and [he hunted seals] from the ocean down there also. He also made a skin boat.

(Up behind their place [at Umkuuk], but not very close to that place, I used to see the old wooden poles from his boat support. Since they probably had been there for years and years they were quite rotten, the logs from his old posts.)

One time the other woman ran in and said a wolf was gnawing and chewing on their boat back there. They apparently chew things since they get hungry.

This was long ago when people always talked [to wolves]. Those seemed to listen and heed, these wolves.

He ran out and saw . . . (The rim [of the boat], they would do what they call *tugucirluki*. They would bind and secure them with a skin line along here, not far from the rim. They tethered the edges with a skin line all the way around. They were nice looking. They were good.)

Ruth Jimmie: (When they put [the skin over the boat frame], is that what they did?)

Tim Agagtak: (Yes, that was their binding material when they had no nails. When they made things, they used appropriate material to bind and assemble them.)

(They also kept everything and salvaged whatever they could from dead animals that they found beached along the shore. They cut and stripped the skins and made strings as thick as the string we find in stores. They made skins into things and used them even though they were skins of animals that had beached on shore. They kept them when I saw them. The stripped skin lines they made were good, they looked good. They call them *pinevkarat*.)

(I tried making skin line, but since I was not skilled, when I would see them and try to make some, the line would cut and break as I stripped the hide.)

Ruth Jimmie: (Did they go back and forth when they did it?)

Tim Agagtak: (Two people faced each other. The other person would put his hand in here [and hold the knife in place]. While he held it like this, [the skin] would go around fast. They were so proficient!)

Ruth Jimmie: (Would he [hold] his knife like this?)

Tim Agagtak: (Yes, he held his knife like this, with [his arm] inside this [hide].)

Ruth Jimmie: (And would that person over there [rotate the hide]?)

Tim Agagtak: (When the other person pulled [the hide], the skin line would begin stretching and get longer and longer. But when I tried making that kind [of skin line] it kept cutting and breaking. I did try making some following the ones I watched, but it turned out very ugly.)

When he went out, he scolded [the wolf] and asked why it was eating [the boat].

unaken tuaten imarpigmek [taqukanek pissurluni]. Angyiluni-llu qecigmek.

(Tua-i yaa-i kelulirneratni mallegteqapiarpek'nak' taukut mayurutellri tang-lallruanka. Canimaaraunritliameng aruk'acagarluki naparyallran murapiit.)

Aipaa taum arnam itqertelliniuq caqerluni pingna-gguq tang kegluneq ang-yaatnek carialria. Cariatullinilriit-am tua-i kailaameng-wa.

Tua-i ak'a qanruqu'urluki pitullermeggni. Niisngacetullrulliniameng-wa ta-makut, makut tua-i keglunret.)

Tua-i-am anqerrluni pillinia . . . (Waten cenait makut wagg'u-q tugucirluki. Nuqilrarturluki maavet, yaaqsigpek'naku qerrlua man'a. Nuqsugucitullruit cenait tua-i uivetmun kassugarrluki. Kenegnaqluteng-am. Assirluteng.)

Angalgaq: (Angyaq-qaa elliaqamegteggu tuaten piaqluku?)

Akagtaq: (Ii-i, tua-i nuqsugutekluku ussukcamek caitellermeggni. Canek taugaam nemerturluki kesianek piuratullermeggni.)

(Cali tua-i piciatun, mallurrateng-llu tua-i qel'kurluki. Pinevkarluki, imutun tua-i pelacinaggartun ellegtariluki. Cakluki tamaa-i tua-i qeciit, malluungraata tua-i. Takumni qel'kaqluki. Assirluteng, kenegnaqluteng tua-i pinevkallrit. Pinev-karat-gguq.)

(Wiinga taugken elluatuunrilama tamatum nalliini, tuaten tamakut tangrra-qamki pilingnaqsaaqngama, kep'arrnaurtut.)

Angalgaq: (Waten-qaa utqetaarluk' piaqluk'?)

Akagtaq: (Ukatmun waten caullutek. Taum aipaan kauqerluku maaggun. Tua-i waten pimaluku piaqan, uivnaurtuq tua-i cukamek. Elisngalarpaa!)

Angalgaq: (Tauna-qaa caviggani waten [tegumiaqluku]?)

Akagtaq: (Ii-i caviggaq tauna tegumiaqurluku waten, una kaumaluku.)

Angalgaq: (Tua-i-llu-q' ing'um waten piluku?)

Akagtaq: (Ing'um-wa tua-i, nuqtaqaku ing'um tapraq tamana neng'aqluni. Wiinga taugken tamakucimek pingnaqsaaqellemni kep'arrnaurtuq. Tua-i ikiuka-cagarluni pingnaq'laryaaqellemni, tamakut tangvallrenka maliggluki.)

Tua-i-ll' pillinia, tua-i nunurluku tuani anqercami ciin nerucianek.

When the wolf noticed him, it was doing something and placed [its paw] on its mouth up there. When it moved [its paw] in this direction, [the wolf] became like this. [The wolf] moved its skin [back] in this direction. [The wolf] removed its hood. [The wolf's] nose was moving and twitching up on top of its head.

Then [the wolf] said, he said that since he was so hungry, he was trying to eat this. Then Ayugutarin said to him, that person would apparently call himself Ayugutarin. He revealed his name. They say his grandmother called him Ayugutarin. Since that was his name, that's what she called him. [Ayugutarin said to the wolf,] "If you are hungry come in and eat."

This is what they said about others besides that [wolf], about how they used to do that, about how they used to remove their hoods [peel back their fur and reveal their human side]. . . .

So, [the wolf] became his companion, and the older sister became his spouse.

Yes, [the wolf] became a human being. He was a person. He became his constant companion. And when he'd hunt in spring, he was his companion, and they'd paddle together in the ocean.

It is said his companion, when he would catch . . . (Back in those days when they followed traditional customs that were said to have consequences when not followed, men were instructed not to chew and crush bones when they ate. And bones were brought [and discarded] in clean areas so they would not be stepped on.) The man noticed that when they ate meat, his guest, the wolf, would eat the meat and crush and break apart the bones as he chewed like a dog.

Ruth Jimmie: Did he chew the meat and bone together?

Tim Agagtak: Yes, he would [eat the meat and chew and] crush the bone at the same time. (They used to make wooden bowls, making the rims of the bowls different. They made them rounded with grooves. They also made bowls for women with flat rims all the way around. There were different kinds. They painted them with red ocher. They were nice looking.)

(Although they were wooden, they bent them. Women's [bowls] were different [from men's bowls]. And men's were also different. These are things you did not catch at all. I saw them, and when a person made a bowl in the *qasgi,* I used to see those people.)

As time went by that one he was staying with [Ayugutarin] caught less and less when they hunted. (I used to hear this story told as a *quliraq.* Only in the evening, they spoke only in the evening.)

[Ayugutarin] caught less and less. Eventually he became pitiful.

In winter, with spring approaching, during midday, the one up there, their small gut windows, or ones made of fish skin, and even burbot-skin ones, those were their small windows above.

Cumikarcamiu keglunrem taum, qaillukuarturaqerluni, pakemna-ll' tua-i qaneni-ll' piluku. Una wani ukatmureskiini waten elli'irrluni. Amini tua-i man'a ukatmurrluku. Nacairluni. Pikani-gguq taugken qengak caqialutek.

Tua-ll' qanlliniuq, tua-i-gguq tang kaissiyaagpakaami mat'umek maa-i nerengnaqell'. Tua-ll' tua-i taum-am pillinia Ayugutarin, taun' Ayugutarimek pilallrulliniuq. Ellminek aperturluku atni. Maurluan-gguq pitullrua Ayugutarimek. Tua-i ateqngamiu, acirluku. "Kaikuvet kitek iterluten neryartua."

Tua-i qanrutkelarait waten, taungunrilengraan, tuaten tua-i, taungunrilengraan, tuaten tua-i nacailallrat. . . .

Tua-i aipaqsagulluku tauna, alqaanek-llu aipangluni.
Ii-i, yuurrluni. Yuuluni. Aipaqu'urluku tua-i. Pissu'urqami-llu up'nerkami aipaqluku malikurluku anguaraaqlutek imarpigmi.

Tauna-gguq tang imna aipaa waten pitaqan . . . (Akaar piciruitullratni tamaani enrit-llu qangqunrilkurrluki. Menuilqumun-llu enrit ayautaqluki tutmanrilkurrluki.) Tauna-gguq tang imna ner'aqamek tamakunek kemegnek, [pinaurtuq] qimugtetun tua-i qangqurluki tauna allanra kegluneq.

Angalgaq: Waten-qaa kemgit nerluki, enrit tuaten?
Akagtaq: Ii-i enertuumaita. (Qancitullruut muraganek cenait makut allarrauluki. Akagenqeggsuga'arluki quagirluki. Makut-llu cali arnat qanciluki cenait mamcarrluki uivetmun. Ayuqevkenateng. Uiteramek mingugluki. Kenegnaqluteng assirluteng.)

(Muragaungraata perrluki. Arnartaat allakarrauluteng. Angutaita-llu cali piit allakarrauluteng. Cayugnailkeci, anguyugnailkeci makut. Tangaaluki, yuk-llu qanciaqan qasgimi tanglallrukenka tamakut.)

Tua-i kiituani tang tauna-w' nunalga picuirusngiinalliniuq. (Waten waniw' qanemciuluku niitetullruaqa man' quliraukluku. Atakumi taugaam, atakurrlainarmi taugaam qanerturatullruut.)
Tua-i-llu picuirusngiinarluni tua-i. Kiituani tua-i ikiurtenglliniuq.
Uksumi tua-i waten, waten iqukvaraqan, waten tua-i ernermiurtaqan, pikna, qilurraat egalrit, wall'u-llu neqet, imkut manignat-llu makut qeltait, tamaa-i egaleqluki pikanirracuar.

(Since they had homes that were square shaped, they made them like this, starting here they would put center beams on them by lifting them up. That was in more recent times. You probably saw [sod homes]. The only [window] was above, and their doorway, their doorways had entrance flaps made of woven grass mats. I, too, used to see [sod houses] like that.)

(The *qasgi* used to be the warmest back in those days because [men] took firebaths inside there, and I know about that, [they were warmer] than homes.)

During winter [Ayugutarin] started making a kayak. [He and his partner] made kayaks. Since he couldn't do anything, that one [Ayugutarin] stopped going over [to his home] from the *qasgi* and started staying there. And his partner stopped entering since he started staying only inside the house.

[His wife] asked [Ayugutarin] why he wasn't doing anything anymore, why he was just not doing anything. She asked what was wrong with him. Even though he didn't have an ailment [he wasn't doing anything]. It was because he wasn't good at catching. Since he stopped catching, although he would go hunting, back when they hunted for caribou with bows and arrows, back when they shot them with bows and arrows. And he didn't catch anymore although he went hunting.

He experienced the consequence of not following that traditional custom of long ago when the practice was around. He lost his ability to catch animals because of the way [the wolf-man] crunched on bones when eating. (In those days I remember they didn't give bones to dogs either, not wanting them to crunch on them.)

[Though she asked why he stayed home all the time] he didn't even react.

So at the end of winter, and during midday after the cold night when the skylight cover up there would have deep frost, and then around midday when someone opened the entrance flap, the woven grass covering of the [entranceway] out there, [the cover up there] would suddenly pop outward.

And when the woven grass flap fell back down and closed, it would pop inward, and then the frost would drop. Since it was midday [and had gotten warmer], [the frost] was no longer stuck [to the cover]. That's indeed what it would do. (I used to see those also. The frost on them would fall and land on the floor in the middle of the room, the frost of the [cover] up there as it was, the snow. That's what it always did.)

(And that also occurred in front of me. But I was useless during that time. I was useless at the time. And I couldn't come up through the entrance hole because I was small. How big was I? I was little, but I was aware.)

(The story I'm telling is still quite far from ending.)

One day she came in and said that they had no more food, that the food she was bringing was the last of what they had. She said the small amount of food they had in storage was gone.

(Enengqetullruameng waten kangirilrianek, waten piurluk', waken ayagarrluki agliraqluki mayurrluki. Canimetuq taugaam taman'. Tanglaryaaqellilriaten-wa. Pikna taugaam, amiigat-wa cali, amiigit cali ikirtuqerluteng tupiganek. Wiinga-ll' tangtullruluki tamakut.)

(Qasgiq kiirtunqurrautullruuq tamaani maqituameng, wiinga-ll' nalluvkenaku, [kiirtunruluteng] enen'i.)

Tua-i arenqialamek, uksumi waten, qayiyaaquq tua-i tauna. Qayilutek tua-i. Casciigalami qasgimek agnanrirluni taun' uitaurangllinilria. Tauna-llu-gguq aipaa iternanringluni tayim' enemi-llu uitauranglliniami tauna.

[Nulirran] pilliniluku ciin waniwa uitavakaucianek, uitangvakallaranek. Qaill' picianek. Apqucinrilngermi. Picunrilami. Pitnanriami tua-i ayaktang'ermi-llu pit-gaquurluki tuntussutullermeggni, pitgaraqluki pitullermeggni. Tua-i ayangermi-ll' picuirucami tua-i.

Piciruirem tamaa-i ak'a tamaani alaitellrani, aturluku. Tamatum-gguq qangqu-lallran picuirutevkarluku taun'. (Enrit qimugtenun-llu takumni tunyuitellruit qangquusqumavkenaki.)

Tua-i umyugaa-ll' pek'arcugnaunani.

Tua-ll' imumek waten iqukvaryarturluni ernermiurtaqami pikna egalrem, ilurpagluku unugpak pirraarluku, tua-i-llu erenrumainanrani, ikirtuqat ikireskata, ernermiureskan, ikireskatni, ikirtuqai ug'um tupigaaraat, elatmun anqerrluni.

Taukut-llu tupigaaraat igeskata, patuqauskata, ilutmun itqerrluni, kanra-ll' iggluni. Tua-i-gguq ernermiurcan nepinganrirluni tamana. Tua-i-w' ilumun. (Tamaa-i call' tanglallruanka tamakut. Iluat-llu kanavet tull'uni natrem qukaanun, ayuqucirramitun ilutellra pik'um qanikcaq. Tua-i piciryaraqluku.)

(Takumni-ll' pilallruluteng tamaa-i tamakut. Ikiulua taugaam tamatum nalliini. Ikiullruunga tamatum nalliini. Amigmi-llu nugesciigataqlua mik'lama. Qaillun tayim' angtallrusia? Mikellruunga, taugaam ayuquciqa nalluvkenaku.)

(Tauna tua-i quli'ir tauna iquklicugnaitartuq.)

Tua-i caqerluni itliniuq, waniwa tua-i neqairutnilutek, waniwa una payu-gutekniluku. Tua-i nangniluki neqtek tamakut qel'kaarratek neqautetek.

At that time [hunters] didn't prepare [for hunts] in the house, but only in the *qasgi*.

[When he heard her say that], [Ayugutarin] finally stopped and thought about his situation, about why he felt sorry for himself, because he was not able to catch and had stopped going out.

Soon after he went out, he immediately caught a caribou. The one they called *cirunelek* [an animal with antlers] when they told *qulirat*. He caught a *cirunelek*.

Starting with that, when he arrived he got material ready to make a kayak. His visitor did as he was doing since he told him to. They built kayaks out of logs, out of these logs.

(They used to say that back in those days, they used to cut large logs only with fire since they couldn't saw them. How did they [cut] them? That was their custom, they would mention it, they would tell stories about it, since they had no saws.)

(But back in those days, they had *ciklat* [pickaxes] made from walrus tusks by tying them on [to a wood handle]. They bound [the walrus tusks onto the handle] like ice picks. Those were their pickaxes. And their bindings were probably not even, they only had strips of sealskin line to bind them with. You've probably seen adzes these days, the small ones that resemble those.)

They finished the kayak. They took it outside. And when the kayak for his partner was done, they also took it outside. [The kayaks] were put on crossed support poles. They placed it on top to dry.

Before it got warm out, during cold weather, they dried the skin out in the cold to make it turn white. (You know how things turn white when they are dried in cold weather today. Then it turned white as it dried in the cold and turned white as it dried. I used to see people processing skin like that. They did that to make the skin look white.)

When they were finished, when they were about to go [hunting], when they were preparing, they put straps [on the outside of the kayak], his companion . . . When some had *apamarrlugutet* [designs along kayak gunwales], those very few kayaks that I saw, I didn't see a lot, but only very few people. They were beautiful. It would have a design.

They dissolved something from down there. They got some black rock and mixed it to use as paint. And they painted a design along the edge of its gunwale, what they call *apamarrlugucirluku* [painting a design along the gunwale of the kayak].

The visitor asked [Ayugutarin] if they should paint designs along the gunwales of their kayaks. He agreed. [The visitor] started painting a design along the gunwale of his kayak.

Like painting. These days, they have started using store-bought paint to paint them. These ink [paints].

Nem'i-ll' tamaani upcuitellratni, qasgimi taugaam.

Nutaan-gguq tang qam' umyugaa pektellria taum, uitaurangllerminek, kana-virqurangellerminek picuitellerminek.

Tua-i-ll'-am ayalriim tuntulluni. Apernassiillratnek tamaa-i cirunelegmek waten quliriaqameng. Cirunelegmek-am tua-i pill'uni.

Ayagneqluku tauna tua-i, tua-i tekicami tamaa qayarkaminek caliluni. Taum-gguq tua-i allanran taum maligtaquluku pisqengani-ll' ellii. Qayilutek muraganek imkunek makunek muraganek.

(Tamaa-i muragpallraat makut tamaani qanrutkelallruit kenerkun taugaam keptuniluki kegglarciigalamegteki. Qaillun pilartatki? Tua-i piciryaraqluku, qanrutkaqluku una, qanemcikaqluku kegglailameng.)

(Ciklanek taugaam imkunek kaugpiit imkunek tugkaraitnek, qillerrluk' tamaa-i pingqetullrulliniut tamaani. Nemerluki tugertun tua-i. Ciklaqluki. Ima-llu-qaa nemrit-llu, taqukanek taugaam pinevkaranek qillerqelluku. Keputet tayim' tangerqalallikten maa-i imkut mikcuaraat tuaten tua-i ayuqluteng.)

Tua-i im' qayaq taqluku. Anulluku tua-i. Taum-llu cali aiparmi qayaa taqngan anullukek. Tatkilukek waten ciligtellriignek. Qaingagnun elliluku kinercirluku.

Imumek tua-i nenglairupailgan nenglem nalliini qercurcirluku. (Iciw' cat maa-i nenglem nalliini qerecqerqateng qat'lalriit. Tuaten-llu tua-i qercurluku kinerluku-ll' qercuinanrani. Takumni-llu tamaani tuatnalallruut. Wagg'uq qatengnaqluku.)

Tua-i taqucamek, ayakataamek, taqngamegneki uptellermegni taprirturluki, aipaa tauna . . . Apamarrlugutengqerraqameng ilait tangerqacuaqalallma, amlleq-wa tangenrilkeka, [taugaam] carraquinrayagaq yuum ilii. Kenegnaqluteng. Qara-lirluni.

Unegken urciluteng. Imumek camek tungulriamek teggalqumek urrluku. Minguluku-llu maaggun apamaan ngeliikun, wagg'uq apamarrlugucirluku.

Tauna aipaa pilliniuq allanra apamarrluguciryugluki. Tua-i anglliniluku. Apamarrlugucillinia tamana qayani tamaaggun tua-i.

Imutun *paint*-arcilriatun. Maa-i mat'um nalliini *paint*-amek piyaureskait makut maliggluki. *Ink*-at makut tua-i.

They would just dissolve and mix that kind [of pigment]. And he used a bird wing feather for a paintbrush to paint it on.

When he was done, he had painted a wolf design on his kayak. When he was finished, it looked like a wolf on his kayak and had legs, and it had designs. It was facing the front.

[The visitor] said, "What about you?" Ayugutarin replied and said that he had no design to put on his kayak. [The visitor] told him that he certainly had one and insisted that he paint it on his kayak as he had done. The visitor was not so kind to [Ayugutarin].

Then [Ayugutarin] gave in and painted a small mink, a mink design on his kayak's gunwale. The painting looked better than [the visitor's] design. He finished painting the small mink. As you know mink are thin. It looked nice, it looked really nice.

[When they were ready] they went down to the ocean. They were about to go, and his visitor said to [Ayugutarin], "Okay now." When they were about to go, they went to the shore. His guest said to him, "Okay, turn and look the other way. After a moment of looking away you can turn around and look at me. You can look at me again."

So as instructed, after looking the other way he turned and saw a wolf standing by the water's edge. It was the same [wolf] he had seen up [behind his home]. Just when he saw the wolf, it quickly dropped its head and lapped salt water. Then after he looked away from him and looked at him again, he looked like the same person as before.

Then [his visitor] asked [Ayugutarin], "Okay, what about you?" [He replied,] "Okay, I can't think of anything else. But after looking the other way for a long time, try looking at me."

[The visitor] turned his back to him. His wily visitor, after turning his back to him, looked at him immediately without waiting and saw a little mink sitting hunched on the edge of the water since it was small. And just as he saw the mink, it dove into the water without a splash and disappeared. When it dove, he scanned the water and waited for it to come up, but it didn't surface.

Soon after, along the edge of the shore ice . . . Perhaps you've seen a kind of little bird that lives in the ocean. They are called *qayingyaar*. They are very small. They are small ocean birds. Or do you not know them?

That kind [of bird], one called *qayingyaar*. Soon after he noticed a little bird like that swimming, following the edge of the shore ice in the water. After it dove in the water he didn't see it again. He waited and scanned the water, and since he was alone, he launched his kayak in the water and left by himself.

Ayugutarin returned home long before it got dark. He caught two bearded seals. So all spring that's what he did. Every time [he went out] he caught two [seals].

Tuaten ayuqelria urrluku taugaam. Mat'umek-llu yaqulgem imumek yaqurranek minguucirluku mingugluku.

Taqlinia maaten tamana tuaten-am pillrullinikii qayani keglunruaruluku. Taqngamiu tua-i keglunertun ayuqluni qayaani maani kanagarluni-llu, qaralirluni. Ciutmun caumaluni.

Tua-ll' pillinia, "Kitak' elpes-mi?" Qanlliniuq tauna Ayugutarin aren ellii-gguq tang tua-i pikailnguq. Pikaitenritniluku pikangqerrniluku, ellmitun waten pisqelluku. Tua-i-gguq taum kenkessiyaagpek'naku allanran.

Tua-i-ll' apamarrlugucillinia imumek tua-i imarmiutayagaq, imarmiutamek. Taumi-llu piliarani assinruluni. Imarmiutayagaq taqlinia. Amitetulriit imarmiutaat. Tua-i assirluni, assirluni-gguq tua-i.

Tua-ll' atrarlutek kanavet. Ayakatarlutek, pillinia, "Kitak' tua-i." Ayakataamek cenamun pilutek. Allanranam tua-i pillinia, "Kitak' yaatmun cauqaa. Caumarraarluten tua-i tangerrniarpenga. Tangerrniarpenga tua-i."

Tua-i yaatmun tunulluku pirraarluni caullinia, kegluneq una mer'em ngeliini nangerngalria. Imna tua-i pikani tangellra. Tangvakartelluni-ll' tua-i taryumek maaken alungcungcunguaqalliniluni. Tua-i-llu ulu'urrluku pirraarluku tangllinia, imutun ayuqluni yuucillmitun.

Tua-ll' pillinia, "Kitak' elpes-mi?" [Kiullinia,] "Kitak' tua-i arenqiatuq wii camek neq'ak'ngaitua. Yaatmun caumamarraarluten tangrruaqaqia."

Tua-i tunulluku. Maaten tua-i, taunalkuk-gguq-am allanra piatmun caurraarluni tangllinia, egmian tua-i uitaqerpek'nani-llu, imarmiutayagaq una quluggluni mer'em ngeliini aqumqeciqtall', mik'lami. Tua-i-ll' waniw' tangvakartelluni mermun maavet cepiartelliniluni, anglluq'alliniluni. Anglluqaan-gguq-am kiartengyaaqaa tua-i tayim' pugyugpek'nani.

Piqerluni-gguq maaggun tuam ngeliikun . . . Tayim' tangerqalallilriaten yaqulecuarnek unan' imarpigmiutarnek. Qayingyaarnek aterluteng. Mikcuayagaat. Imarpigmiutayagaat. Wall'u-q' nalluaten?

Tamakuciq, qayingyaarmek at'lek. Tauna imna piqalliniuq tuam ngeliikun merkun kuimalria tamana tamakuciq, tuaq cenirrluku. Tua-i-ll' tayim' tangenqigtevkenaku anglluan. Kiartengyaaqvigminek-gguq, tua-i kiimelami-llu, qayani tamana atrarrluku ayagluni.

Tua-i-am tauna tua-i Ayugutarin uterrluni unugyugnaunaku. Malrugnek-am tua-i pilluni tungunqugnek. Cuna-gguq-wam' up'nerkarpak ayuqucirkaa. Tua-i malrugnek taugaam piqu'urluni.

Now his companion, just when the sun was setting he was seen approaching home. When he arrived they saw that he had caught a little bearded seal. And that was the only [seal] he caught during that entire spring.

Since he had caught first and had gone up to shore first, his bowl, long ago when they always went to the *qasgi* when they arrived, and not to the home, [his spouse] took his bowl and brought it to the *qasgi* with a cooked rib. She gave him the bowl and said "Okay, now. . . ."

Before that time when food was brought to him, [the visitor] ate the meat and bone together, cracking and crunching as he chewed. As she handed his bowl to him she said, "Okay, now you can eat and crush the bone as you chew." He ate and cracked and crunched the bone as he chewed his food.

He still [didn't catch anything]. His visitor kept going and hunting, but he couldn't catch. He would arrive without having caught anything at all. However, the one he was staying with [Ayugutarin] would come home with two bearded seals long before sunset every time he went out.

One day just before dark, [the visitor's] kayak was seen approaching home. They waited, and soon [Ayugutarin asked] his wife who usually checked for his arrival, "Why has the one who you said was about to arrive not come in yet, why hasn't he arrived?" He asked her to go out and check on him. His wife went out and looked, but he was gone. And she didn't even see a kayak down there. There was nothing there.

After she scanned the area down there, she turned and looked toward the land back there and saw a seal hunter going up [the hillside]. [*laughs*] You know those small hills down the coast. He was heading straight up toward them towing his kayak. [*laughs*]

After observing for a moment she ran inside and said that he was up there climbing and towing his kayak. She said he was going straight up toward those small hills up there, going straight toward those small hills.

Everyone in the house ran out and looked and saw the seal hunter going straight up [the mountain] towing his kayak.

While they were watching he got to the top of the mountain. And as soon as he got to the top, he rolled around up there along those small hills for a moment. After he got down and rolled around on the ground several times, he suddenly stood up as a wolf.

Then the wolf somersaulted toward the other side and was gone. Those who told the *quliraq* would say the following: Later on they found out that the aspiring hunter of Pamalirugmiut [the home of the dead] down there had come and tried to take away the wife of Ayugutarin, [but he had not succeeded]. [The wolf-man] left his wife behind and never returned. [*laughs*]

Tauna tua-i aipaa, akerta unavet-wa tua-i ellirluni, unavarluni pinrakun tua-ll' agiirtelliniuq. Tekitelliniuq maaten imumek tua-i pitlinilria angenrilnguarmek tungunquyagarmek. Cuna-gguq waniw' up'nerkarpak kiingan pitarkaa, tauna tua-i.

Elliin-llu taum, tua-i pitellruami, tua-i ciumek tagellrulun', qantaa tua-i, qasgimun ciunirrlainatullratni tamaani ak'a, enemun-llu piyuunateng, qantaa teguluku agutelliniluku tulimamek imirluku. Tunllinia qanerluni tuaten, "Kitag' nu-taan. . . ."

Tamaani-gguq payugtaqani, tua-i kemeg-un' enertuumaan ner'aqkii qangqurluku, enra-ll' ilakluku. Tunngamiu qanlliniuq, "Kitag' nutaan enertuumaan qangquryaaqiu." Tua-i-am neraa cingqurruluni neryaaqellinikii, qangqurluku.

Tua-i cakaniryugpek'nani pit'lallra. Tua-i ayagyaaqellininaurtuq tauna tua-i allanra picuunani. Tekitaqluni tua-i catengssaarpek'nani. Tauna-gguq taugken nunalga, nunalga tauna unugyugnaunaku tekitaqluni malrulluni tua-i tungunqugnek.

Tua-i-ll' caqerluni-am tua-i tayima atakuyartungqertelluku tua-ll' cama-i alarutliniluni qayar' un'a una-i agiitellria. Tua-ll' tauna tua-i nulirra paqtestek'lallra [pillinia], "Ciin imna tekiteqatarnillren iteryunripakarta, tayim' tekicunripakarta?" Paqteqaasqelluku. Anluni tauna tua-i nulirra anluni piyaaqelliniuq cataunani tua-i. Qayartaunani-ll' un'a. Cataunani tua-i.

Maaten tua-i piqalliniuq, kelutmun cauluni, un'a kiarcaaqvigminek, pilliniuq qamigalria qulmun. [ngel'artuq] Imkut ugkut nallunrilketen ingirrraat. Ciuneqluki qulmurrlainaq qamigalria. [ngel'artuq]

Tua-i tangvakarluku itqerrluni pilliniuq, pagaa-i-gguq tang mayulria qamigarluni qayartuumarmi. Ingirrraat-gguq pikegkut, imkut pikani waten ingirrraat urenkelluki.

Anqerrluteng pilliniut qulmurrlainaq qamigalria mayulmuarluni.

Tua-i tangvakainanratni kanglliartelliniluni. Kanglliarteqerluni pika-i, ingirrraat maani-w' tua-i akuliitni, akagualria. Pika-i qaillukuarturaqerluni, akaguarturaqerluni nang'ertelliniuq kegluneq ayuqucimitun.

Tua-i-ll' tayima amatmun ulpiartelliniluni. Waten-wa tua-i qaneryarilallrukiit quliriqestain: cunawa-gguq ava-i pamkut Pamalirugmiut nukalpiarata nulirriryarturyaaqellinikii tauna tua-i Ayugutarin. Tua-i nuliani tauna unilluku cakaarluku ayalliniluni. [ngel'artuq]

This is how the story ends. This is how they tell it.

Ruth Jimmie: So, is that how Umkumiut was established?

Tim Agagtak: Yes. That is how the village got started.

❧ *Small One Who Drifted Away* ❧

John Phillip of Kongiganak with Roland Phillip, George Billy, Alice Rearden, Mark John, and Ann Fienup-Riordan, Bethel, October 2006

John Phillip: Okay now, I am now going to begin the story of Atertayagaq. We don't know his story from the time he was young. But the story of Atertayagaq, they would ask him to tell his story while he was still able to go down to the ocean, but he couldn't tell the story while he was still able to travel and hunt. These are things that he told to my ears.

I didn't know who Atertayagaq was at first, but my late wife was that person's [Roland Phillip's] mother's sister's daughter; she and my *ilurapak* [cross-cousin, Roland Phillip] here and [my wife] had mothers who were sisters. [My wife's] mother was that person's [Roland Phillip's] aunt. And when she married him, I came to know Atertayagaq. She married him when her husband died.

When he married my mother-in-law, my wife's mother, he lived in my village [Kwigillingok] for over a year, and they lived in my home. When she married Atertayagaq during the summer . . . I cannot say what year she married him. But downriver [along the lower Kuskokwim] you know about my fish camp downriver when you were little; when he was there, across from us, my mother-in-law, my wife's mother, married Atertayagaq.

I didn't know anything at that time, and I didn't know that he would tell the story. We returned home from fish camp. One day when we returned home, one Sunday, people his age set a time for him [to tell the story].

When Atertayagaq was about to leave to go seal hunting at that time [when these events took place], he prepared to go seal hunting. This is the beginning of the story that he told.

When he stood, when he was about to give a testimony inside the first church over in Kwigillingok, he told the story in my very presence. When he stood, when they asked him to and he was able to tell it, when he no longer traveled down to the ocean . . . He evidently couldn't tell the story while he was still able to go down to the ocean [and hunt]. That was his state of mind. And when he was about to speak, he said that he wouldn't mention his most painful experiences, like Roland said. He said that he couldn't tell his most painful experiences.

Waten tua-i iquklit'lartuq. Waten qanrutkelaraat.

Angalgaq: Tua-i-q' tua-i Umkumiut ayagnillrat?

Akagtaq: Ii-i. Nunaurtellrat tauna tua-i.

❧ *Atertayagaq* ☙

Ayagina'ar, Nacailnguq, Anguteka'ar, Cucuaq, Miisaq, Ellaq'am Arnaan,
Mamterilleq, October 2006

Ayagina'ar: Kitak' tua-i, waniw' tua-i ayagniqatarqa augna Atertayagaq. Tayima ayagyuallranek ayagluku nalluaput. Taugaam Atertayagaq tauna waten qanemciq, ak'a wani qanemcisqetuyaaqelliniat piyugngaluku, unavet ayagayugngaluku, taugaam qanemcisciiganani waten ayagyugngaluni cali. Qanellri maa-i makut wangnun ciutegemnun qanellri.

Tauna Atertayagaq nallullruyaaqaqa, taugaam aipangqellruunga ing'um wani aanalgutiinek; aanalutek alqaqellriignek, una-llu ilurapaka. Aanii tauna ik'um anaanakluku. Cali-llu taumeg' aipangellrani nutaan wii Atertayagaq tauna nallunritellruaqa. Aipaqsagulluku aipani tuqullrani.

Tauna cakiqa, aiparma aanii nuliqsagutellrani, nunamni uitallruuq allrakuq cipluku, enemni-llu uitalutek. Nutaan tamaani kiagmi aipaqsagutellrani Ater-tayagaq tauna . . . allrakuq-am waniw' aperturciigataqa aipaqsagutellra. Taugaam uani, nallunritarpenga mikcuaraullerpeni, neqlillrenka ugkut; tuani uitallrani, akimteni tuani, tauna Atertayagaq aipaqsagutellrua taum cakima, taum aiparma aaniin.

Tamaani tua-i cameg' nallulua wii, qanemcillerkaanek-llu nallulua. Nutaan wani uterrluta amavet neqlillernek. Utercamta cat iliitni, Agayunret iliitni wani, pillerkiulliniat taukut augkut pitatain.

Tauna tua-i Atertayagaq tamaani taum nalliini ayakatallermini qamigarluni uptelliniuq. Waniw' una ayagnillra.

Nangercami qanertuq, apervikuaqataami agayuvigmi yaani ciuqlirmi Kui-gilngurmi, takuq'apiaramni pillruuq. Nangercami, pisqelliniatni, nutaan pi-yugngariami, imarpigmun ayagnanriami . . . Ayagyugngaluni tamana qanrut-kesciigatellrullinia. Tuaten ayuqellrulliniuq umyugaa. Cali-llu qanqataami qaner-luni, arcaqalriit elliin nangtequallni qanrutekngaitniluk', qanellruciatun Roland-aam. Arcaqalriit qanrutkesciigatniluki nangtequallni.

When he was about to travel [and hunt], that was also the first time he had acquired a kayak. He acquired a kayak for the first time. One feels uncertain when one acquires a kayak for the first time and goes down to the ocean for the first time. But before we acquired kayaks, they always spoke to us about how we should travel down on the ocean. Or they spoke about ocean faring, or about its current and the winds, or about the waves and the ice. He had those [instructions] stored in his mind.

At that time, he prepared to go down for the first time. That was the first time he was to go seal hunting, he acquired a kayak for the first time. At the time they lived over at Kuiggluk, around Kuiggluk, right down below the village of Kipnuk.

Atertayagaq said that when he was about to leave, he prepared his kayak. He prepared. And since he wasn't ready and needed another day to prepare, the person he would accompany — he said his seal-gut rain garment wasn't finished yet — since they weren't finished yet, [the person he was to accompany] told him to stay behind. And since the things that he was preparing weren't ready, the one who would accompany him, this is what [Atertayagaq] said. . . . Oh no, I forgot a part of the story.

When [Atertayagaq] stood along the back of the church, he asked when he stood, "What do you want to hear?" He first asked what they wanted to hear when he stood along the back of the church to give a testimony, "What do you want to hear?"

This person's late father-in-law stood from behind me and said to him. [Roland Phillip's] grandfather said to him, when he stood along the back of the church and said, "What do you want to hear?" This is what [Atertayagaq] said. When he asked, Cegg'aq stood from behind me, [Roland Phillip's] grandfather said to him from back there, "We want to hear about the tragedy you faced down on the ocean, about how you were adrift on the ocean." That was his only reply. I know the one who asked him. Then he sat down.

When he sat, when [Atertayagaq] spoke, he said . . . during that time, Peter Jimmie went down to the ocean for the very first time to go seal hunting, Peter Jimmie over there. [Atertayagaq] told him to come next to him and had him stand. He had the one who had just gone down to the ocean to hunt for the very first time stand next to him, and I knew that [he had gone down for the first time] during that time [when Atertayagaq told his story]. When he had [Peter Jimmie] stand, he said, using that person as an example, for those of you who understand English, having that person who had gone down to the ocean for the very first time stand as an example. He said that he was that person's [Peter Jimmie's] age.

It was the first time that he had gone seal hunting at that time, and Peter Jimmie was probably fourteen years old or something at that time. We know of the time

Tuani tua-i nutaan ayakataami, nutaan-llu qayangluni. Qayangluni nutaan. Qayangeqarraalleq, atraqarraalleq qaillun picirkaitnarquq. Taugaam ciumek qayangvailemta imarpigmun ak'a qanruquralallruitkut qaillun imarpigmi ayala- llerkamtenek. Wall'u-qaa qaillun imarpim qaillun un'um aturyaraa, wall'u man'a carvanra, wall'u anuqii, wall'u qairet-llu, wall'u cikut-llu tamakut qanrutkelallruit. Tamakut tamaa-i elliin qamiquminun ellimaluki tamakut.

Tuani tua-i nutaan ayakatarluni uptelliniuq. Nutaan qamigaqatarluni, qa- yangeqarraarluni. Yaantellrulliniut Kuigglugmi, Kuiggluum nuniini, Qipnermiut ketiitni.

Tuani-gguq ayakatallermini waniwa tauna Atertayagaq uptellruuq, qayani tamana upluku. Tua-i upquralliniuq. Tauna-llu maligkani, maligkaan taum, nuq- litlinian ernermek ataucimek — qasperek-gguq taqeksaituk — taqeksailagnek uitasqelluku. Uptellra-ll' cali tauna wani qaqimanrilata upqurallri, pillinia taum aipaan, maligkaan, waten qanertuq. . . . Arenqia nalluyaguciunga.

Nangercami agayuviim egkuanun qanertuq waten, kiavet nangercami aptuq, "Camek niicugceci?" Apteqarraallruuq agayuviim egkuanun *testimony*-qatarluni qanrami, "Camek niicugceci?"

Uum wani cakiirutiin tunumnek pamaken nangerrluni qanrutaa. Imum apa'urluan taum, qanrutaa, waten pia, apcani tauna, kiani agayuviim egkuani, aptuq nangercami, "Cameg' niicugceci?" Waten qanellruuq. Qanran tunumnek maaken nangerrluni tauna wani Cegg'aq, taum apa'urlua, taum kiugaa pamaa-i, "Unani imarpigmi arenqiallugtellerpenek ayagall[erpenek] imarpigmi unani pektell[erpenek], tamatumek niicugtukut." Kiingan taumek kiuga. Tua-i tauna apcestellra nallunritaqa. Nutaan-llu aqumluni.

Aqumngan nutaan qanrami qanertuq . . . Peter Jimmie qamigaqarraallruuq taum nalliini, ingna Peter Jimmie. Taisqaa caniminun nangertelluku-llu. Nanger- cetaa nutaan qamigaqarraalria, tamaani nalluvkenaku-llu wiinga. Tauna nangerce- camiu wavet qanertuq, una *example*-aaqluku, apqiitnek elpeci Kass'atun taringetul- riani, ayuqeltassiigutekluku, qamigaqarraalriamek taumek, nangertelluku. Uutun- gguq waten ayanitallruuq.

Tua-i nutaan ayagluni, qaill' tayim' taum nalliini, *fourteen, something*, Peter Jimmie pitallruuq taum nalliini qamigaqarraarluni. Tayim' nallunritarpuk

that he had gone seal hunting, but his father stayed with him [while he hunted]. He used [Peter Jimmie] as an example of how old he was [during the time he drifted away].

When he stood, that's what he said before he started [telling his story]. After having him sit, when he started, he said what I mentioned, that when he was about to go seal hunting at that time, when he was about to accompany that person, he prepared the things he would use. And he said the person who took care of him, his stepmother [or aunt], made him skin boots. We had long skin boots in the past, long ones like this, one pair of long boots and the other pair was a short pair. And I had boots like that, too, ones that were waterproof.

He evidently wore those when he went. And the person who would have accompanied him went down to the bay first.

When he went down, the next day, [the one who would have been his hunting partner] told him to go down the next day when he was fully prepared by towing his kayak following his tracks; he went on foot. He told him to go down following his tracks. His hunting partner would wait for him down there. I think they said that it was Moses Strauss's, Aperyaq's grandfather, Amauq. They say that he was supposed to be his hunting partner. He was going down for the first time.

He prepared at that time. [His hunting partner] told him to go down the next day when he had finished getting his things ready. He prepared all day, and he got his kayak completely ready, so that he could just take it and go down.

But [Atertayagaq] said that he didn't have one thing, his seal-gut rain garment. He didn't have a seal-gut rain garment. His seal-gut rain garment hadn't been finished. That's the only thing that he didn't have. But he said that he had fish-skin mittens that are used in wet conditions. He evidently had those.

Then he went to sleep. Since he would leave the next day, he went to sleep. Just as he lay down, he fell asleep.

When he slept, he dreamed that he went down following his hunting partner's tracks. [Using] his kayak, he dreamed that he left following [his tracks]. As he continued on and got far from shore, he saw a wooden building in the area ahead. A wooden building appeared just ahead. He arrived there following those tracks. He went to the doorway, and he went inside there.

Now pay attention to his story. When he went inside, when he went through the doorway, he looked to his side and saw two pictures that were situated across from one another. There were two pictures that were situated across from one another, and he didn't know what they were. They say there was nothing placed inside [the building] at that time.

Before he left that place, he suddenly woke. When he woke, he immediately looked and saw that it was just starting to get light outside. Then immediately, although his seal-gut rain garment wasn't finished, when he woke, after eating a

una-llu tamaani qamigaqarraallra, atiin taugaam malikurluku. Tauna tua-i cuqyutii, cuqyutkellra.

Nangercami tua-i tauna tuaten qanrutkaa ayagniqatallermini. Nutaan-llu aqumevkarraarluku ayagniami qanertuq aug'utun, tamaani-gguq qamigaqataami, tauna maligteqatarluku ayakataami, uptuq tua-i atu'urkani piluki. Taum-llu-gguq aulukestiin, anaaniin piluguliluku. Imumi pilugungqetullruukut taktuanek, waten taktuagnek, ataucimek taktuagnek, nanilnguaraagnek aipirlukek. Wiinga-llu pilugungqelallruunga tuaten, tamakucignek, ivrucilegnek.

Taukunek tua-i aturluni pilliniluni. Tauna-ll' tua-i maligkaqsallra atralliniluni ciumek tuavet kangimun.

Atraami, nutaan unuaquan, pillinia unuaqu tua-i upingarikan atraasqelluku tumemikun qamigaarluku; piyuagurluni waten. Tumemikun atraasqelluku. Uta-qaarkauluku camani taum wani malian. Auguuningatellruat Moses Strauss-am, Aperyam apa'urlua Amauq. Taum-gguq tua-i malikeqatallruyaaqaa. Atraqatarluni nutaan.

Nutaan tua-i uptelliniluni. Piluku unuaqu atraaraasqelluku qaqiskaki tamakut pillri. Upquralliniluni tua-i ernerpak, qayani-ll' tamana atraqainaurrluku.

Taugaam-gguq ataucik qasperek piituk. Qasperituq. Taqeksaunatek qasperek. Taukuk taugaam tua-i piinatek. Taugaam-gguq arillugluni imkugnek meliurcuutegnek. Taukugnek tua-i pingqelliniuq.

Tua-i-llu nutaan inartelliniluni. Unuakuan tua-i ayagarkaungami inartelliniluni. Inarcami tua-i qavalliniuq, inarutmini qavaqalliniuq.

Qavaami tua-i qavangurtulliniuq tamakut, taum malimi tumellri aturluki atrarluni. Qayani, qavangurturluni, aturluki ayagluni. Ayainanermini unani ke-ssigiqerluni, ciunra ing' laavkaartangulliniluni. Laavkaartanglliniluni ciunra ingna. Tekitelliniluku taukut tumet aturluki. Amiiganun tuavet piluni, iterluni-ll' ellii tuavet.

Murilkelluku piniarci tauna, qanemcia man'a. Tauna tua-i itrami, tamaani itrami waten takuyalliniuq itrami amigkun, tarenrak ukuk akiqliqlutek. Akiqliqlutek tarenrak. Cauciinakek elliin. Tua-i iluni-gguq ilukluku tamatum tamaani.

Tuaken tua-i anvailegmi tupakalliniluni. Tupakaami tua-i egmian pilliniuq ella qakemna tanqigiarallinill'. Egmian-llu-gguq tua-i taukuk qasperegni taqek-sailengraagnek makcami nerqerraarluni, tamakut tumaikun atrarluni imarpigmun.

small meal, he followed [his partner's] tracks and went down to the ocean. Since they were visible, he towed his kayak on a sled and went down.

When he was on his way down and got far down on the ocean, when he wasn't too far from the water, he came upon a new crack, a small crack. When he got to it, he continued on since the crack didn't look unsafe.

Again, right beyond it, he came upon a crack that was wider. He said his kayak sled *?nikimalutek* like this. We here, we two [Roland Phillip and I] know about it. When cracks move, they *?nikituut*. That [crack] had moved. You know, *?waten pillrek aviqesngalutek*. Even though that was the case, since he didn't know any better — that crack was wider than that other one and was new — he continued on.

Before he got too far . . . he said that he walked along some freshly fallen snow. Before he got too far, when he got pretty far down on the ocean, the wind arrived from the north.

When a fresh layer of snow falls, [when the wind blows] the snow immediately begins to drift along the ground. The snow began to drift along the ground and began to billow.

When it became impossible to continue on, he went back to where he came from following his tracks. He said the ice broke off while he was still a ways down there. When he got to that crack, [the ice] had already drifted far from shore. And he said snow was falling and there was a blizzard, too. That's what he said.

He said the [ice] along the shore behind him was visible, but he said that he didn't have a seal-gut rain garment. When he was about to go down [into the water], he got in [his kayak] along the windward side since he was able, and he headed back toward shore. But he said when large waves started to form there and the water started to splash on him, he thought that if his clothing became wet, he wouldn't be able to function normally if he got wet since he didn't have a seal-gut rain garment.

He said that he could have attempted to go to the side. And he said he saw some ice that had beached along shallow areas along the side, but worried that he would get wet. . . . He said that his fish-skin mittens were okay, and he put them on, but he said that he didn't have a seal-gut rain garment.

When the waves began to splash on him, he was thinking; he thought of the *qanruyun* [instruction] that he had heard [about getting wet], and he went down [and returned] to that sheet of ice. He got onto the ice along a good place and climbed up. He towed his kayak far inside [the ice sheet]. He also thought, "When [the waves] break the ice, the waves will reach me." He went far inside [the ice], and when he got far away from the edge, he sat down.

They say he had two *qangiarak* [two man's brother's children, either niece or nephew]. They were probably Nemercuk and his younger sister, the two who his aunt was taking care of at that time. He said that thinking of the two who he was

Alailata qamigaarluni atrarluni.

Atrallermini tua-i unani kessigiqerluni imarpigmun, una-i tayima mer' yaaqsinrirluku, qulinermek tekitelliniuq waten nutaramek, qulinermek qupne-rramek. Tekicamiu tua-i ayalliniluni canrilagnek tamakuk qulinrek.

Cali yaatiini nutaan qulinermek aivkaqaninruluni tekitelliniluni. Tama-kuk-gguq qamigautek nikimalutek waten. Wangkuta, nallunritapuk tauna-llu. Qulinret *move*-araqameng nikituut. *Move*-aumaluni tamana. Iciw' waten pillrek aviqesngalutek. Pingraan, nalluami — tamana aitangqanruluni tamatumi, nuta-rauluni cali — ayalliniluni.

Yaaqsigissiyaagpailgan . . . tuani-gguq qaninerraralleq aturluku tamana pill-ruuq. Yaaqsigissiyaagpailegmi, tua-i kessigiqerluni, atam piqerluni anuqa teki-tellinill' negeqvamek.

Egmian-llu taman', imumek qaninerra'arqami natquingelalria. Natquiggluni, puyingelliniluni.

Aren piyunaircan tua-i ataam utertelliniluni aturluki tumni tamakut. Tua-i yaaqsiggarluku-gguq tauna pillruuq. Qulineq taman' tekicaaqellinia ak'a kessi-gillrullinill'. Man'a-llu-gguq qanirluni pircirluni qanungluni tuaten. Tuaten tua-i qanellra ayuquq.

Tua-i pava-i kelua alaicaaqluni keluni, taugaam-gguq qasperituq. Atraqataami, tua-i man'a, asgulirnerakun ekluni, tua-i piyugngiimi ayagyaaqelliniuq tua-i kelutmun. Taugaam-gguq man'a qailinga'artellrani, ciqertanga'arcani, umyuar-tequq qaini man'a meciqaku elluatuungaicukluni, elluatuungaicukluni meciqaku qasperilami.

Pingnaqsugngayaaquq-gguq maavet taqumun. Pava-i-gguq etgalqitaat-llu alaunateng, maa-i taqruani, taugaam-gguq mecungellerkaminek. . . . Taukuk-gguq tua-i arilluuk canricaaquq all'ukek, qasperituq-gguq [taugaam].

Man'a tua-i qaiq, ciqertanga'arcani umyuarteqliniuq; imna tamana qanruyun ak'a niitelallni umyuaqluku, tamaavet cikumun atralliniluni. Ataam ekluni tuaggun piyunarqellriakun mayurluni. Qamigalliniuq temeqvaarnun. Umyuarteqluni cali, "Man'a navguqaku tekiciiqaanga qairem." Temeqvaarnun nutaan, temeqvanun yaaqsigian nutaan tamana tua-i aqumelliniluni.

Taukugnek-gguq malrugnek qangiarangqellruuq. Imumek Nemercumek, nayagaanek aipirluku pilliuq tauna, anaanami aulukaagkegnek taukugnek. Tau-kuk-gguq tua-i angungnatugararkagni elliraungagnek-gguq umyuaqlukek tuavet

to hunt for, since they had lost their parents and had no one to provide for them, when he sat there, he cried out loud, and he was sorrowful. This is what he said. He said he cried out loud and was sorrowful, and he made crying noises. He said that was the only time that he cried, giving in to his feelings of desperation. He wasn't thinking of himself, but he thought of the two who he was to support through hunting, his nephew and niece. That's what he said when he spoke.

After [he cried], he stayed there although it was windy. And the ice surrounding him didn't break from any direction. He stayed there.

He said when it was time, when the weather improved, those mountains across there, you see them. He said that he would head toward them, but he said when he couldn't continue on, he would stop. He would head toward them [to no avail].

During that time, he started to stay down on the ocean. He would travel like that [on foot] when conditions were good, but he couldn't reach those [mountains] across there. He had no path. And although he wanted to go up to shore, there was no way to go as a lot of ice surrounded him. He saw those mountains across there for some time.

I probably won't remember parts of the story; I won't tell the parts that I forgot.

He said that while he was there, when he wanted to eat, with his [limited] provisions in mind, when he became hungry, he shot a bearded seal. When he shot that bearded seal, he ate that. He never cooked.

But he said when he was thirsty . . . he said that he had some matches. And he had a few bullets. He also conserved his bullets. He'd take parts of that bearded seal and eat them raw. He was also careful with and saved his provisions, and he also ate from his provisions.

He would tow his kayak toward those mountains, but when his path was no longer safe to travel on, he would stop.

He said when he first went . . . I forgot to mention another part of the story. He said when he first left, that moon up there, it was a half-moon during winter. He said he used that [to count the months] while he was down on the ocean.

And he said that while he traveled, he would tow his kayak on foot along the ice. Eventually his boot soles wore away. But he said he would only slip on his other pair of skin boots when he was about to go to sleep.

And when he was thirsty, he said that he conserved his matches. When he was thirsty, he would remove one of the slats of wood from his wooden kayak seat, break it to bits, pour a little seal oil on it, [light it], and melt some ice to prepare drinking water. That's what that one said about his journey.

He would travel at that time, and even go toward those [mountains] across there. He said eventually when his boot soles wore away, he switched his skin boots and continued to wear them.

aqumngami nutaan, qiallruuq neplialuni ilutequaluni-llu. Waten qanerluni. Neplia-luni-llu qiallruuq-gguq iluteqluni, neplialuni-llu. Tua-i-gguq ataucirqumek tauna qialqaa, ataucirqumek nanikuallni tua-i niilluku. Ellii pivkenani taukuk taugaam angussaagarkagni umyuaqlukek qangiaraagni. Tuaten tua-i qanllermini qanertuq.

Nutaan tua-i pirraarluni tamaani uitalliniuq anuqlingraan tua-i. Tamana-ll' avatii tua-i naken cali navgurpek'naku. Uitaurluni tuani tamaani.

Tua-i-gguq piyunarian, assirian, ikegkut ingrit, ikaan' agkut agaa-i tanglaraten. Tungiitnun ayalaryaaquq, arenqiatuq-gguq piyunairutaqan arulailartuq tamaani. Ayalaryaaqluni.

Tamaani tua-i imarpigmi uitanglliniuq. Tuaten ayagaqluni man' piyunariaqan ayalaryaaqluni, tekitesciiganaki taugaam ikegkut. Tumaitaqluni. Tagyung'ermi-llu tumkaunani man'a cikulirluni. Ukut tangerkengaqurluki ingrit ikani.

Tua-i tamaani akulii tayima tamalkuan neq'akenricaaqeciqaqa; qanrutekngai-caaqaqa ilii nalluyagutelqa.

Tamaani-gguq tua-i uitangllermini, tua-i makunek-llu, neryungami, taquani taukut umyuaqurluki, neryungami maklagmek nutellruuq. Nutgami-llu tua-i maklak tauna neqekluku. Keniyuunani.

Taugaam-gguq tua-i meqsugaqami . . . kenerluni-llu-gguq. Imai-llu-gguq ukut ikgenateng. Taukut tua-i imani aninqurluki cali. Taum tua-i makliim akluinek tamakunek tegulluni nerlalliniuq qassaraqluni. Taquani tua-i aninqurluki cali tamakut, ner'aqluni-llu taquaminek.

Qamigarluni ayagyaaqaqluni taukut tungiitnun ingrit, tumni man'a pi-yunairutaqan arulairaqluni.

Ayakarraallermini-gguq . . . Nalluyagutelliniaqa-am cali. Ayakarraallermini-gguq pikna *moon*-aq, *half full moon*-arluni, *half*-aaruluku uksumi. Tauna-gguq tua-i aturluku imarpigmi unani uitauq.

Tamaani-llu-gguq tua-i ayainanermini, qamigalaryaaqluni tamaani. Kiituan-gguq imkuk piluguuk nat'riutuk. Taugaam-gguq taukuk aipakek pluguugmi inarteqatarqami tua-i as'artaqlukek.

Cali tua-i meqsugaqami, keneni-gguq tua-i aninqurluki. Meqsugaqami aqum-gautami ilaitnek ciamciqerluni uqurrarmek piluku ekuavkarluku, kucirturtelluku ciku merkiuraqluni. Taum tua-i tuaten qanrutkaa ayallni.

Nutaan tua-i tamaani ayalaryaaqelliniuq ikegkut tungiitnun. Kiituan'-gguq nat'riucagnek taukuk piluguugni, mumigglukek cali tua-i pilukek.

Eventually, while he was down on the ocean, the half moon was all gone. Another moon came. Another month came. That's also what he said.

But he said that he gradually lost sight of the mountains, the capes across there, the ones across from our area, while he was there.

He would tow his kayak on the ice. He said it never got windy. And he said after a while the ocean ice began to freeze, it iced over. He said that it never got windy. It iced over. He said it froze, it became smooth. But he said he would go along [ice sheets] that were steeper and had thick snow on them.

When he was there for some time, the sea mammals . . . As he was there, when the second month came, he said he seemed to become akin with the sea mammals. He said when they were gone and he hadn't seen them for a while, he would feel sad and lonely over not seeing sea mammals.

He continued to use the moon [to count the days] while he was down there [on the ocean]. He said eventually his skin boots became lower. He tied them, he switched them, and made this section that was here [around his ankle] lower. When the boot soles wore out, he would switch them.

Sometime when he saw a walrus, he went to it and shot it. And since it didn't completely die, he tried to kill it, and when he cut its throat, it finally died.

He said that he also shot its tusks along the base and broke them off and stowed them. After keeping them for some time, and thinking of the time when the ocean would become entirely water, he cut [the walrus] intestine to use as a water container. But he said that when he was tired of keeping them in his possession . . . he kept them stored away at that time.

And that moon got full, turned, and started going back while he was down on the ocean. He said that while he was there, it seemed that he became akin to the sea mammals.

One day, he stopped seeing these [mountains], he stopped seeing the mountains across there. He began seeing mountains that he had never seen before. He had never seen them before; the mountains were steep. He would travel toward them, but there was no way to reach them. He couldn't reach them.

One day, when [the ice] became smooth, while he was on his way, a crack formed, a lead opened [in the ice]. He went toward [the mountains] through that crack.

The second moon had also turned in the opposite direction at that time. He used that moon to tell [the days] as he continued on foot. The first half moon had ended.

While he continued on, when [the crack] closed in, he stopped and climbed [onto the ice].

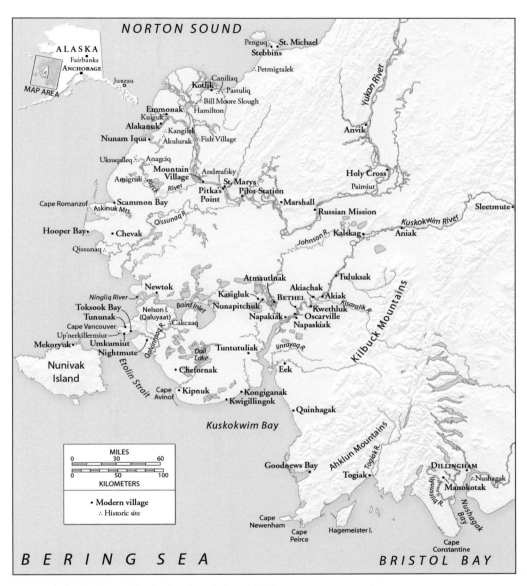

Map of the Yukon-Kuskokwim delta, 2015. Patrick Jankanish

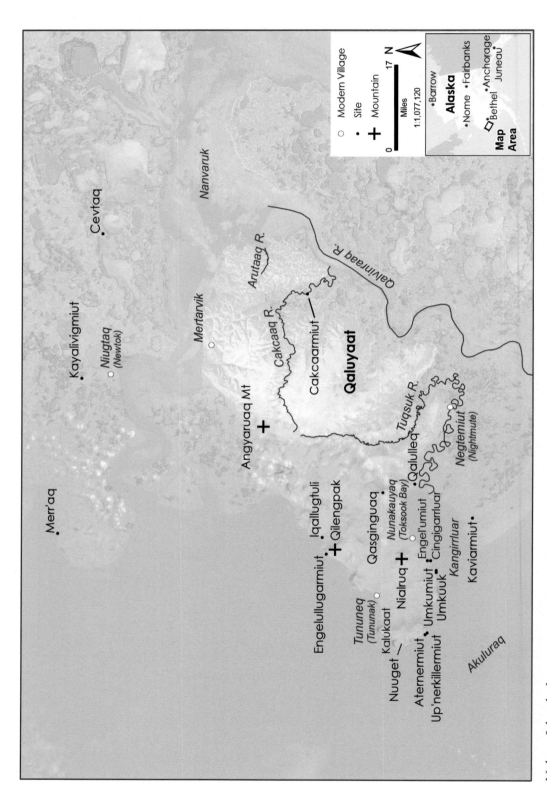

Nelson Island place names. Michael Knapp

Modern Village ○
Site •
Mountain +

N

0 ⎯⎯ 17
Miles
1:1,077,120

Alaska
• Barrow
• Nome   • Fairbanks
          • Anchorage
    Bethel • Juneau
**Map
Area**

Merr'aq •

Kayalivigmiut •

Cevtaq •

Niugtaq ○
(Newtok)

Nanvaruk

Mertarvik ○

Arutaaq R.

Cakcaaq R.

Qalvinraaq R.

Cakcaarmiut •

Qaluyaat

Angyaruaq Mt +

Tuqsuk R.

Negtemiut ○
(Nightmute)

Qalulleq •

Iqallugtuli •
Qilengpak +

Qasginguaq •

Nunakauyaq ○
(Toksook Bay)

Engel'umiut •
Cingigarrluar •

Kangirrluar

Kaviarmiut •

Engelullugarmiut •

Tununeq ○
(Tunanak)
Nuuget ⎯ Kalukaat ○
Nialruq +
Aternermiut •
Umkumiut •
Up'nerkillermiut • Umkuuk •

Akuluraq

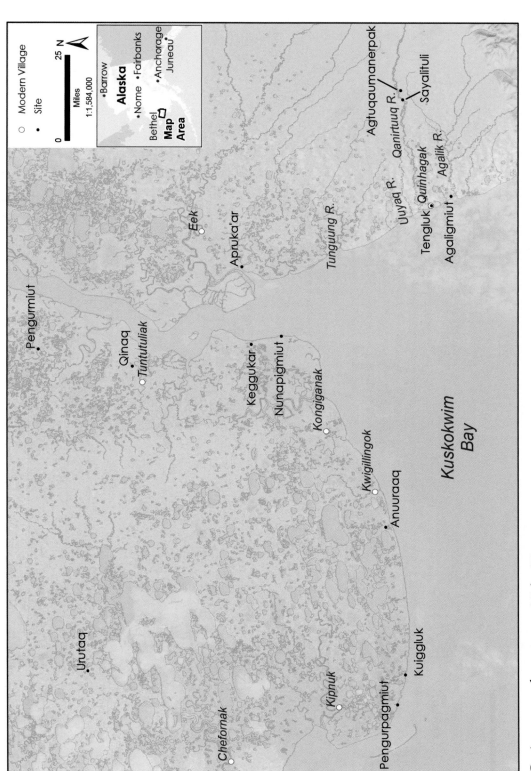

Canineq-area place names. Michael Knapp

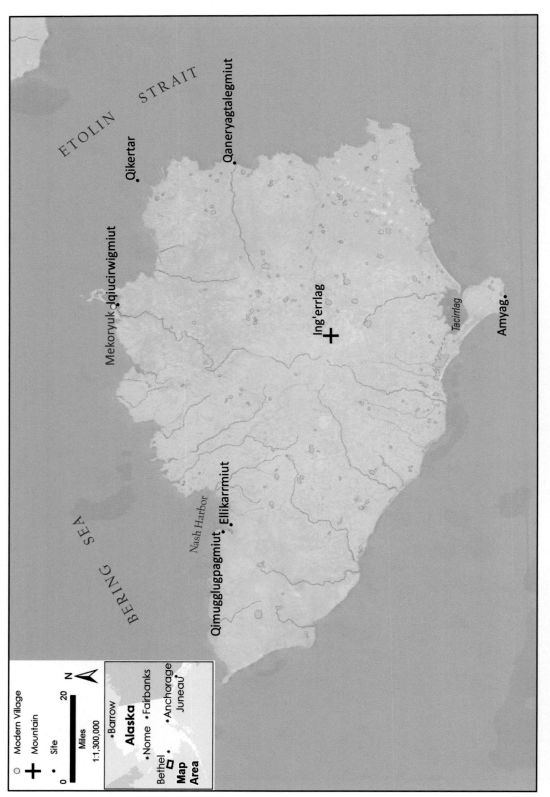

Nunivak Island place names mentioned in Jack Williams's story. Robert Drozda and Michael Knapp

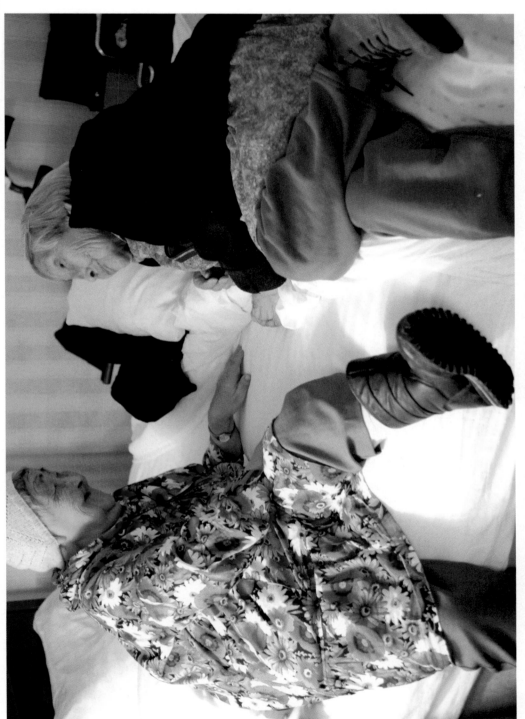

Elsie Tommy of Newtok relaxing in her hotel room with Albertina Dull of Nightmute while on a visit to the National Museum of the American Indian, October 2012. Ann Fienup-Riordan

Elsie Tommy of Newtok during her visit to Washington, DC, October 2012. Ann Fienup-Riordan

Nick Andrew of Marshall bending wood for a fish trap that he and Tim Myers built at the Yupiit Piciryarait Museum in Bethel, November 2006. Ann Fienup-Riordan

Simeon Agnus of Nightmute sharing information at Qalulleq during the circumnavigation of Nelson Island, July 2007.

Ann Fienup-Riordan

Paul John of Toksook Bay documenting the history of Kaviarmiut on the southern shore of Toksook Bay with a group of elders and students, July 2007. Ann Fienup-Riordan

Michael John of Newtok during his circumnavigation of Nelson Island, July 2007. Ann Fienup-Riordan

Frances Usugan holding inflated seal intestines outside her home in Toksook Bay, 1980. James H. Barker

Magdalene Sunny of Nightmute, playing with her grandchild at home in 1985. Ann Fienup-Riordan

Umkuuk, the rock outcrop on the north shore of Toksook Bay, on top of which Ayugutarin had his home and small *qasgi*. Ann Fienup-Riordan

Dick Andrew dancing in Bethel, 1975. James H. Barker

Dick Andrew watching a dance in Bethel, 1980. James H. Barker

"Beetle Mask," collected along with its story by Otto William Geist in 1934 at Old Hamilton. Karinna Gomez and Mahriena Ellanna, University of Alaska Museum of the North 64-15-4

Atertayagaq as a lay pastor in Quinhagak, 1930s. Moravian Archives,
Bethlehem, PA

An above-ground grave like those Mary Napoka and Frances Usugun described in their stories. O. W. Geist, Tununak, 1933, Anchorage Museum at Rasmuson Center

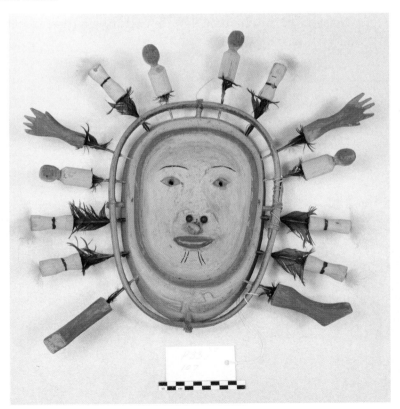

Mask collected by Knud Rasmussen in 1924, said to represent "Husband seeker," who killed her husbands and then used them for mattresses. Anna Mossolova, National Museum, Copenhagen, P.33.107

Nick Andrew tells the story of the shaman Neryull'er during a trip down the Yukon River, May 2017. Ann Fienup-Riordan

The hill named Iquggaq, which Nick Andrew described as the *qasgi* into which Neryull'er looked and saw animals which later became his *tuunrat* (spirit helpers). Ann Fienup-Riordan

Atam tua-i piinanermini unani tua-i imarpigmi, tauna tua-i iraluq nangllini-ll' imna tua-i *half*-aq. Alla pill'uni iraluq. Pill'uni iraluq. Cali tua-i tuaten.

Taugaam-gguq ukut wani ingrit tangenririinarluki, ikegkut nuuget, ikegkut ikani wangkuta ukut akiqliput, tamaani tua-i pillermini.

Atam tua-i qamigaraqluni. Anuqliyuunani-gguq. Man'a-gguq piqerluni cikungluku, man'a imarpik ecirluku. Anuqliyuunani-gguq. Ecirluku. Ecirluku tua-i, manigiluni. Taugaam tua-i makunun qertuuralrianun qanikcalegmek mamtulriamek, tamakunun piaqluni.

Tamaani tua-i uitangllermini, unguvalriit elliin . . . Tamaani uitangllermini tauna iraluq pill'uni kinguqlia, unguvalriit-gguq elliini wani ilaksagusnganaki. Cataitaqata-gguq tua-i tangerrnaciaraqami, aliayugnaurtuq makunek imarpigmiutarnek.

Atam tua-i tauna iraluq call' tua-i una'anlluni call' tua-i aturluku. Kiituangguq taukuk aciqsigiuk piluguuk. Qillerrlukek iqukek mumigglukek, imkuk maantellrek aciqsigilukek. Natriutaqagnek, nang'aqagnek mumigtaqlukek.

Atam tua-i caqerluni-am asvermek tangrrami, ullagluku asveq taun' nutlinikii. Tua-i tuquqapigtenrilan-llu-ggur-am pingnaqluku qakerlaa kepluku nutaan piani tuquluni.

Taukuk-llu-gguq-am tua-i tugkaraak cali kangikegen'gun nuteglukek ayimllukek qemagtellinilukek taukuk. Nutaan tua-i qemangqayaaqerraarlukek, cali-llu umyuarteqluni tamana merrlainaureskan imarpik, umyuangqerrluni qiluanekgguq kepucaaqellruuq mervigkaminek. Taugaam-gguq tua-i tegulngungamikekllu . . . taukuk tamaani qemangqaurlukek.

Tauna-ll' tua-i iraluq kingutmun cauluni unanelnginanrani. Umyugaa tua-i elliini tamaani uitallermini ilaksagusnganaki-gguq elliin umyuamini imarpigmiutaat.

Atam tua-i caqerluni piinanermini, ukut tangenrrirluki, ingrit ikegkut tangenrrirluki. Allanek makunek tanglangllinilria ingrinek tangnerrayagnek. Tangnerrarluki taukut; qertuluteng ingrit. Ayalaryaaqluni-gguq tungiitnun tekitesciiananaki. Qaillun tekitesciiganaki.

Atam tua-i caqerluni tamana manigillrani, ayallermini-am quplinilria qupneq, waten qupneq aitarrluni. Tamaaggun tua-i qupnerkun tungiitnun-am anguarluni ayalliniluni qupnerkun.

Iraluq tua-i man'a cali kinguqlia waten mumiggluni piluni. Tauna tua-i iraluq cuqyutekluku taugaam kangarluni. Tauna ciuqlia *half*-aq nangellruluni.

Atam tua-i ayainanermini iqua quungan arulairluni mayullini-ll' tauna.

When he went up [onto the ice], he dragged his kayak farther back and was sitting there, from his north side, a small walrus appeared. He said the walrus was continually making noises. They call the ones that have short tusks *puyurtat*.

It came toward him swimming through that crack in the ice, and it hadn't gone underwater. And he said when it got to him, it hung its small tusks [on the ice] right below him. It stopped right down below him.

These are parts of the story that he told that I haven't forgotten. He said that it went right below him and faced him. He said it seemed to be telling him something, but he couldn't understand what it was saying. He said it was there for a while. He said it seemed to be saying something, but he couldn't understand what that small walrus was saying.

After [talking to him], after a while that small walrus swam away along the edge of the ice where the crack was. He said it continued to make noise, and then it stopped making noise and disappeared. It left.

When he was tired of being there, he went down and went after it using his kayak, following the path that [the walrus] had taken. When he continued on, while he went on his way, a kayak appeared in the area ahead. He said three kayaks appeared ahead of him. There were a group of people there.

He approached them. He said that he was shy, and was thinking that they were people from Quinhagak.

While he was stopped there, he said one of them took a kettle and walked up and was chipping ice. That's what [Atertayagaq] said. He chipped some ice and filled his kettle. Then he went down.

He said there were people over there. He said he was shy, and he continued to approach them by paddling. He was thinking that they were people from Quinhagak. When he was about to reach them, and he said their gaffs were visible. And their kayaks had windbreaks, and their gaffs were staked [in the ice]. They had windbreaks.

While he was on his way, and was just about to climb up there, and was just about to reach those kayakers, and was about to reach them as they were in human form, as he was on his way, as he was paddling, he happened to see something out of the corner of his eye, something appeared along the corner of his eye. You know how things are visible when they [move alongside us].

When something appeared along the water along the corner of his eye, and he was about to climb up to the ice, when something appeared along the corner of his eye, he quickly looked at that, and he looked away from those people. After looking away from them, he saw that [the thing along the corner of his eye] was a sea mammal. After looking away for a brief moment, when he turned to look at the kayakers, he looked again and saw only walrus. He said when he turned his head to look at what had been kaykers before, after looking at that thing and looking

Mayuami tua-i mayurluni keluqvaarnun qamuqaniqerluk' uitallrani, atam piinanrani tamaaken neglirneranek asveyagar' man'a alairutellria. Qalriagurluni-gguq asveq. Tua-i-w' puyurtanek pilarait augkut tulurralget takenrilngurnek.

Tailliniluni kuimarluni anglluqsaunani qulinerkun tamaaggun. Tekicamiu-llu-gguq kanavet ketiinun tulucuaraagni taukuk agarrlukek. Arulairluni ketiinun kanani.

Maa-i makut qanengssallri nalluyaguteksailkenka. Ketiini-gguq kanani cau-luku. Camek-gguq tua-i qanrut'larngacaaqekii taringesciiganaku elliin. Wanirpak-gguq ak'anun. Tuaten-gguq tua-i qalarrngat'laryaaqluni-gguq elliini camek, camek taugaam taringuciinaku taun' asveyagaq.

Piyaaqerraarluku tua-i, pilngungami taum asveyagaam ayalliniluni kuimur-luni tamaaggun call' cikum engeliikun tamatum qupnerem. Qalriagurluni-gguq tayim' pellaluni tua-i arulairluni. Ayagluni.

Uitalngungami tua-i tamaaggun ellii atralliniluni qayani aturluku tamana maliggluku, tamaaggun tumellrakun. Ayiimi tua-i ayainanermini, atam ayai-nanrani ciunra ing' qayartangllinill'. Pingayunek-gguq qayanek yaa-i ciunra qayartangluni. Yugyualuteng.

Tuaten tua-i ullalliniluk'. Talluryugluni-gguq umyuarteqluni, Kuinerrarmiu-nguyukluki-llu-gguq umyuarteqluni taukut.

Tamaani tua-i uitangllermini, iliit-gguq saaniigmek tegulluni, tagluni piyualuni, cikuliurluni yaa-i pikili. Tuaten tua-i qanemcillruuq. Cikuliurluni imiqiliu tauna wani saaniini. Atrarluni-llu-gguq tua-i.

Tua-i-gguq yuut ingkut yaani. Talluryugluni-gguq tua-i ullagturallinikai anguarluni. Umyuarteqaqluni kiingita Kuinerrarmiungunguartelluki elliin umyua-mini. Tua-i waniw' tekiteqatarluki, negciit-llu-gguq imkut alaunateng. Qayait-llu makut uqruta'arluteng, uqruta'arluteng-gguq, negciit-llu kapusngaluteng. Uq-ruta'arluteng.

Atam tua-i piinanrani, waniw' tua-i mayurarkaurrluni tuavet wani, taukunun qayanun tua-i tekiteqatarluki, yuuluki tekiteqatarluki, maani-am ayainanermini, anguarturainanermini maani nani qigcilkira'artellinill', qigciminek ca im' tua-i piqalliniluni. Waten iciw' tua-i alaitelalriit waten cat piaqameng waten.

Mermi maani qigcilkira'arcan, taukut waniw' mayurarkaurrluni, qigcilki-ra'arcami, tangerqalliniluku tauna, uluqerluki taukut. Uluqerraarluki tua-i tauna pillinia unguvalriarullinilria tauna. Uluqerraarluk' takuyallinii imkut qayat, piqerluteng ukut ayivret ukut. Maaten-gguq tua-i taukut imkut qayaullret taku-yarai, tauna tangrraarluk' uluqerluki, ayivret-llu makut kingupirmeng atraryartur-luteng, kingupiarluteng. Atrarluteng tua-i.

away from them, [the walrus] were moving backward. They went down [into the water].

When they went down and went underwater, since they were scary, he quickly went up to where they had been [on the ice]. Since they mentioned that [walrus] were dangerous, he was afraid of them.

When they went down [into the water], he quickly climbed up [onto the ice]. He said that he was very regretful because he was just about to reach them as they were in human form. And he said one of them, just as I said, went up and was filling his kettle using his gaff [to chip ice].

Feeling regretful, he went up to where they had been. After a while, they surfaced. When they appeared, after looking up at him, they breached and left.

He also talked about those. He thought that if he hadn't looked away from them, he would have arrived with them in human form. He said when he looked away for a second when he saw something out of the corner of his eye, he turned his head to look at them and saw walrus going down to the water. He regretted [looking away].

He had gone after the small walrus. He went up there [on the ice] and stayed there.

He said that he no longer minded being there, but he said that when he didn't see sea mammals for a while, he would feel lonely because of not seeing sea mammals. That's what he said. He said that he would feel lonely.

After [the walrus] left, he regretted that he had looked away from them. Afterward he thought that he would have reached them as they were in human form. They say walrus take people home. That's what I heard about them. I'm just adding that.

After that, the mountains here got closer. And he said that month, the other month ended.

I'm probably not telling parts of the story in between. I probably forgot some parts; I'm telling you about the things I remember. If I forget some parts, Roland will be able to tell those sections, if I missed some parts of the story.

He said at that time, those mountains; the month ended. And he said the second month came around. The half moon ended. But he said that it wasn't too cold any longer. And he said the newly frozen ice started to smooth out. It iced over. That's how it became. And he said that it hadn't gotten windy.

While he was walking on foot, his skin boots got lower. He continually switched them. When he'd tow his kayak, when he couldn't continue on, when the ice became thin, he would stop.

One day, when the ice became smooth, when the third month came around, he became extremely thirsty. The ice that he was on became salt water, it became *elliqaun* [newly frozen ice]. He was extremely thirsty. And he said the *elliqaun* was

Atraameng tayim' anglluata, alingnaqngata tuavet ellii mayu'urtelliniluni mayuumallratnun. Alingnaqluki qanrutketullruitki alikluki tua-i.

Tua-i atraata may'uqerrluni. Qessanayugluni-gguq tua-i cakneq taum yuuluki tekiteqataryaaqellerminek. Iliit-llu-gguq tua-i aug'utun ava-i qanllemtun piyualuni tagluni negciminek saaniigminek imiriluni.

Tua-i qessanayuami mayurluni nuniitnun. Piqerluteng tua-i puggliniluteng. Pugngameng piavet takuyarraarluk' qakluteng ayalliniluteng tayima.
Tua-i taukunek call' tua-i qanerluni. Yuuluki, ulunrilkuniki yuuluki teki-caryaaqsukluki piluki tuaten. Uluqallrani-gguq tua-i taumek qigcilkira'arte-llermini, takuyarai-gguq, ayivret ukut atralriit. Qessanayugluni.

Taum tua-i asveyagaam kinguakun ayagluni. Mayurluni-am tua-i uitalliniluni tamaani.
Tauna-ll'-am tua-i tamaani, tua-i-gguq tamaani cangalliunrirluni, taugaam-gguq makunek imarpigmiutarnek tangerrnaciaraqami aliayungaqluni, makunek unguvalrianek. Tuaten tua-i qanerluni. Aliayungaqluni-gguq tua-i.
Nutaan tua-i tamaani tuaten taun' ayaggaartelluki, tua-i qessanayugluni taumek pillrulliniuq ulullerminek. Yuuluki tekicaryukluki taukut umyuarteqsaaqelliniuq kinguakun taukut. Makut tua-i ayivret qanrutek'larait ut'rucituniluki yugnek. Niigartellruanka. Taumek ilaqerluki pianka.
Tua-i-am kinguakun, makut wani, ukut ingrit canimellilliniluteng. Imna-llu-gguq man'a iraluq, iralum aipaa nangluni.
Tayima tua-i akulii pinricaaqellikeka. Ilii nalluyagucaaqellikeka; neq'akelqa tua-i waniw' qanrutkura'arqa. Tayima ilii pillrunilkumku Roland-aam piyugngaci-qaa katagillrukuma camek.
Tua-i-gguq tamaani ingrit tamakut; una nangluni iraluq. Una-gguq tua-i cali pill'uni kinguqlia. *Half*-aaq una nangluni. Taugaam-gguq imkungluni tua-i, man'a-w' tua-i nengllissiyaanrirluni. Manigiluni-llu-gguq man'a elliqaun. Ecirluku tua-i. Tuaten ellirluni. Anuqliqsaunani-llu-gguq tua-i.
Tamaani tua-i pektellermini kankuk tua-i piluguuk aciqsigillinilutek. Mu-migqurlukek. Qamigaryaaqaqami tua-i ayagvigkairutaqami mamkelliaqan aru-lairaqluni.
Tua-i-am caqerluni waten tamana manigillrani tauna tua-i avga, pingayuak pill'uni iraluq pillrani meqsupiarluni. Tamana taryuurrluni elliqautngurrluni. Meqsupiarluni. Tamana-llu-gguq mey'unaunani tua-i tamana elliqaun. Elliqautet

undrinkable. *Elliqautet* [pieces of newly frozen ice] are not good to [melt and] drink as they are thin pieces of ice.

He stayed there with his head down like this. After staying with his head down, during the time when he was extremely thirsty, he looked up, and on top of his kayak sled, he saw what looked like a snowball. You know how we make [balls] with snow. He said that snowball was on top of the back of his kayak sled. He said it looked like someone had made the snow into a ball and placed it there. And it wasn't much. It was only enough to fill the palm of his hand.

He took that, and following the teaching for it, he bit part of it and melted it in his mouth. They say not to chew new snow, that it makes you tired [when eating it]. He melted it first [in his mouth] following the *qanruyun* [oral instruction].

Following the *qanruyun* at that time, sometimes he would come upon those obstacles on his path. He stayed down on the ocean, constantly recalling the *qanruyutet* [oral instructions]. They say he followed the *qanruyutet* while he was down on the ocean, constantly recalling them. After that, he melted [the snow] and was no longer thirsty.

Just as the [ice was about to melt] and it was going to become all ocean, the *cikullaq* [newly frozen ice], the ocean, became like that at that time. He said it was as though he was akin to the sea mammals, as though he became akin to them. When he'd say that, he even told stories in my home about the time that he was there, that it was as though he became akin with them. Just like I mentioned, he'd feel lonely [when he hadn't seen them].

After a while, when it became like that, the weather outdoors became warm. Those mountains got close. He'd never seen them before. They weren't our [Kilbuck] mountains across there that he'd seen before.

And he said the shore wasn't too far at that time, and the land started to become visible. But he said that while he tried to go up to shore, the ice made it impossible to go up. And he did attempt to go down there, but he would no longer have a path as the ice was packed and crowded. He couldn't find a path to travel on because this was his first experience on the ocean.

He probably could have found a way if he knew [the ocean]. While we were down there, and when [Roland Phillip] and I would go together, sometimes when the current flowed a certain way, one could usually find a way out. When continuing on, leads formed in the ice. He wasn't thinking of those things.

When [the ice] was at that point, he said that the ocean down there never got windy at that time, the entire time he was down there.

He attempted to go up [to the shore] behind him when he could. The current out there is very strong. You all know that fact. It's stronger than here. He said the ice was compacted, it was scary. The ice tended to close in tightly. He couldn't go up [to shore]. And he said that the cliff up [along the shore] behind him was visible at that time.

mey'unaitelartut mamkit'laameng.

Uitaurallinill' pusngaluni waten. Pusngarraarluni tua-i meqsullermi nalliini pusngaurarraarluni, ciugtelliniuq qamigautegken qaingagni tuar'-gguq waten imna qanikcaq. Waten pililalriakut qanikcamek. Qamigautegken-gguq qaingagni, kinguani, elliqaumaurluni-gguq taun' qanikcaq. Tuar'-gguq yuum waten piluku pirraarluku tuavet ellikii tauna qanikcaq. Tua-i angevkenani-llu. Tumiim tua-i imaqluku.

Tua-i teguluku tauna piciryaraq aturluku iliinek kegqaulluni urugciarluku. Qanikcaat tamakut tamuasqessuitelarait nutarat, taqsuqnaqniluki. Tuaten-am urugciarluku qanruyun aturluku.

Qanruyun aturluku tamaani tua-i tamakut, iliini tumkaituraqluni tamakunek. Una'antaralliniluni neq'aku'urluki tamakut qanruyutet. Qanruyutet-gguq tau-gaam aturluki tamaani piurallruuq unaantellermini, neq'aku'urluki. Tuaten-am tua-i tauna pirraarluku urugciarluku meqsuirtelliniluni.

Tauna tua-i tuaten merrlainaurqaartelluku ava-i, augna-wa cikullaq waten ellir-luku, imarpik tuaten ellirluni, ellirluni tamaani. Tua-i tamakut wani unguvalriit elliin ilaksagutellriatun-gguq ellirluki, ilaksagutellriatun. Qanraqami tuaten, qa-nemciqalartuq-llu enema iluani tamatumek uitallermini, ilaksagutellriatun tua-i ellirluki. Aug'utun ava-i aliayungaqluni.

Atam tua-i piqerluni tuaten ellillrani, nenglairutengluni qakemna ellii. Tamakut tamaa-i canimellilliniluteng ingrit. Tangnerranaqluki, tangnerrarluki elliin. Imkuuvkenateng augkut elliin tanglallri ukut ingriput agkut agaa-i.

Man'a-llu-gguq kelua yaaqsinrirluni tamaani, kelua tamana, nuna-ll' alaingluni. Taugaam-gguq tua-i tagengnaq'laryaaqellriim ciku piyunaitaqluni. Tuani-llu cali uavet pingnaqsaaqaqami tumkaituraluni, cikuq qerrleraqluni. Tumkaituraaqluni, tua-i-wa nutaan imarpigmi pilriaruami.

Tumkangyugngayaaqellilria ilii nallunrilkuniu. Wangkuta unani uitaaqamta, wangkuk-llu malikaqamegnuk, iliini carvaneq qaillun piaqami tumkangtuyaaquq. Ayakcaarluni, aitara'artaqluni. Tamakut umyuaqevkenaki.

Tamana-gguq tua-i tuaten ellillrani, unani tua-i-gguq anuqliyuunani tamaani, tua-i-w' unaantellran taktaciatun.

Tamakut tamaa-i kelumini piyugngariami taglaryaaqelliniuq. Carvaneq atam avani tukniuq. Nallunritarci. Mat'umi tukninruuq. Arenqiatuq-gguq qerrlelartut cikut, alingnaqluteng. Eqsugluteng cikut. Tagesciiganani tua-i. Ekviaq-llu-gguq alaicaaqluni pava-i keluani tamaani.

Around that area, [the land] behind him appeared. He would attempt to go sometimes. He said his skin boots had gotten lower. When he was able to go up onto the ice and it could withstand his weight, he'd go toward [shore], and he didn't just stay put.

Then finally one day from his sleep, he'd go to sleep, but he'd slip on the other pair of skin boots that he had when he lay down. He said he conserved those two, those things. And he said that he had few bullets left. He would only shoot [sea mammals] when he ran out of food. He said the warm sea mammals tasted like cooked food to him. The warm ones tasted like they were cooked to him.

One day, after sleeping, he woke to find the sky cloudy. He woke and the wind would gust from a certain direction, toward him. He paid attention and saw that the wind was blowing in his direction while he had a windbreak. He turned his windbreak around in the direction of the wind. He said that all the ice in the area surrounding him was frozen over. It wasn't thick.

After a while, when he woke, he saw that the sky above was cloudy. It was cloudy. He said the wind would gust from this direction, and it was worrisome as it was cold. He thought, "Now finally. The wind out there that is finally going to kill me is probably coming." He became insecure when the wind was blowing, when strong gusts of wind came. And he said it was cloudy.

After switching his windbreak toward the direction of the wind, those grass windbreaks, when he became curious about the windward side, he looked and saw a small cloud that was dark along the horizon, what looked like a small cloud.

He noticed it. But as I said, he thought, "The weather that will surely kill me is probably coming." He said that because a wind that strong had finally arrived.

Oh yes, I forgot to mention that during the time when he drifted away, when he left, I forgot to tell part of the story. I'm going to mention it now that I've recalled it.

He said that when he left, when he disappeared, the people in his village had the mother of the person who they used to call Tuguyak, a person named Qassayuli; they had that person keep watch over him. It is said they would go to that person and ask her [about him]. [It was] because the mother of Tuguyak and her siblings was sort of a shaman.

They say when his relatives became curious about his situation, they would go to that person and ask her how he was. They say that person would fill a bucket with water and look inside it. This is what they said about that person who kept watch over him. That is part of his story that the people where he was from experienced and told, the people of his village. It is said they would let that person look in on him. She apparently watched him. After looking [inside the bucket], she would say that he was okay. She would say that he was okay.

Taum tua-i nuniini tamana alairluni kelua. Piinanrani tua-i ayalaryaaqluni. Taukuk-gguq tua-i aciqsigilutek piluguuk. Tua-i ugcugngariaqami tamatum tungiinun ayalaryaaqluni, uitqapiarpek'nani.

Nutaan tua-i caqerluni qavallerminek, inartellermini-w' tua-i qavaraqluni, taukugnek taugaam tua-i as'artaqluni-gguq piluguugmi aipagkenek inarteqatarqami. Taukuk aninqurlukek-gguq tua-i taukut. Puulini-ll' taukut ikegliluteng-gguq tua-i. Neqkairutaqami taugaam nutgaqluni tua-i. Makut-gguq tua-i unguvalriit elliini keniumalriatun puqlanilriit ayuqluteng. Puqlanilriit tua-i keniumaluteng elliini.

Atam tua-i caqerluni qavarraarluni unuakumi tupalliniuq amirluluni ella pakemna. Uitelliniuq naken maaken anuqa pakemna piaqluni, tunglirneranun. Cunawa-gguq maaten murilkelliniuq, anuqii tuavet tunglirneranun pillinilria uqrutarallrani. Uqrutani tua-i mumiggluki tunglirneranun elliluki. Man'a-gguq tua-i tamarmi eciumaluku avatii tua-i tamarmi. Tuaten mamtuvkenani.

Piinanrani tua-i tupiimi pilliniuq amirluluni qakem' pakemna ella. Amirluluni. Una-gguq anuqa waken taigaqluni, tua-i-w' uluryanaqluni kumlanani. Umyuarteqliniuq. "Nutaan. Tua-i-w' qakma nutaan pistekaqa piqatallilria." Tua-i ellminek augtaryagulluni anuqa pillrani, anuqa tekitelallrani ang'urluni. Amirluluni-llu-gguq.

Uqrutani tua-i mumiggluki tuavet tunglirneranun ellirraarluki uqrutani, imkut kangcirat can'get, caqerluni asgulirnera paqnakluku amna piamiu anuqem tunglirnera pilliniuq, ca amna amirlurraq tunguluni, mat'um engeliini tunguluni amirluquinerngalnguq uitalria.

Tua-i pilliniluku. Umyuarteqluni taugaam aug'utun ava-i, "Qakma-w' tua-i nutaan piunrircestekaqa piqatallill'." Anuqa tua-i nutaan tekican tuaten pitaluni.

Tamaani imat'am ayallrani, tua-i ayiin, nalluyagutelliniaqa call' ilii augna. Neqaamku qanrutkeqatarqa waniwa.

Tamaani-gguq ayallrani catairutellrani, kingunrin taukut, kingunrin taukut aug'umun wani uum wani Tuguyagmek pilallrata, Tuguyagmek pilallrata aaniin, Qassayulim-gguq taum wani; taumun tangvaumavkallruat. Tauna-gguq tua-i ullagluku aptaqluku. Imkuullinian tua-i cakuyuk tuunrangayakuyuk tauna Tuguyiinkut aaniit.

Taum-gguq tua-i paqnakngaqamegteggu ilain tauna ullagluku aptaqluku. Taum-gguq waten qaltaq mermek imirluku, qaltaq uyangtelaraa. Waten-am call' qanrutkaat tauna, tangvagtellra tauna. Aug'um avatiini qanemcian taukut kingunrita man'a pikaat man'a, kingunrin taukut. Uyangcet'laraat-gguq taumun apluku. Tangvaumalliniluku elliin. Uyangqaarluku-gguq qanernaurtuq, canrituq-gguq. Canrituq-gguq.

When they wanted to, following those months, sometimes they would ask her. That woman named Qassayuli would look in and say that he was okay. That's what she would do while he was away down on the ocean. They would ask her [to check on him].

Now I've just included part of the story that I forgot to mention, about the people in his hometown who were watching him.

Now going back to that small cloud. He later became curious about what he thought was a small cloud, and he looked and saw that it had become larger. It had grown.

After a while, because it was distinctly shaped, he watched it. The wind came from that direction. He said the mountains up there [that he was facing] were steep. When checking it a third time, he saw that it had gotten larger, and it looked as though there was something beneath it. He began to watch it closely as it quickly became more visible. The wind was coming from its direction, with the mountains up there. He said [the water] surrounding him was frozen over. That [ice] was *cikullaq* [newly frozen ice].

When he looked at it for the third time, something appeared beneath it. He began to watch it at that point. He saw that it was a ship.

They call those up there *aluyalget,* those that have sails. It was a ship. He saw that it was a ship with a sail. He said it became larger and more visible as it came toward him. It came toward him. He watched it closely there.

When it got close, he thought, when he discerned what it was and figured out it was a ship, and knew that there were white people in it, he thought . . . He said that he was afraid of white people at that time. And we, too, were afraid of white people. White people were scary back in those days. We couldn't get close to them. And I, too, was afraid of them.

Ann, afraid [of you]. [*laughs*]

That's what that person said. I'm using his words. Indeed, white people were scary. He was afraid of them. He thought in his mind, "I will surrender myself to these people. I could have died a long time ago. Let me give myself over to them."

The sail got close. He knew that the bottom was a ship at that point. He was intently focusing on the area beyond it. He finally faced that ship, and he decided that he would surrender to them although they would kill him.

When they got close, when the people in it started appearing, when that particular *qanruyun* came to mind, when the people began to appear, he took his paddle and placed one of his pieces of clothing on it. It is an instruction for us on the ocean; he lifted it up and waved it from side to side. He placed his clothing on the paddle and waved if from side to side.

Piyungaqamegteggu tua-i tuaten iralut tamakut aturluki iliitni aptaqluku. Canritniaqluku tuaten uyangqaarluni taum arnam Qassayulim. Tuani tua-i nutaan tuaten pilalliniluni tamaan' ayaumallrani unaantellrani. Tua-i aptelalliniluku.

Nutaan tua-i tuani tauna augna katagaqa aqvaq'erluku ek'aqa avavet, tang-vaumastellrinun kingunrinun.

Nutaan tauna wani imna amirlurraq. Ca-w' amirlurrauyukellni kinguakun paqnaklinia, anglirikanillinilria. Anglirikanillinilria tauna.

Nutaan tua-i piqerluni elucqeggan, murilkellinia. Anuqii tunglirneranek ta-maaken. Pava-i-gguq paugkut ingrit qertuluteng, piluteng. Atam tua-i pirraarluku pingayiriluni pillinia anglirikanillinill' tuar-llu-gguq acia catangqellria. Nutaan murilkenga'artellinia cukamek misturian. Anuqlii tua-i tunglirneranek tailuni paugna tua-i, paugkut ingrit pavani. Man'a-gguq tua-i waten tamana ecirluku. Cikullauluni tamana.

Atam tua-i pingayiriamiu tuani, tangrramiu acia catangellinilria kan'a. Nutaan tua-i murilkenga'artelliniluku. Maaten-gguq tua-i pia imna sun'aq.

Paugkut-wa aterpagtelaqait aluyalegnek, imkut tengalratulit. Sun'aq. Sunau-llinilria tamana tengalrarluni. Tungiinun-gguq tua-i misturiinarluni tailuni. Tungiinun tua-i maavet. Murilkuralliniluku tua-i tamaani.

Atam tua-i canimellingarcan waniwa umyuarteqliniuq, tua-i caucia nallunria-miu, sunaucia-llu, kass'anek yungqerrucia nallunriamiu, umyuarteqliniuq . . . Kass'at-gguq alikellrui tamaani elliin. Wangkuta-ll' alikellruaput kass'at. Alingnar-qellruut kass'at avani. Mallegcesciiganaki. Wiinga-ll' alikellruanka.

Ann, alinge. [ngel'artuq]
Tauna tua-i tuaten qanertuq. Qanellratun qanertua waniw'. Ilumun kass'at alingnarqellruut. Alikellrui. Tua-i qanlliniuq, umyuamikun pilliniuq, "Tua-i ma-kunun tunciqua. Tuquyauciqa akaurtuq tua-i. Ellaitnun tunlii."

Atam tua-i canimellingartellinilria tengalrautaq. Tua-i acia sunaurciluku tua-i. Man'a-gguq tua-i urenkessaaqekni, yaakarii taugaam urenkelluku. Tua-i taumun nutaan caulliniluni, tun'arkaurrluni taukunun tua-i tuqutengraatni-llu ayuqluni tuaten.

Atam tua-i canimellingarcaki yui alaingarcata, imna-am qanruyun umyuami-nun ekngan, maa-i tua-i yuut alaingarcaki, alaingarcata, tamana anguarutni piluku aturami iliitnek. Unani alerquutnguuq wangkuta; napautarluku arulatlinikii. Anguarutminun piluku, aturani elliluku waten arulatliniluku.

When they got close, since they were visible, after watching him, after a while [the ship] beyond him brought down all of its sails. But he said they left the [sail] up in front standing.

It passed right beyond him, breaking the newly frozen ice right beyond him as it passed. He thought, "Oh well, I'm going to surrender myself to those people over there. I had many chances of dying."

He went over. He went over towing his kayak on his kayak sled, and he went in the water along where the ship had passed, along the crack in the ice. He paddled over.

As he approached them — those ships, [Roland and I] used to work on ships [on the Kuskokwim River] — they let down a ladder made of rope toward him. They let it down. He paddled toward it with a kayak.

He paddled to them. When he got close, that white person went down the ladder there and was motioning [for him to come].

When [Atertayagaq] got to him, he handed that man the skin line that was tied to the tote hole of his kayak. He said there were white people along the side of the ship; they were watching. The people of that [ship] watched him, the ones who he feared.

When he handed [the rope] to him, he took the rope and handed it to the person above him, and the person above him took it. He had gone down and was standing on that ladder. When he extended his arm down at him again, [Atertayagaq] lifted his arm up. When [Atertayagaq] extended his arm up to him, the white person took him here [on his arm]. He reached down to him and took him with one arm. And when he took him, from his kayak down below, he took him with just one arm and handed him to the person above him with just one arm. Then the one above took him with just one arm along his upper body and lifted him and placed him inside [the ship].

See how young that person was. He was young like you. He was apparently a small person. That person wasn't a big person. That Atertayagaq wasn't a big person like us. He was probably as tall as me. He wasn't tall. He wasn't a large person.

When that person placed him inside [the ship], after putting him inside, those people lifted his kayak into [the ship]. They put it inside [the ship].

While he was inside there, he was thinking in the way that I mentioned earlier, that he was surrendering himself to them. Then they lifted the sails and [the ship] took off.

After a while, the captain, the one who happened to be the captain came to him. When he came, the captain took him by the arm and brought him to his room.

Atam tua-i canimellingarrluteng, alailameng, tangvakarluku, yaa-i tua-i piqerluni imkut tengalrautani atrarqellinikai tamalkuita. Ingna-gguq taugaam yaani imna ciungani, ciulitni uitalluku.

Maaggun tua-i yaakariikun qupluku taman' cikullaq kitulliniluni. Umyuarteqliniuq, "Tua-i ingkunun waniw' tua-i tunqatartua. Tuquyauciqa amllertuq."

Aggliniluni tua-i. Agluni qamigautni piqerluk', qamurluk' qayani tamaavet tumellranun ekluni, qupellranun cikum. Aggliniluni anguarluni.

Ullainanrani — imkut sun'at augkut, wangkuta sun'ani calitullruukuk — imkunek *ladder*-aanek ilavkugnek atrarcilliniluni, mayuryaranek, tunglirneranun. Atrarciluteng tua-i. Ullagturalliniluku qayakun anguarturluni.

Anguarluni ullagturalliniluki. Tua-i-ll' waniw' canimelliyartuan kass'aq taun' atralliniluni tuavet mayuryaranun tuavet elucira'arluni.

Tekicamiu tua-i imna tapraq maani qayami ukinqucuanun qillrusngalria tunqerluk' tunlliniluku taumun. Pagna-gguq tua-i sun'am cenii tamakunek kass'anek; tangvagluteng. Yuinek tamatum tangvagluk' tuani, imkut alikekngain.

Tua-i nutaan tauna tunqerraarluku, qulliminun pikavet teguluku tamana ilavkuk, ca, tapraq tunngaku, qullian teguluku cali. Atraumaluni *ladder*-aani taukuni. Yagtenqigcan yagtelliniuq. Yagcan uuggun tegullinia taum kass'am. Inglupiarrarmek kanavet tegullinia. Teguamiu-llu-gguq taum kanaken qayaanek inglupiarrarmek teguluku talliakun waten pikavet inglupiarrarmek tunluku, qulliminun. Taum-llu-gguq kangiakun teguluku inglupiarrarmek ekluku tamaavet.

Tang ayagyuaryaaqellinilria tauna. Elpecicetun waten *young*-arluni. Mikellrulliniuq. Angenrilami-llu-w' tauna. Augna Atertayagaq angenrituq wangkucicetun. Wangtun tayima angtalliuq. Angevkenani. Yugtuvkenani.

Nutaan ekluku, taum ekngani, ekraarluku, qayaa tamana tamaavet mayurtelliniluku taukut. Ekluku tua-i.

Tua-i-gguq ekumallermini tua-i umyuarteqellruami aug'utun tua-i waniwa, tunluni ellaitnun tua-i piluni. Nutaan tua-i tamakut mayurqelliniluki tengalrautni ayagartelliniluni.

Piqerluni-ll' tua-i augna tailliniluni *captain*-aarullinill', *captain*-aaqellinikiigguq tailliniluni. Taingami teguluku tass'urluku *room*-aminun agutelliniluku taum *captain*-aam.

When he brought him inside, they sat down at a table. When that white person brought him in, he pulled open some cabinets and took out a bottle of alcohol and put it down. Then from somewhere, he set down two small glasses. He set down a small glass. He filled the small glass.

When he filled it, poor [Atertayagaq] thought, "He's probably going to give me something deadly that will kill me now." He said, "He's probably going to give me something that will kill me."

After filling it, he handed it to him, but [Atertayagaq] didn't take it. Since he didn't take it, since that man probably understood why [he didn't take it], he drank it himself. The captain drank [the glass] he had filled. When he drank it, he thought, "It isn't entirely deadly after all." [*chuckles*]

"It isn't entirely deadly after all." When he filled it again, he finally drank that glass after he had filled it again. He drank it.

These are parts of the story that I tried not to forget. He said when he drank it, it went down. He said it went down his throat, and when it got to his stomach, he said he could feel it disperse down there. I tried not to forget the things that he said. He said it dispersed. Then, not giving him another to drink, [the captain] took him outside, holding him by the arm. When he brought him outside, he brought him over to the kitchen. When he brought him over, he told the cook to give him some food, and he had him eat.

He said that the captain watched over him. And he also gave him a room, a place to sleep. He said [the captain] had the cook watch over him, their cook.

He said when he stayed with the cook, he stayed with the cook when he cooked meals. The cook would teach him [English] words, starting with these words that are most common. But he said when he couldn't say them, he became abusive toward him when he tried to get him to say words, and he couldn't. Also when he didn't want to [say words], he became abusive toward him.

One of the times he did that to him, he ran off. When he was beating him, he ran outside. When he ran outside, he slammed his two fingers on a door on the ship. It burst and [his fingers] began to bleed. While he held his hand over the water, being careful not to let it drip on the ship, as he was letting [the blood] drip down as the ship was moving, the captain was apparently watching him from someplace on the ship. He went out and approached him and took [his fingers].

When he asked him what happened, he pointed to the person who had done that to him. When [the captain] went over with [Atertayagaq], he reprimanded the cook without any caution about abusing him. He probably told him not to abuse him, but [Atertayagaq] didn't understand what he said. Then another person bandaged his cuts and took care of them.

Itrucamiu tua-i waten estuulumun aqumellinilutek. Itrucamiu taum kass'am, atam makut cat amuktaqerluki qulqitet putiilekaamek una elliillinill'. Piqerluni tua-i naken cali imkunek *glass*-acuaraagnek elliilliniluni. *Glass*-acuarmek taumek elliilliniluni. Imilliniluku taum *glass*-acuar' taun' mikcuar.

Tua-i imiaku-am umyuartequrlulliniuq. "Waniwa-w' tua-i tuqunarqelriamek piqatallikiinga." Qanertuq waten, "Waniwa-w' tua-i tuqunarqelriamek piqatallikiinga."

Imirraarluku tua-i, yagucaaqekii waten, tunluku, ciuniunritlinia. Ciuniunrilaku-gguq taum wani, taringartelliamiu elliin meraa. Taum *captain*-aam taun' imillni merluku. Mer'amiu tua-i, mer'ani umyuarteqliniur-am, "Tuqunarqeqapiaranritliniuq." [*ngelaq'ertuq*]

"Tuqunarqeqapiaranritliniuq." Nutaan iminqigcaku, mell'iniluku tauna imna *glass*-aq allamek piluku. Mell'iniluku.

Maa-i makut qanengssai avauryaaqevkenaki pillrenka. Mer'ani-gguq tua-i atralria. Atralria-gguq tua-i maaggun igyaraakun, anrutaanun-llu-gguq tua-i tekicami camaa-i tua-i saggluni nallunaunani. Tuaten tua-i qanellri maa-i avauryaaqevkenaki. Saggluni. Nutaan-gguq tua-i aipirivkenaku nutaan anutaa tass'uqluku. Anucamiu amavet kenirvigmun agutelliniluku. Agucamiu-tua-i tauna kenirta piluku, neqkainek nutaan nerevkalliniluku.

Tua-i-gguq murilkelluku elliin taum *captain*-aam. Tua-i-ll' *room*-arkaanek cali cikirluku, qavarvigkaanek. Taumun-gguq tua-i kenirtemun qaunqurtelluku, kenirtiinun taum.

Taum-gguq tua-i kenirtem tamaani aipiraqani, aipaqu'urluku keniraqan tauna, tuantaraaqluni tua-i tauna aipirluku. Ayuqucirtuagaqluku-gguq tua-i qaneryaranek pilaryaaqluku, makunek arcaqalrianek nutaan, waniw' makunek qaneryaranek tauna ciumek. Taugaam-gguq tang aperciigataqaki, nangetruyiyugluku pingnaqevkaraqamiu, tua-i pisciigataqaki. Piyuumiitaqan cali tuaten-am taum pilalliniluku, nangetruyiluku.

Tuatnavakartelluni-am pillrani, qimagarcaaqelliniuq. Nangetruyiini anqerrluni. Anqertellermini imumek amiiganun sun'am ukug' yuarak malruk patuqautelliniuk qerremqaullukek *door*-amun. Qagerrluk' aunrarlutek. Tua-i-gguq unavet sun'amun pillerkaak piluku, tamaavet auni uqlallerkaa qigcikluku, ayallrani tauna unavet mermun kucirtuartellukek piinanrani, naken-gguq tangvalliniluku taum *captain*-aam. Anluni tailuni ullagluku taukuk tegullinilukek.

Tua-i piani tauna ellucira'arluku tauna pisteni tauna. Agngami-gguq malikluku tauna nutaan kenirta tauna wani mulngakevkenaku pillrua taum kenirta tauna nangetruyilallranek. Tuaten pisqevkenaku pillikii tua-i tayima, taringumavkenaku taugaam elliin. Taukuk-llu-gguq tua-i caqulukek allam auluku'urlukek.

They continued sailing up [northward] at that time.

And during the time that he went on the ship, when the people at home wanted to, as I mentioned earlier, they would have that person check on him. And they say when the people at home checked on him, when the people at his hometown asked that person to, after looking in on him, she said she lost sight of him. But she said that his body heat was okay. She said he was with people who he wasn't related to.

That's what Qassayuli evidently said about him. She said that he was okay. But she would say that he was with people who he wasn't related to. That's what they say she said. That's what the person who was watching him from his hometown said.

Then they left. They followed the mountains and went [northward].

One day a ship appeared in the area ahead. When they got to it, they went beyond it and put down [their ship's] sails and anchored. That ship was close by.

When they anchored, after a while, they took out [Atertayagaq's] kayak and brought it down to the water. His kayak had been upside down during that time, since they had stored it upside down. When they brought it down, they motioned for him to get inside. They gave him a piece of paper, a piece of paper like this, asking him to bring it over to the ship over there.

When he brought the piece of paper over, those people let a ladder down again. He went to them. When he got to them, many white people on the ship stood along the side, watching him. They were probably in awe of his kayak, too. While they peered down at him, they gave him various things, cookies. He'd place them here along [the bottom] of his hooded garment, happy for those gifts. They evidently also gave him apples, giving him things that he didn't know about; those people there gave him apples.

After he tied that note [onto a rope] and they lifted it up, not long after, they tied a small box [onto the rope] and let it down. They gave it to him. After untying it, when they motioned for him to go across, he returned to that ship. When he went across, after lifting [that box], they also lifted his kayak. He said his kayak filled with water as the stitches began to open at that time. He spilled the water that had entered [the kayak] through the open sitiches out on the water.

After a while, those people on the ship began to smoke cigars. Apparently, they had let him go and get cigars from that other ship over there. [chuckles] They had him do a chore for them, having him go and get the cigars with that kayak. He said those people began to smoke cigars after that.

After doing that, [the ship] headed up, following [the mountains] again. When they left, they headed up to the area down below, to the mouth of Igyagik [Igiugig] River.

He said that ship had a large load of boards on it. The top of the ship was loaded only with boards, it had a load of wooden boards.

Ayalliniluteng tua-i tamaani tua-i kiatmun tengalrarluteng.

Nutaan cali tua-i tamaani ekluni sun'amun, ukut kingunrin piyungaqamegteggu aug'utun qanllemtun paqcetaqluku taumun. Tauna-gguq-am tua-i taum kingunrin paqtellratni tuani, aptellratni tauna kingunrin taum tangvagtiin uyangqaarluku qanertuq, tamaria-gguq. Taugaam-gguq puqlii canrituq. Ilakumanrilngurnun-gguq ilaruiguyutuq.

Taum tua-i imum' Qassayulim tuaten qanrutekliniluku. Canritniaqluku. Waten taugaam piluni, ilakumanrilngurnun-gguq tua-i ilaruiguyutuq. Tauna tua-i tuaten qanercilaraat. Kingunrin taukut tangvagcetellrat tua-i tauna tuaten pilliniuq.

Nutaan tua-i ayalliniluteng. Pava-i-gguq paugkut ingrit aturluki kiatmun.

Piinanratni amna ciunrat tamakucirtanglliniluni, sun'artanglliniluni. Tekica-megteggu-llu-gguq tua-i yaatiinun imciluni kicarluteng. Yaaqliqluku taun' sun'aq.

Kicaameng tua-i uitaqerluteng anulluku-am qayaa tamana atrartelliniluku. Palungqallrulliniami qayaa tamaani, palurrluku ellilliniatni. Atrarcecamegteggu qayaanun ekesqelluku tua-i elucira'arluku. Kalikarrarmek cikilliniat, waten kalikamek, yaavet agucesqelluku sun'amun yaaqlianun.

Agucamiu tua-i tauna kalikarraq agucatgu taukut-am, ataam imkunek *ladder*-aanek atrarcilliniluteng. Ullagluki tua-i. Tua-i-gguq-am tekicateng makut taum sun'am kass'arugaat makut ceniini nangreskilit, tangvagluku. Irr'ikluku tamana qayaa-llu pillikiit. Tua-i-gguq pikani uyangqallratni canek cikirturluku *cookie*-nek. Qaspellraurluni wavet elliurluki, quyakluki tamakut. *Apple*-aanek tuaten pilalliniluku, nallukengaminek tamakunek; makunek atsanek taukut tua-i cikirtulliniluku.

Tauna tua-i kalikaq qilqaulluku mayurqaarluku tayima uitaqerluni, ak'anun pivkenani, atam yaassicuaraak ukuk qillerrluk' atrartellinikegket. Taillukek tua-i. Angiqaarlukek, agaatmun eluciraraatni ataam tuavet utertelliniluni sun'amun. Agngameng tua-i, agngami ataam taukuk tua-i mayurqaarlukek, qayaa-ll' ma-yurrluku. Imangelliniluni-gguq aivkanglliniani qayaa tamaani. Mermun tua-i tamaa-i imangii kuvqerluku aivkangellran.

Ukut-gguq piqerluteng, tamaani taukut sun'am yui piqerluteng-gguq ukut cikalartunga'artellriit. Cunawa-gguq cikalanek aqvacetlinikiit yaaken sun'amek allamek. [*ngelaq'ertuq*] Kevgaqluku tamaaggun qayaakun, cikalassaagtelluku tuaken. Tua-i cikalartunga'arrluteng-gguq taukut.

Nutaan tua-i pirraarluteng, ayalliniluni kiatmun, aturluki cali. Ayiimeng tua-i yaavet nutaan Igyagim ketiinun painganun tagglliniluteng.

Tamana-gguq tua-i sun'aq tuskanek qaimigluni. Qainga imarluni, tus-karrlainarnek imarluni qainga tamatum tuskarugarnek uciluni, tuskarugarnek.

He said at the mouth of Igiugig, Igyagik, the ship beached along shallow water and couldn't enter the river. The tide no longer came up at that time. They stayed there for quite a while. They waited there for a long time and couldn't leave until the tide started to become higher.

He said that while they were there, when they wanted to leave, they unloaded the top of their cargo onto the surrounding water. He said there were many boards from their cargo afloat around them at that time. He said when their ship finally floated, they returned down to Ugashik [on the Alaska Peninsula], and they anchored down below Ugashik, down below a place called Ugashik. There is a place called Ugashik right down from Igiugig.

When they anchored, they stopped there. After anchoring, the captain put the small boat they used to go up to shore down in the water and went up to shore. When he went up, after being gone for some time, he went down [to the ship]. When he went down and arrived, they put his kayak down on the water. After putting it down in the water, he motioned with his hands for him to go up to shore. It so happened that the captain went to find him a place to stay.

When he went up [to the village], there was a boy in the direction he was heading, as he was paddling up to shore. When he'd turn his kayak a little in another direction, the boy up there would follow him. When he'd turn a little, [the boy] would follow him.

Since he wasn't going to move out of the way, [Atertayagaq] went up to shore toward him. He said it turned out that [boy] was waiting there to meet him. He was evidently the son of their Russian Orthodox priest. When he got there, after pulling his kayak up to shore, [the boy] told him to go to his father's home, to their home. He could evidently speak [in Yup'ik]. Those people could evidently [speak in Yup'ik]. When he led him up, he followed.

The villages outside of our area, because their banks are steep, have a dock that leads up to shore with stairs along the slope of the mountain. That's what the villages outside of our area are like. They have docks that lead up [to the village].

He said when he reached the dock, there were many people. The people of the village were lined up across from one another. They were standing across from each other, waiting for him, watching him, probably curious about his kayak when [the boy] went to get him. He said that they stood across from each other in two rows for him to walk through at that time.

He went up to the village following that boy. While he was going up, among the women who were there, one of them looked at him, she had him stop and looked him over. When she saw his parka, she had him stop and looked at the designs on his parka, his family designs. That woman was apparently his maternal aunt. Through his clothing, the designs . . . Our ancestors didn't just do things any old way. They had their own distinct designs, too. They recognized one another

Tuani-gguq paingani yaani Ikikim, Igyagim paingani etgalqilluni sun'aq iterciigatellruuq. Ulnanriulluku. Tuani uitaqalliniut akaarnun. Akaarnun tua-i ula anglinatkaanun ayagciiganateng.

Tamaani-llu-gguq tua-i uitallermeggni tamakut ucimeng qaingit ayag-yungameng maavet mermun yuularluki tua-i taukut. Amllerrluteng-gguq pug-tangluteng avatiitni tuskat tamakut ilait. Pugtercateng-gguq tua-i nutaan ataam uterrluteng uavet Ugashik. Ugashikaarmiunun ketiitnun kicalliniluteng, uaq-liitnun uavet Ugashikaamun. Ikikigmiut uatiitni Ugashikaartangqertuq nunanek taukunek.

Kicaameng tuavet arulairluteng. Nutaan kicarraarluteng, tauna wani *captain*-aaq tamana tagurassutseng angyacuarteng atrarrluku taggliniuq tayima tauna *captain*-aaq. Tagngami tua-i tayima muluqerraarluni atralliniluni. Atraami teki-cami nutaan qayaa tamana atrartelliniat. Atrarqaarluku elucira'arluku tua-i tagesqelliniluku. Cunawa-gguq ciunerkaanek yuarucartullinikii, uitavigkaanek taum *captain*-aam.

Tua-i tagngami, tagellrani, pingna tan'gaurluq, ciunrani uitalliniuq tagellrani anguarluni. Qaviqaniryaaqaqan maligtaqluku ping'um. Caqiqaniryaaqaqan ma-ligtaqluku.

Tua-i pingaitellinian ciuneqluku taggliniluni. Cunawa-gguq utaqallinikii taum ciuniurnaluku. Cunawa-gguq tauna wani, taukut wani agayulirtiita Kass'alugpiat qetunraqlinikii. Tua-i maa-i tekican, qayaa taman' tagqaarluku pillinia aataminun enemeggnun pisqelluku. Qantulliniluni-gguq. Qantulliniluteng. Tua-i tagucani malikluku.

Augkut atam yaaqliput qertuameng tagyarangqetuut, mayuryararluteng ingrit uvernerit waten. Avani augkut yaaqliput tuaten ayuqelartut. Tagyararluteng.

Tauna-gguq tagyaraat mayuryaraat tekicarturaa, yugugaat. Taum yui taukut akiqliqluteng. Akiqliqluteng utaqalriit, tangvagluk' irr'iluteng tamatum qayaanek pillranek-wa tua-i pillilriit, aqvallrani. Amigpitnilartuq, amigpitellruat-gguq tuani.

Nutaan tua-i tag'uralliniluni taun' malikluku tua-i, taun' maliggluk' tan'gaurluq. Atam piinanrani mayuinanratni, arnat tamakut tamaani uitalriit, iliit atam tangvakallinikii, arulaiqertelliniluk' tangvagluku. Aturai tua-i taukut atkui tangrramiki arulairtelluku tamakut aturain qaralit tamakut tangaallinii, alngai, qaralit. Cunawa-gguq tauna wani anaanii. Taum tamaaggun aturaikun, qaraliikun . . . Makut ciuqliput piciatun piyuitut. Qaraliteng-llu qaraliqluki.

through those [designs]. That's what that person apparently did to him. She knew she was related to him through the designs on his parka. That woman was evidently his maternal aunt. She recognized him through the designs on his parka, although his home was far away.

When [the boy] brought him up [to the village], he went inside that home. That man was apparently the priest of the people of Ugashik. He was a Yup'ik man and he spoke Yup'ik, but he was a priest. They were Russian Orthodox. The captain brought him there after searching; the captain went up to the village and searched for someone who would take good care of him. He brought him to that place.

After he went up to the village, the captain went up again, the captain of that ship. When he went up and went inside, using the priest as an interpreter, the captain asked [Atertayagaq] where he came from. He told him that he came from here in Canineq [the lower Kuskokwim coastal area], from right below the village of Kipnuk.

The captain told him that he would leave him here. He told them that he would have brought him to the Kuskokwim River if that was where he was heading. But since he wasn't heading there, he was going to leave him there [at Ugashik]. He told him to accompany others who were traveling and try to get to his village that way.

When we begin to go seal hunting, we normally go seal hunting in March; we start during that time. We also started in April in those days. That [captain] told him to accompany others who were traveling toward his village and head that way.

Then this is what the captain told him. [The captain] said that before they reached him down on the ocean, they came upon a vessel like his, they saw a kayak just like his. He said the person looked awake, but he didn't move. [The captain said] the man didn't do as [Atertayagaq] did.

He said that when they first saw him, they thought he was an insect [possibly a crab]. He said they saw a kayak exactly like his. But he said because the person inside didn't move, they left him. He said he had a kayak like his. [Atertayagaq] apparently wasn't alone at that time. That's what [Atertayagaq] mentioned when he spoke.

Then he said to him that since [Atertaygaq] moved, they stopped and took him. He said that they passed by the other kayak just like his, passing not far from him. He said although that person looked awake, he said he didn't move. They thought that he died of dehydration.

From that time on, he went up toward his home by accompanying others who were traveling. Then . . . oh my, [I missed a part]. At that time, that priest . . . he said that was the first time he had seen a priest, before there were any [missionaries] out on the coast. And since that person was evidently a priest, the Russian Orthodox priest baptized him.

Tamaaggun elitaqutaqluteng. Taum-am tua-i tuaten pilliniluku. Qaraliikun cakucia nalluvkenaku atkuikun tauna. Cunawa-gguq tua-i tauna anaanaklinikii elliin. Taukutgun qaraliikun taum elitaqluku atkuin, yaaqsingraan kingunra amna.

Nutaan tua-i tagucani tuavet enemun itliniuq. Tauna wani agayulirteklinikiit-gguq taukut Ugashikaarmiut. Tua-i-w' qantuluni yuuluni, agayulirtenguluni taugaam. Kass'alugpiaruluteng. Tuavet tua-i ciuniutelliniluku taum tua-i *captain*-aam yuarluni; elluarrluni pistekaanek-am tagluni yualliniluni tua-i tauna *captain*-aaq. Tuavet tua-i ciuniutelliniluku.

Nutaan tua-i tagenrakun tauna nutaan *captain*-aaq taggliniuq ataam, sun'am tamatum *captain*-aara. Tagngami itrami tauna nutaan agayulirta tauna tua-i uitavia qanertekluku apqaullinia taum *captain*-aam, naken pillrucianek. Tua-i nalqigtelliniluku maaken Caninermek, avaken Qipnermiut ketiitnek pillruniluni.

Pillinia taum *captain*-aam tua-i wavet yuuqatarniluku. Maavet taikuni Kusquqvagmun piyaryaaqniluku. Taugaam pinrilami tua-i tuavet yuuqatarniluku. Tuaken ayagluku tua-i maligaruqurluku kingunranun tekitengnaquraasqelluku maligarutaqluku.

Tua-i tayima qaillun, uksumi qamigangaqamta March-aam nuniini qami-ganglalriakut; tamatum nalliini ayagnirluta. Tamatum tua-i April-aam-llu nu-niini pilalriakut avani. Taum tua-i pillinia, maligaruqurluku pisqelluku tuaten kingunranun ayagturaasqelluku.

Nutaan pillinia taum *captain*-aam. Unani-gguq tekipailegmi uatiini un'gani tuaten assigtiitun ayuqellriamek tekicaaqut, tangellruyaaqut cali elliitun tamatutun qayaatun ayuqelriamek. Tauna-gguq yua maktangacaaquq, pektenrituq-gguq. Elliitun-gguq pinrituq.

Ellii-gguq piqarraallrani ciissiuyuksaaqaat. Tuaten-gguq ayuqeqapiaralriamek qayaatun assigtiitun tangerrsaaqellruut. Tauna-gguq taugaam yua uitiin ilang-cillrunritaat. Tuaten tua-i qayaan ayuqiinek. Kiimetellrunicaaqelliniluni tamaani. Taumek tua-i qanertuq, qanllermini qanellruuq.

Nutaan tua-i pillinia aug'utun taum, ellii tua-i pekcan tua-i arulairulluku tegullruniluku taukut tuaten. Tauna-gguq tua-i elliitun tamana qayaq yaataillruat yaaqsigpek'naku. Tauna-gguq yua maktangacaaqellriim, pektaituq-gguq taugaam. Quligyukluku piluku, piunriryukluku tuaten.

Nutaan tua-i tuaken ayagluni, tuaken ayagluni kiatmun uterquralliniuq maligarutaqluni. Tua-i-am . . . arenqia. Tuani tua-i taum agayulirtem . . . nutaan-gguq agayulirtemek-llu tangerrluni tamaani, tamaani catangvailgan unegna. Taum-llu tua-i agayulirtengulliniami angllurcetliniluku tuani taum agayulirtem, Kass'alugpiam.

When he baptized him, he named him. When he baptized him, he called him Isaac, Ishaak, Qiatuaq, Atertayagaq. He mentioned those names. Isaac, Ishaak, Qiatuaq, Atertayagaq. He gave him four names. The name Ishaak is probably a Russian Orthodox name, Isaac. That's what he said. He said he named him Ishaak. That's how that [priest] baptized him.

He finally learned that there was a [Christian] God at that time. Well, he learned about priests for the first time at that time. At that time, there were no missionaries in the coastal area. He [drifted away] during a time when there were no priests.

They say after that person baptized him, he continued to travel [home]. But he said that sometimes the people he stayed with would be troublesome. But he said that those people including those who were drinking alcohol never touched him.

Those people didn't touch him. Although he was among people who were intoxicated and fighting, he said that those people never laid a hand on him.

And he said at one time, he witnessed a murder that took place among people who were intoxicated. He said those people never laid a hand on him. They didn't do anything to him.

Those are the things that he told in his story. He said that he returned home by traveling little by little. He would accompany others who were traveling and gradually traveled from that place like the captain had told him to.

He drifted away during winter, spring. And summer came. Then he came this way little by little accompanying other travelers. And he even accompanied other travelers during winter. He continued to travel by accompanying others like [the captain] had told him to do.

Winter came, and then it was spring. He evidently arrived in Goodnews Bay in early summer. Then he arrived in Quinhagak when the king salmon [run began]. This is what he said. He said he arrived in Quinhagak just as the king salmon run started, just as they began fishing for king salmon.

From there, from Quinhagak across there, they brought him downriver to Papegmiut, to Nunapigmiut from Quinhagak. His family was up at Keggukar.

When he arrived, one of the fishermen yelled from downriver that Atertayagaq had arrived. He said [Atertayagaq] had arrived.

They passed the message upriver, reaching Keggukar. They say his poor family was initially happy and excited about the news they heard from someone downriver, but they said after a moment of joy, "You've probably heard wrong. Don't react." His family thought he was someone else because they thought the person [who had passed the message] had heard wrong.

He finally arrived there among his family in summer during the king salmon run to Keggukar downriver.

Angllurcecamiu-gguq aciraa. Waten angllurcetlermini pillinia, angllurce-camiu-llu-gguq acirluku Isaac, Ishaak, Qiatuaq, Atertayagaq. Taukut aperluki. Isaac, Ishaak, Qiatuaq, Atertayagaq. *Four*-aanek. Ishaak-wa Kass'alugpiartaullilria ateq tua-i, Isaac-aam pia. Tuaten qanellruuq. Ishaagmek. Taum tua-i angllurtelluku tuaten.

Nutaan tua-i elliin Agayucetangqerrucia nallunrirluku. Tua-i-w' agayulirtet nu-taan nallunrirluki. Tamaa-i cataunani unegna, agayulirtetaunani. Agayulirtetang-vailgan piluni.

Nutaan-gguq tuani taum angllurcecani tua-i kinguakun ayagturtuq. Taugaam-gguq tua-i iliini ciunri, ciunrin iliini uitavia, tua-i-wa pinerrlugtaqluteng pi-laryaaqut. Taugaam-gguq ellii wani agturaksaitaat, tamakut-llu taangiqellriit.

Agturaksaitaat tamakut. Taangiqellrianun callulrianun-llu pilangermi, agtu-yuunaku-gguq ellii.

Caqerluni-llu-gguq tua-i tuqucilrianun tamaani tangvagyaaqluni taukunek taangiqellrianek. Tamakut-gguq agtuqsaitaat. Piksaitaat.

Tua-i tamakunek tamaa-i qanengssagluni. Tua-i-gguq wani ayakaniqaqluni. Maligarulluni ayakaniqaqluni tuaken taum pillruciatun *captain*-aam.

Uksumi, up'nerkami ayagluni, aterrluku. Kiagluku-llu. Tua-i-ll' taigurluni, taiguralliniluni maligarutaqluni. Tua-i uksuan-llu cali maligarutaqluni. Ayagtu-ralliniuq tuaten maligarutaqluni, taum qanruyuciatun.

Tua-i uksurluni, up'nerkarluni-llu. Ikavet Goodnews-amun wani tekitelliniluni kiakarluku. Tua-i-ll' wavet Kuinerramun tekitelliniluni nutaan taryaqviit [tuc'ata]. Waten-wam' qanelria. Taryaqviit tut'eqertelluki Kuinerramun tuavet tekitelliniluni, taryaqvagnek neqsuqertelluki.

Nutaan tuaken, nutaan tuaken Kuinerramek ikaken uavet Papegmun, Nunapigmiunun uavet taitelliniluku, tuaken Kuinerramek. Ilai tuanlluteng kiani Keggukarmi.

Tuani tua-i tekitellrani iliit qayagpalliniuq uaken kuvyalriit, Atertayagaq tekitniluku. Tua-i-w' tauna tekitniluku.

Ayagcetaat-gguq kiatmun Keggukar tekilluku. Taukut-gguq tua-i ilaurluin, iliit qanerniluku cakmaken tauna piluku, ilai tua-i ukut ilai quyaqeryaaqerraarluteng pilliniut, "Niitecurlalliuci. Uitaci." Ilain taukut kingunrin allauyukluku, ta-ringecurlagyukluku pillratni.

Nutaan tua-i taun' tekitelliniluni tuavet kingunerminun kiagmi taryaqviit nalliitni tuavet Keggukarmun uavet.

They say when he arrived, he didn't tell this part of the story himself. They had him briefly take Qassayuli, who had watched over him, as a wife. Not long after they got a divorce. [*laughs*] He evidently left her probably because he didn't want [to be married to] Qassayuli. [*laughs*]

That's what they said about him; that's what someone said about him.

He had just arrived at that time. After being married to her briefly, he probably left her. After that, when he was able, he married his first wife.

The [first] missionaries evidently arrived here [at that time]. I think Atertayagaq was one of the first lay pastors.

George Billy: Yes. I used to see him once in a while down there when the first [lay pastors] would gather down there.

John Phillip: He was evidently among the first group of lay pastors to be ordained. Atertayagaq was evidently one of the first Moravian lay pastors to be ordained. When they ordained him as a lay pastor, he first learned about the teachings of the Bible during that time.

They evidently placed him across there in Quinhagak. Finally when he went down to Quinhagak, before he began his work, before he used the church where he would minister, when they made him into a lay pastor and assigned him there — let me tell the entire story. When they assigned him as a lay pastor there, before he used that church, he went to look at it before he spoke inside it.

He went in through that door, through the church's doorway. When he went inside, he appeared through the door and saw the two pictures across from one another. They looked like the two [pictures] he had seen in his dream just before he went seal hunting with his kayak. He had evidently seen the two pictures of Jesus [in his dream]. He had seen Jesus' picture for the first time when he was about to become a lay pastor and learned that it was [Jesus'] picture. Those two pictures that he had seen before he went seal hunting, he said those two were located in their original place. And the inside of that place resembled what he saw in his dream.

You see. Although he didn't know what was to come in his future, he was meant to reach that time in his life. And although there hadn't been a [Christian] God before, they had learned about God at that time. He [had that dream] because he would evidently reach that time [and experience].

He recognized those two [pictures] that he had dreamed of right before he went seal hunting, before he left to the ocean. Since he was destined to reach the time in his life where he would see those two [pictures], although he experienced tragedy and suffering down on the ocean, he was destined to live the part of his life that was shown to him in his dream.

Like I said, if I forget to tell parts of the story, Anguteka'ar [Roland Phillip] will probably be able to tell the story, if I forget some of what [Atertayagaq] said. But

Tua-i-gguq tauna wani tekican, ellminek qanemcikenricaaquq. Tauna im' tangvagcetellrat Qassayuli nulirqeqercetellruat. Ak'anun pivkenani *divorce*. [*ngelaq'ertuq*] Unitelliniluku Qassayuliryuumiitelliami. [*ngel'artuq*]

Tuaten tua-i qanrutkaat; qanrutkaa aug'um qanemcia.

Tua-i nutaan tekilluni tamaani pilliniluni. Tua-i nulirqeqarraarluk' tua-i unitellikii. Kinguani nutaan tamatum piyugngariami tua-i, nuliangluni-llu aug'umek ciuqlirmek nuliallerminek kassuulluni.

Imkut *missionary*-t maavet tekitellrulliniut avani ciuqliit. Ellii tauna ilakngataat tuyut ciuqliit Atertayagaq.

Nacailnguq: Yaa. Tangerqatullruaqa kanani ciuqliit quyurtaqata.

Ayagina'ar: Ciuqliit tuyulilriit ilakellrulliniat. Ilakellrulliniat tuyulilriit taukut, ukut Moravian-aat Atertayagaq. Tuyuliatni tua-i tamaani nutaan nallunrirluku man'a qaneryaraq.

Ikavet Kuinerramun ellilliniat yaavet. Kuinerramun tua-i anelraami nutaan, tuani pivailegmi, nutaan tauna agayuvik atu'urkani aturpailegmiu, elliatni tuavet, tuyuurcatni, *lay pastor*-aarurcatni . . . tamalkuan piluku piqerlaku. Tuyuurcatni tua-vet, aturpailegmiu taun' agayuvik paqtellinia aturpailegmiu, qalarpailegmi iluani.

Itliniluni tuaggun amigkun, amiigakun agayuviim. Itrami puggliniuq, imkuk ukuk tarenrak akiqliqlutek. Qamigaqatarluni qayarluni qavangullerminek, taukugtun ayuqlutek. Jesus-aam tarenrakek taukuk tangellrullinilukek. Cau-cingluku nutaan tarenraa Jesus-aam tamaani tuyuurtellerminek ayagnirluni. Imkuk taukuk qamigaqatarluni, tuani-gguq enemegni uitalutek taukuk. Tamana-llu-gguq tuaten tamatutun qavangullratun ayuqluni ilua.

Tang. Tamaa-i waten taum tekitarkani nallungermiu tamana tekitarkaulliniluku. Agayutaitellrung'ermi-llu Agayutengluni. Tekitarkaulliniamiu pillrulliniuq.

Tuaten tua-i taukuk elitaqa'artellrulliniak tamaani qamigaqatarluni taukuk qavangullregni, ayagnirpailegmi, ayagpailegmi imarpigmun. Taukuk tua-i tekitar-kagni tekitarkaulliniamikek, unani wani arenqiallugnaq nangteqnaq-llu atunger-miu tauna tua-i qavangullni tuavet ek'arkaullinian piluku.

Aug'utun tua-i ava-i ilii katakumku Angutekaraam piyugngaciqsaaqaa tayima, katagikuma qanellran iliitnek tayima. Taugaam tua-i aug'utun ava-i pitaluku

that's how long the story was that I heard. The church was quiet in Kwigillingok when he gave his testimony. But he sang a song when he finished telling the story. I brought the song that he sang with me, the song that he sang when he finished telling his story.

He sang that song last when he gave his testimony. It's inside [that songbook].

We should end with that [song] if Anguteka'ar has nothing to say. Speak if you have something to say.

Roland Phillip: Before you sing the song, I know his story. Two months and half of the third month; it's a long period of time. But like I said earlier, those who experienced hardship and tragedy cannot tell their entire experience, but just a small part of it. If he had told his entire experience, we two probably would be talking all day. Only a few experiences are told. [John Phillip] told the story like I heard it. I cannot add to it. He told the story like I heard.

But [I'm now going to include this], even though it's not part of that story. We young men, when we were young men we were instructed. And that person [Atertayagaq] was also instructed like us. He was probably given more instructions than us when he was young. And we, too, were instructed, and before we went down to the ocean, before we hunted. And since we were given instructions up to that time in our lives, we recognized the instructions that we were given from our instructors [as we experienced them]. We recognized what we heard about the ocean being a joyous place, how it's a dangerous place, and how the currents vary, and [what to do] when a large amount of ice accumulates; we recognized those things that they mentioned as we experienced them.

This is also what I heard about Atertayagaq out in the general public. They say while he was there . . . This is what I heard, what he said out in public and not in church, the following that he said, that he mentioned.

He said while he was down on the ocean and faced tragedy there, he said those experiences are all in his mind and he cannot speak of them. But we had those woven grass bags, *issratet*. Our provisions were inside those woven grass bags in the past. And I had one, too. Things that I needed to use were stored inside those. It wasn't a box container. Things that I needed to use, my bullets, my provision, and other things were stored inside there.

This is what Atertayagaq said about [the grass storage bag]. He said while he was there on the ocean, the instructions that he was given before he experienced being on the ocean, his [instructions] were inside that grass storage bag. He said when he came upon a certain obstacle, he would take that *qanruyun* and use it, the one in his mind. . . . You know the mind, for you, for all of us, the things that are in our heads, the things that we have not forgotten are here in our minds. We will not lose them, we will always recall them.

niicugnillruaqa. Nepaitellruuq agayuvik *testimony*-llrani Kuigilngurmi. Taugaam atullruuq yuarutmek taqlermini. Malikaqa tayima augna yuarun atullra, atullra tuani taqlermini.

Tauna nangneqluku atullrua tuani *testimony*-llermini. Taum iluani uitauq.

Nangenruluku wani qanerkailkan Anguteka'ar. Qanerkangqerquvet qanerluten.

Anguteka'ar: Aturpailegpet tua-i augna ava-i nallunritaqa qanemcia augna. Ava-i tua-i iraluk malruk pingayuak avguluku; amllertuq taum ilua. Taugaam tua-i ava-i qanellrucimtun watua, tamakut arenqiallugtellriit ayuqucillerteng tamalkuan qanemcikesciigataat, carraq taugaam. Tamalkuan qanemcikekaku ayuqucini taum wani tua-i ernerpak tayima qanrumayartukuk. Carraat taugaam augkut tua-i ava-i qanrutkumaut. Tua-i niitellemtun ava-i qanemcikaa. Ilasciiganaku. Niitellemtun qanrutkaa.

Taugaam waniwa aug'um ilakenrilengraaku. Wangkuta tan'gaurlurni, tan'gaurlurni, tan'gaurluullemteni ayuqucirtuumallruukut. Tua-i-llu tauna cali ayuqucirtuumaluni wangkucicetun. Amllenrulriamek tayima pillrullilria tauna ayuqucirtuutmek ayagyuarluni. Wangkuta-llu tua-i ayuqucirtuumaluta, imarpigmun-llu unavet pivailemta, pingnatugpailemta. Tamana-llu tekilluku piamta imkut qanruyutek'lallrit elitaqu'urluki qanrucestek'lallemta. Elitaqaqluki imarpiim nunanirqucia, alingnarqucia, carvanret-llu ayuqenriluciat, ciku-ll' amllerraqan; tamakut qanrutkelallrit elitaqluki, elitaqaqluki.

Tua-i tauna waten cailkami cali niigartellruaqa Atertayagaq. Tamaantellermini-gguq . . . Ava-i niigartelqa wiinga, elliin qanellra agayuviunrilngurmi, waten taugaam qanellra, qanrutkellra.

Tua-i-gguq tamaantellermini imarpigmi, arenqiallugtellermini tamaani, tua-i umyuamini, umyuamini uitaniluki qanrutkenritai. Taugaam augkunek tupi-ganek issratengqelallruukut. Cat tua-i ekumaaqluteng taquaput avani canegni tupigarni. Wiinga-ll' pingqellrulrianga. Tua-i aturyuk'nganka tuani uitaaqluteng. Yaassiiguvkenateng. Aturyuk'nganka, imanka, taquanka, allat-llu cali tuani uitaluteng.

Taum Atertayagaam waten qanrutkaa. Tua-i-gguq tamaantellermini, imarpigmetlermini, imkut qanruyutek'lallni, aturpailegmiu imarpik, issratem-gguq taum iluani, iluani uitaluteng. Camun-gguq tekitaqami, tauna-gguq teguluku aturaqluku qanruyun, umyuamini. . . . Iciw' tua-i una umyuaq elpet, tamalkumta, cat umyuarteqelput, nalluyagutenritelput, wantut umyuamteni. Pikenrirngaunaki, wangkuta tua-i neqaumaarkauluki.

And I've said the following in the past, I've mentioned it many times. My mind, when I come upon a situation, my mind admonishes me. My mind cautions me. I recall the *qanruyun* that I was given and refrain from acting, not following and taking part in it.

But my other mind also tells me to do this. My mind tells me what to do. This is what [those instructions] apparently are, "Help a person who is in need and do not ignore him. Do a chore that needs to be done at home. If it needs to be dumped, go and spill it out, even if you hadn't heard anyone tell you to do it." Those good [instructions] are there [inside my mind]. Those good [instructions].

But these bad things, the teaching that if my fellow has committed a wrongdoing against me, [my mind] cautions me not to repay him. That is what that person, Isaac, Ishaak, Qiatuaq, Atertayagaq said. He said the *qanruyutet* that he heard were inside that grass storage bag. And he said that when he got to a certain situation, he would just take it [from the storage bag] and use it. That's what that is. What [John Phillip] talked about is good starting from that point.

And now what [John Phillip] mentioned when he just started telling the story. [Atertayagaq] knew that he wouldn't be capable if he got wet, he just went back to that place where he would be safe.

For us young men, in other situations besides that, when the conditions were potentially unsafe, we avoided things that they instructed us about. We knew when something was potentially unsafe, and we knew it, we tried not to take part in it. That's what they are like.

What [John Phillip] talked about is good. And like I said, if [Atertayagaq] had told the story about his entire journey, we would talk all day. And we probably wouldn't finish the story today. Yes, okay, that's it.

John Phillip: We should all sing this song; you two should join me. You two know it. I want you to help me as I won't be able to sing one section. This song.

George Billy: [Atertayagaq] has a song. When the first lay pastors started their work down on the coast, he sang it a number of times, and I heard him sing. Thank you so much. A person who knows his story [has brought it up], and I, too, heard the story, as stories become clearer [when told]. This is a song I used to hear, and his daughter always sang it after he passed on. Are we going to sing it now?

John Phillip: Yes, we're going to sing it. Anguteka'ar [Roland] can join us.

He sang this song when he finished [telling his story]. [The title of the song is] When I feel desperate, Christ is here.

Roland Phillip: Okay now.

John Phillip, George Billy, and Roland Phillip:
When I am desperate, Christ is here.
And although temptation is around, he holds me fast.
He is holding me. He is holding me. My Savior loves me so. He is holding me.

Waten-llu waniw' wiinga qanlalrianga, amllerqunek qanrutkelaqeka. Um-yuama, camun tekitaqama, umyuama inerqularaanga. Umyuama inerqularaanga. Imna tua-i qanruyutek'lalqa neq'erluku, uitalua-llu maligtevkenaku tauna.

Taugken umyuama cali aipaan ellimerturaqlua waten pisqellua. Umyuama ellimerturlua. Makuulliniluteng iciw', "Ikayurnarqelria yuk tangrrinarpek'naku ikayuqiu. Kevgiuqina ca tangerquvgu enem iluani. Ciqitnarqekan ciqiskiu qanel-riamek niitenrilngerpet." Tamakut uitaluteng assilriit. Assilriit.

Taugken imkut makut assiitellriit, ilama qaillun pingraanga tauna akisqevke-naku inerqurlua. Tamaa-i tamakut taum Issac, Ishaam, Qiatuam, Atertayagaam tuaten qanrutkaa. Imkut-gguq niitellni qanruyutet taum issratem iluani. Tua-i-llu-gguq tamaavet tekicami tauna teguqerluku aturluku. Tamaa-i tamana. Assirtut augkut ava-i qanrutkurallri tuaken ayagluni.

Tua-i-llu augna ayagnillermini, ayagnillermini ava-i qanrutkellrua. Tua-i elliin nalluvkenaku elluatuungailami mecungekuni, tua-i taugaam tamaavet pinru-llerkaminun tua-i ataam piluni.

Tua-i makut wangkuta tan'gaurlurni-llu, ca taungunrilengraan, piyunai-teqataqan, qanrutkelallrit avitaput, avitelaraput. Atuyunaiteqatarqan nalluvkenaku tua-i, pingnaqeksaunata. Tuaten ayuqut.

Tua-i augna ava-i, assirtut qanrutkurallri augkut tua-i. Qanrucimtun-llu taum qanellri qanemciku'urluku tamalkuan ayallni pikuniu ernerpak qanrumayartukut. Nangucanritliukut-llu mat'umi ernermi. Ii-i, kitaki, tua-i.

Ayagina'ar: Una tamalkumta aturluku; elpetek ilagarlua piniartutek. Nallun-ritartek. Atauciq una wani pisciigaciiqngamku piunga. Una wani yuarun.

Nacailnguq: Yuarutengqertuq. Tuyut unani piqarraallratni atulallrua qav-cirqunek, wiinga-llu niicugniluku. Quyanaqvaa. Tua-i-am waniw' nallunricestii, wiinga-ll' niitaqluku qalamcillra, qalamci man'a, taringnaritulliniameng. Waniw' una niitetulqa, panian-llu catairucan aturturatullrua. Waniw' atuqatararpuk-qaa?

Ayagina'ar: Ii-i, atuqatararput. Ilagarniaraakuk Angutekaraam.
Uumek wani taqlermini atullruuq. Nanikuagaqama wii wantuq kristussaaq.

Anguteka'ar: Kitaki.

Ayagina'ar, Nacailnguq, Anguteka'ar-llu:
Nanikuagaqama wii, wantuq Kristussaaq.
Picetaarun-llu pektengraan, tegumiaqaangaa.
Tegumiaqaanga. Tegumiaqaanga. Anirturtem Kenkaanga. Tegumiaqaanga.

Because my faith is weak, I hope he holds me.
And because my love is not enough, he holds me fast.
He is holding me. He is holding me. My Savior loves me so. He is holding me.

In his sight, I am someone precious. He will hold me fast.
He is happy for those he saved. He will hold me fast.
He is holding me. He is holding me. My Savior loves me so. He is holding me.

He won't let me get lost. He is holding me.
He has bled for me. He will hold me fast.
He is holding me. He is holding me. My Savior loves me so. He is holding me.[13]

George Billy: The last verse hits the message perfectly. That song that was just sung, when the lay pastors first started ministering down there. . . . They are all gone now; all the first lay pastors I used to see are all gone now. They spoke only in Yup'ik. They were mainly elders.

Based on what [John Phillip] briefly mentioned, I recalled some parts of the story earlier. Since the person who knows the story has told the story, we two [Roland Phillip and I] know the story. We used to hear it in the past.

Stories are told for a good purpose. It is no wonder when people told stories in the *qasgi* in the past, when we imagined what they were like in our minds in the past before there were white people around, they would speak for some time about good teachings, about things that we would encounter in our future.

Pinialan wii ukveka, tegumiaqlia-tuq.
Kenkutka-llu ikgelan, tegumiaqaanga.
Tegumiaqaanga. Tegumiaqaanga. Anirturtem Kenkaanga. Tegumiaqaanga.

Qununarqua takuani. Tegumiaqnauraanga.
Anirtullni angniutekai. Tegumiaqnauraanga.
Tegumiaqaanga. Tegumiaqaanga. Anirturtem Kenkaanga. Tegumiaqaanga.

Tamaumavkarngaitaanga. Tegumiaqnganga.
Aunrautekaanga elliin. Tegumiaqnauraanga.
Tegumiaqaanga. Tegumiaqaanga. Anirturtem Kenkanga. Tegumiaqaanga.

Nacailnguq: Nangnermi nall'artuq. Augna ava-i yuarun, tuyut kanani piqarraallratni. . . . Tayima nang'ut; tamarmeng nang'ut tangtullrenka tuyuu-
qerraallret. Yugturrlainaq qantuluteng. Ciulirnerpalluullruut.

Tua-llu waniwa mat'umek maa-i qanqallermini, ava-i elitaqiuranka ilait.
Waniwaurlur'-am una tua-i waniwa nallunricestii qalamcian, waniwa-ll' wangkuk
nalluvkenaku. Niitetullruluku.

Man'a cali qalamci assilriamek kangingq[ertuq]. Anirtim' augkut-llu qasgimi piaqameng, qalamciurarqata, tangrruarturaurlurqamteki augkut, kass'ar-
tangvailgan, mat'umek maa-i alerquutmek assilriamek qalarquraqatuut, te-
kitarkamtenek.

GRANDMOTHER AND GRANDCHILD

– *Grandmother and Grandchild* –

Elsie Tommy and Marie Meade, Anchorage, June 1992

Marie Meade: Do you know any other authentic legends?

Elsie Tommy: I do know an authentic *quliraq,* but I think I have forgotten part of the story. I think I may forget part of it.

Grandmother and grandchild along a river, along a little river, they lived there.

Again and again she had told her grandchild, "Down at the mouth of our river, *angu, angu* [no, no], without stopping there you must go by it when you travel."

Then since her grandchild couldn't speak when he was hunting with his bow and arrow, he suddenly realized that he had come to the mouth of their river.

Then instantly he was subdued with fear. "My grandmother has told me not to come to this place. If my grandmother hears my voice perhaps she will help me."

Then after he was there for a while, he went down to the sandy beach. He started walking up calling his grandmother, [singing].

My grandmother *iyarrarayaa*
My grandmother *iyarrarayaa*
Give me your wooden bowl
Give me your wooden bowl
And I will repay you with *?eqnermek eqnermek.* [*chuckles*]

He walked up singing the song, singing about his grandmother.

Then when he arrived at the place where his grandmother was staying, he stopped and called her,

"Grandmother-r-r-r! Granmother-r-r-r!"

His grandmother did not reply.

ANUURLUQELRIIK

◆ *Anuurluqelriik* ◆

Nanugaq Arnaq-llu, Anchorage, June 1992

Arnaq: Qulirapianek-qaa allanek nallunrituten?

Nanugaq: Qulirapiamek-wa tua-i qulirarrangqerrsaaqelrianga, taugaam ilii nalluyagusngataqa. Nalluyaguciiqngataqa.

Anuurluqelriik kuigem ceniini, kuilqurraam ceniini uitalutek.

Tua-ll' tauna tutgarani qanrutliniaqekii, "Kuimegnuk paingani uani, angu, angu, arulaiqsaunak caqcaararqavet kitulaqiu arulairvikevkenaku."

Tua-i-ll'-am qanerciigalami tauna tutgarii piteggniallermini-am tua-i, maaten-gguq tang ellanguq tauna kuimek painga tekitellinikii.

Alingallalliniluni. "Anuurluma-ggem wavet tekitesqessuitaanga. Anuurluma-wa erinaka niiskuniu ikayurciqlikiinga."

Tua-llu-gguq tuani tua-i pirraarluni, atrarluni qaugyam qainganun. Itralliniuq anuurluni tuqluraurturluku, [aturluni].

Anuurluma iyarrarayaa
Anuurluma iyarrarayaa.
Qantarrlugaan taiyarru
Qantarrlugaan taiyarru
Nunulirniamken eqnermek eqnermek. [*ngelaq'ertuq*]

Tuaten-am tua-i aturturlun' itralliniluni tua-i anuurluni yuarutekluku.

Tua-i-ll' tauna anuurlumi nallii tekicamiu arulairluni qayagaullinia,

"Anuurluu! Anuurluu!"

Angeryugpek'naku-gguq anuurluan.

211

Then he came farther up.

"Grandmother-r-r-r! Grandmother-r-r-r!"

She didn't answer him.

On the third try he called loudly, "Grandmother-r-r-r, give me your wooden bowl *?eqnermek, eqnermek*." [*chuckle*]

At the end of his call his grandmother replied, "*Aa-a*. I wonder who will help you. You cannot speak. Continue on through that [path] there."

His grandmother told him to do that.

He couldn't get up onto the land up there, but he only remained on the sand.

He traveled up the river, he went up.

He spoke to one of the gulls gliding up there,

"Hey you gull up there, would you help poor old me. My grandmother is not assisting me. I'll reward you with . . . (What was it that he offered as a reward?) I'll reward you a *qauqauqau*."

Then the gull, flapping its wings and looking down at him, said to him,

"You are not going to reward me with the call *qauqauqau* we [gulls] make."

Since it had refused to accept his offer he continued on. As he went along, was it when he heard a long-tailed duck, he called to it:

"You old *aarraangiiq* [long-tailed duck], you awful long-tailed duck, would you help poor old me. I'll grant you an *aarraangiiq*."

Then the long-tailed duck swimming in the usual fashion said to him . . . (What was it again the long-tailed duck had called him?)

"*Quuqeqniiq*, who would possibly reward you when you have belittled me." [*chuckle*]

Again it just ignored him.

He continued to travel along since it had not helped him. As he was going along up ahead there was something swimming in the water. When he got closer he noticed it was a little muskrat.

"Hey, little old muskrat, would you help poor old me."

Little muskrat quickly turned its head toward him.

(They've mentioned the reward he offered. I guess I don't have to say what reward he offered.)

Little muskrat said, "*Aa-a. Quuquuquu. Quuquuquu* will not match me. *Quuquu, quuquuquu*."

After saying that to him, muskrat left him.

And then he suddenly fell on his bottom on the sand. When he fell he cried out, "*Aa-a. Aa-a. Aatatatata*." [*chuckle*]

That was the way he cried out.

Nugkanilliniur-am.

"Anuurluu! Anuurluu!"

Tuamtell' kiunritlinia.

Pingayiriami qayagpalliniuq, "Anuurlu-u-u, qantarrlugaan taiyarru eqnermek, eqnermek." [*ngelaq'ertuq*]

Anuurluan-gguq taq'ercan kiugaa, "Aa-a. Kia-kiq tua-i ikayurniartaten. Qanerciigatuten. Tamaaggun ayii."

Tua-i-gguq anuurluan tua-i tuaten qanrulluku.

Tua-i-gguq pagaavet nunam qainganun nugesciiganani, qaugyam taugaam maavet qainganun.

Tua-i itralliniluni, itrarluni.

Naruyat tengaulriit pagaavet uputellinii,

"Naruyaaq pagsuuq, ikayuqaurluqernga. Anuurluma tang ikayunrilkiinga. Nunulirniamken . . . (Cameg' ima tam' nunuliryukii?) Nunulirniamken qauqau-qaamek."

Tua-llu-gguq taum naruyam, kanaviarlun' yaqiurturlun' tuaten pillinia,

"Qalriucimtenek nunulirngaitarpenga qauqauqaamek."

Tua-i-am niitenrilani ayalliniluni. Ayainanermini-am tua-i allgiarmek-qaa niicami tuqullinia:

"Aarraangiilleraaq, aarraangiilleraaq, ikayuqaurluqernga. Nunulirniamken aarraangiimek."

Tua-ll'-am aarraangiim [allgiaraam] imumek kuimarluni tuaten piqallinia . . . (Kitumek imat'anem tauna allgiarmun tuqlurnillrukiit?)

"Quuqeqniiq, kia-kiq tua-i nunulirniartaten caunrilkellua arivakevnga." [*ngelaq'ertuq*]

Tua-llu-ggur-am ilangcivkenaku uitalluk' tayima.

Tua-i-am ayalliniluni tua-i ikayunrilani tua-i. Ayainanermini tuallitua kuimal-riartanglliniuq ciunra. Elitaqnariuq-gguq maaten kanaqlayagaq.

"Kanaqlaarrluar usuuq, ikayuqaurluqaqernga."

Takuyaartellinia kanaqlaarrluaraam.

(Cameg-am nunulirniluk' piyaaqaat. Tua-i taun' nunuliutii qanrutkenrileng-ramku.)

Kanaqlaarrluar pilliniuq, "Aa-a. Quuquuquumek-kiq tua-i. Quuquuquuq-wa ayuqengailkeka wiinga. Quuquumek, quuquuquu."

Kanaqliim-am tuaten tua-i tuqluqarraarluku unitellinia.

Tua-i-llu-gguq tauna imna aqumkallalliniluni qaugyam qainganun. Aqumka-lliimi qalrillalliniluni, "Aa-a. Aa-a. Aatatatatata." [*ngelaq'ertuq*]

Tua-i-gguq qiaguq.

❧ *One Who Changed the Weather* ❧

Lucy Inakak, Tununak, May 1976

Lucy Inakak: I will [tell a story] although it's short.

There were once a grandmother and grandchild living along a river. Their river flowed out to the ocean. Her grandchild was a boy.

When fall came, they would do things, and her grandchild would hunt birds and hunt caribou.

Then one day, it started to rain, there was a very heavy rain.

Above his grandmother was a hanging drum.

Then her grandchild said to her, "Grandmother, what purpose does that drum have that it hangs behind you?"

Then she said to her grandchild, "It's just hanging here for no reason."

"Hurry and try to change the weather."

When [her grandchild] *?kasngupakaani,* she attempted to change the weather.

"Okay then, since you're pleading with me, let me know right away when the visibility gets good." He agreed.

Then she sang:

(How does her song go again?)

"*Angiuret, angiuret, angiuren-ka-rra-ngiuren-ka-rra. Atkaling-maliga-rra, puyungu-ta-rra, ka-suraa-suraa-nga,* hurry up and go outside."

Then he went out and saw that their small elevated cache was visible.

Then thinking about how he was entertained, he wanted to lie to her.

Then when he entered, he said to her, "It hasn't changed."

[Then she sang,] "*Angiuret, angiuret, angiuren-ka-rra-ngiuren-ka-rra. Atkaling-maliga-rra, puyungu-ta-rra, ka-suraa-suraa-nga,* hurry up and go out."

When he went out, he saw that it was very sunny. It had already melted. There were caribou up behind them eating. And there were different birds flying. It was very joyous.

Running away from the heat, he ran inside. He said, "It hasn't changed."

His dear grandmother [sang] with more enthusiasm:

"*Angiuret, angiuret, angiuren-ka-rra-ngiuren-ka-rra. Atkaling-maliga-rra, puyungu-ta-rra, ka-suraa-suraa-nga,* hurry up and go outside."

He went outside and it was burning outside. And he saw that their small elevated cache had already burned with a huge fire.

When he ran outside, he said to his grandmother, "It's time for you to stop! It's burning outside!"

His grandmother said to him, "I thought I already told you to tell me!"

❧ *Ellaliulleq* ❧

Negeryaq, Tununeq, May 1976

Negeryaq: Tua-i carraungraan piciqua.

Tua-lli-wa-gguq ukuk anuurluquralriik ukuk uitaurarqelriik kuigem ceniini. Kuigak imarpigmun anumaluni. Tauna-gguq tutgarrlugii tan'gurrauluni.

Tua-i-gguq uksuarutaqatek caqcaarlutek tua-i, tengmiarrsurluni-llu tutgarii, tuntussurluni-llu.

Tua-i-ll' caqat iliitni ellallunglliniluni, tua-i ellarvagluni cakneq.

Anuurluan-gguq-wa quliini cauyaq agauralria.

Tua-i-llu tutgariin pillinia, "Anuurluu caunaluni taun' cauyaq keluvni agaaqa?"

Tua-llu-gguq tutgarani [pia], "Cauvkenani-w' tua-i waniw' agaaqelria."

"Amci ellaliuqaa."

Kasngupakaani-ll' tua-i ellaliurluni.

"Kitak' tua-i pisqevvakararpenga, kiarnariqerrutaciatun tamaa qanruskia." Angerluni.

Tua-ll' aturtuq:

(Qaillun imat'am yuarutii ayuqell'?)

"Angiuret, angiuret, angiuren-ka-rra-ngiuren-ka-rra. Atkaling-maliga-rra, pu-yungu-ta-rra, ka-suraa-suraa-nga, kitag-am ani."

An'uq-gguq maaten mayurrvicualleraak alaitellinilria.

Tua-i-ll' umyuarteqliniluni anglanillerminek iqluyugluku.

Tua-i-ll' iterngami pia, "Cakaniqsaituq."

"Angiuret, angiuret, angiuren-ka-rra-ngiuren-ka-rra. Atkaling-maliga-rra, pu-yungu-ta-rra, ka-suraa-suraa-nga, kitag-am ani."

An'uq-gguq maaten akerkagakacagarluni. Ak'a tua-i urulliuq. Tuntut-gguq-wa paugkut nerelriit keluagni. Tengmiat-gguq-wa cat tengauralriit. Tua-i nunaniqluni cakneq.

Puqlamek qimagluni itqertelliniluni. Pilliniuq, "Cakaniqsailnguq-wa."

Anuurlullrii-gguq-am pikanirtuq:

"Angiuret, angiuret, angiuren-ka-rra-ngiuren-ka-rra. Atkaling-maliga-rra, pu-yungu-ta-rra, ka-suraa-suraa-nga, kitag-am ani."

Anlliniuq ella man' ekualria. Ak'a tua-i mayurrvicualleraak-llu ekurpangell-rulliniluni.

Itqercami anuurluni pia, "Taqnariaten! Ella tang ekelria!"

Anuurluan pillinia, "Ak'a-ggem-tam' qanrucesqellruyaaqua!"

Quickly digging inside her bag, and from the bottom of her grass bag, she gave him a weasel skin, "Chew on the inner side of that, and then blow on it and put it on."

They both chewed the inner side of the skin. Then they say they blew at them at the same time and put them on, and when they dug in the ground and quickly entered, the tips of their tails were singed.

They say the tips of their tails that singed, these days the tips of weasel tails are black.

Then they lived like that, and they didn't remove their skins and they were weasels. These days, they continue to be weasels, they are weasels.

It has ended. There is nothing else to say about it.

ᐁ   *One Who Transformed into a Water Beetle*   ᐁ

Stephanie Nayagniq, Tununak, May 1976

Stephanie Nayagniq: A grandmother and grandchild lived. . . . They were living along a river.

Her grandmother was able to do things, and she would bring her grandchild here and there. They lived together, and they never saw a person.

(I will [tell it] although I'm in a hurry.)

When she began to sit and not do things, her grandmother said to her, "Okay now, grandchild, when I am unable to do things, now that I am unable to do things, don't continually leave me. And don't head toward the headwaters of our river down there. I'm such that I shouldn't be left as I am unable to do things and cannot prepare things myself."

Then her grandmother would just sit. Her grandchild would take care of her urine container. Her grandchild was a girl.

One day when she was outside, as she watched the headwaters of their river, she started to yearn to travel there. And she started to wonder why her grandmother admonished her not to go toward the headwaters of their river.

Then after tightening her bootstrings, she headed toward the upper part of their river.

She went, she climbed a hill, she climbed it. When she got on top and looked over, she saw a house down there. And down there next to it, she noticed a raised cache.

Then she headed toward it. After a while, she came upon a path. When she got on it, since it headed toward that home down there, when she got on it, she followed it and went.

Aglulaakarluku kellarvillrani issrallugaam camaken terr'anek narullgimek cikillia, "Angulaluku kitek' tua-i tauna cupqerluku atniaran."

Angulallinilutek tamarmek. Tua-i-llu-gguq ataucikun cupqerluku as'arrluku elagtuullutek-llu-gguq nevum akuliinun itqertellragni, pamyukenka nuukek elek'arluki.

Tua-i-gguq-am tamakut pamyuita nuvuit ek'ullakallret maa-i narullgit pamyuita iquit tunguut.

Nutaan tua-i tuaten tua-i yuulutek, amiirpeg'natek-llu tua-i narullgiulutek. Tua-i maa-i narullgiulliaqelriit tayima, narullgiuluteng tua-i.

Tua-i iquklilluni. Qaneryararkairulluku.

⨕ *Melnguurtelleq* ⨏

Ceturngalria, Tununeq, May 1976

Ceturngalria: Anuurluquralriik ukuk uitaurarqelriik. . . . Uitaurarqelriik kuigem ceniini.

Tua-i tauna anuurlua piyugngall'erluni, ayagataqluku-ll' taun' tutgarani. Aipaqlutek tua-i yugmek-llu tangyuunatek uitalliniaqelriik.

(Tua-i patagturangerma piciqua.)

Tua-i tamaani aqumengengami taum anuurluan pia, "Kitaki tua-i tutgarrluk, waten-wa tua-i wiinga pisciigalilua pingkuma, waniw' pisciigalilrianga, unitaarpiiqnii pilaqia. Cali-llu un'um kuimegnuk kangian tungiinun ayaksaunak pilaqina. Tua-i waniw' unitaayunairutaanga wiinga pisciigaliama, wangnek-llu arrliurciigalilua."

Tua-i-ll' im' anuurlua tauna tua-i aqumgastenguaqelria. Qurrullugiurqekii taum tutgariin. Nasaurluuluni tayim' tutgarii.

Caqerluni tua-i ellamqenillermini qaugna kuimek kangia tangssuarallermini, ayagyuumingluni tua-i tamaavet. Ciin-llu anuurluminun inerqurpakalallminek kuimek tungiinun, kuimek kangianun ayagcecesqumanrit'lallerminek paqnayungluni tua-i.

Tua-i-ll' cingigni cagniqurarraarlukek ayagluni tua-i kuimegnek kangian tungiinun.

Ayagluni, qemir' man'a mayurluku, mayuarluku. Yaaqsigiami mayuarluku uyangtellinia, ena camna. Kan'a-w' call' caniani mayurrvik kana-i nallunaunani.

Tua-i-ll' tungiinun ayagluni. Piuraqerluni tumyaranun makunun kana'arrluni. Kana'arcami kat'um enem tungiinun ayiita, kana'arcami atu'urrluku ayagarrluni.

Then after a while, [she came upon] two lakes; between them was a narrow stream with water in it.

She went to it and when she got to it, after quickly looking inside it, since it seemed she would be able to make it to the other side if she leaped, she aimed and ran down, and she happened to glance at the bottom of the water, a very large water beetle down there was watching her up there. It was really watching her. Then she jumped, and when she got across, she ran and took off.

She was getting close to that home. There was an elevated cache next to it.

As she slowly went inside its porch, the porch was very clean, no debris was inside it, even though it was made out of sod. She slowly went in, she bent her head down inside its doorway and listened, but she didn't hear anything.

She then stepped down and slowly went in [through the entrance]. Ancient people of long ago had *igcarat* [underground entryways] that dropped down.

Heading in, she slowly peeked in through its *pugyaraq* [entrance hole where one emerges], but no one was inside.

She climbed up, and when entering, here toward the right side was a mattress. Up there, up there was a mangy caribou parka, and there was also a man's squirrel parka.

Then since there was something to cook, she cooked, she prepared caribou. They were done cooking. She ladled them out.

Then she took that mangy, old parka and saw that a hole was in its armpit. Since there was a hole, she searched for a needle. When she found a needle, she sewed that closed to the end. And when she was done with it, she put it back in its place.

She would go out and search her surroundings once in a while. One of the times she went out, she searched her surroundings and saw a person approaching back there.

And when she went inside, she stood down there and looked around, but she couldn't find a place. She went across behind piled, folded caibou skins in a confined space and hid.

Then as she was there, there were thumping noises outside. He entered down there and made noises like a man, it was a man.

She was afraid.

Then when he sat on his bed across there, she peeked through a small crack and saw that he was sweaty. He lay down across there. He would say he was hot and sweaty. He would say across there that when he cooled off, he wanted to prepare food. He said he wanted to prepare food.

Then he got up across there and said, "And where is my [old parka] I wear when I'm hot?" And he took the ones she had sewn across there. He said, "Oh yes, I forgot it has a large tear."

Tua-i-ll' piuraqerluni nanvagnek ukugnek [tekiarrluni]; waten tua-i una wan' akulnguyarauluni merluni.

Ullagluku tua-i tekicamiu uyangarqaarluku, tua amelvakuni nurusngail-ngalami, uqliqerluni atraqerrluni mer'a, un'a terr'a tangerqallinia ik'ikik' mel-nguk'utagpallraam kat'um pikavet tangssukii. Tua-i tangssugluku cakneq. Tua-i-ll' qecegluni akilliarcamiu, aqvaqurluni ayagarrluni.

Tua-i tuavet enem'un tekicartuarluni. Mayurrvik-wa elatiini.

Itqataralliniuq elaturraanun elaturraa taman' menuaraunani, caarrluaraunani nevurrlainaungermi. Itqata'arturluni kanavet amiiganun pull'uni niicugniuryaa-qellinilria, camek niitevkenani.

Ayumian tua-i atrarluni itraqataarluni. Igcarangqetuameng tamakut akaar qulirat.

Itraarluni tua-i kiaggun pugyaraakun pugyartuaralliniuq, tua-i man'a yung-ssagaunani.

Mayurluni pilliniuq, wani itellriani tallirpiim tungiini aci una cururluni. Paugkut-wa pava-i, tuntuvialuaraak pingkuk, qanganat-wa cali pingkut atkuut angucinrauluteng.

Tua-i-llu kenirkartangqellinian kenirluni tuntuliurluni. Tua-i uuluki. Ipugluki.

Tuamtell' taukut atkullraaraat ak'allikai tegullinii unra tua-i man'a ulling-qaluni. Ullingqallinian, tua-llu-w' mingqutkaminek yuarluni. Nalkucami tua-i mingqutmek tamana tamaa-i nunguqurluku mingeqkiliu iquklilluku. Taqngamiu-ll' tua-i enellritnun elliluki.

Anluni kiartaqluni. Caqerluni anluni kiartelliniuq paugna yug' agiirtellria.

Iterngami-ll' tua-i kanavet nangerrluni takuyartaaryaaqluni tua-i nanllikiarluni, nanlucirkaunani. Agaavet agkut tuntut imgumalriit qalliqluteng pamavet keluat-nun qerteqcarluni tua-i iilliniluni.

Tua-i-ll' uitainanrani qakma migpallaraluni elatiini. Itliniuq cama-i angu-tuaqaqluni, angutnguluni.

Alingluni tua-i.

Akma-ll' tua-i aciminun aqumngami, maaggun tua-i-am calqurrarkun qinquu-ssaagarluni tangerqallinia kiiryugluni. Tua-i taklarrlun' ika-i. Kiiryugniluni qa-naaluni. Nengllaqaqani-ll' neqkiuryugluni akma qanraqluni. Neqkiuryugluni qan-raqluni.

Tua-i-ll' ika-i makluni, "Nauwa-ll' imkut kiirnilissuullugaanka?" Teguluki-ll' ika-i imkut mingqellri. Qanertuq, "Aren allganerpaurlulriit-llu imat'anem."

Then he started to search across there, "Where is it? I thought this had a large tear. I evidently sewed it here. I don't think I sewed these stitches. These aren't stitches that I sewed."

Then he put them on across there. When he was about to prepare food he said, "And look here, I evidently cooked. [*laughs*] I have some food. There is cooked food here. My, maybe there's a person here! If there is someone, I won't do anything to them. If there is a person who has arrived, where is he/she? Is he/she here?"

Then he went outside. He was talking outside and kicking his feet, agitated. And he probably went to check his partially underground cache.

Then when he entered, starting from the side wall across there, as he pulled back his things, he uncovered a person. That one suddenly became extremely frightened.

"My, indeed there is someone. What did you think I'd do to you that you've hidden? And I've been lacking someone who is like that, constantly lacking [someone]." He took her and brought her down. He invited her to eat with him. [He said], "Okay then, let's eat."

They ate. She was shy. Since it was the first time she'd seen a man, she was shy.

This was toward falltime. It was toward winter when it starts to frost. That was the time she had left for the first time.

That one she came upon took her as a wife right away. He was her husband. She was his wife.

They made a living there. Her husband, he was proud that he had gotten a wife to help him.

Then winter came and their river down there froze. When it started [to freeze], her husband instructed her. He said that he wanted to return after being in camp, that this is where he goes fall camping, and no one preferred that place. He said he had family down there, that his family was living down in the village.

He had her cut some caribou back fat into pieces. He had her cut the back fat in pieces a little larger than a mouthful and had her fill a grass bag until it was completely full. She placed something around the top and tied it. She was finished with it.

That one said that he wanted them to go down the next day.

She also suddenly became curious about those they would go to.

He loaded skins onto a small sled with a raised back and handlebar, filling it with many caribou skins. And he had her get in on top. He brought her along the glare ice since it was glare ice.

They headed downriver. They looked around one of the bends, after going around many bends, it came into view, a village was downriver.

Tua-i-ll' akma yuangartuq, "Nauwa? Allganerpaullruut-ggem ukut. Maa-i tang mingqellrullinikek'a. Aling tavaq makut mingqelqanka. Mingqelqenritanka makut."

Tua-i-ll' akma all'uki. Neqkiuqatarluni pirraarluni piuq, "Tang waniwa-ll' kenillrullinilrianga. [ngel'artuq] Neqkangqelliniunga. Waniw' kenirartangqelliniuq. Aling yugtangqelliuq! Yugtangqerkuni atak' caciqenritaqa. Kina im' yuk tekitellrukuni nauwa? Maancaaquq-qaa?"

Anluni-ll' tayim'. Qakma tua-i qanaaluni-ll' kitngiarluni arenqianani. Elagyani-llu-w' paqtellikii.

Iterngami-ll' tua-i ikaken caniqamek ayagarrluni makut tua-i cautni ketmun pakigluki piinanermini yugmek uumek pakikengluni. Tauna alingallak'acagarluni.

"Aren qayumi tua-i yugtangqerciqelria. Canayukluten waniw' iircit? Tuaten-llu waniw' ayuquralriamek wiinga kepquralalrianga, kesianek kepqurlua." Teguluku atrarrluku. Nerucugluku. [Piuq], "Nernaurtukuk kitek'."

Nerlutek tua-i. Talluryugeurlurluni tua-i ellii. Nutaan-llu waten-ll' ellii angutmek tangerpaaluami talluryugluni.

Uksuaryartullrani. Imumek tua-i qakurnaqungluni uksuqatangellrani. Tuani tua-i ayagpaalullruluni.

Aling taum imum tekiskengaan nuliqsaguareskiliu. Tua-i uikluku. Nuliqluku.

Tua-i yuungnaqaqelriik tuani tua-i. Tauna tua-i angutii caluni, tua-i picuggluni tua-i aiparminek uumek ikayungllerminek.

Tua-ll'-im' tua-i uksurluni un'-all' kuigak cikuluni. Pingan taum imum angutiin alerquaguraraa. Tua-i kacecungniluni waniwa, ellii wani wavet uksuiyatuniluni, yugmek-llu cucukestaunani. Ilangqerrsaaqniluni tayima cakma, cakmani nunani uitaniluki, uitaniluki taukut ilani.

Tunugnek ingqivkaqiliu. Tua-i imumek iqminruaraam angnerarainek tunuq ciamqurluku ingqivkarluku issran imircetliniluku tua-i muiqaarluku. Camek taugaam pailinguarauciqerluku nuilrarluku. Tua-i taqluku.

Tua-i unuaqu anelraryuglutek piluni tauna qanaaluni.

Tua-i-am cali tua-i paqnayullagluni-ll' ellii taukunek tua-i ullagarkamegnek.

Ikamrarraak qulelgek uciliqek tua-i qecignek, tuntunek, tuntunek qecignek imirlukek. Pakmavet-llu kangragnun ellii ekevkarluku. Ayautelliniluku tua-i cikulraaraungan cikulraam qaingakun.

Kuigkun cetulutek. Qipneret iliit igvallinia, igvarpakarlutek, tua-i qipepakarlutek igvallinia, nunat ugkut.

They approached it; he mentioned the name of his village down there. He said to his wife, "Okay now, they don't fail, they will [do that]. They always do that when I am approaching. Give everyone who comes upon us those small pieces [of caribou back fat] that were cut into pieces." He said he always gives them some when he arrives after camping in fall.

They went on their way. Just when they were about to arrive, the people came toward them forming a line. When he told her to, she gave to the ones who came to them and she gave them all of those pieces of caribou back fat. And that very large grass bag emptied. There were none left. Then they arrived.

There was a very large *qaygi* back there, a very large *qasgi*. And next to it back there was a very large home. He stopped down below it.

After a while, a girl up there ran out. Then another girl ran out. And again, another who was older than those others ran out.

Those who ran out greeted him with great affection. Her husband told her that those were his siblings. He said that was his younger sibling, and [the older one] was his older sister.

He brought her inside. When she entered, she saw that she had already become a daughter-in-law. Across there two people were also sitting along the side wall. Across there were a man [and woman]. An elderly man and elderly woman. His wife acted as if she knew that she was her daughter-in-law. They were apparently her husband's mother and father.

[Speaking in a high-pitched voice] "A daughter-in-law, a daughter-in-law, hurry up and prepare her bed back there in the center!" Her sisters-in-law started preparing her bed. They were beside themselves and showed her great affection. They were very grateful for her.

They lived there.

They say the sibling after their oldest sister, their middle [sister], even if they were small things and nothing, she was easily amazed by things. She was easily awed. And when she saw insects, she wouldn't ignore them. When she saw them, she always studied them closely.

Then after being there all winter, and summer came, after spring camping, toward falltime, toward fall, her husband once again wanted to bring her to his fall camp. The woman wasn't lazy at all to do things, and she was really good to have as a family member.

They left. They headed up with a boat. When they arrived, they lived there.

Right when he would make thudding noises out there, his wife would run out and quickly go to her husband, meeting him.

Then that one left one day. After he left, as she was there, there was some kind of noise, and a person down there was peeking out from her doorway.

Tua-i ullagluki; ua-i ugkut nunani aperturluki. Pia tauna nuliani, "Kitaki tua-i atam pinricuitut, piniartut atam. Agiirtaqama pirrlainatuut. Tua-i tekitellriit tuaten tuaken ingqiayagarnek tamakunek cikirtuarqiki." Cikirtuaratuniluki elliin waten uksuiyaumarraarluni tekitaqami.

Ayaglutek. Tekitniaraqanragen'gun ayumian makut yuut tungiignun tailuteng nengluteng. Tua-i kitakiirngani tekitellriit tuaten cikirtuarluki aruquralliniluki tau-kunek tununek. Tauna-ll' imna issralvall'er imairulluku. Nangluteng. Tekillutek-llu tua-i.

Pingna-wa pia-i qaygirpall'er, tua-i qasgirpall'er. Caniani-wa cali pingna nerpall'er. Tuavet tua-i ketiinun arulairluni.

Piuraqerluni neviarcaq pingna anqertuq. Tuamtell' alla neviarcaq anqerrluni. Cali tuamtell' alla, taukuni tua-i ak'allaunruluni, anqerrluni.

Arenqianaku tua-i ungaciqilin'gu taukut tua-i anqertellret. Taum tua-i qanqaulluku angutiin taukut tua-i elliin anelgutekniluki. Nayagaqniluku, tauna-ll' imna [ak'allaunrulria] alqaqniluku.

Itrulluku tua-i. Maaten-am imna itertuq ak'a tua-i ukurraurtellrulliniluni. Ikegkuk-wa cali aqumgalriik nakirnermi. Tua-i angutenkuk ikegkuk. Angut-ngurrlutek arnaurrluni-llu. Ukurraitenritkacagarluni taun' nulirra. Cunaw' ika-i angutiin aanak aatii-llu.

[Cuyarrluni] "Ukurrar, ukurrar, aciliurluku amci piluku kiavet qukamun!" Aren aciliungartaat ikegkut cakirain. Tua-i arenqianateng tua-i ullyulluku. Quyakluku cakneq.

Tua-i yuuluteng.
Tauna-gguq tua-i taum tua-i alqaqliata tungii, qukaqliak, calqurraungraata, tua-i caunrilengraata iillatartuq cakneq. Tua-i ucurtarluni. Cissilqurraat-llu makut tua-i-gguq ulurngaunaki. Tangrraqamiki yuvriarturluki kesianek.

Tua-ll'-am tua-i uksurpak uksirraarluteng kiagluni-llu, up'nerkirraarluteng, uksuaryartunga'arcan-am taum, uksuaryartunga'arcan tua-i-am ayaucugluku tuavet tua-i uksuiviminun angutiin taum. Tua-i qessaitkacagarluni una arnaq tua-i cakneq tua-i yuksunaqluni.

Ayaglutek-am tua-i. Angyarlutek itrarlutek. Tekicamek tua-i tuani yuugurlutek.

Tua-i qakma migpallaruciatun tauna im' nulirra anqertelliniaqelria tua-i tauna aipani ullagarrluku, paiqerluku.

Tua-i-ll' imna tua-i caqerluniam tua-i ayagluni. Ayallran kinguani, uitau-raqanrakun qaillun tua-i cavallartell', kina yuk kan'a amiigakun pugumaartuq.

When she climbed up, it was a small woman down there, and her body was shimmering. She was wearing a cormorant parka. Her cormorant parka was very dark and shiny.

She went to her. [She said,] "Let's trade parkas."

"I won't trade."

"Hurry, let's trade parkas."

"I won't trade. I don't want that kind of parka."

Removing her parka, she said, "Hurry, let's trade parkas. My parka here is good."

My, when the poor thing removed her garment, when she undressed, she was wearing nothing, she was naked.

Then when she took that one, she pulled her. Although she didn't want to, she removed her parka and quickly put it on. And after having her put on her parka [she said], "Why is this darn person so unwilling? Because she is so unwilling, she's unwilling to put on my parka."

And after putting them on her, she felt as though she shrunk, and it was very tight for her. She threw [the girl] into the underground passageway down there. "Why is this darn person so unwilling?" Then [the girl] lost consciousness.

She lost consciousness for a long time. When she gained consciousness in what seemed like her own self, she looked around and saw that she had landed in the center of where their *igcaraq* [underground entryway] headed inside. It was daunting for her to go up there, and she was also afraid that she might be stepped on.

She headed out slowly toward that place where one first ducks one's head when entering the passage. Then when she went out to a place where they wouldn't step on her, she stopped.

Then when it was time for her husband to arrive, when he arrived, he was doing things and making noise out there. Then he came inside from out there saying, "Why is that poor one in there not quickly coming outside as usual?"

He entered. Up there, up there when he ducked his head to get inside the entrance tunnel, she yelled at him as loud as she could. He actually stopped for a second, seemingly hearing something. Then he passed by her and entered.

Then when he entered, he said to his wife, "You made me worry since you didn't run out. Are you okay?"

The awful one answered him, "I'm fine."

They say she was ignorant, that awful person didn't know how to have a husband.

Then after a while, when he went out, once again [the girl] yelled at him as loud as she could, really [loudly], really [loudly]. Once again, pausing a little longer than he had when he entered earlier, he seemed to hear something, but then he went out.

Maaten nug'uq arnalqurraq kan'a, qainga-w' qevlerpak. Uyalegnek atkugluni. Tungurpak uyalgi qevlercenateng.

Ullallinia. [Pillinia,] "Atkupuk navrutnaupuk."
"Navrusngailngua-wa."
"Kiiki atkupuk navrutnaupuk."
"Navrusngaitua. Tamakucinek atkungqerrsuumiitua."
Matarteliurluni tuaten, "Kiiki navrutnaupuk atkupuk. Assirtut atam ukut atkuunka."
Aren, nakleng imna mata'arcami, maaten mata'artuq, tua-i cangssagaunani, matarrayagarluni.
Tauna-ll' teguamiu cayugluku. Qessangraan tua-i atkui yuuluki elliin as'arrluki. Taukunek-llu atkullraminek ac'equarraarluku [pia], "Ciiqtar' una qessaqtarpakarta? Qessiimi-qaa atkuunka qessakai at'enritnaluki."

Ac'equarraarluku-ll', ayuqucia-ll' man' eq'errluni tua-i calturluni cakneq. Kanavet igcaramun egqualuku. "Ciiqtar' una qessaqtarpakarta?" Cacini-ll' tayim' nalluqerluku.
Tua-i nallumaluku tua-i. Maaten tang imna ellmini tua-i ellamini ellanguq, kiarquralliniaman'akananiimumiigcaramekimkuaniitraqercaraani,qukartuulluni tut'ellrullinill'. Tua-i paugna ullallerkaanek caperrsugluni tutnayukluni tuaten aaryugluni.

Uavet tua-i put'eqarraaryaramun anelraqcaarturalliniluni. Tua-i-ll' uavet tut'arkaunriatni, tua-i arulairluni.

Tua-ll' imna tua-i tauna angutii qakma tekicungami tekicami, cavallarayaa-qelliniaqelria qakma. Tua-i-ll' qakma iteryarturtuq qanerluni, "Ciurluq qamna qayuwa anqercunripakarta?"
Iterluni tua-i. Pagaa-i pika-i, kalvagteqatarluni put'ellrani tua-i erinitacirrami-tun qayagpagayaaqelliniluku. Tua-i pinritevkenani-gguq tua-i arulailkiqeryaaq-luni cameg' niisnganani. Tua-i-ll' kiturluku ava-i itliniluni.
Tua-ll' iterngami tauna nuliani pillinia, "Peng'gallagcetarpenga tua-i qayuw' anqertenripakaavet. Tua-i-q' canricaaquten?"
Kiuqtaraa-gguq, "Canricaaqelrianga-wa."
Tua-i-gguq ńalluluni, uingqeneq nalluluku tauqtam.

Tuamtell' tua-i piuraqerluni anngan, cali tua-i pitacirramitun qayagpa-gayaaqelliniluku, tua-i cakneq, cakneq. Cali-gguq tua-i, watua-am itellran pikani-neqluku tua-i, camek tua-i niigarrnganani piyaaqerraarluni-am, tayim' anlliniluni.

Since he wouldn't hear her . . . and that wretched one, her husband found his wife to be strange. (And did he not pay attention to her face?)

Since he was beside himself, he told his wife when the winter season came, "Okay now, let's return to our village. Prepare some things to give away like before." And he showed her the caribou back fat, the back fat.

My, she didn't know how [to cut it]. He saw that she still had not cut them into pieces.

He got impatient and told her to hurry and cut [caribou fat] into pieces and fill the grass bag. He asked her why she had been acting strange.

That wretched one cut [the fat] into pieces and filled it.

And that poor thing that she had thrown [down inside the *igcaraq*], that seal-gut rain garment that was usually filled with caribou back fat, the one that he usually brought inside the house, she went to it, she took a long time to go to it.

And she finally climbed up through the underground passageway back there and got inside their home up there. She headed toward it slowly and finally came upon it after a long time.

Then when she came upon it, she went through the small openings and went inside, trying to reach those pieces of caribou fat. Then she finally got inside.

They say she continally ate caribou fat from there.

Then her husband took that one, the seal-gut rain garment filled with caribou fat, and placed it inside his sled out there. The two out there started going home.

Once again, when the people got in line, when he told her to start [giving away caribou fat], the darn little woman didn't act. She stayed and wouldn't distribute to them. The people just stayed like her and weren't given any.

He told her to hurry and give to those people. They say being upset, her husband said that. Then she finally started giving to them. She gave to them and they finished. They arrived.

Then when they arrived, her in-laws were finding their daughter-in-law strange. She acted strange, and she was even lazy. She wasn't like she had been before.

They say they would have the Bladder Festival there since they lived in a village. After summer passed, when fall came, they planned to have the Bladder Festival. When it got cold, they would have the Bladder Festival.

They would say, the people there would say, "Why has that daughter-in-law changed? She has apparently returned to her usual [bad] self [implying that she had acted like a proper daughter-in-law earlier in her marriage but was actually not well behaved]."

Then when they were about to make *akutaq*, when they were going to deflate [bladders], they took that supply of caribou fat. He grabbed it, but it was light. Then that person shook the contents of the bag onto the floor. And when he shook it, the poor thing landed on the floor.

Tua-i niitarkaunritliniani . . . taunangssak-gguq-wa tua-i, allaliarrluni tauna angutii taumek nuliarminek. (Kegginaa-llu-mtaq murilkeksaitelaraa?)

Arenqialami tua-i pillinia taun' nuliani uksuurtenga'arcan-am tua-i man'a, "Kitaki-ata tua-i kingunemegnun uterrnaurtukuk. Imucetun-ata tua-i aruqutkiurturqina." Tunuq-llu aperturluku, tunut.

Aren, tua-i-gguq nalluluni. Pinauraa-gguq cali ingqiksaitelliniaqell'.

Tua-i qemitaakengluku amci issran imiisqelluku una ingqiluku. Ciin qaillun pivakallranek.

Tua-i ingqiqcaarluni imiqtarluku taum.

Tauna-ll' tua-i imna egquraurlullra, tuamtell'-am tua-i imkuk imarnitek tunurnek imangqetulik, qamavet itrautetukek, ullaglukek tua-i ullaumalliniaqekek.

Tua-i-am mayuryaqlirluni-ll' kiaggun igcarakun pikavet enem'ek iluanun. Tungiignun tua-i ayagturluni tekiteqcaarturainallinilukek.

Tuamtell' tua-i tekicamikek, tua-i makutgun qelpaksiurneruarteggun qamavet, tunut taukut tekingnaqluki, iterturalliniluni. Tua-i-ll' iluagnun iterturainarluni.

Tua-i tununek tuaken nereqcaartura'arqelria-gguq tua-i.

Tua-ll' imna, taukuk-am tua-i imarnitek tunenek imalgek angutiin taum tegulukek, qakma ikamragminun eklukek. Qakma tua-i uterrlutek.

Tua-i-am tamakut yuut ukatmun nengeng'ata, kitakiiryaaqekiini-am, una arnakcualler uitakili. Uitalun' tua-i aruqsugpeg'naki. Makut-gguq-wa tua-i maliggluku tuaten cikirciuryugpeg'nateng.

Amci tamakut cikirtuusqelluki. Umyugaa-gguq assirpek'nani-gguq taum angutiin tuaten qanerluni. Nutaan tua-i cikirtunga'arrluki. Tua-i cikirturluki nangluki. Tua-i tekillutek.

Tuamtell' tua-i tekicamek, ukut tua-i taukut cakirai uumek ukuarmeggnek allayugciluteng. Qaillun-gguq una tua-i ayuqluni tua-i, qessamkauluni tuaten. Imutun ayuqevkenani.

Tua-i-am Nakaciutuut-gguq tamaani taukut nunaungameng. Kiagurraarluni uksuaran Nakaciuqataqallinilriit tua-i. Aren tuani-w' pacetaqan Nakaciutullruut.

Tua-i qanraqluteng, qanraqluteng taukut yuut, "Qaillun augna ukurraq ayuqlirillinia? Tua-i-w' ava-i egkuagminun piami assiirutlinilria."

Tua-i-ll'-am' akuteqatarluteng tua-i elciqatallermeggni, taukuk tua-i tunuutegteng tegulukek. Teguleryaaqelliniak tua-i uqiggenateng. Tua-i-ll' taum natermun evcuarquleryallinilukek. Evcuarquakek-ll'-am tua-i natermetqaurlurluni.

Again, afraid that she might be stepped on, she slowly went back underneath a log headrest. And when she came to the log headrest, she went underneath it. She stayed there and waited for it to get dark.

The people up there were talking about something going missing. They said the caribou fat that was inside the seal-gut rain garment had finished. What was left was all crumbs.

They made *akutaq*. When they were doing something and not paying attention, she headed inside [toward the back of the home] underneath the log headrest, she slowly headed inside.

Then back along the place where they put the lamps, they had a place for the lamps like this. Then they put the clay lamp there and left it on. She slowly went up on that so she would be seen when someone turned on the lamp. That one who was easily amazed by things, she went up to the lamp of the one who was easily in awe of things.

When they were about to light the lamp, "Hurry up, it's getting dark, turn on the lamp." The lamp, poor, back when they had no matches. . . .

[I forgot] part of what I should have said. Before that small woman entered, when her husband left, when he was far away, remembering her grandmother, she ran to see her. And she approached her. As she was approaching her, she heard that one over there suddenly crying out over there inside their small home.

When she arrived upon her, she slowly climbed the side of their small home and slowly peeked through the window, poor, her grandmother down there was trying to put on skin boots. Her grass insoles, since they used to wrap grass around their feet for insoles, when she would [fold] them like this, the grass would suddenly get cut.

When she looked at them closely down there, the toes of her feet, her small toes all had mouths on them with small teeth. [The mouths and teeth] would cut the grass she had wrapped around her feet for insoles by biting on them.

When she saw her like that, she slowly went down. When she passed [her grandmother's house], she ran home to their home there.

Then the middle sibling after their eldest, when she was about to light her lamp, when she lit the wick over there and brought it over, she lit its wick and happened to see [the daughter-in-law who had become an insect].

When she saw her, she wouldn't leave her at all. She was in awe and excited looking at that very large insect down there.

Then she called her older sister, "Older sister, look at that insect down there!" She quickly came over. After quickly looking inside she moved away in fear, "Throw it away! Kill it!"

She wouldn't kill it at all. She put something small underneath it and pulled it toward herself and started to study it.

Aren tua-i-am tutnayukluni pavavet akicillrem acianun tua-i tageqcaaralliniluni. Akicilleq-llu tekicamiu tua-i acianun qerrluni. Tuani tua-i tan'gerinerciarluku.

Paqriciluteng-gguq pakemkut qanaaluteng. Tunut-gguq tang imkut tayima wani imarnitegni nangllinilriit. Taugaam-gguq ciamelliniluni tua-i ciamlinrurrluni.

Tua-i akulluteng. Imumek tua-i caluteng murilkevkenateng pillratni, akicillrem aciakun itraaralliniluni, itraqcaaralliniluni.

Tua-i-llu kiaggun kenuraucetaakun, waten kenurraucetangqetullrulriit. Tuavet-llu tua-i qikuq kenurraq elliluku kumavkarluku. Tamaaggun tua-i mayuq-caarturluni pikavet, imumek tua-i kumareskaku tangrrarkaurcelluni. Tauna tua-i iillatalria, iillatalriim kenurraanun mayurluni.

Tua-i kenurraqatarluteng waniwa, "Amci-am tan'geriuq kenurrarci." Kenurraq imumek, nakleng, spickayuilameng-llu. . . .
Iliinek qanrutkarkamnek [katagilliniunga]. Tuani imna arnangssagaq iter-pailgan, angutni ayagngan, tayim' yaaqsigian, imna maurluni umyuaqluku aqvaqurturluni ullakii. Tua-i-ll' tekicarturluku yaa-i. Maaten imna tekicarturluku tekicartuararaa, amna qalrillagauraurlulria ama-i iluanek enacualleramek.
Tekicamiu tua-i, qacarnerakun im' enacualleramek mayuqata'arluni egalrakun uyangqataralliniuq, nakleng, maurlua kan'a pilugungnaqelria. Imumek tua-i piineni, piinirluteng carangllugnek pitullruameng, waten piluki piaqaki, ugkut imkut caranglluut kep'arrnaurtut.

Maaten kanavet cumikluki pillinii it'gain ugkut yuarai, yuarayagai ugkut tamarmeng qanerluteng kegguksuarluteng. Tamakut tamaa-i piinri kep'ar-telliniaqekait keggurqelluki.
Tuaten tua-i tangrramiu, atraqataarturluni tuamtell'. Pellugngamiu aqva-qurturluni uterrluni tua-i nutaan tuavet enemegnun tuavet.
Tua-i-llu tauna alqaqlikacagiita, akunleqliag' una, kenurrani kumarteqatarluku, imumek tua-i kumarun yaaken kumarrluku tailluku, kumarutii kumarrluku tangerqalliniluku.
Tangerqaamiu-am tua-i unicugnaunaku. Tua-i iillakluku kan'a ciisvall'er aren-qianani.
Tua-i-llu alqani tuqluraa, "Al'alkuniing, atam kan'a ciissiq tangerrsartuqarru!" Taigarrluni. Uyangarqaarluku uniquallinia alingallagluni, "Egesgu! Tuqusgu!"

Tuqucugnaunaku-am. Imumek calqurrarmek aciiqerluku cayugluku aren yur-vinga'artellinia-am.

When she would look at it down there, it was as though she had a human face down there.

Then that insect she was holding yelled at her, "Hurry, break open my shell and split it open!"

After putting her ear to it, she said, "I think this one is speaking! [*laughter*] Older sister, come over and listen to it! It will seem like it's speaking!"

Then she came over. Being squeamish she would leave it and say, "Drop it and kill it!" That one wouldn't kill it at all.

My, after putting her ear to it, "What?" When it would speak again down there, "What?" She would reply to it.

Then as she was doing that, she understood what it said, "Split open my shell and remove it." My, she tried to split it open. Although they tried, they were afraid of it. Something, they say her shell was completely hard.

After many tries, it made a popping sound and split open, and there was a baby inside it. My, she quickly took it. When she looked at it closely and recognized her, it was the face of their daughter-in-law, their wonderful daughter-in-law.

My goodness, when they realized who she was, that one grew quickly, she started to inflate and fill out and grow. When she quickly grew, they saw that she was their daughter-in-law.

And their small daughter-in-law, they took her along some part of her body and took her outside and threw her out, [and said], "No wonder this person is so ugly! We really thought she was very different since she acted differently."

Then finally their daughter-in-law, their wonderful daughter-in-law told them that after her husband had left, that small woman entered her home using a cormorant parka and the surface was shiny, and her small ruff was tundra-hare skin.

She told them that [the small woman] had removed her parka, she removed her small parka, and although she was unwilling, she removed her parka and forced her parka on her. And she had put on her parka. And she told them after putting [the parka] on her, she had thrown her down inside the doorway, inside the underground entranceway.

She told her family the story. And she said when her husband would go out, she would yell to him, but that after staying there for a second, he would just pass by while she was down in the doorway.

He said that it was no wonder when he went out, he would seem to hear something. He said since he didn't know, he just ignored her. He said he was feeling guilty, and he scratched his head [and said], "My goodness, how disappointing, it's because I didn't know [you were there]!"

Then finally, she went back to her normal self. She was good, she felt light. She didn't just sit there ungroomed and not taking care of herself [lit., "with her

Kanani-gguq tua-i piaqani, tuar-gguq tang kana-i eyinrarmek kegginangqe-lalria.

Tua-i-ll' taum imum tegumiaran ciissim qayagpalliniluku, "Ampi, caquteka tamana navegluku ulliiresgu!"

Tua-i ciutni maniqerluku pirraarluni, "Una tang qaneryugnarqelria! [ngel'artut] Al'alkuniluug'am' tailuten atam niicugniyartuqarru! Atam qanerngatniartuq!"

Tua-i tailuni. Ii-qungvagyugluni uniquaciqaa, "Peggluku tuqusgu!" Aren taum-ggu-qam tua-i tuqucugnaunaku.

Aling tua-i ciutni maniluku pirraarluni, "Ai?" Allamek cama-i qanelkitaqan, "Ai?" Angraqluku.

Tua-i-ll' piinanermini taringelliniluku, "Caquteka tamana ullirrluku aug'arru." Aren, ullircessaangartellinia. Un' pingraatni tua-i alikluku. Camek-am tua-i, tegkacagarluni-gguq taman' caqutii.

Pingnaqvakarluku cingqullagluni ulli'irtelliniuq mikelnguyagaq kan' iluani. Aren, teguqalliniluku. Maaten-gguq tang wavet elitaqluku pia, imna una ukurraata kegginii, ukurraqegtaariita.

Aling aren, tua-i-ll' im' tauna elpekngamegteggu, elpekngamegteggu ang-turriturnirluni qerruryarturluni angturrilliniluni. Angturriqertuq maaten waniw' tua-i ukurraat.

Tauna-ll' imna ukuacuallerteng natiikun teguluku anlluku ellatmun eg-telliniluk', "Anirtima tang un' ikiuqtarpakalartuq! Allayukekacagalaryaaqekvut tua-i allaungat'larpakaan."

Tua-i nutaan taum ukurraata, ukurraqegtaariita, qanemcitliniluki aiparmi ayallran kinguani arnangssagaq augna itellruniluku eneminun uyalegnek atkug-luku, qainga-wa qevlercenani, negipsaarii-wa qayuqegglirraq.

Tuaten tua-i taukunek, atkuni yuuluki, atkullrani taukut yuuluki, ellii qe-ssangraan matarqualuku, taumek tua-i atkullraminek ac'equallruniluni. Ellii-ll' atkuinek all'uni. Ac'equarraarluni-ll', acetquarraarluki-llu kanavet amigmun igcaramun egtellruniluku.

Qanemciquralliniluki tua-i taukut ilani. Aipani-ll' tauna an'aqan qayagpaga-laryaaqniluku, tua-i qarilkicuaqangraan, camek pivkenaku kitularniluku amigmi kanan' uitallermini.

Anirtima-gguq tang tua-i, an'aqami-gguq tang tua-i cameg' imumek nii-gartetullruyaaqell'. Nalluami-gguq uitat'laraa. Arenqianani-gguq tua-i qessana-yugluni, qamiquni-ll' kumegluku [qanerluni], "Aling aren qessanaqvakar, na-lluamken-wa!"

Tua-i nutaan imutun-am tua-i ayuqucirramitun ayuqluni. Assirluni, tua-i ayuqucia uqgenani. Aqumluni kivengllugtevkenani. Imutun-am tua-i

pants slipping down her legs"]. She went back to her normal self, and they stayed together as they did before. And now the story has ended. There is nothing left to say about it.

∝ *Long Nails* ∾

Stephanie Nayagniq, Tununak, May 1976

Stephanie Nayagniq: Then again, a grandmother and grandchild were living along the shores of a small river. They say their river was like this. It would get narrow and suddenly widen; many sections widened like lakes along it.

Her grandmother would constantly admonish her like before [in the previous story, "One Who Transformed into a Water Beetle"] not to go to the headwaters of their river. Obeying her, she wouldn't go.

Then one day, there is nothing to say. One day, she started becoming curious about her grandmother's admonishment. She started traveling to the upper part of their river.

Then she crossed along one of the narrows. After a while, when she came to a trail, she traveled along it. Then the trail ended along a home over there. She approached it.

She slowly crept in, she crept inside. Like before [in the previous story], that porch was very clean. And that was the only home there like before. She slowly looked in on the person inside, and when she came into view, she was sewing a bearded-seal intestine rain parka.

When she looked at her nails back there, she saw that her nails were copper. Those very long nails were extremely sharp. (How did she hold her needle?)

She was very scary looking.

Then after heading out toward the exit, as she pretended to enter, [the woman with long nails] grunted and suddenly grasped her hands and [made a whimpering noise], "*Eng*. Maybe she saw them." Then the one she was referring to said, "What?"

"I thought you saw them."

She said she hadn't seen anything. "Okay, then sit. My, because you got tired of being obedient, you have broken your admonishment. Your grandmother has been constantly warning you not to come here because of me. Okay, now sit across there and eat. What do you want to eat?"

Up there along her hanging rack were small fish that had been cut to dry with oil dripping from their foreheads. They looked appetizing.

Then she wanted to eat from up there.

ayuqucirramitun nutaan tayima aipaquralliniaqelriik. Nutaan tua-i iquklilluni. Qaneryararkairulluni.

⊷ *Cetugpak* ⊶

Ceturngalria, Tununeq, May 1976

Ceturngalria: Tuamtell' ukuk anuurluquralriik uitaurarqelriik kuicualleraam ceniini. Tamana-gguq tua-i kuigak waten ayuquq. Nequturiqetaarluni; nanviuqerrneret amllerrluteng.

Tua-i-am taum anuurluan inerquaralliniaqekii cali tamaavet kuimek kangianun ayaasqevkenaku. Niilluku tua-i ayayuunani piuralliniaqluni.

Tua-i-ll'-am tua-i, camek qaneryararkailnguq. Piinanermini-am tua-i paqnakengluku inerquutii tamana anuurlumi. Kangirtenglliniluku kuigtek.

Tua-i-ll' quuyat iliitgun arvirluni. Piuraqerluni tumyara'arnek makunek kana'arcami-am aturluki ayaagalliniluni. Tua-i-ll' ing'umek enem'ek yaa-i iqungluni. Ullagluku tua-i.

Itqata'arluni, itqataralliniuq. Tua-i-am elaturraq tamana menuaraitkacagarluni cakneq. Kiimi-ll'-am tua-i eneguluni tauna. Igvaqatayangiirturluku kiavet yua igvallinia, imkunek tua-i tungunqinraagnek qilunek iqrelria.

Maaten-gguq tang kiavet cetui tangrrai, kanuyat-wa cetui. Imkut cetugpallraat cakneq ipegluteng. (Qaillun-mi-tanem minguqtni teguluku?)

Tua-i alingnaqluni.

Tua-i-ll' nutaan anelrarraarluni cakmaken itqataruarluni pillrani, engaaqerluni unatni qes'artellinii, "Eng. Tangllii." Tua-i-ll' ciunran taum pillina, "Ca?"

"Tangerrsukluki."

Camek tangenritniluni. "Kitek' aqumluten. Aling, inerciryalnguavet tua-i inerquutan navgan. Anuurlurpet inerquararqekiiten taisqevkenak wiinga piteklua, wii taugaam inerquumavkalaraaten. Kitek' aqumluten ikavet neri. Camek neryugcit?"

Pagkut-gguq-wa initaani ceg'ayagaat agalriit cung'umegteggun uqurrarnek kuciqniyagarluteng. Aglumanaqluteng tua-i.

Tua-i-ll' pagaaken neryulliniluni.

"Okay then, take some yourself and eat." Then she took some food and ate, finding her food delicious.

Then as she was eating, a child down there, a girl appeared through her doorway. When she appeared and faced her across there and whispered, her mother said to her, "Aa, you won't eat." She wanted to eat the small fish that were cut and drying up there. "You won't eat!"

That small girl ran out and said, "How awful the one in there with copper nails."

She quickly got up and ran after her. And when she ran after her, out in the porch, she suddenly cried out a little.

And when she entered, acting as though she hadn't done anything, she sat and just held her hands together.

She continued eating, suddenly frightened.

Pretending not to, when she was done eating, she tightened her boot laces down there and tied them tightly until they seemed as though they wouldn't come undone.

Then she told [the old woman] that she felt like urinating, that she wanted to go and pee. When she said yes, she went out. [She said,] "Come in right away." She said yes.

She went out to the porch, and she saw that poor thing who had entered for just a short while with her belly split open from one end to the other. She stepped over her and went out.

Then from outside, she flew toward home as fast as she could!

After a while, just as she was getting close to that small river, from behind her she made noise, "That wily one pretended to want to pee, one who had a plan. I promise, for the rest of your life, I'll go after you!"

She quickly looked back and she was approaching back there. She would do this with her nails and had them make clanging noises. They made noise like a bullet blast.

She lept forward and ran fast! Then when she came upon their small river and through a place she thought she could cross, through the widest part, and here [the old woman] was going to catch up to her! Her nails back there would make clanging noises. Through the widest part, she lept forward and landed on the other side.

My, behind her, there was a loud splashing noise. Following that one, [the old woman] had jumped, but she was short and didn't make it across.

They say their small stream had a strong current. That one down there started to drift away. And she just watched her down there.

"Kitek' elpenek tegulluten neri." Tua-i neqkaminek tegulluni neraqcaarallini-luni neqnililuni.

Tua-i-ll' piinanrani, nernginanrani kan'a mikelnguq, nasaurlurraq pugqallini-luni amiigakun. Pugngami-ll' tua-i ika-i cauluku akma qaneksuaraan, aaniin pia, "Aa nerngaituten." Pagaaken neryugyaaqluni ceg'ayagarnek. "Nerngaituten elpet!"

Anqerteqtalliniuq tauna nasaurlucuar qanerluni tuaten, "Ik'atak kiugna ka-nuyanek cetulek."

Nang'errluni maligartelliniluku. Maligarcani-ll' cakma elaturrami iqupku-ggarmek qalrillacuaqalliniluni.

Iterngami-ll' tua-i caqallruaranrilngurtun tauna im' canermek taqluni tua-i unatni taugaam qesngaurluki.

Tua-i neraqcaarluni alingallagluni.

Pinrilnguarturluni tua-i tuani nernermek taqngami cingigni camkuk cagnit-linilukek tua-i, qillerqurlukek-llu tua-i egumqerrngairusnganakek.

Tua-i-ll' pillinia nakaciniluni, yuqercugluni. Tua-i-ll' anluni angqerngan. "Tamaa itqina." Angraluni.

Anluni elaturramun anlliniuq imna una itqaurlulleq aqsiik iqukliarrlutek ullingqalutek. Amllirluku anluni.

Tua-i-ll' keggaken tenglliniluni kingunermi tungiinun tua-i aqvaqurluni cakneq tua-i pitacirramitun!

Piuraqerluk' tamaavet tamaa-i kuicuallermun alegnaringeqanrakun, ama-i kingunranek nepelkilluni, "Yuqercuguallerallinilria umyuangqerrngulria. Ungu-varpeni tuani taqciqamken pillra!"

Kingyaq'alliniuq uka-i. Cetuni waten piluki avirlurcetaqluki. Imumek tua-i imarpallaraluteng qalriagaqluteng.

Tua-i tengluni ellii aqvaqurluni! Tua-i-ll' tamana kuicuallerani, kuicuallertek tekilluku tua-i uuggun alkekngamikun, ameltunqurrakacagarkun maa-i-w' angu-qataqii! Avirlurtaqluteng pamkut cetui. Ameltunqurrarkun tenglliniluni tua-i agaavet akianun-llu tull'uni.

Aren, kingunrakun mecarpak. Tauna imna maliggluku qecegyaaqellriim nurulluni.

Carvanqektartuq-gguq taman' kuicualleriik. Aren tua-i atertenga'artellinia un'a. Elliin-llu unavet tangssuarluku.

And since [the stream's] sides had a high bank, she would head up to shore and poke in her very long nails, but the land would break off. When she would poke in her other very long nails again, the land would break off since her nails were too long.

[She begged her] to lift her up, to pull her up. She wouldn't pull her up at all and said she wouldn't listen to her.

She continued to do that. And she arrived upon their small home. That poor one passed by. She couldn't climb up since her clothes were wet. When she would poke her nails in, they would break off the land. When she poked the other side, they would break off the land. They would cut off [the land] and come off.

When she arrived at their home, their small home, she headed up and entered and sat as though nothing had happened to her. Her grandmother looked across at her and said, "Mmmmm, grandchild, you are so disobedient! Okay now, walk around as much as you want upriver! [*laughter*] You no longer have an enemy!"

There are no more words to this story. It's the end.

The Little Needlefish

Wassillie Evan, Akiak Culture Camp, July 2002

Wassillie Evan: That [story] about the porcupine. . . . *Aa-a,* [I won't tell it,] it's too long. But this [story]. The story about a small fish approaching a grandmother and grandchild. Yes.

There once lived a grandmother and grandchild along a river.

So during that time, they hadn't experienced anything [out of the ordinary].

Here at that fish camp, there were paths. There was a path over there to the smoke house. There was another path to the place where they went and got wood to smoke fish.

The grandmother and her grandchild resided there; they had paths.

Then one day, yes, one day, at that place, since her grandmother always got up early, one morning she went outside.

They say after she went out the grandmother woke her grandchild [and said,] "Grandchild, something is approaching us. From downriver, it is coming this way toward us."

Then that one said, "Now go and listen."

Then the grandchild got curious when she told her to go out and listen, and she went to listen.

Penarenqektaami-llu-gguq avatii tamana, tagluni-gguq pavavet cetugpallrani kapucaaqngateng, ussutnaurtut. Allat ukut cetugpallrani kapucaaqngateng ussutaqluteng cetugpaussiyaagami.

Mayurteqaasqellun', qeluqaasqelluni. Qeluyugnaunaku niisngaitniluni.

Tuatnaurluni imna. Tekitelliniluku-ll' enacuallertek. Taunaurluq tayim' kitulliniluni. Mayurciiganani mecirngani. Cetullerani kapucaaqngateng ussutaqluteng. Akiit kapucaaqngateng ussutaqluteng. Navgulluteng pilaulluteng aug'artaqluteng.

Tua-i tauna enesek [tekicamiu], en'acuallertek, tagluni iterluni aqumqalria, tuar-gguq tang callruuranrilnguq. Anuurlurluan-am ikavet tangrraa, "Mmmmm tutgaarluk, inerciigapagcit! Kiteg' nutaan umyuan aturluku qavani pekayalaqina! [ngel'artut] Anguyairututen tua-i!"

Tua-i-am qaneryararkairulluni. Iquklilluni.

❧ *Quarruugaurluq* ❧

Misngalria, Akiaq, July 2002

Misngalria: Augkut-am issalu . . . Aa-a, taksiyaagtuq. Una taugaam. Tutgara'urlurluqellriinkuk neqcuaraam agiireskiik. Ii-i.

Tua-ll'-am taukuk tutgara'urlurluqellriik tamaani kuigem ceniini uitallinilriik. Tua-i-ll'-am tamaani tua-i camek pilutek piksaunatek.

Maa-i waniwa-ll'-am ukut neqlillret tumyararluteng tua-i. Tuamtallu cali waten makut tumyararluteng yaavet, pimun puyurcivigmun. Tuamtall' aruvagkanek cali aqvacaraq tumyararluni.

Tua-i-am taukuk-am tuaten uitaurlullinilriik maurlurluqellriik; tumyararlutek tua-i.

Tua-llu-am caqerluku, ii-i, tua-i-ll'-am caqerluni, tamaani tua-i piqerluni tauna, ak'a-ll' tauna uicaratulliniami maurlurlua, caqat iliitni atam unuakumi anllinilria.

Tua-i-llu-gguq anllermini taum maurlurluan tutgara'urlurluni tupar—qaa, "Atam tutgarrluk, cam agiireskiikuk. Cakma uatemegnek ukatmurrluni tungmegnun."

Tua-i-ll' taun' imna, "Atam niicugniyartuqaa."

Tua-i-llu piqerluni tauna tutgara'urlurlua camek paqnayuallinia, anesqengani, niicugniyartuusqell[uku], niicugniyarturtuq.

Then she heard its voice down there.

When she went inside, when she went inside their little house, oh my, they quickly got ready to flee and turned their little open canoe upright.

The things, including the pathways, the paths they took to urinate, and the paths they took to dump their trash, I wonder how they picked them up? They placed them all inside their canoe.

Then after they loaded those, they also got their little cooking pot and other things and loaded them in their canoe because they were scared of the thing down there that was approaching. It was scary because it was singing as it was approaching.

After everything was done, they went down. It sounded like it was in their river. It had reached the area down below them.

While they were there, it seemed the thing had reached the area down below them, it seemed that it was just about to arrive down there. After a while, that one, the grandchild, went down to the canoe. And her grandmother followed her.

When she went down, she went down and it was singing down there, "The two over there, the two dear old women on the other side of the small point, I wish I could eat them raw, cutting them down their middle, *ki-yaa aa-rru-rra-yaa ki-yaa.*"

Because it seemed like it was coming from the water, her grandmother checked in the water and saw that it was a poor needlefish going upriver, singing a song.

Then since their things were inside their canoe, including cooking utensils, bowls and things, she searched for her little ladle, a ladle, and there it was.

And when the needlefish swam [right by the canoe] singing, she dipped it out of the water. What they call a *quarruuk,* a poor little needlefish, she cut it in the middle because it had been purposely scaring them.

Then the grandmother ate the front part [of the needlefish] and her grandchild ate the tiny tail part. That is how long [the story] is.

Also the things they had gotten ready, their paths and things, they put them back. [*chuckles*] The various things including their path to go and dump things and their small urine containers, they were back in their places.

It so happened that the poor needlefish had sung to scare the grandmother and grandchild.

After putting those things back, the grandmother and grandchild stayed there without fearing anything. The little needlefish had apparently tried to scare them. This is the length [of the story].

Tua-i-llu tuani erinii cakma piluni.

Tua-i-ll' itrami, necualleramegnun itran, aren, upngartuk qimakatarlutek aguuksuallertek-llu tamana makluku.

Cat tua-i, tumyarat-llu makut, yuqercaratek-llu, ciqiciyaratek-llu, qaillun-kiq avurtanki? Tuavet aguutmeggnun ekluki tua-i.

Tua-i-llu-gguq tamakut pirraarluki, cali imkut egaksualleratek-llu, cat tua-i ekurluki aguutmegnun alingamek cakmumek agiirtellriamek. Arenqiatuq aturluni-llu agiirtelliniami.

Tua-i-llu cat tua-i qaqirmirteqerluki waniw' tua-i atrarlutek. Tuar-gguq tua-i tamaani kuigagnek. Tua-i cama-i ketiignun ellirluni.

Tua-i-llu-gguq tamaani pillermegni, ketmegnun ellirnganani, tua-i cama-i tekiteqatarnganani. Piqerluni, tua-i taum pia, tutgara'urlurlua aguutmun tuani atrarluni piluni tua-i. Tua-i-llu maurlurluan cali maliggluku.

Maaten-gguq atrartuq, atrartuq cama-i aturluni, "Ingkuk-tur' yaani-ii, cingiggaaraam amatiini arnarkaurluuk qassarlakek-tur', qukaagnegun kep'artaqlukek, ki-yaa aa-rru-rra-yaa ki-yaa."

Maaten-gguq mermek pingalan, taum maurlurluan, piqertuq un'a cukituliurluq asgulria aturpagluni, yuaruterluni.

Tua-i-ll' aguutmegni, taukut imkut, kenircuuteurlutek-llu cat-llu qantarrateklu taukut carratek-llu ekumiita, arulamiruksuallerani ipuun, ipuuksuallerani kiarartaa, waniwa.

Tua-i-llu-gguq unavet quarruuk taun' aturpagluni pillrani, qaluqerluku nuggluku. Apqiinek tauna quarruuk, *needlefish*-ayagaurluq qukaakun kep'arrluku alingcetaallruatek.

Tua-i taum maurlurlua keggatiinek nerluni tauna-llu tutgara'urlurlua nuuksuggiinek tua-i nerluku. Tua-i waten taktauq tua-i.

Aren-wa tua-i imkut ataam pitek, upcaaqeltek, tamakut imkut tumyaratek ellilarluki. [*ngelaq'ertuq*] Cat ciqiciyarraurlutek-llu tua-i, qurruksualleratek-llu-wa tua-i tamaavet ataam enemeggnun pillinilriit.

Cunawa-ggur-am taum quarruugaurluum, *needlefish*-aurluum aturpagluni alingcetaallinikek taukuk tutgara'urlurluqellriik.

Tua-i tamakut cat pirraarluki, nutaan tua-i camek alingevkenatek tuani uitauraurlulliuk tayima taukuk tutgara'urlurqellriik. Quarruugem, *needlefish*-ayagaam alingcetaallrullinilukek. Tua-i waten taktauq.

WHEN EXTRAORDINARY BEINGS WERE PRESENT

∽ *Ircenrraat Stories* ∾

Frances Usugan with Cathy Moses and Ann Fienup-Riordan,
Toksook Bay, July 1985

Frances Usugan: Qasginguaq. What are these *ircenrraat* [other-than-human persons] who have been around for a long time? Some people happen upon *ircenrraat*.

Now, my older brother Cyril Canaar, did you not see him?

Cathy Moses: I used to see him.

Frances Usugan: Oh, you used to see him? He heard people drumming and singing coming from Qasginguaq up there. And that winter when they had the Messenger Feast, he composed numerous songs with *ircenrraq* origins.

It is said when people hear *ircenrraat* singing, they learn [their songs] right away.

Nuyarralgem Atii [the father of Nuyarralek], when we went to Qalulleq to go summer camping, from up there he evidently went to get *uiteraq* [red ochre] by walking to Angyaruaq across there, a great distance away across there. When he was young he walked a great distance in summer.

Then as he was returning home, he heard some people singing. It was evidently from Qasginguaq. Although they were far, although the *ircenrraat* were far, he heard them singing. It is said that the closer he got to Qasginguaq, the quieter and quieter they became. Then when he arrived upon it, they got quiet.

What are these *ircenrraat*?

They used to also bring [people] inside. I used to hear stories that the *ircenrraat* would bring some people inside their land.

When they brought them inside they would spend a night. When they let them out, they would go out and realize that they had gone out the next year after having slept overnight. That's what I used to hear about *ircenrraat*.

CAT PAIVNGALLRATNI

   Ircenrraat Qanemciit

Piyuuk, Keggutailnguq, Ellaq'am Arnaan, Nunakauyaq, July 1985

Piyuuk: Qasginguaq. Tua-i-w' ircenrraat makut ukanirpak caugat? Yuum ilii, nall'arkenglalriit ircenrrarnek.

Tua-i-llu anngaqa Cyril Canaar, tangerqallrunritan?
Keggutailnguq: Tanglallruaqa.
Piyuuk: Oh, tanglallruan? Pikaken pika-i Qasginguamek cauyalrianek niitell-ruuq atulrianek. Uksuan-llu Kevgiata ircenrrartarnek yuaruciquluni.

Ircenrraat-gguq waten niitaqamegteki aturtelluki elitetuit egmian.

Ellii-am Nuyarralgem Atii, kiaken, Qalullermun kiagillemteni, pekqurluni-am uitertelliuq ikavet Angyaruamun, ak'akik akmavet. *Young*-allermini yaaqvanun *walk*-arluni ayagluni kiagmi.

Tua-i-llu uterrnginanermini atulrianek niilluni. Cunawa tua-i Qasginguamek. Yaaqsingraata, ircenrraat makut yaaqsingraata atulriit niiqurluki. Tauna-gguq Qasginguaq tekisngiinallra maliggluku qaskelliinarluteng. Tua-i-llu tekilluku ne-pairulluteng.
Ircenrraat makut caugat?
Cali itrucitullruluteng. Tua-i-w' qanemcinek niitelallrulrianga ilii yuum itru-taqluku ircenrraat nunameggnun.
Itrutaqateng qavartarluteng. Anevkaraqaceteng, anenaurtut-gguq allrakuan anllinilriit unugpak qavarraarluteng. Tuaten-am niitetullruanka ircenrraat.

Are you recording it? Is it recording?

Ann Riordan: Yes, it's good.

Frances Usugan: Yes, I don't know a great deal about these *ircenrraat*, but I've heard stories about them.

I also heard the following story. It is said they brought a man inside. I'll tell you these particular stories as they come to mind. That man they brought inside, he wasn't a *nukalpiaq* [great hunter]. He had a bird parka made of different kinds of birds, different kinds. Back when people were poor, those who weren't great hunters just had parkas made of all sorts of small birds.

Then when the *ircenrraat* brought him inside, back when those poor people wore parkas without cloth hooded garments over them, men wore their bird parkas with the feathers on the outside.

After the *ircenrraat* messed with him at first . . . this is how I heard the story. Those *ircenrraat* asked him questions about his parka; they would ask who caught this one [particular bird]. That one there, that one with the parka would say that they were caught by his various family members.

Since these people were wise . . . That's what I heard about that. When [the *ircenrraq*] asked about this [particular bird], because he lacked [birdskins], the poor thing wasn't wearing a parka made of just one bird species. His parka had skins of different small birds.

When [the *ircenrraq*] asked about this one, he would say his father caught it. "Who caught this?" When he asked about another, he would say his paternal uncle had caught it. [He'd say] that his uncle caught it. [He'd say] that his cousin caught it. [He'd say] that his grandfather caught it. He would say that a certain family member had caught [a particular bird]. Those people were wise.

Then those *ircenrraat* evidently said to him, "Don't mess with that one down there and let him out. Evidently there are many people who will fight for him if harmed." They were afraid to harm him. "He evidently has many people who will seek revenge if he is harmed by anyone. Let him out without bothering him."

This is what I hear about *ircenrraat*. When they are about to go out, it is said there are three doorways. What are these *ircenrraat*? He evidently told him to go out through the middle [door]. Some others evidently told him to go out through the bottom one; they told him to go out through the top one.

Then one of the elderly men said, "Don't mess with him, and let him go out through the one in the middle."

Some of them there were cruel to him. If he had gone out through the [doorway] on the bottom, he wouldn't have returned home, he would have gone out through the lower or upper doorway and not found his way home.

They were afraid when he said that his various relatives had caught [the birds] on his parka. He lied, since those people in the past were clever. Thinking that he

Tua-llu-q' imiran? Imirtuq?

Ellaq'am Arnaan: Yaa, assirtuq.

Piyuuk: Yaa, tua-i-wa arcaqerluki ircenrraat makut nallunritenrilkenka, taugaam tuaten qanemciuluki niitetukenka.

Cali-llu waten qanemcimek niitellruunga. Angun-gguq tauna itruskiit. Tua-i pugugtaarluki. Angun-gguq tauna itruskiit imuuluni tua-i nukalpiaruvkenani. Tengmiqcaaraat-wa-gguq atkui tamat, ayuqenrilnguut. Waten tua-i avani arr-saagaaullermeggni, nukalpiarunrilnguut tengmiqcaarnek atkungqerraqluteng.

Tua-llu ircenrraat itrucatni, tamaa-i atkugteurlutullermeggni qaspermek-llu caunateng, waten yaqulkussagaat atkuteng elatmun caulluki angutet.

Tua-i qaillukuaryaaqerraarluku ircenrraat . . . waten tua-i qanemciq niitell-ruaqa. Ircenrraat taukut apqaulliniluku atkui tamakut apyutkurluki; una camun pitaqellranek. Taum wani, taum wani atkulgem caminun pitaqniaqluki.

Tua-i umyuartulaameng makut . . . Tuaten tauna niitellruaqa. Una wani ap-yutkaqaku, pikaitem ugaan tua-i kesirrlainarnek atkugteurlurpek'nani. Teng-miqcaaraat makut qecileguaraat tamaqcaaraat atkukluki.

Una wani apyutkaqaku ataminun pitalqeniaqluku. "Una kia pitallra?" Alla cali apyutkaqaku ataataminun pitalqeniaqluku. *Uncle*-aaminun pitalqeniaqluku. *Cousin*-aaminun pitalqeniaqluku. Apa'urluminun pitalqeniaqluku. Caminun tua-i pitalqeniquluki. Tua-i umyuartulaameng makut.

Tua-i-llu ircenrraat taukut pilliniluku, "Ataki kan'a qaillukuarpek'naku anev-karciu. Pistekalilliniuq." Alinguqluku. "Pistekalilliniuq. Anevkarciu qaillukuar-pek'naku."

Waten wani ircenrraat niitetuanka. Anqataraqata waten amiiget pingayun-gguq. Ircenrraat makut caugat? Waten pilliniluku qukaqlirkun anesqelluku. Ilaita piyaaqluku aciqlirkun anesqelluku; qullirkun anesqelluku.

Tua-llu iliita angullugaat pilliniluni, "Qaillukuarpek'naku qukaqlirkun anev-karciu."

Waten wani tamakut ilaita ilacukluku. Aciqlirkun ankan piciuyarpek'nani acitruulluni qang'a-ll' ellatruulluni piyalliniluni.

Alinguqluku tua-i tamakut atkuni caminun aperturturaaki. Iqluquluni, um-yuartulaameng avani. Ilumun pistekalipigcukluku ircenrraat tamakut alinguqluku

really did have many people to do things [seek revenge] for him, the eldest of those *ircenrraat* were afraid of him, back when those who were appointed to lead their people were their leaders.

One of the elderly men evidently said not to mess with him, but to let him out. And although those people there said for him to go out through the middle, the top, and the bottom, they scolded them not to mess with him but to let him out through the middle [doorway].

When he went out, he went out to our world here. That's how I heard that *ircenrraq* story, since those people used to constantly tell stories.

That's that one. The short stories, I really don't know various short stories well, but only about people doing things.

Stories about people who happen upon *ircenrraat*, I heard them as short stories like this and not long [stories], just like that.

And Kalukaat [Mountains] down the coast, ones they call Kalukaat along Nuuget [the capes on the west shore of Nelson Island], when we go around [the cape], those high [mountains] up there, they say they are *ircenrraat*. And they also say these killer whales are *ircenrraat*.

And down the coast at Nuuget, when a person hears it, after making the noise of kayaks preparing to take off, they say that killer whales breach and dive very close to shore heading down away from shore. Those from Kalukaarmiut, they say residents of Kalukaat make kayak noises like ones getting ready. Although they don't see anything, after hearing them [get ready], killer whales evidently breach and dive heading down away from shore from very close to the shore.

And again when [killer whales] catch a seal, when they are fighting a seal, it is said the [person] watching them, it is said there will be blubber around for the one watching them. It is said [killer whales] are giving him a share of their catch, *nengirluku* as they say.

They say [the blubber] looks exactly like something that they had cut with a knife. In the past since they used to divide a seal equally when they pursued seals in open water, they said [the killer whale] was giving him a share of the blubber.

That's the length of that story also.

[*Ircenrraat*] also used to make rumbling noises [kicking their feet repeatedly]. When a shaman was going to die among [the people], the [*ircenrraat*] would make rumbling noises [by repeatedly kicking their feet], the *ircenrraat* would make rumbling noises. We used to hear *tukaralriit* [ones making rumbling noises, kicking their feet]. One that was far was loud, it was loud. Some people would say that it sounded like it was coming from Kalukaat.

And again, our *maallugaaq* [name for a grandmother], our *maallugaaq*. The people across there [at Tununak], those two across there, Louise, you know

teggassagaita, ataneruarateng avani ataneqtullermeggni

Tuaten tua-i angullugaat iliita pilliniluku qaillukuarpek'naku anesqelluku. Tamakut-llu tamaa-i qullirkun-llu, aciqlirkun-llu anesqessaaqekiit, qaillukuarpek'-naku qukaqlirkun anesqelluku nun'urterluki.

Anngami tua-i maavet ellamtenun anluni. Tua-i tuaten niitellruaqa tauna qanemciq ircenrraq qanemciuluku, qanemcingssaarturluteng pilallruameng.

Tua-i-wa tauna. Qanemcingssaaraat, wiinga tang qanemcingssaaraat arca-qerluki nallunritenrilkenka taugaam tua-i pingssarturaqlriit.

Ircenrraat nall'artellrit tua-i takevkenaki qanemcingssaaraat niitetullruanka waten taktuaruvkenaki-llu, tuaten tua-i.

Cali ugkut Kalukaat, Kalukarnek pitukait Nuugni, uivaqamta qertuluteng ak'akik' qulvani pikegkut ircenrraunilarait. Makut-llu arrluut ircenrrauniluki.

Waten tua-i uani cali Nuugni ua-i, yuum niitaqani, qayarpallaraurluteng pirraarluteng, arrluut-gguq qaktelartut cenak'acagarmek maaken ketmun. Ka-lukaarmiut, tua-i-gguq Kalukaarmiut tamakut qayarpallaraurluteng imutun up-tellriatun. Camek tangvanrilngermeng niiterraartelluki, arrluut ketmun qakte-tullinilriit cenak'acagarmek maaken.

Tua-i tuamtellu waten taqukaskuneng, taqukamek callukuneng, tangvagteteng-gguq tauna, tangvagtiit-gguq tauna iciw' uqumek, uqumek paivngaliqerciquq. Nengirluku-gguq tua-i.

Tuarpiaq-gguq imna caskumek pilagtuaqapiarallrat. Avani taqukaq man'a naacuqa'arrluku malirqaqameng pitullruameng, uqurcilluku-gguq tua-i.

Tua-i tuaten tua-i tauna cali tuaten amllertacia.

Cali tukaratullruluteng. Tua-i ilangarteqatarqata camek angalkumek tukara-tullruluteng, imumek tem'iqtara'arluteng ircenrraat. Tukaralrianek niitetullruukut. Yaaqsilria qastuluni, qastuaqluni. Waten yuut ilait piaqluteng, Kalukarnek-gguq pingatut.

Tuamtell'-am maallugaarput tauna, maallugaarput. Ikegkut, ikegkuk-wa ika-i, Louise-aq, iciw' Louise Qanrilaq, Qanrilankut *grandma*-rat. Ukut-wa cali

Louise Qanrilaq, the grandmother of the Qanrilaq family. And she was also the grandmother of Qulvarkaq and family. There was the mother of Qulvarkaq and sibling's father's mother and Louise Qanrilaq and sibling's mother's mother; those two who are brother and sister across there.

Those across there [at Tununak], and those two dear small elderly women across there. You know how the other over there, the small one over there has the last name Aluska. The other [has the last name] Post. You know how Post's spouse died this past winter, the poor thing dying inside an airplane.

Those across there are family, they are siblings. The very small one across there whose name is Nalugalria in Yup'ik, the small one with the last name Aluska across there. She had adopted her younger sibling, that Pete Aluska. That's their youngest sibling, he's the baby of their family. But since she couldn't have children, his older sister adopted him. The poor one who got married down there, the father of the one who got married.

Our *maallugaaq* evidently would say, she was our *maallugaaq*, that when she was about to die that Kalukaat would make rumbling noises [kick their feet]. She was a shaman. Then that woman, our *maallugaaq* was a shaman.

Then one day the Kalukaat evidently made rumbling noises. When they *tukararqameng* as they say, [pounding on the floor or table] they make rumbling noises. It is said when their *tarnaq* [*tarneq*, "soul or spirit"] arrives among them, the *ircenrraat* say "oh boy" when their *tarnaq* arrives upon them.

Cathy Moses: Their *tarnat* [spirits or souls]?

Frances Usugan: They probably call them their *tarnat*. In the past, they were probably referring to the souls of those poor people. I think they were referring to their souls. And since they didn't mention anything, and they never spoke of their *anerneret* [spirits, souls], they only spoke of their *tarnat*, their *tarnat*.

Then our dear *maallugaaq* when the Kalukaat made rumbling noises, she said she didn't know what to do, and the poor thing evidently cried. They said that our *maallugaaq* moved to that place [Kalukaat] when the poor thing died.

Qulvarkaq across there, Bob Hooper, since he likes to clown around, while he was seal hunting down on the ocean, he evidently would pretend to call out to his *maallugaaq* down the coast at Kalukaat. [*chuckles*] His *maallugaaq*, not wanting him to be in a desperate situation down in the ocean. [*chuckles*] Their oldest brother over there.

I don't have any more stories to tell about *ircenrraat*.

Qulvarkankut *grandma*-qluku. Qulvarkankut atiita aanii, Louise Qanrilankut-wa aaniita aanii; anngaqelriik taukuk.

Ikegkut ika-i, arnassagacuaraurluuk-llu ikegkuk ika-i. Aipaa iciw' Aluska-mek *last name*-arluni mikcuayaar ikna. Aipaa-ll' Post-amek. Iciw' Post-am aipaa tuqullrulria uksuq tengssuutem iluani piurlurluni.

Taukut ikegkut ika-i ilakut, anelgutkut. Nalugalriacuayaar Yugtun ikna, Aluska-mek *last name*-ayagalek ikna. Aug'um, uyuraminek *adopt*-allrulria aug'umek Pete Aluska-mek. Uyuraqaat, piipiqaat. Taugaam irniangyuitellruami alqaan ik'um *adopt*-aaqellrua. Kassuuteurlulleq kan'a, kassuutellrem atii.

Waten qanlliniaqluni maallugaarput tauna, maallugaaqellruarput, waniw' tuquqataquni Kalukaat tuka'arciqniluki. Angalkuuguq. Tua-i-ll' arnaq tauna angalkuuguq maallugaarput.

Tua-i-llu cam iliini Kalukaat tukaralliniluteng. Tukararqameng tem'iq-tara'arluteng pituut. Tua-i-gguq tarnaata tekitaqateng imkulartut, imkurluteng-wa tua-i ircenrraat imkut, "*oh boy*"-aaraluteng tarnaita tekitaqateng.

Keggutailnguq: Tarnaita?

Piyuuk: Tarnaitnek-wam pilallikait. Anernerit-kiq piurlutullrulliit avani. Anernerit pilarngatellrullinikait. Camek-llu qanyuitellruameng, anerneritnek-llu qanyuunateng taugaam tarnaitnek, tarnait.

Tua-i-ll' maallugaurlurput tauna Kalukaat tukaraata tua-i, tua-i cacirkaitniluni qiaqcaaraurlulliniluni. Tua-i maallugaamtenun-am upagvikellruniluki taukut tuqu'urlullrani pillruut.

Ikna Qulvarkaq, Bob Hooper-aaq, picingssaungami, imarpigmi-llu kanani qamigaqcaararqami-am maallugaani tuqluruatullrullinikii Kalukarni uani. [*ngelaq'ertuq*] Maalluugaanek tangerkengaqlua imumek imarpigmi nanikuas-qevkenani. [*ngelaq'ertuq*] Anngaqlikacagiita ing'um.

Tua-i ircenrrarnek qanemcikairutua.

∾ *Ircenrraat and Inglugpayugaat* ◌

Mary Napoka, Rachel Sallaffie, and Ann Fienup-Riordan, Tuluksak, May 1989

Rachel Sallaffie: What happens to a person who gets lost? You know as we are outside in our world, when one is walking, they say things will be hanging in the trees. They say if he takes those things, he will get lost.

Mary Napoka: Those are probably things belonging to those [*ircenrraat*].

And also that poor person, Kamek'aq who was missing back there [inland], I think those [caused him to get lost].

Arsall'er and her husband's [child] . . . you know how the poor thing got lost back there [inland].

Since he wasn't too wise, when he was traveling somewhere inland, he evidently got lost. He said that he saw trees around. He said that he once saw two really nice dolls up there, but he couldn't reach them. He couldn't reach them.

And he said that sometimes he would see a great many necklaces. When he took one, he evidently brought it home. The necklace that he showed us had sinew for thread. I think those *ircenrraat* displayed those things to him.

Rachel Sallaffie: What if he traded for it?

Mary Napoka: It is said that they trade those [things they find] for something small and take them. It is said [*ircenrraat*] don't do anything to us at all when we exchange [things] for something and take them.

And upriver at Caniqerrarmiut, above that place, those crosses, not looking like crosses; a piece of wood was shaped like this with a lot of nails on it. It was evidently where things had been hanging.

The only thing hanging there was a small red bracelet. Mayuaq down there, my child down there wanted to take it. I cautioned her not to take it, thinking it was something, thinking it was something bad. And when we looked underneath it, there was a very nice looking small pot. I think it was this big. It wasn't tall, it had a lot of small designs on it. She also wanted to take that, so that we would have it in our home for decoration. We also didn't take that.

Rachel Sallaffie: What do they do when they take those?

Mary Napoka: When they trade them for something small, a small amount of food or something small, they're good. Although she wanted to take it, I cautioned her, thinking something would happen to us since that entire place was filled with graves. We had evidently set up tents in the midst of graves.

Rachel Sallaffie: And nothing happened to you?

Mary Napoka: And nothing happened to us; we never got haunted. But from Tuluksak, they told us never to chop with axes there. But they told us to chop wood far down toward the shore.

⨾ *Ircenrraat, Inglugpayugaat-llu* ⨽

Mary, Maayaaq, Ellaq'am Arnaan-llu, Tuulkessaaq, May 1989

Maayaaq: Pellalleq-mi qaillun pitua? Camek iciw', waten ellamteni uitangi-nanemteni, tarriskuni, tua-llu napami-gguq cat agaluteng. Teguskan tamarciq-niluku.

Mary: Tamakut-wa pik'lallikait.

Cali imnaurluq Kamek'aq imna cataitelleq im' pavani, tamakut pillru-yaaqsugnarqaat.

Imna Arrsallrenkuk . . . tamaurlullrulria iciw' pavani.

Usvingqessiyaanrilami-w' ayaganguallermini nani pavani ayuquciirutliniluni. Pinaurtuq-gguq makut napat. Irniaruaqegtaaraagnek-llu-gguq-am pika-i tangerr-saaquq, nurlukek. Qaill' pisciiganakek.

Iliini-llu-gguq pinaurtuq uyagmigugaat. Tua-i atauciignek tegucami ut'rutell-ruyaaqelliniuq. Augkut uyamiit nasvallri imumek yualunek nuvuterluteng. Tamakut ircenrraat pilaryaaqsugnarqaat tamaani, paivutaqluku tamakunek.

Maayaaq: Cimiuskani-mi?

Mary: Carrarmek-gguq cimiqerluki tegularait tamakut. [Piyuitaitkut-gguq] watqapiar cimiqerluki teguaqamteki.

Tua-i-ll'-am cali kiani, tuani Caniqerrarmiuni, im' quliitni tamakut kelistat, kelistangqerruciinateng; waten murag' man'a waten pimaaqluni, ik'ik' ussu-kcalirluni. Cunaw' cat agallrit.

Augna talliracuayaaq augna kavirliyagaq kiimi agaurall'. Maayuam kat'um, irniama kat'um teguyugyaaqaa. Inerqurqa wii tegusqevkenaku cauyukluku, assiilnguuyukluku. Maaten-llu piukut aciani kanani egaksuakegtaar. Waten ang-tayugnarquq. Sugtuvkenani, tua-i qaraliaralirluni. Cali taun' teguyugyaaqluku, tangnircautekniarput-gguq enemteni. Teguvkenaku cali tauna.

Maayaaq: Qaill' tuaten tamakut piaqamegeki pituitki?

Mary: Camek-wa tua-i carrarmek, neqkarrarmek wall' carrarmek cimiqerluki piaqameng, assituut. Tua-i-am teguyungraagu wii inerqurluku qaill' pinayukluta qungurrlainaullinian-llu. Pelatekallinilriakut-llu qungut akuliitni.

Maayaaq: Cavkenaci-llu-q'?

Mary: Cavkenata-ll'; alangruayuunata. Taugaam maaken Tuulkessaamek qanrutaitkut watqapiar piqertuaqsaunata tamaani pisqelluta. Unani taugaam ket-vani-ll' eqiulaasqelluta.

They told us not to chop with axes on top of where those deceased people were.

Then these ones suddenly wanted to move after a while. I was happy, and we moved since I was constantly afraid after I noticed those graves.

And after a while we discovered a large *qasgi* down there. And the logs that were inserted [into the ground] along the edge weren't rotten. They were in good shape.

That there, they told us, "When you are going to do something, give them an offering of food and water, *aviukarrluki* [give them an offering]." The men there would throw an entire Canada goose as it was over to the corner, asking for animals to be available to them. The next morning we'd see that [the goose] was gone.

Rachel Sallaffie: They were probably grateful for it.

Mary Napoka: Yes. Since I started to become afraid, when they said they wanted to move, I got happy. [*laughter*] We got happy and went home.

Rachel Sallaffie: They could have taken all of you [as a whole].

Mary Napoka: How frightful! There was a wonderful birch tree [grave where a shaman was buried] that was standing bound by trees. Its roots were wrapped around that birch tree [grave]. They said that was a shaman in the past. And here, unafraid of it, we lived around [the tree] for a long time.

Rachel Sallaffie: Since you probably continually gave them things, they probably liked you.

Mary Napoka: Yes, these men including these boys, after hunting, when they'd arrive, they would throw the whole Canada goose across there.

[My tent] was the highest up there. This area was stretched out, and then it suddenly got smooth down there. Behind [someone's] family's tent was that deceased shaman. The one Elena was named after mentioned that that one whose [grave] was bound [by roots] like that was once a shaman. I was constantly afraid. But we didn't experience anything at all, and we weren't haunted.

It turned out that we [had set up a tent] at a place with many graves. They say the ones who moved from there, from upriver, they split up like this. Many people died when there was a big flu epidemic. It is said when a few of them were left, they split up. Some went downriver, and some went upriver. [These ones] went upriver to Ayimqeryararmiut. But these ones evidently moved to Kuigeurluq and not around people. But they say some of these went upriver to where there were other people. [The place] evidently lost residents like that. No one lived there any longer.

Rachel Sallaffie: What about the next ones, when there was no longer anyone living there, how did they bury the next ones?

Mary Napoka: The next ones had coffins made out of various things. And after splitting logs and preparing boxes for [the deceased], although they were thick, they made them as thin as boards.

Tua-i-w' yullret qaingatni piqertuaresqevkenata.

Tua-i-ll'-am piqerluteng-am ukut upagyunga'artut. Tua-i wii quyalua upagluta alinguralaama taukut qungut elpekngamki.

Maaten-llu caqerluta piukut kanani qasgirpall'er. Waten-llu muriit mengliini waten kapurqumalriit arumavkenateng. Assirluteng.

Tua-i tuavet, piatkut tua-i waten, "Kitaki tua-i caqatarqavci aviukarrluki pilaqiciki, aviukarqaqluki." Ik'iki-am ukut angutet ukut lagiq-llu eluciatun ikavet kangiramun egtelaqiit, pitarkameggnek-llu paivutesqelluteng. Unuaquani pinaurput cataunani.

Maayaaq: Quyak'lallikiit-wa.

Mary: Ii-i. Tua-i wii alingengama upagyuata quyaqerlua. [*ngel'artut*] Quyaqerluta utertukut.

Maayaaq: Elucirpet teguksailkiitgen.

Mary: Ila-i! Augna-wa tang elnguqegtaar man' naumalria waten napat nemrumaluku. Imkut camkut kevraarcinrain nemrumaluku waten, augna qasruq. Tauna-gguq tua-i angalkulleq. Tua-llu-w' alikevkenaku nunalguciumallrukvut.

Maayaaq: Cikirturiivciki-w' assikellrullikiiceci.

Mary: Ii-i ukut, tan'gaurluut-llu ukut pissurraarluteng tekitaqameng, lagir' eluciatun ikavet egtaqluku.

Wiinga qulliulua pikani. Tauna waten man'a ceturrluni unani-ll' manigiqerluni. Maani [kinkut]qankut pelatekaata tunuqviini avani tauna angalkulleq uitalliniuq. Tua-i Elena-m atran qanrutekluku angalkullruniluku tauna nemrumalria waten. Wii tua-i alingura'arqellrianga. Amtall' cayuunata watqapiar, alangruayuunata-ll'.

Cunaw' qungurugarnun [pelatekalillinilriakut]. Tua-i-gguq tuaken, kiaken anelrallret avvluteng, waten. Quserpallratni-gguq yuirulluteng. Ikgelingarcameng-gguq waten avvluteng. Ukut uatmun, ukut-llu kiatmun. [Ukut piluteng] qamavet kiugkunun Ayimqeryararmiunun. Ukut taugken wavet Kuigeurlurmun pillrulliniluteng yugnun pivkenateng. Ukut-gguq taugken ilait kiavet yugnun. Tuaten nanglliniluteng. Tua-i taun' yugtairulluni.

Maayaaq: Qaillun-mi kinguqliit yuirutellrani qungulallruitki, kinguqliit?

Mary: Kinguqliit qungulallruut tua-i canek, canek-wa tua-i carrluarnek. Muriit-llu cakilluki waten yaassiigkiurraarluki, tuskatun, mamtungraata tuskatun ellirluki.

Rachel Sallaffie: Someone said that they saw coffins upriver that are visible.

Mary Napoka: Yes. Some [were put in coffins] made of wood; people who died in spring were probably not [buried] properly.

It was because those first people weren't afraid of things. I still haven't forgotten the things that I saw.

Rachel Sallaffie: What other things did you see?

Mary Napoka: I've seen various things, and evidently also these *ircenrraat.* And they would speak of something called *inglugpayugaat* [lit., "ones that have one of something," from *inglu-,* "other one of a pair"]. They say back when they constantly made *kalngat* [grass storage bags] out of grass, making containers for fish, when they always made *kalngat,* they say they used to braid this part [on the bottom of the bag] into one and sometimes two. It so happens that those would be their legs.

[The legs] of the *kalngak* [storage basket].

Rachel Sallaffie: Then what did those do?

Mary Napoka: They filled them with fish, they filled them with fish and also filled them with frozen fish to eat. They say back then that those, the *kalngat* that people made, used to start walking around. Although they were filled with fish, they walked around. They say some had just one leg. And they say some had two.

Evidently these days they no longer do that.

They say those [grass storage bags] are visible to [people] who they find to be bright.

Ones who they find to be bright, they are visible to people they like when they want to be visible.

The [storage bags] walked around, they had legs.

❧ *Those Pretending to Arrive* ❧

Frances Usugan with Cathy Moses and Ann Fienup-Riordan, Toksook Bay,
July 1985

Cathy Moses: What about those. . . . What was it again? She said those who had gone to attend a dance festival, when they returned home, they didn't arrive. Are they called *agiirrnguat* [those pretending to arrive]?

Frances Usugan: Agiirrnguat. *Agiirrnguat* also, up at Cakcaaq River, we see the trail that the *agiirrnguat* took. They used to say to us not to continually search our surroundings, anxious and impatient for someone's arrival.

Maayaaq: Kina-ggem qanellruuq kiani qungunek tanglarniluteng iciw' pugumalrianek.

Mary: Yaa. Muragnek ilait; up'nerkami-wa tua-i pillret picuvlagluki-llu pilallikait.

Alingyuitellruameng-llu-w' imkut ciuqliit. Wii tua-i tanglallrenka maa-i nalluyagucuitanka.

Maayaaq: Canek-llu tanglallrusit?

Mary: Tua-i-w' makunek canek tanglalrianga, cunawa-ll' makunek ircenrrarnek. Tuamtallu-am caneg' imkunek inglugpayugarnek qanernaurtut. Imumi-gguq kalngiuratullratni canegnek neqet caqukiurluki, kalngiuratullratni una-gguq piirrilaraat atauciuluku, iliini-llu-gguq malruuluku. Cunawa-gguq irukait.

Kalngiim.

Maayaaq: Caluteng-llu tua-i tamakut?

Mary: Tua-i-w' imirluki-w' neqnek, neqnek imirluki canek, kumlanerkanek tuaten imirluki. Tamaani-gguq-am tamakut tua-i tarringelallruut kalngiarit yuut. Neqnek imangqeng'ermeng tarritaqluteng. Ilait-gguq atauciirrarmek iruluteng. Ilait-llu-gguq malrugnek.

Kiituani-am maa-i pinanrirtut.

Tua-i-gguq-am tamakut cat tanqikekmeggnun alaitetuut tamakut.

Tua-i-w' tanqikekmeggnun, assikekmeggnun alaitaqluteng alaicugaqameng.

Tarrilluteng, iruluteng.

&ea; *Agiirrnguat* &so;

Piyuuk, Keggutailnguq, Ellaq'am Arnaan-llu, Nunakauyaq, July 1985

Keggutailnguq: Augkus-mi. . . . Canek-ima? Ukut-gguq yuraliyalriit utercaaqellermeng tekicuunateng-gguq. Agiirrnguat?

Piyuuk: Agiirrnguat. Agiirrnguat cali, kia-i Cakcaami agiirrnguat tumellrat tanglaraput. Waten pitullrukaitkut nerinilluta kiarquraasqevkenata.

And I saw with my eyes the trail that *agiirrnguat* took. The village of Cakcaarmiut upriver, Cakcaarmiut, these days they travel to Cakcaaq [River]. Cakcaaq is located along the outlet of Qalvinraaq [into Baird Inlet].

Those people there evidently went to attend a Messenger Feast since Messenger Feasts had been their tradition since long ago. The people of Cakcaarmiut evidently went to attend a Messenger Feast on the other side of the mountains.

Then those two who were a grandmother and grandchild were among the group who stayed back to watch over things. Those who had gone to attend the Messenger Feast were delayed in their arrival, they weren't arriving.

Because her dear grandchild was so anxious and impatient for their arrival; and from [the top of] small homes, they would look at their surroundings. When there was a sled that had left or when their husbands had left, they searched their surroundings once in a while to check for his arrival, so that they could make it comfortable for him when he arrived and also put out food for him.

When we got husbands since we were instructed to think about their stomachs, they used to do that once in a while. But because of that poor thing, I think it became an admonishment [not to be anxious for someone's arrival]. The trail that the *agiirrnguat* took up there is a deep gorge. They evidently passed through [making a gorge], just barely missing the village.

Her grandchild, probably because of her hungry stomach, she probably did that; she climbed on top of the home and looked toward where those who had gone to attend the Messenger Feast had headed.

Anna, hand me my hooded cloth garment over there.

While the poor thing was looking in the direction of the area where they had headed, then the mountains . . . Upriver at Cakcaaq, you know how there's a mountain. The spot that she was looking at from Cakcaaq was a small mountain. From the small mountain, toward evening those up there evidently slid down. Then when she went inside, she excitedly told her grandmother that they were arriving.

It is said they slid down from that mountain all evening, all evening long, all day, traveling extremely slowly. She would go out and check on them many times and see that they had only reached this place slowly.

It is said they got faster as the evening progressed. It so happened they were *agiirrnguat*. When [the grandchild] would go inside, [she'd tell] her grandmother.

For that reason they used to tell us not to search our surroundings too much, that we would experience seeing *agiirrnguat*. We were afraid of that. They would tell us not to search our surroundings too much, that we would experience seeing *agiirrnguat*. Searching one's surroundings too much was dangerous.

Then they said that after traveling all evening, when they started traveling faster, their noise started to become audible, making creaking noises. You know how some things make creaking noises.

Iigemkun-llu qava-i agiirrnguat tumellrat tangellruaqa. Tua-i Cakcaarmiut kiugkut nunat, Cakcaarmiut, Cakcaamun ayagalartut maa-i. Qalvinraam igyaraani tua-i Cakcaaq.

Taukut curukallinilriit waten ukanirpak Kevgiq pikngamegteggu. Amalirnermun akmavet ingrit amtiitnun curukallinilriit Cakcaarmiut.

Tua-i-llu taukuk maurluqura'urlulriik tua-i pailriit ilaklukek. Tua-i curukat imkut tekicugpek'nateng, utercugpek'nateng.

Tua-i tutgara'urlua una nerinitem ugaan'; enerrlugarni-llu waten nacelluteng-llu. Ikamramek ayagciangqerraqameng, qang'a-ll' aiparmeggnek ayagciangqerraqameng tua-i agiirtellerkaa piqerluku kiarartetullrulriit, imumek ciunqegcarnaluku neqkainek-llu paivcitnaluku.

Waten tua-i aipangaqamta wangkuta anrutait-llu qanruyutngullruata, tuaten tua-i piqatullrulriit. Taugaam tua-i tauna-am pitkeurlurluku inerquutaularyugnarqelriit. Qava-i atam agiirrnguat, agiirrnguat tumellrat tevaumakacaartuq. Nunat tua-i ukut uniurcecuarluki pillrullinilriit.

Waten-am tua-i tutgara'urlua tauna, tua-w' anrutarani-ll' niilluku pillilria; enem qainganun mayurluni curukat imkut ayallrata tungiinun.

Qaspeqa ing' taiteqerru Anna.

Ayallrata tungiinun kiarqura'urluinanrani, tua-llu ingrit . . . Kiani kia-i Cakcaami, iciw' ingritangqellria. Tua-i Cakcaamek tangvallra ava-i ingricungaq. Ingricungarmek tua-llu atakuyartumi tua-ll' pagkut tua-i ellulliniluteng. Tua-i-ll' maurlurluni itrami tavulluku agiirrniluki.

Tua-i-gguq imna atakurpak tamaaken tamaa-i ingrimek elluumalriit, atakurpakutarpall'er, ernerpak, cukaitkacagarluteng. Tua-i ak'akik' tua-i anluni paqnaurai wavet elliqcaaralliniriit.

Atakullra-gguq maliggluku cukariinarluteng. Cunawa-gguq tang tamaa-i agiirrnguat. Maurlurluni tua-i [qanrutaqluku] itraqami.

Taumeg'-am tamana pitekluku anagulluta kiarquraasqevkenata pitullruitkut, agiirrnguarciqniluta. Tamana alikellruarput. Anagulluta kiarquraasqevkenata agiirrnguarciqniluta. Alingnaqluni-am tua-i kiarqurassiyaallerkaq.

Tua-i-llu-gguq atakuan, atakuyarturpak cukariameng, nepait-gguq alairtut kekingerrluteng. Iciw' qalriayaaralalriit cat kekingerrluteng.

When I asked about those, they said they were many old-style [above ground] coffins, *cit'at*, many coffins. This is what I heard about them. Since they used to bury people like this and not bury them underground, these logs were their coffins, they were their coffins on top of the land. And someone who was greatly loved, they made a post for him that was high. That's how they used to [care for the deceased].

Her dear grandmother, she asked her if they were those, [saying] that they had gotten faster as they were approaching. And when their noise became audible, her dear grandmother, using her ability, doing something, with her mind she hoped that they would miss them, and she did a ritual in hopes that [the *agiirrnguat*] wouldn't go right through that village.

Since those dear people tried things, and since some elderly women's and elderly men's minds were powerful, and also it's like they used to pray constantly as they lived. They evidently did things with purpose.

And one who was going through training to become a better hunter, what they call *cilkiagurluni*, one who was constantly handling debris and refuse, a young person who worked on dirty jobs, who worked dumping urine containers when he was trying to become good at catching animals, God evidently heard his [prayers].

The *agiirrnguat* arrived right along the edge of [the homes of] those people there. They hollowed out the ground in winter. There is a trench along the edge of Cakcaarmiut, the trail that was taken by the *agiirrnguat* since they were probably real. That's how [the story] ends.

When I have a few stories that I know, I tell them to you.

And now [what else]? . . .

Cathy Moses: She's asking what, what other teachings you were given like that one? Like the other [instruction] not to look around for no reason.

Frances Usugan: Yes, we were given that admonishment, that although we do search our surroundings from time to time, that like that one's grandchild, even though we are impatient and anxious for their arrival, not to continually search our surroundings.

They would tell us, "You will experience seeing *agiirrnguat*. You will experience seeing *agiirrnguat*." We were afraid to do that, to continually search our surroundings. Even though it wouldn't happen to someone. When things happened, those admonishments came to exist; they became admonishments when things happened. When something happened to people and there was a story about it, they told us not to engage in it.

Tua-i tamakut apyutkellemni cit'arugaat-gguq, qungurugaat. Waten-am niitellruanka. Waten wani qungiciurlutullruameng tua-i elautevkenaki, muragat makut tua-i qunguqluki, waten tua-i qunguqluki nunam qaingani. Ilii-llu kenkataq naparyirluku qulvarluku naparyirluku. Tuaten tua-i pitullruit.

Tua-i maurlurluni, tamakunek tamaa-i tua-i tamakuulliniciitnek, uka-i cukariniluki. Nepait-llu alaillratni, maurlurluan taum tua-i pirraminek, qaillun-wa tayima, umyuarramikun tua-i uniurteqaasqellutek, nunat taukut tumkekacaaranritqaasqelluki qaillukuaqcaaralliniluni.

Pingssaaraurlurluteng pitullruameng, ak'allaraam-llu arnassagaam, angullugaam-llu iliin, umyugaa cagnitullruami, cali-llu waten tamana tamaa-i imutun agayuuralriatun pitullrulliniut yuullermeggni. Ca man'a umyuarcirturluku pitullrullinilriit.

Waten-llu cilkiaguralria, apqiit cilkiagurluni caarrliurturalria, ikiuguralrianek yun'erraq caliarluni, qurrutnek caliarluni picungnaqaqami tamaa-i, Agayutmek niicimalallrull[iniuq].

Taukut menglaicuarluki taukut agiirrnguat tekitellruut. Tua-i nevu nayugluku uksumi. Qava-i tua-i Cakcaarmiut mengliitni tevaneq augna agiirrnguat tumellrat tua-i-am piciullrulliameng. Tua-i tuaten iquklilluni.

Tua-i nallunritaraqemnek qanemcinek pikangqevguararqama pilaramken.
Tua-llu? . . .
Keggutailnguq: Canek-llu-gguq-qaa, canek-llu alerquutangqellruuten iciw' aug'utun? Call' aug'utun kiarrnguaresqevkenaki.
Piyuuk: Yaa, tua-i-w' tuaten inerquumalallrulriakut kiarteqaqu'urluta pingramta, aug'utun ava-i tutgara'urluatun anagulluta nerinitlerput pitekluki kiangqauraasqevkenata.

Waten piaqluta, "Agiirrnguarciqaaci. Agiirrnguarciqaaci." Tamana tamaa-i alikellruarput, kiarqurassiyaagluta [pillerkarput]. Pingailengraan. Tayima piqallruaqata inerquutaulartut; inerquutaulallruut piqallruaqata. Pillruaqata qanemcitangqerraqan, tuaten pisqeksaitelallruakut.

❧ *Person Who Came upon Wolf Pups* ❧

Dick Andrew and Marie Meade, Bethel, August 1992

Dick Andrew: There was a person who came upon wolf pups as he was going along the seashore. They were along the ground in a nest of grass. He stood briefly and looked down at the cute pups. He had a gun. It was after they had acquired guns that you load. Then after looking at them he continued along past them without touching them.

Then later on in the day he heard the sound of breathing behind him. He looked back and discovered that a wolf had already caught up with him. Then when she caught up with him, she ran past him and whipped him with her tail. Oh, it hurt so much when she hit him with her tail. Then she continued to hit him. Soon there were two of them, her and her male partner.

Then he was about to collapse, when his legs were about to buckle since he was in pain. . . . When [the two wolves] turned their tails and hit him as they ran by, the impact was like the force of a club. He began speaking to them, "I didn't do anything to your pups. I walked past your pups without touching them. I didn't bother your pups." She resented that he had looked at her pups.

Then since he was hurt, as his legs began to fail, he told the other [wolf], "Since you two will not listen to what I'm saying. . . ." Though he had told them what he had done, they wouldn't stop. [He told them,] "I will give you fire from the other side of the ocean which you cannot escape."

Then as one of them ran past him and turned sharply, he shot it on the leg. When he shot one of them, they quickly disappeared, taking off.

Then he discovered that it was beginning to get dark. Since his legs were in bad shape and realizing that he could not reach home right away, since it was a little windy he sat on the leeside of willow bushes and rested.

Just when night fell, when he heard some talking behind him, he looked back, since he had settled in front of the mountains, and he saw two young men coming chatting to each other. Two handsome young men were chatting.

When they arrived they told him that [the men] in the settlement back there had asked them to come get him so that he could spend the night at their place. Then they took his arms and lifted him up and held him on both sides and slowly brought him up.

When he looked back he saw houses with light coming out of doorways. Then when they came to the middle one, the [middle] doorway, when they came to it one of them pushed him. As he pushed him, [the man] fainted.

❧ *Keglunyagarnek Tekitelleq* ❧

Apaqutaq Arnaq-llu, Mamterilleq, August 1992

Apaqutaq: Tauna-ggur-am ayainanermini imarpiim ceniikun keglunyagarnek ukunek tekitellinilria. Maani tua-i cailkami ungluluteng, taugaam cururluteng canegnek. Kumekluki kanavet tangvaagalliniluki. Nutegluni. Nutengneratgun pillrulliniami imiriyaranek. Tua-i-ll' tangvaagaqerraarluki tua-i yagtevkenani, agtuqerpek'naki-llu kitull[iniluki.

Tua-i-ll' man'a erneq qaill' pitariqertelluk' kingunra anertevkalriamek [pitangelliniluni]. Kingyaartelliniuq keglunrem ak'a tekitellinikii. Tua-i-ll' anguamiu ayakarluni qip'arcami, pamyuminek piqerrluku kitu'urtelliniluku. Akekataki-gguq irua akngirrlun' cakneq pamyuminek piqellrani. Wanirpak tua-i. Kiituani-gguq malruurtuk, anguteklinikni-ll' tauna.

Tua-i-ll' uyungarkaurcami, tua-i irugni uyungarkaurcagnek nangteqngami . . . Kaugtuutartun-gguq pitauk pamyukek piqrutaqatkek qip'arrlutek kitu'urtaqagni. Qanrut'ngelliniak wavet, "Irniaten qaill' pinritanka. Qaill' piqerpek'naki kituranka. Unitanka irniaten qaillukuarpek'naki." Irniani tangvallrit pitekluki taum.

Tua-i-ll' akngircami, akngingqengeng'ami, irugni camkuk, uyungarkaurcami, aipaa qanrutlinia, "Tua-i niicunripakarpetegnga. . . ." Cakaniyuunatek-gguq tuaten qanrutengraatek. "Imaam akian kenertaanek avicunailngurmek cikirciqamtek."

Tua-i-ll' imna arenqialami tua-i, aipaa kitu'urtellrani avavet irua nutliniluku. Nutgan nutaan avallaqerlutek tayima catairtellinilutek, ayagarrlutek, tauna aipaa nutgani.

Tua-ll' pilliniuq atakuluni man'a. Tua-i irugni camkuk assiilagnek, uterteng'ermi-ll' kingunisngailami tamaa, uqvigarraat waten napalriit uqratnun anuqliaraan aqumqerlun' uitauralliniluni.

Tan'geraaraqertelluku pamkugnek qanemciuralriignek niicami takuyalliniuq kelutmun, ingrit manuatni pilliniami, yun'erraaraak makuk agiirtellriik tua-i qanengssaullutek. Tua-i qanengssaullutek yun'erraqegtaaraak ukuk.

Tua-ll' tekiarcamegnegu pilliniak pingkut-gguq aqvasqengagnegu waniw' aqvaak pamani uitasqelluku, uitasqellug' unugpak. Tua-i akiqliqa'arrlutek tallig-ken'gun teguqerluk' taguquralliniluku.

Maaten-gguq tang ciunrak paugna keluni tangrraa enet paugkut kenurrarluteng amiimeggnek. Tua-i-ll' uumun qukaqlirmun tekicamegnegu, amiiganun waten, tekicamegnegu cingqaqalliniluku aipaan. Cingqaqaani cacini nalluqalliniluku.

When he regained consciousness, he found himself in a *qasgi* on top of the floor boards. He looked all the way around the *qasgi* and found people everywhere. And on the platform in the back he noticed a *nukalpiaq* on his back complaining about his leg. His leg was in pain, and he was rolling around. The wolf that was struck by a bullet was a human, a *nukalpiaq*.

Then one of the people said, "Oh my, you have harmed that one back there. You help him get well. You harmed him. He said you harmed him intentionally."

Then he walked up to him and examined his leg and saw that the wound was at the exact spot where he had shot. Since he had a little knife, he pulled out the bullet with his little knife.

Then he said that he had given him the fire [bullet] from the other side of the ocean when [the wolf] was beating him and hurting his legs earlier that day. He said it was because they were beating him and wouldn't stop. He said that the action was not deliberate, but because they kept hurting him and after a time of caution.

Then one of them said, "I thought he said it was done deliberately." Then they said, "Would you hang him up down there."

Then they poked a hole here in the bridge of his nose. They threaded something through [his nose], and that tether was moving continuously like an inflated intestine. And they tied the line to the post out near the entrance. He hung there. He hung there, and he didn't feel any pain.

Then as he did something he fell down. When he fell one of them spoke, "*Yii-i!* The artery of the earth which has never been cut has finally been cut by someone. Don't bother him anymore. Let him go."

The old man across there said, "If you bother him . . ." He was the grandfather of that person. He had recognized him. "If you bother him *ull'uciiqamci* [?I will destroy you with a big wind]."

When they were about to let him out, he saw that there were three doorways vertically up and down. Then they said to him, one of them said, "Where are we going to let him out? Should we let him go through *acitruucaraq* [?the way that is taken to go underneath]? Or through *ellangqerrucaraq* [?the way that is taken to go through the sky]?"

Then the [old man] yelled at them again, "If you bother him, I will [destroy you] with a big wind." The others went down and attempted to let him go through the bottom [door] and again through the top. Then [the old man] went down and had him step on his spine and let him out through the middle doorway. He went out.

When he went out — it had been spring at the time [he entered the *qasgi*] — he found that the grasses were pale [dead]. Then he went home.

Ellangartelliniuq qasgim iluani nacitet qaingatni unkut. Kiarquralliniuq ena man'a, qasgiq man'a avatek tua-i yugyaglutek. Qaugna-wa tang inglermi nukalpiaq qaugna tua-i ngirtellria tua-i iruminek uumek. Nangteqluni tua-i iruminek akagturluni. Puulim tut'ellra kegluneq yuuluni tua-i qavani nukalpiaq qaugna.

Tua-ll' iliit qanlliniuq, "Aling qaugna qavani qaillukuallruan. Qaillukuallruan elpet kitugesgu. Qaillukuallruan. Pitsaqluku-gguq qaillukuallruan."

Tua-i-ll' maaten tang ullagluku [pia], imna tua-i waniw' nutellran nallii. Nuussicuallerrangqerrami, nuussicualleraminek ikuggluku antelliniluku.

Tua-ll' qanlliniuq tuaten, nangpakaagni ernermi, irugni akngirqevvakaagni cikillruniluku imaam akian kenertaanek. Nangpakaagni tua-i. Tua-i pitsaqevkenakek pillrunritnilukek, tua-i nangpakaagni taugaam tua-i inerquryaaqviminek.

Tua-ll' iliit qanlliniuq, "Pitsaqluni-ggem-tanem pillruniuq." Tua-i-ll' pilliniut, "Agarteqerciu kanavet."

Ayumian-am uuggun akuliraakun putuluku. Cameg' mat'umek nuvlliniat, tua-i qilutun qerruratun uitavkenani man'a uskuraa. Aglumun-llu uavet qillrulluku. Agaqalliniluni tuani agauyaarluni. Tua-i qaillukuarturluni agauyaarturalliniuq akngirtevkenani-ll', akngiringavkenani.

Tua-i qaill' piqalriim igtelliniluni. Igcan iliit-am qanngartelliniuq, "Yii-i! Nunam atam taqra kepestengyuilnguq kepestengurainalria. Qaillukuarpek'nak' anevkarciu."

Imna ikna angukara'urluq pilliniuq, "Qaillukuaquvciu . . ." Apa'urlua-gguq taum. Ika-i elitaqluku. "Qaillukuaquvciu ull'uciiqamci."

Tua-i-ll'-am anevkaqataatni pilliniuq, ukut-gguq amiiget waten pingayuuluteng atliqluteng. Tua-i-ll' iliit-am pilliniuq, "Naugg'un anevkaqatarta? Acitruucarakun? Wall'u-qaa ellangqerrucarakun?"

Tua-i taun' qanleryalliniluni call', "Qaillukuaquvciu ull'uciiqamci." Atrarluteng-am imkut tuc'etnauraat uuggun aciqlirkun, qullirkun-llu. Atrarluni taum qemirrluminun tut'elluk' uuggun akuliignegun anevkalliniluku. Anluni.

Anlliniuq — up'nerkaullruluni-gguq — can'get makut qakiluteng, qakimaluteng. Tua-i-ll' utertelliniluni tua-i.

When he got home everyone back home was very surprised to see him arrive. Apparently, to the *ircenrraat,* one year is like one day to them. One year is a day for them. He had stayed with them for an evening and all night, and the next day when he went out a whole year had already gone by. [*chuckle*]

After he returned he never experienced that again. *Ircenrraat* are some kind of beings. They used to say that they were former *angalkut* [shamans].

I think that is how long the story is. It seemed like it was long enough. Did it not fill up [the tape]?

Marie Meade: It's just right.

❧ *At Cuukvagtuli* ❧

Mary Napoka, Rachel Sallaffie, and Ann Fienup-Riordan, Tuluksak, May 1989

Mary Napoka: And again, one day when I was a girl out at Cuukvagtuli [northwest of Kasigluk], our lay pastor's daughter and I liked to play together. We liked playing together and constantly stayed up late at night playing.

Then one day we filled their grandmother's canoe with things, filling it with old things, and moved sailing through a slough. We traveled by sail going over there. When we arrived we went up.

When we went up, I happened to notice, when I stood and looked around, I saw some old houses that were obvious. Their entryways looked like little sloughs.

Rachel Sallaffie: Were they going crosswise?

Mary Napoka: Outward. The entryways. And here there was that old house pit that looked like a small lake.

Then I happened to notice, poor, there were a great many clay pots turned over outside of [the houses]. They were very nice, and their edges had small designs on them. I didn't mind, thinking that they were always there.

There were different things. Lamps, old urine containers, bowls. Those large ones were probably their large mixing bowls.

Rachel Sallaffie: Did you not trade for them [take them, leaving something in return]?

Mary Napoka: And we didn't think about trading for them. We played with them all night. We cleared out an old house; its floor was like this. It was extremely hard.

We cleaned it and used it as our home and played all night. We would pretend to cook with those small [dishes], moving about. We lost track of time and played on. Then suddenly, I noticed that the sun was about to come up.

Kingunitellrani-gguq tua-i alangaalriit ukut tekiyucianek. Cunawa-gguq ircenrraat makut allrakumek tua-i ernengqetullinilriit. Allrakuq tua-i erneqluku. Atakuyarturpak uitarraarluni, unugpak uitarraarluni, unuaquan anllermini, allamikuan anlliniluni, antelliniluku. [*ngelaq'ertuq*]

Tua-i tekicami nutaan tua-i tuaten pinqigtevkenani. Ircenrraat-am tua-i caugut. Tamakut-wa angalkullrunilaqait tamakut.

Ava-i-wam' tuaten taktangalnguq qanemcika. Ngelqinganaku piyaaqaqa. Tua-llu-remtaq nangenritaqa?

Arnaq: Ngelqiuq.

❧ *Cuukvagtulimi* ☙

Mary, Maayaaq, Ellaq'am Arnaan-llu, Tuulkessaaq, May 1989

Mary: Tuamtell'-am piqerlunuk, wiinga nasaurluullemni avani Cuukvagtulimi, augna-llu aiparniklunuk tuyumta pania-llu. Aiparniklunuk tua-i unugmi peggaarqellriakuk naanguarlunuk.

Tua-ll' atam piqerlunuk-am augna maurluata aguutii imirluku canek, callernek tua-i imirluku upagtukuk tengalrarlunuk kuicuarkun. Tengalrarlunuk aglunuk yaavet. Tua-i tekicamegnuk taglunuk.

Maaten tang tagngamegnuk murilkua, nangerrlua kiartellemni murilkua, makut enellret maa-i nallunaunateng. Maa-i tuartang amiigit kuicuaraat.

Maayaaq: Qeratmun-qaa?

Mary: Elatmun. Anyarat. Una-w' enellrullinilria, tuar nanvarraar-llu.

Tua-i-ll' maaten murilkua, akleng, makut imkut qikut egatet amlleqapiggluteng elataitni palungqalriit. Tua-i assiqapiarluteng menglait-llu makut qaraliarluteng. Nutem tuantetuyukluki wii cangalliurpek'nii.

Cat ayuqenrilnguut. Kenurrat, qurrutellret, qantat, tua-i. Makut-wa miiskaaqelallikait angelriit.

Maayaaq: Cimiutevkenak-qaa piksaituten?

Mary: Cimiutnalunuk-llu umyuarteqevkenanuk. Tua-i naanguaqluki unugpak. Una-am enelleq carrirarpuk; tuartang im' natra waten. Tua-i tegqapiarluni.

Carrirluku enekluku naangualriakuk unugpak. Tamakutgun imkucuarteggun keniruaraqlunuk peklunuk. tua-i-am nauwa tayim'. Maaten murilkartua pivakarlua akerta pugniarallinill'.

Then I said to my companion there, "Our families are about to get up. We should return home."

Then she said to me, "What about our toys here?" Then I said to her, "We should turn them upside down and leave them, so that we can use them again when we play again." My, and we didn't bring any of them home.

We left. And when we left, from down there, the whole experience escaped my mind. And I forgot about it. It so happened that my playmate did the same thing.

But when she started to get sick . . . She had moved to the village of Napakiak. She had gotten a husband. When she started to get sick, evidently when she was going to die the next day in the evening, she suddenly recalled those things.

When she recalled them, she told her mother that in the past, she and I, since we always played together, had strange toys, things that aren't seen around here. She said our toys were numerous.

Then [her mother] said to her, "Then why didn't you bring home a small thing or even a small old lamp?" She said that we weren't thinking of bringing anything home, but she said that we were thinking of playing with them again when we went to them again. It so happened, when we left them, they disappeared.

Rachel Sallaffie: So if you had placed them [upright] like this, one of them would have been there?

Mary Napoka: Yes, if they were placed upright. We placed them all upside down. I was thinking, "The rain will fill these things." When we left they were turned over. It so happened that they disappeared.

They say that they went to check on them after my playmate died. Then it is said her mother said, "Gee, although you two played with those things, you are going to leave us." Then she said she was going to leave us now that she had become weak. Then it is said her mother said, "Hopefully, your playmate, the one you played with will live for a little longer [than you]."

[Those things] disappeared when we left them. They would tell us, even after my playmate died, they'd tell me the following. They said that we were actually very rich, but we thought nothing of [those old things].

I thought that they had always been there, thinking that they belonged to that place. But here when we'd go egg hunting there, we never saw anything. We would only see old house pits. And we never saw anything around.

Tua-ll' piaqa aipaqa, "Tang ilapuk tupagniarallinilriit. Wangkuk taugaam ut'reskumegnuk."

Tua-ll' pianga, "Makus'-mi naanguapuk?" Tua-ll' piaqa, "Palurqurluki-w' uniskumegneki, cali naanguaryartuqumegnuk aturniapuk." Aren, iliitnek-ll'-am ut'rutevkenanuk.

Ayaglunuk. Wii-ll' tua-i ayiimegnuk kanaken, tayima umyuamnek tayima. Nalluyagulluku-ll' tayim'. Cunaw' aiparma-llu.

Tua-i taugaam naulluungellermini . . . Naparyarrarmiungurrluni. Uingellruluni. Naulluungellermini, waniwa-gguq cunaw' unuaqu atakumi yuunrirciqluni, neq'erluki.

Neqaamiki-gguq aanani qanrutaa, imumi-ggem wangkuk wiinga-llu aipaquralaamegnuk, naanguangqellrunilunuk allayugnek, maani tangrrumayuilngurnek. Naanguapuk amllerrniluki.

Tua-i-ll' pillinia, "Ciin-mi iliitnek camek carrarmek kenurracuarallermek-llu ut'rutenricetek?" Ut'rutnalunuk-gguq umyuarteqenritukuk, taugaam-gguq ullakumegneki call' naanguaqnaluki. Cunaw' unicamegneki tua-i tevillinilriit.

Maayaaq: Waten-qaa ellikuvtegneki iliit uitayartuq?

Mary: Ii-i makqurluki ellikuneng. Palurqurluki elliapuk. Waten umyuarteqlua wii, "Ellalluum makut imirciqai." Palurqurluki-ll' tayim'. Cunaw' tua-i tayim' tevirluteng.

Paqcaaqait-gguq, tauna-w' tua-i aipaqa yuunriumarian. Tua-llu-gguq aanii taun' qanertuq waten, "Aren cunawa tamakunek naanguallrungerpetek, tua-i elpet uniteqataqevkut." Tua-i-gguq qanertuq, tua-i-gguq-wa uniteqataqiikut waniw' cirlaurcami. Tua-llu-gguq qanertuq aanii, ikika tua-i aipan imna aipaqellren yaaqvaarnun unguvauraqerciquq.

Tua-i tayim' unicamegneki catairulluteng. Tua-i pilaqaitkuk, aipaqa-ll' taun' yuunriumariluku, pilaqiitnga-llu waten. Tukuuyaaqelliniukuk-gguq wangkuk, wangkuk-gguq cauyukenritliniapuk.

Wii-w' tua-i nutem tuancukluki, taumun piksukluki. Amta-llu tang tuavet peksussa'arqamta-ll' camek tangyuunata. Makunek taugaam enell'ernek maani. Camek-llu tangyuunata.

✑ *One Who Became What He Saw* ✑

Theresa Hooper, Tununak, May 1976

Theresa Hooper: There were a mother and son living somewhere.

Then in the fall, her son prepared to leave to go in search of material to make a hat. He had a bow and arrows.

Then he left. They say as he was going along, when he saw something that looked like a window, he went to it and looked inside and saw that it was a window.

He opened it along the corner and looked inside, there were two people inside. Out in front of the doorway was some water. It was filled with fish, king salmon that were alive and moving.

On the other side was a person sitting with a mole on one side.

There was a caribou hanging down along the back wall.

There was also his/her companion sitting across from him/her.

Then as he/she was sitting there, he/she suddenly got angry and went down and took the caribou and started to break it apart with his/her right hand.

Then he/she got angry and once again, from one side, from the side that was [?dead], he/she started to break it apart. There were popping noises.

And he was watching them, and those two didn't know he was there.

Then after a while, his/her companion who was sitting across laid down.

As he/she was laying there, he/she got larger and larger, and he/she became a very large person, he/she was very long.

After a while, from his/her side a log started to grow, and when it hit the beam of the house, it stopped growing.

And he/she continued to sleep.

Then again, from his/her ear, a muskrat ran out. And when it took a piece of grass from the mattress down below, it ate it. And when it was done, it ran inside his/her ear.

Then after a while, that tree shrunk next to him/her, and then it disappeared.

Then after a while, that person got smaller and smaller and became his/her normal size. He/She woke.

Then that person, when he thought of something, he got up, after watching for a short while, he saw that his bow and arrows had gotten pale, they had gotten worn from the weather.

Then he thought, "Gee, I thought I left just a while ago."

He got up and looked around, and it was such that it was melting rapidly, it was becoming summer.

Then when he got up from there, he headed home.

❧ *Tangvallermitun Ayuqlirilleq* ❧

Ackiar, Tununeq, May 1976

Ackiar: Taukuk-gguq aanakuralriik uitalriik nani tayim'.

Tua-i-ll' tauna uksuarmi, qetunraa tauna nacarkarrsuqatarluni-gguq aya-katarluni. Urluvengqerrluni pitegcautai-gg'.

Tua-i-ll' ayagluni. Ayainanermini-gguq uumek egalrungalngurmek tangerrngami ullagluku uyangtellinia egalrullinill'.

Kangiraakun iki'irrluku uyangtelliniuq, yugluni malrugnek. Ugna-wa-gguq amiigem ciuqerrani mer' ugna. Tua-i-gguq neqnek imarluni, pektellrianek taryaq-vagnek.

Ikna-wa-gguq yuk akiani aqumgaluni inglua-gguq tuqunqurluni.

Tuntuq-wa-gguq agalria kanan' egkumi.

Aipaa-wa-gguq cali ikna ika-i akiani uitall'.

Tua-llu-gguq tuan' uitainanermini qenqullagluni atrarluni tuntuq teguluku ayimcinga'artelliniluni tallirpiminek mat'umek.

Tua-ll' qenqerrluni tuamtell' ingluanek tamaaken nalamalriim tunglirneranek ayimcinga'artelliniuq. Cingqurruluni-gguq tua-i.

Elliin-llu taum tangssuarlukek, nalluluku-ll' taukuk.

Tua-ll' piuraqerluni aipaa tauna imna ikaantauralria inartelliniluni.

Inangqaurainanermini-gguq kana-i angturriinaqili, yugpallraurrluni-ll' tua-i takek'ayagluni.

Tua-ll' piuraqerluni, caniqerranek waken muragaq nauyartulliniluni, pagaa-vet-llu-gguq enem agluanun puukarluni arulairluni.

Qavarturallra-llu-gguq cakaniyuunani.

Tuamtellu-gguq ciutiikun kanaqlayagaq anqertelliniluni. Acimek-llu-gguq unaken carangllugmek teguqaucami nerluku. Taqngami-llu-gguq im' ciutiikun itqerrluni.

Tua-i-ll' piuraqerluni, napaq tauna mikliriinalliniluni caniqerrani, tayima-ll' tamarluni.

Tuamtell' piuraqerluni yuk tauna mikliriinalliniluni angtacimitun-ll' ang-tariluni. Tupagluni.

Tua-i-ll' tauna camek umyuarteqngami makluni pilliniuq, wanirpaagaq tangssucuaqerraarluni, ak'a man' urluvra pitegcautai-ll' qakiluteng, ellaluki.

Tua-ll' umyuarteqliniluni, "Aling watua-ggem ayallruunga."
Makluni-gguq kiartelliniuq, urugyukapiarluni-gguq tua-i, kiagyugluni.

Makcami-ll' tua-i tuaken utertelliniluni.

As he was heading home, he came upon a river. It had a very swift current.

As he was going along, since he couldn't step over that, since he couldn't cross it; he had [previously] traveled on land back there somewhere.

When he came upon that river, since he had no way of crossing, he sat there. It had willows along its shores.

After a while, a log came out from the middle of the river. When the current pushed it down, it sank.

It started to surface periodically there.

He thought, "I should jump down there and take a leap to the other side."

Then when it surfaced, he jumped down there and he leaped to the other side. And he thought nothing of what he had done.

When he looked back at it, he saw that what he had stepped over was a very large river. It had a very swift current.

Then he went to their village.

As he was arriving, he saw smoke rising from their small house over there.

He went over and entered. When he entered he saw that his poor mother was sitting with messy hair. She had cooked. She had already ladled caribou into dishes down there.

When he entered, after looking at him out there she said to him, "Those that resemble [my son] enter like this."

Then he said to her, "Mother, what's wrong? You shouldn't be acting that way now. I'm that person, I'm me. Be nice and put your hair back in place. I haven't died. I've arrived now. I'm that person now."

The poor thing looked at him and suddenly got happy. [She said,] "My, are you really that one?" He said he was that one. He said that she should feed him. He said that since he left, he hadn't eaten at all. And he said he hadn't slept at all either. He said after eating, that he would sleep. He told her to clear the back wall of their small home, the place where he would sleep.

Then his dear mother cleaned it.

He said to her, "If I should do something strange when sleeping, even if I change, don't be afraid."

When he was done, when he was done eating, he went to bed back there.

My, they say after sleeping a while, he started growing larger, and he filled the back area of their home until it was full. And she didn't suddenly get scared since he told her not to get scared.

Then after a while, alongside him, a large log started to grow. It grew, and when it grew when it reached the top, it stopped. His poor mother watched in awe.

Uterrnginanermini tua-i mat'umek kuigmek tekitelliniluni. Carevpagluni-gguq tua-i.

Tamaa-i-gguq ayallermini tamana tamaa-i amllirciigalamiu, arvirciigalamiu; naugg'un tua-i tayim' pavaggun nunakun ayallruluni.

Tekicamiu tua-i taman' kuik qaillun arvirciigalami uitauralliniluni. Uqvi-garnek-gguq cenengqerrluni.

Piuraqerluni muragaq kan'a anlliniluni kuigem qukaanek. Imumek tua-i carvanrem negcani tayim' kill'uni.

Pugqetaangartelliniuq tua-i tuani.

Umyuarteqliniluni, "Kanavet taugaam qeckaquma, akianun-llu amlliq'erlua."

Tua-i-ll' pugngan tuaten qeckalliniluni kanavet, akianun-llu amlliq'erluni. Cangakevkenani-llu-gguq tua-i ellminek.

Maaten-gguq tang kingyarluku pillinia kuigpall'er tamana amlliq'allra. Carev-pagluni.

Tua-i-ll' aggliniluni tua-i nunameggnun.

Maaten-gguq tua-i tekicartulliniuq, en'arrlugaurluak ing' puyirturallinill'.

Agluni itliniluni. Maaten-gguq itertuq aanaurlua tauna nuyavlugciluni-gguq tua-i uitalria. Kenillrulliniluni-gguq. Tuntunek ipullrulliniluni kana-i.

Iterngan-gguq uavet tangerqerraarluku pillinia, "Ayuqnguat-llu tua-i waten iternaurtut."

Tua-i-ll' pillinia, "Aanaa qaill' pisit? Qaill' piyunaitaaten waniw'. Imuugua, wanguunga. Assircaarluten nuyaten-llu taggluki. Tuqunritua. Waniw' tekitua. Imuugua tua-i waniwa."

Tangerqaurlurluk' quyaqalliniluni. "Aren tua-i-r' imuuguten?" Imuuniluni waniw' tua-i. Nerevkaasqelluni. Waniw' ayaggaanerminek nerengssaaqsaitniluni. Qavangssaaqsaitniluni-ll' cali. Nererraarluni taqkuni qavarciqniluni. Qaugna qa-vani enellerameg' egkua carriisqelluku, acikaa.

Tua-i-ll' taum aanaurluan carrilliniluku.

Pillinia, "Qaillukuangerma qavaquma, qaillun ayuqliringerma alingyaqunak."

Tua-i taqngami, nernermek taqngami inartelliniluni kiavet.

Aren qavaqerluni-gguq una inarteqerluni angturiyartulliniluni enellera-mek-llu-gguq qaugna egkua imirluku tua-i muirluku. Ellii-ll' alingallagpek'nani alingallaasqellrunilani.

Tuamtell' piuraqerlun' caniqerrakun muragpall'er nauyartulliniuq. Nau-yartulliniuq, naungami-ll' pagaavet aklicami arulairluni. Irr'ikluku aaniin tang-ssuaraurlullinia.

Then after a while, when a muskrat ran out of his ear, it took a piece of grass from the mattress and started eating. And when it was done, it quickly ran inside [his ear].

He became exactly like that one who he had watched closely.

It has ended.

Tuamtell' piuraqerluni ciutiikun kanaqlayagaq anqercami acillermek maaken carangllugmek tegulluni nerngartelliniuq. Taqngami-ll'-am tayim' itqerrluni [ciutiinun].

Imutun tua-i tangvak'acagallermitun ayuqlirilliniluni.

Tua-i iquklituq.

SPIRIT HELPERS

✌ *Neryull'er* ✍

Nick Andrew with John Phillip, Paul Kiyunya, and Alice Rearden,
Anchorage, October 2006

Nick Andrew: Some of you have probably heard of a person named Neryull'er. He was from the Yukon River area.

John Phillip: I've never heard of him. I don't know who he is.

Paul Kiyunya: We don't know who he is.

Alice Rearden: He just said his name is Neryull'er, Neryull'er.

Nick Andrew: They say that man lived about eight miles upriver from our village [of Marshall] on the other side of the river. It's a short [trail] to that river back there. There are two rivers. That man evidently lived along the confluence of those rivers. During winter . . . It's a long [story] though. I shouldn't have told it. [*chuckles*]

Since they weren't idle when winter came, he got his snowshoes and left to the area across [from his camp]. There is another river across from that place, upriver. Upriver there are Ingrilukaat [Mountains] that head down from up there. Just as they end, there is a hill there that looks like a *qasgi*. It's along the end of those mountains that head down, but separate from them. They call that [hill] Iquggaq [lit., "One at the end"] since it is the end of those mountains.

While he was walking across there right after it had snowed, he saw some martin tracks. Since they were new [tracks], he followed [the martin]. He followed it, and he started thinking that he would leave it since it continued on for too long.

Just as he was thinking that, he saw that its other foot print, its other hand print had turned into a human foot print. Out of curiosity, he started to follow it.

They say after a while, even its other footprint would transform into a human footprint. Eventually, they started changing form, the other footprint would change. Eventually they were no longer martin footprints. Another type of [animal] track would appear. He began to follow it in earnest because he was amazed.

TUUNRAT

❧ *Neryull'er* ❧

Apirtaq, Ayagina'ar, Kayungiar, Cucuaq-llu, Anchorage, October 2006

Apirtaq: Augna-qaa ilavci tayim' niiteqallrungataa-ll' aipaagni yug'atengqerrluni Neryull'ermek. Kuigpagmiunguuq.

Ayagina'ar: Wii niiteksaitaqa tauna. Nalluaqa.

Kayungiar: Nalluarput.

Cucuaq: Neryull'er-gguq, Neryull'er.

Apirtaq: Tauna-gguq angun kiatemteni *about eight miles* akilirnermi uitallrulliniuq. Markituq atam kuigmun pamani. Kuigek-wa malruulutek. Kassigluagni
tuani uitallrulliniuq taun' angun. Uksurngan . . . Tak'uq taugaam. Ciin-tanem
qanemciksia. [*ngelaq'ertuq*]

Uksurqan-wa tua-i uitaurayuilameng, tanglullraagni pilukek ayalliniluni aki-
lirnermun. Ikani cali kuigtangqertuq akiani, kialirnermi. Kiani-wa Ingrilukaat
qamaken anelralriit. Nangqerluteng ingrirtangqertuq waten tuarpiaq-llu qasgiq.
Augkut anelralriit ingrit waten iquatni, ill'arrluki taugaam. Tauna tua-i Iquggarmek
acirlaraat iqukngatgu tamakut ingrit.

Agaani pektellermini qaninerrarluku qavcicuamek tumcilliniuq. Nutaraungata
maligtelliniluku. Wanirpak-gguq maliggluku, umyuangluni-llu ayagpakaan unit-
naluku.

Tuaten-gguq umyuarteqengqerluni pia maaten it'gaan-gguq inglua, unatiin
inglua yinrarmek inglurluni. Umyuaran cumikarrluni maligtelliniluku.

Piuraqerluni-gguq pinauraa it'gain-llu ingluit yinraurtaqluteng. Kiituani-gguq
caurtaangut, ingluit piaqluteng. Qavcicuam-llu tumkenrirluku. Allanek tumai
pingaqluteng. Maligtelliniluku tua-i iillayuami cumigtengluni.

When he reached the [hill] I called Iquggaq . . . The end is easy to climb. It isn't slanted [steep], but it's good. He saw that the [martin] had ascended. Since it had climbed, he went up following it.

Just as he reached the top, he saw that [the martin] had gone inside what appeared to be a window. It was the window of a *qasgi*. He saw that it had gone inside.

They say when he lay face down and peeked inside, many people were down there inside the *qasgi*. Down below them there was something that was upright. Some of them even had wolf heads on them. The people had animal heads in front of them. And he saw the one who he had followed down there who had a martin's head.

He went around in a circle, watching them down there. All the different animals were down there. He circled the place [with his eyes]. When he had looked all the way around, to him it didn't seem that he had looked all the way around at them for a long time, [but] when he stood, this [front] part [of his clothing] stayed behind. It had rotted. [*laughs*] They say the front of his parka here stayed behind since it had stuck. It had rotted.

He saw that it had already turned into summer. He thought, "I wonder how I will reach home now?" And there was no ice, and he had no boat. He was wondering how he would reach his village across there.

While he was looking around . . . The Yukon River is visible down there [from Iquggaq]. While he was looking around, he saw a log down there with its end sticking up that was drifting along. When it seemed to reach the area around his village, he said at the same time that he lifted his leg, "I wish I could step from here, and when I step again, set foot right outside my home."

He saw that he was moving in the air. When he stepped there, when he lifted his other [leg], he went and landed outside his home. He stayed there.

After a while, [he] began drumming. He had evidently become a shaman. All the ones that he saw, the animals, had become his *tuunrat* [spirit helpers]. They say that one wasn't a shaman before that.

They say he would drum. The others there started to get tired of hearing him drum, and since he would constantly drum, they asked him, "Why do you start drumming constantly at night?" [*laughs*]

He replied, "I drum at night looking for fish for the Yukon River." When he gave that reply, they left him. He continued to drum when night came as usual.

One day he said that he had found a fish over at Iilgayaq [Nushagak River]. They say the fish at Iilgayaq used to be fat long ago, really nice fish. But they say the fish on the Yukon River had no fat.

Tuavet Iquggarmek aplemnun tekicami tang . . . Iqua atam mayuyunarquq. Uvertevkenani, assirluni taugaam. Mayurtuq-gguq waniwa. Mayullinian mayulliniluni maliggluku.

Pakmani kangranun tekiteqerluni itliniuq uumun egalruluni-gguq waten. Qasgim egaleqluku. Itliniuq waniwa.

Maaten-gguq tang palurrluni uyangtuq, ik'iki unkut yuut qasgimi. Ketiitni-wagguq napalria. Ilait-gguq keglunrem-llu qamiqurranek pitangqerraqluni. Pitarkat qamiqurritnek manuqlirluteng tua-i yuut. Imna-llu maligtellni kana-i tangerrluku qavcicuamek, qamiqurranek pingqerrluni.

Unavet tua-i uivuralliniluni tangvagluku. Tua-i-gguq pitarkat tamarmeng una-i unaanlluteng. Uivuralliniluku. Kassugyaqliamiu, ak'aninrilnganani-wa tua-i kassugngamiki nangertellriim-gguq man'a unegtuq. Arulliniluni. [ngel'artuq] Man' atkullraan-gguq un' manua unegtuq neptellrulliniami. Arulliniluni.

Maaten-gguq tang murilkuq kiallrullinilria-ll' ak'a. Umyuara atam pillinilria, "Qaillun-kiq waniwa kingunitniarcia-llu?" Cikutaunani-ll' angyaunani-llu. Qaill' agaavet nunaminun pillerkaminek [piluni].

Tuani kiarrnginanermini . . . Kuigpak atam una-i tangerrnarquq. Kiarrnginanermini un'umek yuraplugmek tanglliniuq aterquralriamek. Ava-i nunami nalliinun ellirngalan, qanerluni tuaten irumi inglua nalukataarallinia, "Tayima-tuq waken unavet amllirlua, aipirikuma-ll' enem'a elatiinun tull'ua."

Maaten-gguq murilkuq ayalria pagg'un. Tuavet-llu tuc'ami, inglua call' naluamiu ayagluni, enem'i-llu-gguq elatiinun tull'uni. Tua-i uitalliniluni.

Atam-gguq una piqerluni cauyalangelria. Angalkuurtelliniluni-gguq. Tamakut imkut tangellni, pitarkat tamalkuita tuunraqsagutelliniluki. Angalkuullrunrituq-gguq tauna.

Tua-i-llu, tua-i-gguq cauyaraqluni. Ilain-am niitellngungluku cauyarpakalaan pilliniat, "Calriavet unugmi cauyangvakalarcit?" [ngel'artuq]

Kiulliniuq, "Tua-i-wa tua-i cauyarlaryaaqellrianga unugmi Kuigpiim neqkaanek yuaralua pilalrianga." Tuaten kiungan tua-i unitelliniluku. Tua-i-gguq cakanirpek'nani tua-i cauyangnaurtuq unugaqan.

Cat atam iliitni qanllinilria, neqmek-gguq nalaqutuq Iilgayarmi amani. Iilgayaam-gguq neqai uquritullruut ak'a tamaani, neqkegtaaraat. Kuigpiim-gguq taugken mat'um neqai uquunateng.

He said that he started to see an image of a fish at Iilgayaq, but he said that two shamans kept watch over it. But he said that he would try to get it. He said that although there were two [shamans], he would try to get it. Those two evidently had strong powers over at Iilgayaq.

They went to the *qasgi* and gathered there, and they carried out various activities with him when he was going to go over. They say he had them bind and tie him up, and they sheathed him in a bearded seal skin. They tied him tightly inside.

While they were tying him, he started to hover in the air. And when they were done with him, when they let him go, he quickly went out making a loud *"cugg"* noise.

After being gone for a while, they say he finally quickly went inside. They untied him. He evidently said, "Indeed, the image of the fish I saw. . . ." He said it was over there. But he said that the two watching over it were too powerful. But although that was the case, he wouldn't stop trying [to get it]. He wanted the Yukon River to have the king salmon.

They say at that time, he started to use his spirit helpers, trying to take it. He said that those two shamans at Iilgayaq, inside the *qasgi* . . . Oh, he took it at that time, he somehow took it. They say he arrived with it, and it was a small fish. He had the people see it. He said it was this fish here, a good fish, a fat one, a fish for the Yukon River.

They say after he took it, those two shamans from Iilgayaq would suddenly enter the *qasgi* during some nights, trying to take that back again.

My, they knew their names. They mentioned them. I have forgotten their names.

They say sometimes they would suddenly enter the *qasgi* trying to take that [king salmon] again. Since that one was a powerful shaman, since he secured it completely, they couldn't take it. That's why they say that the king salmon today in the Yukon River were stolen by that shaman. [*laughter*]

Then one day, they told him when they had a dance festival to *kanaqlaguaresqe-lluku* [use his spirit powers to try to make *kanaqliit* (muskrats) readily available (to catch)]. Since he wouldn't refuse when they asked him to, he used his spirit powers to try to make muskrats readily available. They say that the river down below his home was a river that was in great condition.

They say when spring came, the rivers were full of muskrats. They say that one [went hunting] with his younger sibling sitting back to back with him [in a kayak]. When he caught one, that one would immediately skin them. He would throw their carcasses in the river.

And when they skinned them in his village, since they couldn't consume them, they would discard them in the water. His river, that wonderful river eventually became choked with muskrat meat. It's an awful river. And it's about this wide at this time, but it's deep. They say that it became choked there.

Pilliniuq neqem tarenraanek tangerkengangniluni amani Iilgayarmi, taugaam-gguq malrugnek angalkugnek murilkestengqertuq. Taugaam-gguq qaillukuarci-qaa. Malruungraagnek-gguq taukuk qaillukuarciqaa. Tuknimilliniuk-ll'-am tau-kuk cali amani Iilgayarmi.

Tua-i-am nutaan qasgimun piluteng katurrluteng anglanillininluku ama-virteqatallrani. Qillerqevkarluni-gguq, maklagmek-llu caquluku. Tua-i qiller-qulluku umciggluku.

Qillerrnginanratni-gguq tua-i qerratarangnaurtuq. Taqngatni-llu-gguq tua-i pegcatni tayim' cugg'erpak anqerrluni.

Tayimngurraarluni-gguq tayima, cayaqlirluni-gguq itqertuq. Angitellininluku tua-i. Qanllininluni tua-i, "Tua-i ilumun tauna neqem tarenraa tangelqa. . . ." Amaa-netniluku. Taugaam-gguq taukuk murilkestek caperrnarquk-gguq. Taugaam pingraan taqngaitniluku. Kuigpagmun ayuqekulluku neqkesqumaluku taryaqvak.

Tamaani-gguq tua-i tegungnaqengluku tuunriaqluni. Taukuk-gguq tang amkuk amani Iilgayarmi angalkuk qasgimun . . . Oh, teguluku imat'am tuani taum, tegulliniluku qaill' tayim' piluku. Tekiutaa-gguq tua-i neqcuayaar. Tangertelluku yugnun. Waniwa-gguq una neqa assilria, uqurilria, Kuigpiim neqkaa.

Tegumariluku-gguq atam taukuk angalkuuk amaken Iilgayarmiuk qasgimun itqertelalriik atakut ilaitni, taumek ataam tegutengnaqlutek.

Aling atkek-llu nallunricaaqagket. Apertullruyaaqagket-am. Tayima-am wiinga nalluyagutagka atkek.

Tua-i-gguq iliini itqerrnaurtuk taukuk qasgimun taun' ataam tegungnaqluku. Tua-i taum tuani angalkurpaulliniami asvairiluku pillrulliniamiu, tua-i tegunrit-ngurtellininluku. Taumek-gguq maa-i taryavqiit Kuigpagmi taum angalkum tegle-gaqai. [ngel'artut]

Tua-ll'-am piqerluteng pilliniat yurallermeggni kanaqlaguaresqelluku. Tua-i pisqevkarngatni-ll' uitangailami kanaqlaguallininluni. Tamana-gguq eniin ketiini kuikegtaaraullruuq tamaani.

Tua-i maaten-gguq up'nerkartuq, ik'iki-gguq tua-i pekaqlugpak kuiget kanaq-lagnek. Tauna-am ellii kinguqlini alrapaqluku [ayagaqluni]. Egmian tua-i pitaqami taum tua-i amiiqeraqluki. Kemgit mermun egtaqluki.

Tuani-llu nunamini amiirqamek, pisciigalamegneki mermun egtaqluki. Tamana kuiga, kuigkegtaar tamana tuvtellininluni kanaqliit kemgitnek. Kuivialuuluni tua-i. Waten-llu iqtutauq watua, taugaam ilutuluni. Tuaggun-gguq tua-i tuvtellruuq.

And his *qasgi* is still visible today. It is deep. I think it's as deep as this place [twelve feet]. And I think it's about as large as this place [ten feet by twelve feet]. It looks like a *qasgi*. They say it's the *qasgi* of that person, the place where his *qasgi* was located.

There is water inside where its fire pit was located. They say when there are going to be [many] muskrats, there is [a muskrat] that is out of the water there resting on top of something small. [*laughs*] Even today.

And nothing has grown on it. Different types of trees have actually grown, even this past year. Now that the weather is warmer during winter, the trees are growing in our area. But nothing grows there at that place. The *qasgi* is obvious. It even has an entranceway [facing] the river.

They say it is the *qasgi* of that powerful shaman, the one who became a powerful shaman. That's the end [of the story].

৵ *One Who Stole Spirit Helpers from a Powerful Shaman* ৵

Raphael Jimmy and Sophie Lee with Alice Rearden, Mark John,
and Ann Fienup-Riordan, Anchorage, April 2012

Raphael Jimmy: There once was a married couple living beside a river along the ocean somewhere. There was a shaman living up north somewhere. He was a shaman, but he was a *qelatuli* [one who practices shamanistic divination in which the paitient's ailment is determined by tying a string around his forehead and testing it by pulling in different directions]. He would take a stick and use a person's head [to carry out divination].

But his fellow [shaman] living beyond in Qissunaq somewhere would practice his shaman spirit powers in a real way. He was also an extremely powerful shaman; he was able to see everything.

Those two, in the *quliraq*, it is said those two sometimes went and visited one another using their helping spirits, and they would spend time with one another and speak to one another using their helping spirits but not in the actual outdoors like this.

Then one day, they say the one to the north of him wasn't a powerful [shaman]. He would actually practice rituals using his helping spirits to heal people, but he was a *qelatuli*.

One day he said to his wife, "Now make me six pairs of waterproof skin boots." Those waterproof skin boots. They are those where you skin a ringed seal. This person here [Sophie] knows what *ivrucit* [waterproof skin boots] are. Those [boots], they made them long like this.

Cali qasgia maa-i tangerrnarquq. Ilutuuq. Mat'utun ilututangatuq. Mat'utun-llu tayim' angtangatuq. Tua-i qasgitun ayuqluni. Taum-gguq tua-i qasgia, qasgillran nunii.

Kan'a-wa kenillran nuniini mengqerrluni. Kanaqlangqeqatarqan-gguq uges-kaartangqerrlartuq tauna. [ngel'artuq] Maa-i cali.

Cam-llu tang nauksailkii. Napat amlleret ayuqenrilnguut nauyaaqut, allragnir-pak-llu. Nenglairtenga'arcan uksumi naugartut napat nunamteni. Tauna taugken cam nauyuunaku. Tua-i nallunaunani qasgi. Iteryarangqerrluni-ll' una kuigem tungii.

Taum-gguq-wa tua-i angalkurpiim, angalkurpaurtellrem qasgia. Nangelria-wa tua-i.

◄ *Tuunrairilleq Angalkurpagmek* ►

Angagaq, Sophie, Cucuaq, Miisaq, Ellaq'am Arnaan-llu, Anchorage, April 2012

Angagaq: Tua-llu-gguq taukuk nulirqellriik kuigem ceniini unani tayima nani imarpiim ceniini. Tauna qagaani angalkuq-gguq tauna qiini qagaani nani tayima. Angalkuuyaaqluni imkuciuluni taugaam qelatuli, qelatuli. Waten equggaq teguluku yugmek nasqirluni.

Una-gguq taugken yaaqlia avani nani Qissunami tayima avani tuunripigte-tuluni. Cali kayulriaruluni angalkurpak; ca tamalkuan tangerrsuumaluku.

Taukuk-gguq tua-i, qulirami, taukuk-gguq tua-i caaqamek maaggun tuun-ramegnegun ullaullutek tua-i waten aipaqlutek tua-i waten qanaatuuk tuun-ramegnegun maaggun tellakun pivkenatek.

Tua-llu caqerluni, tauna-gguq negeqlia kayulriarunrituq. Tuunralguyaaqluni taugaam qelatuliiuluni.

Caqerluni nuliani pillia, "Kitaki ivruciliqernga arvinlegnek." Ivrucinek. Imkut nayiit iciw' amiirluki. Nallunritai uum ivrucit. Tamakucinek, waten takluki.

Then when he was about to leave from there, he put on the first pair of waterproof skin boots and carried the others on his back. He traveled along the ocean shore and had for food some dead animals that he found beached along the ocean shore.

When those waterproof skin boots down there would tear, he would discard them and put on another pair. He traveled along, he traveled along the ocean shore. When he came upon rivers, he would build himself a boat out of logs and cross, down along the ocean shore.

Then after a while he was wearing the last pair of waterproof skin boots; he knew things through his helping spirits. When he put on his last pair of waterproof skin boots, he was about to reach the shaman over there. Those waterproof skin boots wouldn't tear until he reached him.

He traveled along, traveled along. As he was going along he said, "Oh dear me, I really have no helping spirits. When I arrive upon that shaman over there, I won't have helping spirits to use."

As he was among some old logs, he saw an *amitatuk,* a weasel. You know how that one is impossible to take, it's impossible to capture. He saw the weasel running around, and it was going in and out of old logs. He said, "How fascinating this is, this one that will be my helping spirit."

Then after a while, he tried to capture it. A weasel is impossible to take. After a while, that weasel let that shaman who was a *qelatuli* take it.

When he took it, I'm not sure which side he placed it on, either on this side or this side. He placed it inside on this side and told it, "Stay there. I will get you when I want to use you." When he put the weasel inside, he didn't feel it. It was gone.

Then he continued traveling. [He said], "My goodness I'm going to reach that shaman and have no helping spirits. I wish I could get some sort of helping spirit."

After a while, he saw a *cek'aviaq* [hawk owl, also *eskaviaq*]. *Cek'aviat* are dangerous; they are fast. What do they call those in English? We call them *cek'aviat.* Those that travel at fast speeds, those that are good at catching.

Their chests are like this; they catch with these [talons]. That kind was flying around. He said, "How fascinating this is, this one that will be my helping spirit."

Then after a while that one he was trying to take, that *cek'aviaq* let him take it. When he took it, he placed it on the other side and said to it, "Stay here. I will take you when I want to use you."

Then finally [he had powers]. Then that shaman over there, he hadn't actually gone to him before, but he knew him through his helping spirits and by having gone to see one another [using their helping spirits].

Then there was a point over there. [The village] was on the other side inside a cove.

Tua-llu tua-i tuaken ayakataami ivrucik taukuk ciuqliik at'ak, ilait atmagluki. Unaggun imarpiim ceniikun caneg' mallunek neqengqerrluni imarpigmi.

Ivrucik kankuk allguraqagnek egglukek allagnek at'aqluni. Eglertuq, eglertuq imarpiim ceniikun. Kuiget makut tekitaqamiki equgnek angyirluni qeraraqluni, imarpiim ceniini unani.

Tua-llu piqerluni waniw' ivrucik nangenrek; tua-i-am nalluvkenakek-llu cali tuunramikun cat. Ivrucik ukuk waniwa nangenrek ac'amikek tua-i amavet angalkumun tekitarkaurrluni. Tekitellranun ivrucik taukuk allgurarkauvkenatek.

Eglerrluni, eglerrluni. Piinanermini pilliuq, "Arenqiapaa-lli wangni, cakneq-lli wangni tuunraipaa. Angalkuq amna tekiskumku tuunrarkaunii."

Equut ak'allaat akuliitni piinanermini piqertuq-gguq maaten amitatuk, *weasel*. Imna iciw' teguyunaituq, teguyunaituq. Maaten-gguq piqertuq amitatuk man'a pangarvagalria maani imkuni equgnun ak'allarnun itqetaarluni. Pilliuq, "Cavagta man'a, tuunrarkaqa man'a."
Tua-ll'-am tua-i piqerluku tegungnatugturallia. Amitatuk teguyunaituq. Tua-i-am piqerluni tauna amitatuk taumun qelatulimun angalkumun teguvkalliuq.
Teguamiu, nalirnermun taugaam piciitaqa, ukalirnermun qang'a-ll' uka-lirnermun. Ukalirnermun qamavet ellillia waten qanrulluku, "Tuani uitaurqina. Aturyungkumken piciqamken." Iterrluku-am amitatuk ellikiin', tayima-gguq elpekevkenaku-llu. Tayima cataunani.
Tua-i-am eglerrluni. "Arenqiapaa-lli amna ama-i angalkuq tekiteqatarqa aling tuunrarkaunii. Camek-kina waniwa tang tuunrangli."
Piqerluni-am maaten-gguq piqertuq imna iciw' cek'aviaq. Cek'aviat alingnar-qut; cukanrartut imkut. Canek Kass'atun pilartatki imkut? Wangkuta cek'avianek pilaraput. Cukanrarluteng imkut, piculit imkut.
Qat'gait waten ayuqluteng; 'gguun pitetuluteng. Tamana tengaulria. tua-i-am pilliuq, "Cavagta man'a, tuunrarkaqa man'a."
Tua-llu-am tua-i piqerluni tegungnatugturallrani, imna-ggur-am taun' cek'aviaq teguvkaqili. Teguamiu wavet ingluanun pillia qanrulluku, "Wantarqina. Aturyungkumken piciqamken."
Tua-i nutaan. tua-i-am ama-i amna angalkuq, nalluvkenaku elliin, teki-teksaicaaqluku, tuunramikun taugaam nalluvkenaku ullautellermegen'gun.

Tua-llu-gguq waniwa amna ama-i cingik. Amatiigni kangiqutami amani uitaluteng.

As he was traveling along, he looked and saw a very large log here! He went to its stump down there, and when he did this to it [encircled it with his arms], he couldn't hold it all the way around [with his arms] since it was thick. It had a stump.

He went toward its tip. When he came to its tip, its very top, the one who told the tale said that its width was the thickness of a pinky finger. You know, the log slowly tapered and became thinner over there. And its very top was about this thick.

Alice Rearden: Like a pinky finger?

Raphael Jimmy: Like this, yes, it was about the thickness of a pinky finger.

He evidently said, "How fascinating, this one that will be my helping spirit." He said that in his mind. But I'm not sure where he put it, either on this side or this side. I think he placed it on this side.

Once again, when he took hold of that log, he placed its tip along his ear and slowly put it inside. He put it inside [his head]. After a while, when he came upon its stump, after putting it inside, he patted [his ear]. It is said he shook his head a little, but he didn't feel that very large log. He said, "Yes, now, let's see how it turns out!"

He headed up, and here was the point. The shaman was living on the other side of it. Like I said earlier, when he got a view of it [he thought], "I wish that the people would stop walking around and settle down." [*laughter*]

Like I did [referring to a previous story]. I'm not actually a shaman, but [I said that] feeling ashamed, since I had no pants. [*laughter*]

Then as he was watching them, those people stopped walking around. When they stopped walking around, he quickly went to the outside of the *qasgi* and quickly looked inside.

He went to the entryway and stayed there and heard people talking inside.

Then after a while, he entered. When he entered he looked inside there, and that shaman, that powerful shaman was back there. That one who he used to visit with his helping spirits was back there.

It is said when he saw him, looking at him he sat facing him out there.

Then after sitting there a while, he said, "Gee, it's hard to sense where the guest came from. Where did he come from?" That one who knew everything didn't know who he was.

He sat down. I think that one replied to him in the following way, "If you arrived at my village, I would know who you are." That person, the *qelatuli* evidently said that to him.

Then after a while he sat down in the center of the *qasgi* in front of the firepit on the floor, sitting like this.

He said to that shaman that he was going to show him something now, that he, too, [should show him something].

Tua-i-am eglerrnginanermini, maaten-gguq piqertuq equgpakayall'er man'a! Acilqurra-gguq kan'a ullagluku, waten-gguq piqeryaaqaa kassugpek'naku cellgan. Nasqunartuumaluni.

Kangranun ayagluni. Maaten-gguq kangra tekitaa, kangkackaa pakemna, taum quliraqestiin waten pillrua iqelqutun ellegtaciirluku. Iciw' equg' amiliinaararluni aminani amani. Kangkackaa-ll' pakemna waten pitaurluni.

Cucuaq: Iqelqutun?
Angagaq: Waten, ii-i, iqelqutun ellegtaurluni.
Pilliuq, "Cavagta man', tuunrarkaqa man'a." tua-i-am umyuamikun qanlliuq. Nalirnermun taugaam piciitaqa, wall'u-q' ukalirnermun wall' ukalirnermun. Ukalirnermun pingataa.

Tua-i-am tauna, equk taman' teguqaamiu waten, ciutminun imna nuuga ek'urluku iterqurallia. Iterrluku. Kitek'-am piqerluni waten tekitaa nasqunaa tekicamiu, tekicamiu nasqunaa iterqaarluku patguuraa. Ungaulukaryaaquq-gguq tayima elpekevkenaku imna equgpakayall'er imna. Tua-i pilliuq, "Ii-i, tua-i nutaan, takuqerli!"

Tua-i itrarluni, una cingik. Ama-i amatiini tauna angalkuq uitaluni. Imutun watua qanemciklemtun igvaamiu pilliuq, "Cavagta yuut-kina pektaiqerluteng uitaqaqerlit." [*ngelaq'ertut*]

Wangtun. Angalkuunricaaqua wii, taugaam kasnguyuglua qerrulliilama-llu. [*ngel'artut*]

Tua-llu kellusnginanrani, piinanratni yuut imkut pektairteqalliut. Pektaircata agqertelliniuq qasgim elatiinun elatii uyangarrluku.

Wavet iteryaramun piqerluni uitaqalliuq qanerturalriit qamkut.

Tua-llu tua-i piqerluni tua-i itliniluni. Itran-gguq imna kiani maaten piqertuq imna tauna angalkuq kian' angalkurpak. Imna ullaglallra tuunramkun kiani uitalria.

Tangrramiu-gguq tangrrauqerluku aqumqaqili cauluku uavet tangvagluku.

Tua-llu-gguq uitaqerluni qanertuq, "Aling allanermi-lli elpegnaipaa. Naken, naken pia?" Nalluluku taum nallutailnguum.

Tua-i aqumluni. Waten tuar taum tuan' kiungataa, "Elpet-wa nunamnun tekiskuvet nalluyanrilkemken." Taum yuum pillia qelatulim.

Tua-i piqerluni kanavet qasgim waten qukaanun kenillrem unavet kellirneranun aqumqalliniluni natermun, waten aqumluni.

Pillia tauna angalkuq maniiteqatarniluku waniwa, ellii-llu pisqelluku.

Then he took that weasel first and took it out. He said to the weasel, "Now, run around all over in here."

It is said when it took off, he said to the people in there, "Try to kill this one by striking it! Kill it by striking it!" Following what he said, those there were trying to strike it. It is said that after a while, one of them finally hit it. When he killed it, he took it and placed it here on this side.

Then after putting it down he said to him, he said to the shaman, "Now you do as I did."

That shaman, his host went down and sat across from him. And after making some kind of noise, after doing something, he took out a weasel from inside himself. He evidently said the same thing that one said, "Okay now, kill this." He let go and the helping spirit of the shaman across there was running around in the surrounding area. "Kill it."

It is said that while they were trying to kill it, that one would disappear. They tried [killing it], but it disappeared.

His guest said to him, "Gee, gee, your helping spirit tends to disappear." That's what his guest said to him.

Then he said to him, "I'm going to do it again." He took out that hawk owl again. When he took it out, he said to it, "Now, fly around here so that these ones will pursue you." When it flew, he said to the people around, "Now, try to kill this." It was flying around and it was in the way. They were trying to kill it once again by striking it.

Then after a while one of them hit it and quickly killed it. When he killed it he brought it over and placed it on this side.

After placing it there, he said to his host, "Now you do as I have done." That shaman, his host, after making noise, after doing something, he took out a hawk owl. He said to it, "Now fly around." He said to the people around, "Kill this one."

Those people there were trying to [kill it], but they lost its whereabouts. They didn't kill it.

Then that one, his guest said to him, "Gee your helping spirits tend to disappear. You are evidently not a very good shaman." He actually knew that he was [a powerful shaman]. He said to him . . . The story is almost at an end now.

He said to him, "You are not someone to be around. I'm going to leave you. I'm going to go out." That log was still there.

When he went out, when he went down into the underground tunnel entranceway, he evidently went out sideways, going out, back when they used to [enter and exit] underground. It is said they used to [enter and exit] under the *qasgi* through the hole down there.

Alice Rearden: The *kalvagyaraq* [underground entrance]?

Tua-ll' imna tauna amitatuk ciumek teguluku antelliniluku. Pillia amitatuk, "Kitek' maani pangarvaga piciatun."

Ayakaan-gguq ava-i pii taukut yui, "Nalatengnaqiciu man' kaugtuarluku! Kaugturluku nalaciu!" Taukut-gguq tua-i imkut maliggluku kaugtungnaqluku tua-i. Cayaqliqerluku-gguq iliita nall'arrluku. Nalacaku-gguq akurturluku ukalirnermun wavet elliqeraa.

Tua-llu-gguq elliqerraarluku pillia, taun' im' angalkuq pillia, "Kitek' elpet-llu wangtun."

Tua-i tauna imna angalkuq, tukua atrarluni ikavet akianun aqumluni. Cali nepangruyaggaarluni-gguq carraarluni, amitatugmek anciuq iluminek. Tua-i taum qanellratun pillia, "Kitek' una nalaciu." Peggluku pangarvagalliuq maani ik'um angalkum qasgim tamatum yuan tuunraa tamana. "Nalaciu."

Nalatengnaqnginanratni-gguq imna tamarnaurtuq. Tua-i cayaaqluku tamariluku tayima.

Tua-i taum allanran pillia waten, "Aling, aling elpet-lli tuunrarpeni tamaryugpaa." Taum allanran.

Tua-i-am pillia, "Ataam piqatartua." Tauna tua-i imna cek'aviar ataam antelliniluku. Ancamiu pillia, "Kitek' tengaura maani ukut piniaraatgen." Tengeng'an pillii ukut, "Kitek' man'a nalatengnaqiu." Maani-gguq tua-i aviraulluni tengaurluni. Nalatengnaqluku-am kaugturluku.

Tua-i-am iliita piqerluku nall'ara'arrluku nala'artelliniluku. Nalacaku-am tua-i tailluku ukalirnermun elliqalliniluku.

Ellirraarluku-am tauna tukuni pillia, "Kitaki elpet-llu wangtun." tua-i-am taun' imna angalkuq tukua nepangruya[ggaarluni], qaillun pirraarluni tua-i-am cek'aviamek ancilliniluni. Pillia, "Kitaki tengaurluten." Ukut pillii, "Man'a nalaciu."

Tua-i-gguq-am imkut pingnaqsaaqluku tayima-llu-gguq tamariluku. Nalatevkenaku.

Tua-i-am pillia taum, allanran taum, "Aling elpeni-lli tuunrarpeni tamaryugpaa. Angalkuuluaqanritliniuten." Tua-i-w' nallunricaaqluku. Tua-i pillia . . . Tang waniw' iquklitniarartuq.

Pillia, "Arenqiatuten elpet nayurniituten. Tua-i wani uniteqataramken. Anqatartua." Imna tauna cali equk uitaluni.

Tua-i anngami kanavet kenillermun kalvagcami, imna tauna canirmi anlliuq, anluni, camaggun pitullratni. Qasgim aciakun camaggun ukinerkun pitullruut-gguq.

Cucuaq: Kalvagyaraq?

Raphael Jimmy: Yes, those *kalvagyarat* [entranceways] underground. He evidently stretched out that log, going out, going out, going out. And when he got to the end, they say he took a couple of steps or three steps and arrived at his hometown. I think that one had traveled for six months wearing six pairs of waterproof skin boots. He either took two steps or three steps and arrived at his hometown when he returned home.

Then after he went out, their elder said, "Go out and check on that one by going outside." It is said they went out but had no way to go out. That *kalvagyaraq* was filled with a log, and there was no way [to go out]. It was plugged.

It is said it took a long time for them to go out by striking it, removing small pieces at a time. Finally when they were able to fit through, they went out. When they went out, they saw that it was a very long log. Its end was only about this wide [like a pinky finger]. Then the story is over.

Then they say that powerful shaman, sometime later, he checked on his shaman powers, his *tuunrat,* and he had none at all. That shaman had taken all of them and brought them with him. [The once-powerful shaman] was suddenly not useful any longer. [His guest] took away his shaman powers, took away his helping spirits, took them away from him. Now the story has ended.

This is the only [tale] that I don't forget, this *quliraq* that Nanuq told. I've heard tales, but I've forgotten many. I wonder why I don't forget this one? I think it's because I tell it from time to time, since I tell the story from time to time. And when my dear children gather sometimes, I tell that story.

When not telling old ways, whatever they may be or even a song, you know about this; if we don't sing a song or we don't tell a story and a *quliraq,* we will lose it. But when we tell it from time to time like this, when we speak of it from time to time, we won't lose it.

Especially our traditional customs and ways, the traditions of our ancestors are something that we should regret losing. It's a good thing. And it is very impressive. That's something that one should be extremely sad to lose.

The *qaneryaraq* [oral instruction] will save a person who is feeling remorse or one who is sorrowful if he obeys it. But if he doesn't follow it, it won't save him. The *qaneryaraq* has a good consequence, the *qaneryarat* of our ancestors.

Angagaq: Yaa, kalvagyaraat tamakut nunam aciani. Equk tamana nengtellia, anluni, anluni, anluni. Iquklican-llu tua-i kingunerminun-gguq, tuarpiaq malrugnek wall' pingayunek amllirluku kingunranun tekitnilaraat. Tauna iraluni *maybe* arvinlegni eglertellrungatuq arvinlegnek-llu ivrucinek aturluni. Malrurqugnek wall' pingayurqunek amllirluni kingunerminun-llu tekilluni utertellermini tauna.

Tua-llu imkut anellran kinguakun taum tuani, teggenrata pillii, "Ataki tang augna paqciu anluci." Anyaaqut-gguq anvigkaunateng. Imna-gguq tamana kal-vagyaraq equgmek imarluni qaill' piyunaunani. Mellaumaluni tua-i.

Imkucirturluku iciw' kaugtuar[luku], ilangarqurluku anengnatuumaut-gguq tua-i. Cayaqliqapiggluteng engelqayagucameng anluteng. Maaten-gguq an'ut ak'aki man'a equk. Iqua-gguq ama-i waten ellegtaurluni. Tua-i-llu iquklilluni.

Tua-llu-gguq imna angalkurpak, qakuani tayima, maaten-gguq imkut angal-kuni, tuunrani murilkai, caitqapik-gguq tua-i. Taum-gguq imum angalkum teguluki tamalkuita ayautellii. Cakaunriqerrluni tua-i ellii. Angalkuirluku, tuunrairluku allurrluku. Tua-i-llu iquklilluni.

Man'a tua-i kiingan nalluyagucuitaqa, Nanum quliraqellra man'a. Quliranek niicaaqua taugaam amlleq nalluyagu[taqa]. Ciin-kiq tayima man'a nalluyagucuicia? Tua-i-w' atuqaquurallma pingataa, qanemcikqaquurlaamku. Waten katurtaqata-ll' iliini ukut-llu yuurluunka katu'urtellratni, katu'urtaqata qanemciqerlartua tama-tumek.

Ca man'a wangkuta ak'allaq piciatun qanemciksuunaku qan'ga-ll' yuarun, nallunritan; yuarun, qanemciq-llu, quliraq-llu qanemciksuilkumteni tamarici-qaput. Taugaam piqa'aqluku waten, anteqa'aqluku piurqumteggu-gguq tama-ringaitarput.

Arcaqerluku man'a piciryararput wangkuta ciuliamta piciryaraa qunu-naqsaaquq tamarillerkaa. Elluarrluni assilriaruuq. Caperrnaqluni-llu. Tamana qununaqsaaquq cakneq.

Yuum ilii umyuarrlulria, qang'a-llu-qaa iluteqellria anirturarkaugaa qaner-yaram mat'um, maligaaskuni. Maligaatenrilkan taugken cali anirturpek'naku. Tuaten iqungqertuq man'a elluatun man'a qaneryaraq, augkut ciuliamta qaneryaraat.

OTHER WORLDS

✍ *Pamalirugmiut* ✎

Elsie Tommy and Marie Meade, Anchorage, June 1992

Elsie Tommy: Some would abstain from things when their children died.

Marie Meade: Perhaps that was the important [instruction].

Elsie Tommy: They considered [abstinence rules] important. If he didn't abstain he would block the way of the person who died. He would block [the dead one's] path to the place of the dead. This is what they used to tell us. They said that the person who had died traveled alone to another place.

And Qissunamiut resident Ap'ayagaq, husband of Laakautarkaq, when we used to winter down there, I never forgot the story he told in the evening.

He told of a girl who was sick. Following her sickness she died. When she died she went to the place of the dead.

Then, you know, they give thanks and have feasting. And they would have another event and have a feast. And again at Christmas they had a feast. They did that long ago, they used to do that.

And also those who honored the bladders, the Bladder [Festival] was another custom they carried out besides feasting.

I saw people honoring the bladders one time, but I was not fully aware of the event. Apparently it was the last time they honored the bladders in Kayalivik. I watched them, but I didn't really pay attention to what they were doing.

The girl had died. When she died in the fall, during the time of thanksgiving, when her family came to the village, [going] to her hometown, she joined her family. They [the dead ones] went inside the *qasgi*.

They all sat around the door here. Then they brought in their dishes and filled them with food. Their relatives brought in food.

Then the one who had died the previous fall, or rather the one who had died the year before, her parents didn't bring food. They didn't. And her brothers and sisters also didn't bring any [food]. They didn't come. That [girl's] bowl was empty. She just watched as gifts were being given to her companions.

ELLAT ALLAT

❧ *Pamalirugmiut* ❧

Nanugaq Arnaq-llu, Anchorage, June 1992

Nanugaq: Tua-i-w' irniateng-ll' ilaita tuquaqata tua-i eyagutaqluki.

Arnaq: Arcaqallilria-wa tauna.

Nanugaq: Arcaqalriaklukek ukuk. Eyanrilkuni tauna tuqulria tumkairluku-gguq. Tuqunernun ayallerkaa-gguq tumkairluku. Waten qanrut'lalqaitkut. Tuqulria tauna allakarmi ayalarniluku nunanun allanun.

Cali-ll' wiinga tauna, tayima imum Laakautarkam angutiin Ap'ayagaam Qissunamium, kanani uksilallemteni qanemcik'lallra atakumi avaullrunritaqa.

Tauna-gguq nasaurluq nangteqluni. Tua-i-ll' nangteqraarluni tua tuquluni. Tua-i-ll' tuqungami tua-i tuqunernun tua-i ayagluni.

Tua-i-ll', iciw' quyalalriit kalukarluteng. Tuamtallu cakuneng cali call' kalukarluteng. Tuamtall' Christmas-aami kalukarluteng. Tuaten pilalriit ak'a, pitull-rulriit.

Cali imkut augkut nakaciutullret, tamakut tamaa-i aipaqluki taukut kalukaryarat nakacuut taukut.

Nakaciulriit ataucirquqapiarmek tangssullruanka, taugaam murilkeqapiarluki pillrunritanka. Cunaw' nangnermek nakaciullratni Kayalivigmi. Tangssugyaa-qellruanka, murilkeqapigtellrunritanka.

Tauna tua-i nasaurluq tuqullinilria. Tua-i tuqungami uksuarmi quyam nalliini, ilani tua-i iluvarngata nunanun, kingunermi, kingunrinun, ilagarluki tua-i ilani tua-i pilliniluni. Qasgimun iterluteng.

Tua-i-llu aqumuraluteng tua-i amiigem pianun maavet. Tua-i-llu qantateng iterqelluki neqnek imirluki. Tua-i tamakut imkut tungelqurrit itruquriluteng.

Taum-llu tua-i uksuaq tuqullrem, aren allragni tuqullrem, angayuqaak itru-civkenatek neqnek. Pivkenatek. Cali-ll' anelgutai cali pivkenateng. Iterpek'nateng. Taum-llu tua-i aluuyaq qantaa imaunani. Tua-i tangssuarluk' ilani aruqutaitnek pillratki.

Then her friend who had received three pieces of blubber, he put the third piece in [the dead girl's] bowl.

He told her, he said to her . . . Those who have told the story have said this, "You poor one, your family never thinks about you. No one at your home thinks about you. They just allow you to starve. They let you suffer." Then he put the third piece of blubber in her bowl.

Then she put [her bowl] by the door. And when her companions were done and were leaving, when she ran out she forgot to take her bowl. When she realized she had forgotten her bowl she went in backward [with her back against the outside doorway] and got her bowl and ran out. Her companions had disappeared. She didn't know which way they had gone.

When she got frightened she stood and looked around along the shade of the *kenurraucetaq* [lamp] in the porch, holding her bowl. [Many people] were walking around. They were going out and coming in.

Then one of the people spotted her. She asked her, "Oh my, is it a person?" Then she answered, "Yes, it is a person."

"Then come forward so I can bring you in."

Then when she brought her in, as they came up [into the *qasgi*] an old man spoke from the side, "Okay then. Thank goodness. Bring her over to her parents' home, holding her hands on both sides. Bring her over, her parents will welcome her."

So then they took her out and brought her into her parents' house. Her parents jumped up with joy as their daughter entered.

Then they sat her on the floor and removed her garments. When they removed her outer garment they found she was wearing the gift that they gave to her last Christmas. She was wearing the parka that they had given to her namesake.

After they removed all of her garments they washed her with [urine] from the urine bucket. They washed all over her body. Then they wiped her. Then after they wiped her, they put clothing on her. They didn't put on what she wore when she died, but they put new clothing on her. She stayed with them after that. They stayed there with her all winter.

Then one day she said . . . In the evening when they were about to have their evening meal her mother gave her a bowl of food.

When she took her bowl she stared at it for a while. Then after she sighed she said, "*?Kanngurtut*, the people of Pamalirugmiut that I have left down below, how fortunate they are for they are eating frozen fish with matching heads." The girl apparently said that. Her parents looked at her for a moment.

When she mentioned that for the third time, her mother had an idea. She took two whitefish, either *akakiigek* [two broad whitefish], *qaurtuk* [two broad whitefish],

Tua-i-ll' *friend*-aan aruqutengqerrami-gguq taukunek tangevkayagnek qe-llukanek pingayunek, pingayuatnek qantaa imiqalliniluku.

Qanrulluku tua-i, tuaten qanrulluku . . . Qanruciilaqiit qanemcikestain, "Nak-leng elpet, ilavet umyuaqsuunak. Kingunerpet umyuaqsuunak. Kaigturcelluten taugaam. Nangteqevkarluten." Tangevkayami pingayuatnek qantaa imiqerluku.

Tua-i amiigem canianun elliqalliniluku. Tua-i-ll' ilai ukut taquraluteng anellratni, anqertellermini qantani tauna nalluyagutelliniluku. Tua-i murilkarcamiu qantani avaullni kingupiarluni aqvalaagluku teguluk' anyaaqlun'. Ilai-gguq imkut tamaqalliniluteng tayim'. Natetmun ayauciinaki tua-i.

Nanikuallermini tua-i qasgim elaturraani, kenurraucetam talinranun nangerr-lun' qantani tegumiaqurluk' waten kiarquralliniluni. Kangalriit tua-i. Anluteng iterluteng.

Tua-i-ll' iliita tangerqalliniluku. Aptaa-gguq, "Waq'ataki yuuguq-qaa?" Tua-i-llu-gguq ciunran kiugaa, "Ii-i yuulria-wa."

"Kitak' tai-tai itrutnaamken."

Tua-i-ll' itrucani, nugngamek maaken angulluat qanlliniut, "Kitaki. Quyana. Angayuqaagkenun aguciu tass'uqluku malruulluku. Aguciu, angayu-qaagken ciuniurciqaak."

Ayumian tua-i anulluku angayuqaagkenun itrutliniluku. Angayuqaak-gguq imkuk tua-i quyaqerlutek nangrallallinilutek tua-i taumek panigmegnek itellriamek.

Tua-i-llu-gguq aqumlluku natermun matarqelluk'. Maaten-gguq matartaak allragni un' Christmas-iutellrak aturluku. Atranun cikiutellrak-gguq aturluku atkuk.

Tua-i matarqerraarluk' imumek qurrutmek [teq'umek], qurrullugmek erullini-luk' qainga. Tua-i erurluk' tua-i qaqilluk' tua-i. Tua-i-ll' perrirluk'. Perrirraarluk' akluluku tua-i. Tauna tuqullrani atullra aturcetevkenak' allamek taugaam ac'elluk'. Cunawa-gguq im' ilakaqkiik tua-i. Ilakluku uksurpak tua-i uksilutek tua-i.

Tauna tua-i caqerluni qanlliniluni waten . . . Atakutami-am tua-i atakutaqa-tallermeggni aaniin-am tua-i qantamek cikirluku.

Qantani taun' teguqaamiu waten waniw' tangssuaralliniluk'. Tua-llu-gguq aneryaarpallarraarluni qanertuq, "Kanngurtut-tanem camkut kingunrenka Pama-lirugmiut atunem nasqulegnek nerngulriit kumlanernek." Tuaten tua-i qanlliniluni taun' nasaurluq. Angayuqaagken tua-i tangvakalliniluku.

Cunawa-gguq tua-i tuaten tua-i qanran pingayiringan aaniin umyuangulluku. Akakiigek, wall' qaurtuk, wall' qassayagaak paangrutkenka, aipaan, paangrutiin

or *qassayagaak* [two Bering cisco] and she cut off the [left] pectoral fin of one and she removed the [right] pectoral fin from the other and placed them [side by side] facing in one direction. One side [of the fish] had a pectoral fin, and the other had none. When she put them together their heads would be matching.

Then she carefully placed them in her bowl. She would hand her the bowl. Then when she took it, she said to her with gratitude, "Oh thank you very much, just like back in Pamalirugmiut where I am from, I'm about to eat a whitefish with matching heads side by side."

I have never forgotten it. I wonder why I never forgot that. [*laughter*]

Marie Meade: Yes. A *quliraq.*

Elsie Tommy: Yes, it's like a *quliraq.* Laakautarkaq and them; Ap'ayagaq from Qissunamiut, the late husband of Laakautarkaq told the story. He told the story in the evenings at our home. He didn't tell it every night, he would tell it to us girls in the evenings sometimes when we wintered in places where they had no *qasgi,* down below Kayalivigmiut.

❧ Ones Who Went Beneath ❧

Martha Mann with Julia Azean and Marie Meade, Kongiganak, July 1994

Martha Mann: When we were about to have Qaariitaaq [a fall festival during which children's faces were painted and they went house-to-house asking for food], they took me to the *qasgi.* When I went in they let me sit next to an old man. My face was about to be painted with *urasqaq* [white clay] and decorated. That old man said, "Okay now, don't run around as you go. Don't horse around, and make sure you hold on to the younger ones as you travel out there." Then he remembered the story about those who took part in Qaariitaaq who went beneath [the ground]. And then he told the story.

He said that one of the young boys had slowed down and gotten behind everyone. When he was coming out of a house the group was already going into the next one. He went over. When he went inside he saw that the other half of the house had no light. He saw a woman caring for a child sitting near the exit on the left side. It was hard to tell if there were people there. Since the back part of the house was dark and also the other side . . . There was only one lamp next to her.

As he was about to come up through the entrance, she told him not to follow the others. She pointed to the back corner, and she told him that they had all left through that place back there. She told him not to go with them.

Then she searched and pulled out a piece of bleached bearded-seal rib bone and said, "I'll give you this, for I have nothing else to offer." Then she told him not

nalliikun kepluku, aipaan-llu paangrutii aug'arluk' ataucimun caugarullukek. Aipaa paangruterturlun', aipaa-ll' paangrutaunani. Kackautaqatek-gguq tuaten atunem qamiqungerrnaurtuk.

Qantaanun tua-i tuaten pinqegcaarlukek eklukek. Tunciqaa-gguq qantaa. Tua-llu-gguq tegukuniu quyalun' qanrutaa, "Quyanarpiitli kingunemtun Pamalirugmiutun atunem qamiqulgegnek nerqatalrianga."

Tauna avaullrunrilkeka tua-i. Ciin-kiq avaullrunricia tauna. [*ngel'artut*]
Arnaq: Ii-i. Quliraq.
Nanugaq: Ii-i, quliratun atam ayuquq. Ukut tua-i Laakautarkankut tua-i; Laakautarkam aipairutiin Ap'ayagaam Qissunamium qaneryaralqaa. Enemteni atakumi qanemciurautellra. Atakut-llu tamaita pivkenak', cam iliini qanemciknauraa tamana wangkutnun nasektaggarnun, qasgiilngurni uksiaqamta, Kayalivigmiut kanan' ketiitni.

❧ *Aciirutellret* ❧

Mass'aluq, Anglluralri, Arnaq-llu, Kangirnaq, July 1994

Mass'aluq: Qaariitaaqatarluta qasgiskiitnga. Itertua tang uum angulluam canianun aqumevkaqilitnga. Urasqerrluku kegginaqa qaralirteqatarluku. Tauna qanertuq angulluaq, "Kitaki ata, aqvaquavkenaci pikici. Ayaniilleci makut unitaarpek'naki ang'aquagurluki, akusrartevkenaci pikici." Ayumian tang neq'erikili taukunek qaariitaallernek aciirutlernek. Tuani qanemcill'.

Tauna-gguq iliit tan'gaurluq nuqliarrluni. An'uq-gguq tang yaa-i nem'um itellriit. Tua-i aggliniluni. Itertuq-gguq tang nem'un maavet, agna nem inglua kenurraunani. Una-wa-gguq iqsulirnerem tungiini uatmi arnaq un' mikelngurmek pill'. Tua-i-gguq yungqerruciinani. Qaugna-ll' tan'gercelan' agna-ll' . . . Kiimi tauna kenurrarluni.

Tua-ll' nugqataryaaqelria taum pillinia, augkut-gguq ilai maligcaqunaki. Egkuq-gguq kiug' niiraa, kiaggun-gguq tang anelriit augkut. Maligtesqevkenaki.

Ayumian-gguq piuq, yuarluni tulimamek mat'umek enermek makliim tulimaanek qakirpak, "Cikiutekaitua taumek cikirnaamken." Tua-llu-gguq pia angurr-

to ever lose it whatsoever. She said someday when there was famine in the world he would use it to survive. He quickly slipped it inside his garment.

Then she said, "Okay now, [don't turn around, but] go out backward [with your back against the outside doorway]. We may look like people, but we are not human. See, look at these here." He looked and saw a line of people with hair down to the bottom. They were moving out toward the exit.

He went out walking backward [as instructed]. And when he came up outside he continued on, walking backward away from there. As he was walking backward outside he suddenly fell on his back and blacked out.

Then someone woke him up. He had been asleep. He asked him why he was sleeping there. He told him to go inside and sleep. He got up and went into the *qasgi* and lay down.

When he woke he discovered that the people in the *qasgi* were other people. He had become aware in another village. Those people took him home.

Oh my, when he got home the mothers of the children who had gotten out through the back corner, whenever they heard them crying from beneath the floor they would begin to dig the ground to no avail. They would do that when the [children] who had gone beneath [the ground] made noise.

Then they say they came back out through the side of Ing'errlugaat [the lava cones north of Nelson Island]. That place out there was where they came out. It looks like a huge door. When Aaska Hall's wife told the story about them, she said that was the place where the *qaariitaat* [children going house to house] came out.

The girls used to throw small rocks at it to predict their futures. Sometimes when a person threw a rock it would go skipping and suddenly disappear. And sometimes [when a person threw a rock] you wouldn't know whether it landed or not. They say if a person was to live a long life it would go skipping and suddenly disappear. However, if a person was to die early you wouldn't know whether it had landed or not. She said she had joined those who had thrown rocks at the place they said *qaariitaat* came out.

Marie Meade: The ones who had gone beneath.

Martha Mann: Aciirutellret [Ones who had gone beneath]. They say when they came back out they brought those *patelpiit* [beads of a certain type] with them. When they began to travel through the big doorway and kicked them along the way, [the things they kicked] would roll sparkling with light. The older ones would pick them up and put them inside their garments. They say they came back with them.

Marie Meade: Paterpiit. Were they rocks?

Martha Mann: They were beads, not rocks. Some of them, back when they wore handmade belts, they would use those as hook fasteners.

They called the red ones *aumat*.

luk pegtesqevkenaku qaill' pingraan. Cam-gguq iliini ella neqailkan kanautekaqaa tauna. Qumikallinia.

Pia-gguq, "Kitak' tua-i kingupiarturluten ani. Yuuyuk'ngerpekut yuunritukut. Atam makut tangerqerki." Maaten-gguq tang, yuut makut nuyait-wa-gguq kanavet. Uatmun-gguq tua-i qimugluteng.

Anllinilria tua-i kingupiarturluni. Nugngami-ll' kingupiarlun' ayaglun'. Tua-i kingupiarinanermini, ellamun ellinermikun, qetqallalriim, ellani nalluqalliniluku.

Tupagtelliniat. Qavalliniluni. Ciin qavaucianek tuan'. Iterluku inarcartuus-qelluku. Tua-i makcami iterluni qasgimun inartelliniluni.

Maaten-gguq tang makcami imkut qasgimiut, qasgiksukluku pillni pia allauluteng. Nunani allani ellangellinilria. Tua-i ut'rutliniluku taukut.

Aren, tekituq-gguq tang tamakut, imkut kiaggun egkukun anellrita aanait, camaken-gguq nunam acianek natermek qalrillaganga'artaqata elagterayaaqnau-raat kan'a nateq. Taukut aciirutellret neplirluteng piaqata.

Tua-i-llu-gguq tang anluteng Ing'errlugaat qacarneratgun. Tauna-gguq tua-i anellrat qakma. Tuar-gguq ikan' amigpall'er. Imum-am Aaska Hall-am nulirran qanemcitaqamikut, tauna-gguq tua-i qaariitaat, anelqenillrat qaariitaanun.

Ciunerkarcuutekluku miluquuratullrukiit nasaurluut teggalquyagarnek. Tua-i-gguq ilii milqerqan matngalkuarturlun' ayagnaurtuq pell'aqerrluni-llu. Ilii-gguq taugken tus'uciinani. Tua-i-gguq ak'anun unguvaarkaq tuaten matngalkuarturlun' ayalalria pell'aqerrluni-llu. Makut-gguq taugken ak'anun unguvanritarkat tus'ucii-taqluteng. Elliin-llu-gguq tua ilagallrui miluquurarqata taukut qaariitaanun anenillrit.

Arnaq: Aciirutellret.
Mass'aluq: Aciirutellret. Taukut-gguq tua-i anellret tekiulluteng imkunek-llu patelpagnek. Tamaani amigpagkun ayangellermeggni, itemkarqaceteng akagar-taqluteng tanqigpallaraluteng. Ayaninrita qumikaqluki. Tekiutellruit-gguq tua tamakut.

Arnaq: Paterpiit. Teggalqut-qaa?
Mass'aluq: Tegglit teggalqurrunrilnguut. Ilait naqugutengqelallermeggni imkunek pilianek nagcalquqnaurait tamakut tamaa-i.
Tamakut tamaa-i kavirtelnguut aumauninaurait.

Oh my, when they told stories . . . Our father went to Qinaq one winter. As he was traveling the weather got bad and began to blizzard. When there came to be a blizzard, he stopped along the way and sat down and made a shelter. As he was sitting there, he heard people talking. When he peeked out he saw [dead] people out there passing by. They passed by and were gone.

Then after a while he heard people talking again. He looked and saw them going back holding bowls of food. Some of the bowls had *akutaq* in them. Some of them had food in them. They would pass him by.

Then he heard one coming complaining, "Why did they even try to follow the traditions? And why have they put it inside this bowl?" He looked and saw [a woman] going by holding a bowl with a fermented fish head in it. One end of the bowl was burnt. [She] was scolding those people in the place she came from, expressing her sorrow for them giving her such a bowl. They went by and were gone.

[The next day] when he woke and the weather was good, he went the rest of the way to Qinaq. This was before the people [of Qinaq] moved to Tuntutuliak.

While he was in the *qasgi* a girl came in and said that she had come to get the old wooden bowl. When they passed it down to her, he recognized it as [the bowl] the [unhappy woman] was holding the night before. The wooden bowl was smeared with fermented fish head and was burnt on one end. It was the one the person felt disappointed about [the night before]. She said why did they even try to follow the traditions. And [she was asking] why they had given her that container. Then the girl took it and left.

When my mother was getting ready for occasions, including Aaniryaraq [a fall festival following Qaariitaaq], [our father] used to tell her to put the *akutaq* and other things in a nice bowl. He would tell her what he had seen [out there in the storm].

Oh my, since I had grown with him around, he used to talk to me all the time. Just when our youngest who lives up [in Bethel] now turned a year old, our father died. And just when she turned three years old there was famine. [It was] after she had gotten bigger. She is younger than my younger sister up there.

There was a famine over in Kwigillingok.

Julia Azean: There was no food on the coast around here. They say there in 19[16] . . .

Martha Mann: The story I told hasn't ended yet. When there was famine in the world, the one who had received the rib bone, when he remembered it, when there was no food in the world . . .

Julia Azean: That happened before that time.

Marie Meade: Yes.

Aren, tua-i qanemciurarqata tua-i . . . Tauna-am atavut caqerluni uksumi Qinartellinilria. Tua-i-ll' pirtungutelliniluku. Pirtungucani tua-i aqumelliniluni, qilirluni taugaam. Aqumgainanrani amkut qanngellinilriit. Qinertuq-gguq tang yuut qagkut yaatmun kitulriit. Tayima-gguq tua-i.

Tuamtall' piinanran' tuamtall' qanngelliniluteng. Pilliniuq qagaa-i utertellriit qantanek [tegumiarluteng]. Ilait-gguq akutanek imangqerraqluteng. Canek-ll' ilait neqnek. Kituraqluteng.

Iliit igvalliniuq nunurturlun' amna, "Maligtaqutengnaqat. Ciin-llu uumek assigcirtatgu?" Pillinia aluuyamek tegumiarlun' tepa-wa-gguq imaa. Taum-gguq aluuyam muriim iqua legcillerluni. Tua-i taukut kinguneni nunurluki taumek ilulliqluni assigciuciatni. Tayim' kiturluteng.

Makcami tua-i assian tuavet Qinarmun tekivsiarluni. Tuntutuliarmun nug-tarpailgata.

Qasgimi im' uitainanrani nasaurluut iliit itliniuq. Imna-gguq aluuyall'er aq-vaa. Atrartaat-gguq tang unuk taum tegumiallra. Aluuyaq kan'a tepluurrluni iqua legcillerluni. Taum tua-i ilulliqluni pillra. Ciin-kiq-gguq maligtaqutengnaqat. Ciin-llu-gguq uumek assigcirtatgu. Tayima-ll' anutelliniluk'.

Tua-i-gguq waten wani Aaniqatarqata-llu, aanaka pinauraa, assigtaqegcarluki makut akutat-llu pilaasqelluki. Taumek tua-i qanemcit'lalliniluku tangvallminek.

Aren, tua-i, tua-i cumigyagterpiimni-ll' ayuqucirtuagurallrukiing'. Qamna qama-i kinguqlikacaarput kassukartelluku taun' atavut tuqullruuq. Allra-kungeqerluni-ll', allrakungluni-ll' pingayunek kaigluteng. Anglinermikun. Tauna tua-i kinguqliqaa qam'um kinguqlirma.

Kaigluteng amani Kuigilngurmi.

Anglluralria: Cenar man' neqaunani. Tuani tua-i *nineteen*-gguq . . .

Mass'aluq: Iquklipailgan augna qanemcika pianga piqanemkun. Tauna imum' ella iluarcaku, taum imum tulimamek cikirciullrem, enermek, neq'aqaamiu, tua-i ellam ilua neqtairucan . . .

Anglluralria: Tamatum ciungani tauna pillruuq.

Arnaq: Ii-i.

Martha Mann: He took it out and began to wash it in a bowl. He also thoroughly washed and cleaned the container for it. After he washed it, he put it on the shelf and covered it. They say he left it sitting there for five days.

On the fifth day he took it, and the rib bone had meat on it and was bloody! It would end up saving his life. And that man shared the meat with the other people there in the house. My, he survived with that [piece of bone].

And after the famine was over, he washed it. After completely eating the meat off the bone, he washed it thoroughly and put it away. It was the bone the dead person had given him. She had given him a bare rib bone. She told him not to lose it, that it would save him when [there was famine] in the world.

❧ *Woman with Long Hair* ❧

Magdalene Sunny, Tim Agagtak, Ruth Jimmie, and Ann Fienup-Riordan,
Nightmute, July 1985

Magdalene Sunny: Once there was a village. A married couple there had five sons, all males. When the youngest boy was old enough, they built him a kayak. And in the spring when they went seal hunting they took him along. They went down [to the ocean] to hunt with him.

My, when strong winds suddenly struck, they towed the youngest brother's kayak and started to head to shore. The youngest boy, as he watched his brothers towing him, he suddenly saw a woman with long hair pop up in the water. Her face was very red. As soon as she surfaced and the tow line broke, he blacked out.

Ruth Jimmie: How did she break the line?

Magdalene Sunny: It was the woman who popped up from the ocean.

Ruth Jimmie: How, by using a semi-lunar knife or . . .

Magdalene Sunny: I don't know what implement she used. Perhaps she used her teeth.

He was unconscious. Then he started to gain consciousness, and he heard someone up there waking him up, [saying,] "Hey, you, stop sleeping. Hurry and get up so we can go up."

When he was awake, when he got up, he fixed his eyes and looked, he realized he was someplace that wasn't his village. He looked at the woman there, and she had long hair and a red complexion. He thought to himself that she looked like the woman he had seen briefly in the ocean.

Then they went up. When they went up, they went inside [a house]. When he entered, he saw that she had parents. Her parents also had red complexions.

Mass'aluq: Teguamiu qantamun ekluku erullinikii. Assigtarkaa-ll' erurluk' erunqegcaarluk'. Erurraarluku-ll' qulqitnun ellimiamiu patuqerluku elliluku. Ernerni tua-i tallimani-gguq uitalluku.

Maaten-gguq tang tallimaurcata tegua, aren tulimar' man'a kemeglun' aunraarlun'! Cunawa-gguq tua-i kanautekaa. Tamakut-llu nelgutni tuaten ciki-qaqluki taum angutem. Aren, tua-i kanauteklinikii imna.

Tua-i-ll' kainriata erurluku. Pukugturarraarluku erunqegcaarluk' erurluku call' qemagtelliniluku tauna imna eneq. Tua-i-gguq waten taum nalamalriim cikiutellra. Enerrlainarmek-gguq tua-i tulimamek cikiqii. Tua-i-gguq qanrulluku pegtesqevkenaku, ella [kaigem] iluareskaku kanautekaqniluku.

❧ *Arnaq Nuyarpaulria* ❧

Missan, Akagtaq, Angalgaq, Ellaq'am Arnaan-llu, Negtemiut, July 1985

Missan: Taukut nunat uitalriit. Nulirqelriik taukuk qetunrarlutek tallimanek anguterrlainarnek. Tua-i tauna uyuqlikacaarteng ayagnariaku qayaliluku tua-i. Up'nerkaan tua-i qamigaameng malikluku. Malikluku tua-i unavirrluteng tayima.

Aren, cayukaucateng tua-i tauna tua-i uyuqlikacaarteng nangcarluku tagluteng, tagyaaqluteng. Uyuraat tauna nangcaat, avavet tua-i anngani tangssugluki piinanrani, arnaq ingna puggliniuq nuyarpauluni. Kegginaa-gguq-wa kavirpak. Pugngami tamana tua-i nangcautii kevkaruciatun, tua-i cacini nalluqerluku.

Angalgaq: Camek kepluku?

Missan: Taum-wa tua-i arnam pugelriim imarpigmek.

Angalgaq: Qaillun uluakun wall'u-q . . .

Missan: Naamikik' camek-wa caskungqerta. Keggutminek-wa pillilria.

Tua-i tayima. Tua-i pivakarluni ellangyartulliniuq, yuum pak'mum tuparqekii, "Usuuq qavarpiiqnak! Amci makluten tagnaurtukuk."

Tua-i tupiimi, makcami iigni kitugqaarlukek pilliniuq, nani tua-i maani nunakenrilkemini uitaluni. Arnaq tauna tangrraa nuyarpauluni kavinqeggluni. Tuar tang una unani imarpigmi tangerqallra.

Tua-i-ll' taglutek. Tagngamek tua-i iterlutek. Itertuk maaten angayuqang-qellinilria. Angayuqaak-wa cali tua-i taukuk kavircenatek.

Since he was overwhelmed, the girl quickly became his wife. After that, he would continually hunt. He hunted all the time.

Then one day his father-in-law told him not to ever go up to the highest peak of the mountain across from their place when he hunted. He would wonder and ask himself why [he had been warned about that mountain]. . . .

One day he followed a caribou that he had injured while hunting.

When he caught up to it, he suddenly realized that he had already reached the top of that mountain. Then he said, "Oh, let whoever wants to confront me do so. And if a scary thing wants to confront me, let it confront me."

Gee, he looked around, he looked around and recognized their two mountains up there. And without warning he felt a deep longing and sadness. He suddenly became extremely homesick.

He went home without getting the animal he had injured. When he returned home and arrived, he told his wife that he wanted to bring her to his village for a visit. He told her to tell her parents.

When she told them, her father said [to him], "If you bring her along you will not reach your destination. You should leave her behind and visit if you want to. And return if you want to."

He really didn't want to leave her behind. Since he insisted, [her father] said, "Okay, then bring her with you and you can return home on the path you took."

When she was completely settled [in his kayak], he went across. And when he got to the mouth of their river, he headed slowly up [the winding river]. He was going around the point and was just about to see what was on the other side. When it came into view, he saw his village upriver up there. They saw the village.

As they approached, from a certain distance people up there began to murmer and walk here and there. They were murmuring, and they heard someone say to alert Amllerrlinkut Atiit [the father of Amllerrliq and family].

They continued going up toward the village. Not far from the village, they saw a man up there go down [to the river] holding a seal-gut garment.

[The man] stopped and performed an incantation back there. And as soon as he blew his breath out, they suddenly stopped moving. [The man] continued to perform an incantation back there. When he would breath out, when he breathed, he moved backward.

That's what they continued to do from that point on. They could hear people speaking upriver, "The one who took your younger sibling, since it wants more, it has attempted to come again."

Whenever the man blew out his breath, [the kayak] would slide farther back. So, realizing that he would not be able to reach [the village], he turned [his kayak] downriver, he turned back.

As he slowly headed downriver, he beached, [and stricken with grief] he started to cry. (Gosh, I used to sing the song, but I can't remember it.)

Arenqialami tua-i tauna arnaq nulirqeqalliniluku. Pissu'urqelria-gguq tua-i. Pissu'urqelria.

Tua-i pivakarluku taum cakian angutem pillinia, pissu'urqan ikavet ingrim qertuqranun mayuqaasqevkenaku. Tua-i-gguq umyuarteqnaurtuq ciin tuavet . . .

Tua-i pivakarluni tuntutani picurlak'ngani maligquralliniluku.

Anguamiu ellangelliniuq taum tua-i ingrim kangranun ak'a ellillinill'. Tua-ll' tua-i qanertuq, "Aa tua-i cam imum piyukunia pikilia. Alingnarqelriim-llu piyukunia pikilia."

Aren, kiartuq-gguq, kiartuq ingriigket pikegkuk. Aren tua-i-gguq atam alia-yullalria. Tua-i aliayullagluni cakneq.

Tua-i tauna picurlak'ngani pivkenaku uterrluni. Utercami tua-i tekicami, tauna tua-i aipani pillinia nunayucugluku. Tua-i angayuqaak qanrutesqellukek.

Qanrucatek tua-i taum atiin pillinia, "Aren maliksaaqekuvgu tauna ciu-nisngaitutek. Uniteng'erpeggu taugaam nunacukuvet nunaten. Taiyukuvet-llu tailuten."

Aren tua-i unicuumiinaku tua-i, unicuumiicaaqluku. Arenqialan tua-i qepircan pillinia, "Tua-i malikiu tumevtegen'gun uterrniartutek."

Aqumkacagaan-gguq tua-i arvillinilria. Kuimeng-llu painga tekicamiu, kaucamek tua-i itraaralliniluni. Cingik tua-i igvaryarturluku. Igvaraa tua-i nunai kiugkut kia-i. Nunarrluut.

Tua-i qaillun tayim' yaaqsigtalria, piinanermeggni qamkut tua-i qaalruangar-telliniluteng kangarluteng tuaten. Tua-i qaalruarluteng, tua-i piaqluteng, Amllerr-linkut Atiit elpengcaasqelluku.

Tua-i itraaryaaqlutek. Tua-i-ll' waniw' yaaqsinrirluki, tua-ll' qaugna angun atralliniuq imarnitegnek tegumiarluni.

Kia-i tua-i qaniqluni. Cupelria-gguq atam egilrallrak man'a arulairtell'. Tua-i kia-i qaniqluni. Cup'aqan, cupelria kingupiaqanilliniluni.

Cunawa-gguq tua-i ayuqucirkaak. Qama-i-gguq tua-i qanernaurtut, "Tua-i uyu'urpeci maa-i man'a pistellra, cangimiami taiyaaqellria."

Tua-i allamek cup'aqan, pikanirluni kingupiarnaurtuq. Aren tua-i tekisngai-telliniamiki, uatmun cauluni, kingutmun cauluni.

Anelraarainanermini tua-i tep'arrluni qiaqcaaralliniluni. (Tang-ata yuarutii nallunritellruyaaqekeka.)

He cried. (I used to sing the song.) He cried and cried. When he finally stopped crying he swiped his runny nose snot and tossed it to the side and said, "Go ahead and boast and see if anyone will come to you in the future."

So they went home. On the way home, since the weather was calm, they spotted beluga whales and tried hunting. They went across with no catch.

Regrettably as they arrived home his in-law was dancing up there. "Who is this person coming dragging ____? *Ayaa, aya-rraa, yi-yaa-anga, aa-angai!*"

[He blurted out,] "What the heck is that one up there doing!" He looked back and saw his seal-poke float dragging behind his kayak. He quickly nudged his partner and said, "Pull that in!" She pulled it. After she took it, he turned to look at her again, but she was just walking up [to the house].

They arrived home. When they arrived, from that time on they lived there and continued to live a long time.

There are no more words to this story.

[singing, recalling the young man's song]

> My family *yaa-rra-aa*, my family *yaa-rra-aa*,
> I am happy to see you after a long absence *yaa-rra-aa*.
> My family *yaa-rra-aa, aa-rr*, my family *yaa-aa-aa*,
> I'm happy to see you after a long absence *rra-aa-aa*.

When he finished [singing the song], I think he took his runny nose snot and threw it down and said, "Go ahead and boast and see if anyone will come to you again in the future."

Ruth Jimmie: So he was human? He wouldn't go to [him] again?

Magdalene Sunny: He wouldn't go to his family again.

That kayak heading up, [the people in his village] apparently saw it as a flame. In the center there was a dark thing. There was a flame heading up along the water, and in the center was a dark thing. The people there were saying that the one who [took] the younger sibling of the *nukalpiat* was approaching once again to try to do it again.

To him he must have thought there was nothing wrong with [how he appeared], but his wife there must have caused them to see him as a flame.

Ruth Jimmie: Yes, those are the hairs of *itqiirpiit* [huge hands with mouths on each fingertip, said to rise from the ocean as a flaming red ball].

Magdalene Sunny: Those they call *itqiirpiit*. They say those with long hair are offspring of *itqiirpiit*, the reddish people. They say other people who see them for the first time see them as a flame with a dark thing along their center.

Tua-i qialuni. (Atulallruyaaqaqa-am.) Qialliniluni tua-i. Tua-i-ll' qialnguami kakeggluugni egtelliniak qanerluni, "Yuum tuani ullanqigciiqaaci picugci."

Uterrlutek. tua-i-am quuniuramek cetuanek maliqsaaqlutek. Pitevkenatek tua-i arvirlutek.

Qessan, tekicarturtuq-gguq-am cakia pingna yuralria. "Kina man'a ?____/ terriyugaa ?____/mavaateni-i qamurluku-uu tailria. Ayaa, aya-rraa, yi-yaa-anga, aa-angai!"

"Caqtarta-mi-llu-t'am pingna!" Takuyalliniuq qerruinaa man'a qamulria. Aipani tauna nuulellinia, "Cayuggu tamana." Cayugluku tua-i. Teguaku tangerrsaaqaa, augna-llu-gguq tagluni.

Tua-i tekillutek. Tekicamek tua-i tuani yuulliniluteng tua-i, yuuguralliniluteng.

Qaneryararkairulluni ava-i.
[aturluni]

> Ilama-yaa-rra-aa, ilama-yaa-rra-aa,
> Aryuquma-yaa-rra-aa.
> Ilama-yaa-rra-aa, aa-rr, ilama-yaa-aa-aa,
> Aryuquma-rra-aa-aa.

Tua-i-w' iqukliutmini kakeggluugni egtellruyugnarqekek, "Yuum tuani ullanqigciiqaaci picugteqtarci."

Angalgaq: Ellii-qaa yug'uluni? Ullanqiggngaunaku?
Missan: Ullanqiggngaunaki ilani tua-i.

Tauna tua-i itralria qayaq tangssullrulliniat kenruluku. Qukaani-wa-gguq tunguuralria. Keneq-gguq man'a merkun itralria, qukaani-gguq-wa tunguuralria. Tua-i-gguq taukut qanerluteng tua-i nukalpiat uyuraata pistii uka-i cali pinaluni taiyaaqniluku.

Tua-i ellramini tua-i qaill' pivkenani piyaaqellilria, taum taugaam tua-i nulirran kenruluku tangercecugnarqaat.

Angalgaq: Yaa, itqiirpiit-gguq nuyaqait.

Missan: Tamakut tamaa-i itqiirpagnek pilaqengait. Nuyarpiit, itqiirpagnun yuknilarait, kavircelnguut yuut. Yuut-gguq allat tangerqerraartaita tua-i kenruluku tanglarait qukaitni-wa-gguq tunguuralriit.

❧ *Qanikcaartuli* ❧

Dick Andrew and Marie Meade, Bethel, August 1992

Dick Andrew: There along a river lived a grandmother and her grandson. Her grandson was little.

They got their food by salvaging animal carcasses, some caribou. They would also salvage some dead sea mammals that beached along their river. They always had those for food.

Some caribou carcasses they found were fresh. They prepared the meat and hung it to dry.

And from the sea mammal carcasses they salvaged from along their river, from those they always had seal oil. They hung those [meats] to dry for food.

Also when summer came — her grandson grew and became a teenager — they'd pick berries since berries grew abundantly in the area where they lived. Since salmonberries grew abundantly near their place, they would just walk over and pick. When their buckets were full of salmonberries, they would go home.

Now, whenever they would go out, they would come upon a little tundra island surrounded by marshland. Going by it during the berry season, the island would be covered with red salmonberries. It would be glowing red when they passed behind it.

His grandmother would tell him, "Grandson, don't ever go down there. Don't ever go on that down there."

His grandmother would just warn him [about the island] and say nothing else. She told him never to go down and step on the tundra island covered with salmonberries, a little island in the middle of the marshland.

So the two continued living and weren't starving and always had food. That was how those two poor people lived.

There's not much to say about this part of the story. Now it's time to go to the next part.

When her grandson was old enough to marry, his grandmother got older and began to slow down. And he started to go berry picking by himself. And since she had warned him, he never went on that [forbidden] island although it had many berries. He would go out alone while his grandmother stayed home. His grandmother didn't like to go out anymore because she wasn't as mobile.

One day the poor young man went out to pick berries. And when he went behind the little tundra island he thought, "My, I wonder why my grandmother always warned me not to go to that place down there."

Then he suddenly felt the urge to just give up and go down.

✌ *Qanikcaartuli* ✍

Apaqutaq Arnaq-llu, Mamterilleq, August 1992

Apaqutaq: Taukuk-am anuurluqellriik uitalliniaqellriik kuigem-am ceniini tua-i. Tutgara'urlua tua-i tauna angevkenani.

Mallurrarnek tua-i neqengqerraqelliniaqellriik, tuntunek. Unaken tuaten kuimek ceniinek mallungaqlutek imarpillarnek. Tua-i neqaicuunatek tamakunek.

Ilait-gguq tua-i tuntut nutaqsignaurtut mallukek. Iniurturluki tua-i tamakunek neqkiulalliniuk.

Tuamtellu tamakunek imarpillarnek, kuimek tamaani ceniinek mallungaqamek, tua-i tamakunek cali uqurtuumaaqlutek, mallurramegnek. Iniurturluki tua-i tamakut kinercequ'urluki neqengqelliniaqelriik.

Cali-gguq kiagutaqatek . . . waten tutgara'urlua tua-i angturringengluni tamaa-i tua-i yun'errarpaurtengluni . . . iqvarqelriik, atsitullinian tamana nunatek. Atsalitullianian yaatsek man'a aylliniaqellriik iqvarlutek. Tua-i qaltatek tua-i imirvigkarairutaqata, qaltatek imangaqata utertaqlutek, atsalugpianek.

Tua-i-gguq ayagaqamek uumek alkignarrarmek, nunapiggarmek kanani caarrluum qukaani tekitaqelriik. Kana-i tua-i atsam nalliini qainga kavirpaulliniaqelria atsanek. Tua-i kavirpagglainaq keluirqagni kana-i.

Maurluan pilallinia, "Tutgarrluk, kanavet atraqeryaqunak. Kat'um qainganun ug'arcaqunak."

Tua-i tuaten camek-llu iquunak' inerqulliniaqekii. Kanavet ug'arteqaasqevkenaku kat'um alkignam qainganun atsilriim, nunapiggaam-wa caarrluggaam kanani qukaani.

Tua-i tuaten yuulliniaqelriik, kaigpek'natek tua-i. Yuulliniaqelriik tuaten tua-i taukurluuk.

Tua-i-wa tuaten qaneryararkailnguq amllermek man'a. tua-i-am caqernarillinikii.

Tutgarii tauna yun'erraurrluku, nulirturnaringarteqerluku waniwa, maurlurluan taum kipulleggluku tua-i qessanaktaringelliniluni. Kiirrarmi-ll' iqvaryaryaurrluni. Taum-llu tua-i nunapiggaq tauna, inerqulallruani, ullakayuunaku atsingraan pilliniaqekii. Tua-i uitaaqan anuurluni kiirrarmi ayagaqluni. Qessanaktaringengami anuurlua tauna tarranqeggialiami.

Caqa'urlurluni-am tua-i tauna tutgarii ayalliniluni iqvarluni. Tua-i-ll' umyuarteqliniuq, tauna keluiramiu, "Aling, anuurluma kan'a calria wani ullakaasqessuipakalartau."

Tua-i-ll' tuatequaguq.

[The island] was always glowing red covered with salmonberries.

Since his bucket wasn't full yet, since that one down there was red [with salmonberries], he gave up [following his grandmother's advice] and started going down.

My, when he reached the island [there were so may berries] he couldn't even walk. Stopping at the edge of the island, he began picking slowly moving in. The ground was red, covered with clusters of salmonberries.

As he picked and slowly moved forward he suddenly saw the toe part of boots. While bending over picking berries, he saw the toe part of boots in front of him.

Looking at them he immediately noticed a pair of small boots. The person's boots were made out of flippers just wrapped around the feet. The person had on seal flipper boots.

When he started looking at it from the bottom up, he noticed that it was wearing pike-skin pants. He continued looked at its hooded garment and saw that it was also made of pike skin.

When he got to the person's face, he saw a homely slender young woman.

She was something to behold. She was wearing snowshoes. Though it was summer she had on snowshoes.

She held two walking sticks. One had a carving of a mink on it, and the other had a carving of *?nuukuk*.

Then she said, "Oh my, I am so happy [you are here]. I know your grandmother warned you [not to come here]. Tired of watching you from yonder and wishing that you were my husband, I now come to get you because I want you to be my husband."

He told her that he was not going [with her], that his grandmother had always warned him not to go down on this [island].

Then she said that she was going to take him away.

When she told him she would take him away, he said, "[If I go with you] will you bring me back here to see my grandmother? Will we come and see my grandmother?"

"We will always come and see your grandmother. We will come and see her. We will come and see her frequently and be with her."

When she said that she wanted to do that, he finally agreed to go with her.

When he agreed, she had him slip inside the bottom part of her hooded garment, and she had him put his arms around her waist.

And just when he put his arms around her waist she spun around. He lost consciousness when she spun, when she lifted off the ground and suddenly whirled.

Tua-i atsirrlainarluni-llu tauna kavirpaurrlainarluni qainga.

Aren tua-i qaltani una imangyugnaitarluku, kan'a kavirpaussiyaagan, tua-tequaluni tua-i ullalliniluku, atralliniluni.

Aren, maaten-gguq tekitaa tua-i tuc'unaunani tua-i. Iquanek waken iq-vaaraqerluni, tagkaniqerluni. Arenqianani kavirpaungan, atsat itukurluteng, mallguqu'urluteng.

Tagkaniqerluni iqvaarainanermini piqalliniuq itgek ukuk. Waten yuum ukuk itgek wani pusngallrani tamaani iqvarluni.

Maaten-gguq wavet tangvakalliniak piluguggaak ukuk. It'gayagaat qipqerrluki pilugungqelliniluni. Taqukam cam imarpigmium it'gainek pilugungqellinilria tauna.

Maaten tang qulmurqurallinia una waten luqruuyiit amiitnek qerrulliggarluni. Qasperrluggii maaten piuraraa, cali luqruuyiit amiit, qasperrluggii.

Maaten wavet kegginaa tekicamiu tangllinia neviarcararall'er una kemeg-kunani.

Arenqianani tua-i. Tangluluni, tanglunek aturluni. Kiagulria-wa tanglunek aturluni.

Ukuk-wa ayaruk. Ayaruk ukuk tua-i aipaa imarmiutaq, aipaa-wa imna, imkuciq ?nuukuk.

Tua-ll' pillinia wavet, "Aling, quyanaqvaa-ll' tua-i [tailuten]. Maurlurpet inerqularyaaqaaten nallunricaaqaqa [wavet taisqevkenak]. Yaatevnek cucul-nguamken tua-i uiknaluten, waniw' uiksugamken, aqvaamken."

Tua-ll' pillinia ellii ayagngaitniluni [maliggluku], maurluminun wavet atraasqevkenani inerqulallruniluni.

Tua-ll' pia ayauciiqniluku.

Tua-ll' pia, wavet ayauciiqniani pillinia, "Tua-ll' ima-qaa maurlumnun ut'rut'larciqerpenga? Maurluqa ullagaqluku piciqerpuk?"

"Ullagturciqerpuk maurluun. Ullagaqluku piciqerpuk. Ak'aniksaunaku ullag-turluku piciqukuk."

Tua-i tuaten piyugngani nutaan anglliniluni.

Angerngan imum qasperrlumi akuakun itercetlinia, qukamikun-llu qet'ev-karluni, qukamikun.

Qec'ani atam una uivqertellinilria. Tua-ll' cacini nalluqalliniluku elliin uivqertellrani, qerratarteqerluni uivqertellrani.

After they traveled for some time she stopped. When she stopped, she said, "Look and see." They stopped but, down below, while standing, he felt like he was still moving and turning.

She said to him, she let him out, she lifted the skirt of her garment and said to him . . . They were on a narrow strip of land, and it was rocking and moving back and forth. As he observed, the ground slowly tipped to one side. Then she told him that this was the heart of the universe. That's what she told him.

Then she said, "Let me leave you right here." [The young man] replied, "You wanted me to come with you, don't leave me. You won't leave me here."

Once again, she had him slip inside [her garment]. Just as she spun around, he blacked out again.

Then the one out there said to him, "You in there, we are here. We have arrived." When he went out, when she had him come out, he looked around and saw a little house, a small house. Next to it there was a little above-ground cache.

Then she invited him into the house. The slender young woman was happy and very hospitable and said, "Let's go inside." They went in.

When they entered the porch, he saw the entrance covered with thin stone. And when she touched it, the stone door opened. As they went into [the house], they passed through five [stone] doors. Each time she touched the stone on a certain spot, it opened.

When they finally entered [the main room] it looked just like a regular little house. On one side he saw a space prepared for sleeping. On the opposite side was another bed. When he looked around the room, he saw a little shelf in the back wall, and on it were several small seal stomachs filled with seal oil.

Then she said to him, "Sit across there. That will be your place."

[She told him that] although he was her husband; he was married to her now.

[She said,] "You will stay across there."

He looked and saw a bed; there was loose grass down under covered with a woven grass mat. That's how houses were in the past.

From that moment on he stayed there and never went outside again.

His wife would go out of the house sometimes in the morning through the doorway. Those doorways; while she was gone he would fight and do everything he could to try and open the stone doors. They couldn't open.

He stayed inside the house.

When she arrived, when she ate, she would give him a tiny bit of food. She would give him a very small amount of food in a dish.

Then soon, because what he ate was so meager, that poor young man got thin. That's what he continued to do. Then one day . . .

[This story] is not too long. It will end before long.

He started to get thin. Beneath his mattress, he felt something that hurt. Whenever he lay down he felt them and they would hurt his body. However he

Tua-i-llu ayainanermegni arulailliniuq. Arulairami pillinia, "Atam." Tua-i-gguq man'a, arulaingqallermini, camna nangerngallrani, tua-i uvaagurluni man'a ayuqucia.

Pillinia, anlluku pillinia, qakuggluni qanrutlinia . . . Nunapiggar una tua-i iqkunani uvaarturluni. Caaqami tua-i uv'ercimaarnaurtuq. Tua-ll' pillinia wani-wa-gguq una ellam ircaqua. Taum [tuaten] qanrutlinia.

Tua-ll' pillinia, "Wavet unillaken." Tua-i pillinia, "Ayaucullruarpenga unicaqunii. Wavet unisngaitarpenga."

Tuamtell'-am tua-i ataam itertelluku [qasperrluminun]. Uivqertellrani cacini nalluqalliniluku.

Tua-ll' qak'mum pillinia, "Usuuq, tekitukuk. Tekitukuk." Maaten tang im' anlliniuq, ancani-ll' tua-i anlliniuq, kiartelliniuq enecuar una, enerr'aq angevkenani. Una-wa cali qulvarviggaq elatiini.

Tua-i-ll' pillinia iteryuglutek. Arenqianaku taum nasaurlullraam, taum kemeg-kilnguaraam arenianaku tua-i, "Iternaurtukuk kitek'." Iterlutek.

Atam itqerlutek elaturramun piqerlutek, amiik una teggalqumek can'ggelngunamek ikirtuqangqell[inilria]. Natiikun piqaqiini, ikirtelliniluni. Aren itliniuk tuaten tallimauluteng ikirtuqat imkut amiiget. Tuaten-gguq tua-i piqa'ar-qateng nataitgun, ikirrnaurtut teggalqut imkut.

Itliniuk maaten enecuar man'a enerr'aq. Acirraq-wa ik' akiani. Ikna-w' cali akiani aci. Kiartelliniuq qaugkut qavani qulqika'armi anrutayagaat uqunek imalget, qulqitiini.

Tua-i-ll' im' tua-i pillinia, "Ika-i tang ikavet aqumi. Tuanciiquten elpet."

Amta-ll' uikluku elliin; uiksagulluku tua-i.

[Pillinia,] "Ika'anciiquten."

Tua-i-ll' pilliniuq aci; tupigarnek qallirluteng unkut can'get. Enet-wa tuaten ayuqetullrulriit.

Tua-i cunaw' anyuunani tua-i tamaantelliniaqell'.

Nulirra tua-i tauna unuakumi tua-i waten caaqami tua-i anlalria tua-i amiigkun. Amiiget tamakut; kinguani callugyaaqelallinii tamakut teggalqut amiiget. Tua-i ikirtesciiganateng.

Tua-i enemiutaurarqellria.

Tekitaqami, ner'aqami tua-i cakuinermek neqkuinermek cikiqalallinikii. Tua-i cakuinepiamek qanciqerluku aug'umek qantamek.

Tua-i kiituani-gguq tang tua-i, nerellni ikget'laata, kemgiutenguq taunaurluq, tauna yun'erraurluq. Tua-i tuatnalliniaqell'. Tua-ll'-am piqerluni . . .

Taksiyaanrituq. Iqukliciiquq ak'anissiyaagpek'nani.

Kemgiutengluni. Cat-gguq tua-i camani aciani akngirnaqnaurtut. Waten tak-lartaqan akngirnaqsugluteng. Elliin-ll' paqnakeksaunaku tauna acini. Curunek

never checked his bedding to see what they were. His mattress was grass padding with a woven grass mat on top. When he sat or lay down, something bumpy beneath his mattress would hurt him.

He began to live in that manner. He got thin. She fed him very little. He got skinny.

Soon he couldn't move much anymore. He could barely get down on the floor below his bed when he tried to get up and walk, when he got up wishing to go outside. He had gotten very bony.

Then, he stayed there all winter; it was in winter.

Then eventually the skylight up there, the seal-gut window panel started to stiffen at times since it apparently had gotten warmer out there and spring had arrived; back then people had seal-gut windows. The sun's heat caused the seal-gut panel to tighten during the day.

So when it began doing that, one day when she left she was gone all day. The daylight hours had gotten longer. She was gone [for many hours]. The poor man would be hungry while she was gone.

As usual when she left, the skylight above, since she had left early in the morning, not long after she went out, when he heard a slight crackling sound from the skylight above, he looked up and saw a woman up there with one eye in the middle of her brow peeking in through the open corner of the window. Then she said, "Oh dear, poor thing." She said, "Is he still alive?"

Since he could reply, he told her that he was alive. [She responded,] "I see, you are alive. After I've watched you in that pitiful condition for a long time and felt sorry for you, I've come to get you. Aa, I've come to see you after having sympathy for you for a long time. I've come to see how you are."

Then she spoke to him and said, "You see, that person with you, this is what she does. Your spouse, she kills many people. Now check and see what is beneath your mattress. Many people have died there in your place."

He pulled back the mattress and discovered that there were bones there, human bones.

She said to him, "Okay, when she returns home tell her this. Tell her that while you are still alive you want to go outside one more time. Tell her that you want to see that world out there where you once lived." Then [she said], "I will clear the sky and the world before you go out tomorrow. When you go out tell her to look for lice in your hair." [She told him to have her] look for lice in his hair.

And then, "When you lay your head on her legs facing [the ocean] have her look for lice. And when you see a little cloud over the water down there say this to her, 'I wish I could eat a fish that is swimming below that [cloud] down there, a king salmon I used to eat.'"

waten, curuluut can'get, tupigat-wa qaingani. Tua-i-gguq aqumaqami, tua-i taklartaqami, akngirnaqnaurtuq tua-i manianani acia.

Tuaten yuungelliniuq. Kemgiutengluni tua-i. Iqemkacuaqercetaqluku-gguq carraquinermek. Kemgiutengluni.

Kiituan' tang pektaarciigaliuq. Kanavet-llu tua-i pegnem tua-i kanavet natermun tut'aqluni waten tarrircugyaaqaqami, anyugyaaqengaqami. Kemengssagairutengluni.

Tua-llu, uksurpak tua-i uksullinilria; uksuuluni.

Tua-i-ll' waten egaleq pikna, up'nerkallinian cagniriqercaurtelliniuq qiluq; qilunek egalengqetullruameng yuut. Cagniriqercaurtelliniluni, akertem waten, akerta puqlangaqan.

Tua-i-ll' tuaten elliqertelluku, tayima-am tua-i anngami-am tua-i tayima ernerpak. Erenret takturiluteng. Tayima tua-i. Kaigyaaqurlulallinill' kinguani.

Tuaten tua-i tayimngullrani-am, egaleq pikna, unuakuqvani pilliniami tua-i, ak'anivkenak' ayallra tayima, ciilerpalla'arcan egaleq tangerqallinia kangiraa ikingqaluni arnaq pikna uyangqauralria iiluni ataucirrarmek uuggun akuliramikun. Tua-i-ll' pillinia, "Aling nakleurluq." Pilliniuq, "Unguvauq-qaa tua-i?"

Tua-i-ll' kiuyugngiimiu kiullinia unguvaniluni tua-i waniwa. "Kitaki unguvalliniuten. Tua-i wii takumcukelnguamken waniw' aqvaamken. Aa, takumcukelnguamken ullagamken. Paqluten tua-i ullagamken."

Tua-i-ll' qanrutlinia, qalarulluku tua-i, "Kitaki atam augna waten pituuq. Yugnek amllernek tuqurqilriaruuq tauna, augna ava-i aipan. Kitaki atam acin tamana paqteqerru. Tamaa-i tuani tuquuralriit amllertut, amllellruut."

Pakikaraa-gguq maaten enernek atlingqellinilria, yullret enellritnek, enritnek.

Tua-i pilliniluku, pillinia, "Kitaki waten qanrutqaqiu tekiskan. Unguvallerpeni pitullren, ella, unguvallerpeni waniw' ellamun anqeryugyaaqniluten. Ellamun waniw', ella qakemna tangvalallren tangvakaryugyaaqniluku." Tua-i-llu, "Ella carrirciqaqa unuaqu. Ankuvtek waten qanruskiu kumakiisqelluten." Qamiqurra kumakirluku.

Tua-i-llu, "Ketmun cauluten kumakirteskina iruan qaingagnun inareskuvet. Mer'em quliini camani amirluarmek tangerquvet waten qanqina, 'Kana-i-kina kat'um acian neqtaanek nerqerli, taryaqvagmek nertullemnek.'"

After she spoke to him she said, "She may catch us, she's going to catch us, I'm going to end our conversation and leave you." So after she instructed him on what to do, [the boy's spouse] arrived.

When she arrived, the next day in the morning, after sleeping, he told her, "While still alive, I wish to go outside and enjoy the world out there like I used to."

Then she began doing something, acting as if she was sad, and she started gasping spasmodically.

Then after a while the one across from him suddenly wanted to bring him outside. Then because the poor thing couldn't move, because he was skinny, she picked him up and carried him out. When she somehow touched [the stone] doors they opened.

When he got outside it was clear and sunny; it was early in the morning. Then he asked her to look for lice in his hair. Since he wanted her to check for lice, she started looking for lice in his hair. Facing [the ocean], he sat back with his head on her legs.

The area above the ocean . . . The sky was blue and cloudless. While scanning [the ocean] he saw a little cloud puff way down there. It was the only speck of cloud down there.

Then he told her, "While I'm still alive, I wish I could eat a fish that swims under that cloud down there, a king salmon I used to eat."

Then she started gasping and sobbing, his selfish wife. Then she said they should go in and she carried him inside. She told him she would try to catch a king salmon for him the next day.

Then [the next day] when he woke up, he saw that she had gotten ready to go out. When he woke up, he saw her across there getting ready, and she had started preparing a berry mixture with seal oil.

As she made the berry mixture he told her that he would like a little taste of the prepared berries.

Then with [the bowl], getting ready to go, she bathed right in front of him using the bowl he usually used when he ate.

My, using the bowl she had used when she washed, she gave him a little bit of prepared berries, just a small amount. The poor thing quickly ate it since he was hungry.

Then she put on a seal-gut garment and snowshoes and positiond herself to take off, motioning back and forth ready to take off across from him. After several moves forward, the [stone doors] suddenly opened, and she leaped and flew. She went out in a flash.

Then not long after she left, he heard a crackling sound from up above. He looked up and saw the same woman with one eye who had come before.

Tua-i tuaten qanrraarluni pillinia, "Anguyuaraakuk tua-i, anguqataraakuk, waten pitalunuk uniteqataramken." Tua-i tuaten ayuqucirtuarraarluku, tua-i-ll' tekilluni.

Tekican tua-i tamatumek pillinia, unuakuan, ercan qavarraarluni, "Waniwa-kina unguvallermini ellamun anluni ellamet'lalle[mtun] uitaqerli."

Tua-ll' piqerluni ikna pilliniuq, ikna canguaqili, caluni tua-i, mangllegaluni.

Tua-i piqerluni atam anucunga'artellinikii ik'um. Tua-i kevegluku elliin pektesciigateurluan kemgilan, anutelliniluku. Amiiget tamakut qaill' piqa'arqateng ikirtaqluteng.

Tua-i-ll' maaten tang an'uq tua-i ellakegciluni akercirluni; unuakuarmi. Tua-i-ll' kumakisqelluni qanrutlinia. Kumakiryuan qamiqurra tua-i kumakirluku. Ketmun caugarrluni waten iruan qainganun piqerluni.

Imarpiim qulii . . . Tua-i ella tua-i avaunani amirlutaunani. Kiarqurluk' pilliniuq amirlurraq camna. Camani amirlurrauluni-ll' kiimi.

Tua-i-ll' pillina, "Kana-i-kina kat'um, unguvallermini, kat'um acian neqtaanek nerqerli, taryaqvagmek nertullemnek."

Una-am manglleganguangareskili, unaller imna nulirruara. Tua-i-ll' im' itrucugluku itrutliniluku. Waniwa unuaqu tamatumek naspaaciqniluni tua-i naspaaluni tamakucimek taryaqvagmek.

Piqerluni tua-i uptellinilria maaten tupagtuq. Tupa'agtuq-wa tua-i, uptellinill' ikna, uqumliluni-llu.

Tua-i-llu uqumlillrani pia wani tua-i piqeryugyaaqluni tamaaken atsamek.

Tua-ll' imuggun, ervuqalria-gguq-wa takuani tuan' ayakatallermini qantaq'la-llranek imumek qantamek aturluni.

Aren, atullminek taumek qancirluku, ervuqervillminek tunkiliu uqum-leggarmek-am tua-i ikgelengraan, carrarmek. Tua-i nerqaurlurluku kaigami.

Ikna atam imarnitegnek all'uni tangluluni-llu akiani uqlialria. Uqliaguraqer-luni, unegkut-llu iki'irrluteng tayima anqertellria. Anqerrluni tayima tua-i.

Tua-ll' ayallra ak'anivkenaku, akaaraurteqertelluku pakemna-am ciilerpalla'-arrluni. Piqallinia imna pikna uumi pilleq iiluni ataucirrarmek.

Then through the skylight she began dropping a swathe, a harness. She told him to try to get inside the harness. He then jostled trying to get in, and when he finally got inside [the harness] . . .

Oh, yes, during that time . . . I have forgotten to mention this part [of the story].

Previously, after [he and the woman with one eye] had spoken briefly, when [his wife] arrived, she said, "How infuriating! The dim-witted one spoke to someone while I was gone!"

[She said,] "The dim-witted one has talked to someone." He told her that he had not spoken to anyone. "Aa, you just said that you had not conversed with anyone. Look up and see that thing." He looked and saw a line of breath flowing up. It was a line glowing red and going up, and one side of the breath line was bright. [chuckles]

Marie Meade: [Was it flowing] up to the window above?

Dick Andrew: Yes, to the window above.

He said to her, "Oh yes. I just recalled, when a McKay's bunting landed up there, I spoke to it. And I told it that it was fortunate to be outside." [She said,] "Aa, so it was that awful thing that talked to you." [laughs] She believed him.

Then finally the [woman with one eye] arrived. I just told the part [of the story] that I forgot to tell.

Then when he [got inside] the harness, when he said he was ready, that [woman] with one eye yanked the line and pulled him up.

When he landed [on top], he saw that she was wearing a seal-gut garment and had on snowshoes like the other woman. When he got on her snowshoes and she spun around, he immediately lost consciousness.

She said to him, "We've arrived. We are here." When he got out he saw a little house. And just like the other place, there was a little cache next to it.

They went inside [the house]. Once they were inside, that woman with one eye gave him some food to eat.

She just left him alone for a few days.

Oh yes, I forgot to mention that she had him do five somersaults before she [took him away]. And after the fifth forward roll, when she shook and brushed his body, dust and debris came off of him like smoke.

Marie Meade: [Did she dust him] when she pulled him out?

Dick Andrew: Yes, when she went to get him, yes, yes.

She had him do five somersaults. She helped him do five somersaults. When she brushed off his body each time, dust and grunge came off him like smoke.

After that, he felt lighter and revitalized, after she brushed him off.

Then when she brought him home, they never left. After a number of days, or perhaps after five days, he felt a tiny bit invigorated.

Atam kalevcillinilria uskurrluugnek, uskurrluut, imkut-wa tua-i uskurat.
Pillinia taukuk tua-i iluagnun ekengnaqeqaasqelluku, ekengnaquraasqelluku.
Qaillukuarluni ek'urainaan . . .

Aa, ii-i, yaa, tuani imat'anem . . . Avaurilliniunga.

Tuani imat'anem tuaten qanaaqerraarlutek tekicami qanlliniuq, "Uuminaqvaa!
Qaneqtallrullniluni!".

Tua-i-ll' "Qaneqtallrulliniluni." Tua-ll' pillinia qaneqsaitniluni. "Aa qaneqsait-
nilriaten. Atam ciuggluten tamana tangerqerru." Maaten pilliniuq anerneq man'a
pikavet mayulria. Kavirialuni mayulria, inglua-ll' man'a tanqigcenani, anernerem
inglua. [ngelaq'ertuq]

Arnaq: Egalermun pikavet?
Apaqutaq: Ii-i, egalermun pikavet.

Pillinia, "Aren. Kanguruar-imat'anem mit'ellani waten qanaatellrukeka. Ella-
melnguucianek-llu ayuqniarniluku." "Aa, taulkuum cunawa pikiiten." [ngel'artuq]
Ukveqerluni.

Tua-i nutaan tauna tua-i tekilluni. Tua-i nutaan avaurilqa piaqa ava-i.

Tua-i-ll' uskurrlugmun [ekngan], kalevcesqengani, tua-i pikaken nutaan
cayugarrluku iilgem taum at;aucirrarmek.

Tuc'ami-am atam pillinia, imarnitegnek atullinilria tanglurluni cali tautun.
Tanglugmi qaingagnun tus'arcan, uivqercan, ayuqucini nalluluku.

Pillinia, "Tekitukuk. Tekitukuk." Anluni pilliniuq enerrar una tua-i waniwa.
Cali aug'utun, mayurrviggartarluni elatii.

Itliniuk. Itramek nutaan neramciurcetlinia taum arnam taum iilgem ataucirrarmek.

Uumirpak tua-i uitatlinia.

Aa, tallimarqunek imat'am ava-i ulpiarcetellrukii tua-i pivailegmiu. Tallimiitni-
llu evcukiini, tua-i caarrlugmek puyirluni tua-i.

Arnaq: Tuani-qaa nugcamiu?
Apaqutaq: Ii-i, aqvallerminiu, ii-i, ii-i.

Ulpiarrluk' tallimarqunek. Ulpiarrluku ikayurluku. Evcugaqluku piaqan
caarrlugmek puyiraqluni tua-i.

Tua-i tamatum kinguani uqeglikanirluni ayuqucia, evcullmi kinguani.

Tua-i-ll' tekiucamiu tua-i uitalutek tamaani. Qaillun qavciatni, wall'u-q' erenret
talliman kinguatni cegg'acuarluni ayuqucia.

One day, they heard a loud bang from right outside [the house]. After the loud bang, she said to them inside, putting her head down on the window, "How infuriating! Iingaqruaq [from *ii*, "eye"] took my husband with her! My husband, give him back to me for he is not your husband!" [*chuckles*]

Then [Iingaqruaq] looked up and nonchalantly said to her, "He's your husband, so just come in and get him."

The poor [young man] got frightened. When he got frightened and said that she might come in, she assured him that she wouldn't come in. She told him that the one out there certainly wouldn't come in.

So for several minutes [the person out there] kept [yelling]. [She said,] "Give me my husband for he is not yours! How infuriating, you dreadful Iingaqruaq!"

She would quickly answer, "He's your husband, come in and get him!"

Every time the young man got scared, that one would tell him that she won't [come in].

Then she said, "How annoying! If you don't give him to me, I will *?qum'acagciqamtek* you two!"

My goodness, after they heard a few rumbling sounds from out there, her house began to drip. It suddenly started to drip water. As soon as the water started coming down she exclaimed, "How annoying!"

Oh yes, it was Qanikcaartuli. I have made a mistake. It was [Qanikcaartuli who said], "How annoying, that awful Iingaqruaq! The awful Iingaqruaq took my husband away!" I had accidentally switched [their names].

Marie Meade: Who is Qanikcaartuli?

Dick Andrew: The woman who tortured him.

Marie Meade: I see, yes.

Dick Andrew: I accidentally switched [their names].

Then she put on her hood and belt.

Marie Meade: Who put on a hat?

Dick Andrew: Iingaqruaq.

Right after she ran out, he heard crashing sounds from out there. It was really loud. Then after the loud noises, it stopped dripping inside. After the crashing noises outside, it stopped dripping.

Then she slowly entered, sweating. Her body and face were wet.

Once she was inside she looked at him and said, "Go out and check the person you feared."

Since he was scared to go alone, she took him out. When they went out, there she was, she had turned into a pile of bones, just bones. Evidently, [Iingaqruaq] had attacked and fought Qanikcaartuli, the one who had tortured him, and she ended up as nothing but a pile of bones. [*laughs*]

Piqerluni-am qakemna migpallartelliniuq erenret iliitni. Migpallarcan, mig-pallarcami pilliniak, qamaviarluni egalerkun pull'uni pilliniak, "Eqnarivakar! Iingaqruaqtam uika ayautelliniluku! Uika uikenritan taisgu!" [*ngelaq'ertuq*]

Tua-ll' tauna qaciggluni pakmavet pillinia, "Uikan ikik' iterluten aqvau."

Alingallageurlurluni tua-i tauna. Alingalliimi [piluku] iternayukluku piyaa-qekiini, iterngaitniluku maavet. Iterngaitniluku qakma.

Tua-i wanirpak. [Pia], "Uika taisgu uikenritan! Eqnarivakar Iingaqruaqtaq!"

Kiugaqluku tua-i, "Uikan ullagluk' aqvau!"
Alingallagyaaqaqan taum pingaitniluku qanrutaqluku.

Tua-ll' pia, "Uuminaqvakar! Taicunripakaquvgu ?qum'acagciqamtek!"

Aren, ella qakemna tua-i tem'irquraqerluni, kut'ngelliniuq man'a enii. Kut'ngallalliniuq. Kut'ngalliin qanlliniuq-am tauna, "Uuminaqvakar!"

Aa, taum imat'anem Qanikcaartulim. Alartelliniunga-am ava-i. "Uuminaq-vakar Iingaqruaqtaq! Iingaqruaqtam uika ayautelliniluku." Mumigutliniagka-am.

Arnaq: Kina Qanikcaartuliuluni?
Apaqutaq: Tauna-w' nangcetellra arnaq.
Arnaq: Aa-a, ii-i.
Apaqutaq: Mumigutliniagka-am.
Tua-i-ll' nacaqerluni, nacaqerluni, naqugarrluni.
Arnaq: Kina nacaqerluni?
Apaqutaq: Iingaqruaq.
Anqerteqerluni tem'inglliniluni qakemna. Tua-i tem'irrluni. Tem'irquraqer-telluku, man'a-ll' kucinriqerrluni. Tem'irquraqertelluku qakemna, kucinriqerrluni.

Itrumaalliniuq, kiiryualuni. Qainga kiiryualuni, kegginaa.
Tua-ll' pillinia wavet itrami, "Atam alikek'ngan paqteqerru."

Tua-i alingluni anenrilkurcaaqellria, anulluku. Pillinia imna una, enerrlainaat ukut, enret. Tauna imna nangtestellra Qanikcaartuli tua-i enrurrluku pegtellinikii taum Iingaqruam. [*ngel'artuq*]

Then after that she kept him there with her and nursed him back to health. He gained strength. She took care of him and never let him go hungry. He soon regained strength and became active and he had no ailments at all.

Once he recovered, he remembered his grandmother and started thinking about her. He started to worry about his grandmother. One day he mentioned his grandmother [to his partner], and he said he would like to see his grandmother.

Without hesitation she replied, "Okay, if you want to go see your grandmother, when you go out you will follow a footpath. You will stay on that path and continue. As you go, you will come upon a sod house with some grass grown on it. When you get there shear the grass on the porch [entryway], and after plucking off the grass on top of the house, go inside."

Then when he was getting ready to leave the next morning, she gave him a small seal stomach filled with seal oil to bring with him.

Then he left.

As he went following the footpath he soon came upon a little sod house covered with grass, and the porch also had a lot of grass on it.

Then after shaving the grass, he went inside and saw a woman across there, an old woman, lying on her belly. She was lying on her belly. Then she said to him, "Grandson."

People in *qulirat,* they used to speak in their own language. "Dear grandson, my grandson, okay then."

Oh yes. This was after he put seal oil in her lamp, after putting seal oil in her lamp and increasing the flame. They had traditional seal oil lamps.

While she lay there, he entered. [She said,] "My grandson." She had gotten up. "Thank you so much, my life had gotten so dark, thank you very much for illuminating my life. Now my grandson, when you leave and continue on, my older sister over yonder will know more about your path and destination."

Then he left again. When he went out, he continued on the same path. When he came upon another little house, after pulling the grass, he went inside and saw another [old woman] lying on her belly.

He came upon three [sod houses] at that time. And in the third house, a woman, he started hearing some kind of noise from her. In each house, after putting more seal oil in the lamps, he would increase the flames.

Then the last [house], their older sister, when he came into the third house where the eldest sister resided, and after he added more seal oil to her lamp, increasing the flame, he sat across from her and waited. The [old woman] across from him never moved.

Then he soon heard a buzzing noise that got louder and louder, and it sounded like a housefly. He listened closely and realized that the sound was coming from across there, from the old woman who had not moved.

Nutaan tua-i elliin aipaqu'urluku aningcaaralliniluku. Piniriluni tua-i. Kaig-cecugnaunaku cakneq aipaqluku. Tua-i piniriluni cegg'anqeggiluni natlugne-riulluni.

Piqanermikun imumek tua-i maurlurminek tua-i umyuarteqenglliniluni. Peng'garrluku tua-i maurluni tayima. Tua-i-ll' maurluni aperluku, tangerrsug-yaaqniluk' maurluni.

Pillinia taum qunukeqerpek'naku, "Kitaki ullagyukuvgu maurluun, ayag-ciquten maaggun tumyara'arteggun ankuvet. Ayagciquten tumyararaat makut. Enemek tekiciiquten qainga piluni, canliqtaarluni. Tekiskuvet elaturraani can'get piluki, kenagqaarluki, qainga-ll' enem cali eritarluku, can'get eritarluki it[qina]."

Ayakatallrani-llu tuani, ayakataan unuaquan, anrutayagarmek uqumek ima-legmek taumek ayautevkalliniluku.

Tua-i-ll' ayagluni.

Tumyara'arteggun ayainanermini ak'anivkenani enerr'armek uumek teki-telliniuq canlirluni, elaturraa-ll' man' canlirluni.

Evegtarraarluki itliniuq arnaq ik' arnassaagaq palungqauralria. Paluquyu-garalria. Tua-ll' pillina, "Tutgar."

Qanruciicetun-am qanercet'lallruyaaqait qulirat. "Tutgarrluga'urluuq, tut-gara'urluqa, kitaki."

Aa. Kenurraa uqirraarluku, uqirraarluku kumaqanirluku-llu. Kenurrapiarlu-teng uqunek.

Uitaqanrakun itliniuq. "Tutgarrlugaqa." Makluni. "Quyanaqvaa-ll' tua-i yuu-cimek, tan'gerivakalria man' ayuquciqa, tanqigivkarluku. Kitaki tutgarrlung aya-kuvet, alqerma ing'um nallunrillruciqaa ciunerkan."

Tua-i-am ayagluni. Anngami ayalliniluni tumyarakun. Tekicami-am enerr'armek tuaten eritarraarluku, itertuq-am paluquyugaralria imna.

Waten qavcinek, pingayunek tekitellruuq tuani. Pingayuagni-ll' wani una arnaq, camek tua-i imumek qalriaguralriamek niiskenganngluni. Tuaten tua-i piqa'aqluki, kenurrait uqirraarluki kumaqani'iqluki.

Tua-i-ll' tua-i nangenrat, alqaat, alqaqlikacagiita ukut pingayun, itellrani, ku-maqanirraarluku, uqirraarluku kenurraa, akianun aqumqerluni uitauralliniuq. Ikna-gguq pekteksaunani.

Tua-ll' imumek, cameg' imumek ciivagngalngurmek qalriaguralriamek niis-kengangellliniluni qasturiinarluni. Maaten-gguq tang murilkuq ikaken pilallinilria, tuaken arnassaagarmek pekteksailngurmek.

Then suddenly she lifted her neck slightly and said, "*Aarrarraarraa!* You have lifted me up into life." That old woman said, "My grandchild, you have given me light and brightened my life. Okay now, I'm the last one [in your path]. You already came to my younger sisters. When you leave here and continue on, you will see the one who will help you on your journey."

Then when he went out he continued traveling on the path. Then as he went, he came upon a huge spider. It was a giant spider. When he came to the spider, it gestured and pointed, since insects don't speak. When he looked in the direction it signaled, he saw a hole. He looked beyond the hole and saw what looked like a world down below. Down below, it looked like the world [he once knew].

When [the spider] readied itself to go down through the hole, when it signaled for him to climb on its back, as soon as he mounted on its back and put his arms around its back, the huge spider began going down, it continued down. You know, spiders navigate on threads. They went down [on a thread] for a long time.

They finally landed at their berry-picking spot beyond their place. After they landed on the ground, the big spider took that same line and started going up again.

[After the spider left] he went inside [their house] and found that his grandmother had died. She was dead. But she wasn't in the condition that [those old women] were in. When he saw her dead, he didn't know what to do, and he didn't know how he was going to live and take care of himself, since he was alone.

The poor thing sat below [his grandmother's body] and wept. After crying, the poor thing went outside. When he went out, he said, "What should I do now? It might be a good thing if I turn into a bird."

Then he put his hood on and dove into their river down there. He wanted to become a common loon at first . . . How does it go again? Then he came up and tried calling like a loon, he made the call *tuyer*. [He sang], "*Tuyer, tuyer.*" Do you know *tusairnaraat* [grebes], the tiny *qaleqcuuget* [grebes]?

Those small grebes. Have you not seen those kinds [of birds]?

Marie Meade: I've probably seen them.

Dick Andrew: Yes. They are very small grebes.

He came out of the water making that sound, "*Tuyer, tuyer!*" Then he dove again after thinking, "Why have I turned into this kind [of bird]?" Once again, he made a wish to change into a bird of his choice. [When he surfaced] once again he called like a grebe, "*Tuyer, tuyer!*"

When he first dove into the water, this is what he thought. He saw a stone in the river. Although he wanted to become [a stone], he realized he would sit and not be able to move. But after he picked the kind of bird he wanted to be, when he surfaced and called, he sounded just like a grebe.

Tua-i-ll' uyaquni piqerluki, "Aarrarrarraa. Tua-i yuucimun qagvirtarpenga." Qanlliniuq taun' arnassagaq, "Tutgara'urluqa tanqigivkarlua-ll' waniwa piarpenga. Kitaki waniwa nangneruunga. Yaa-i kinguqligka kituragken. Ayakuvet pekyutestekan tekiciiqan, pekyutestekan."

Tua-i-llu anngami tua-i ayalliniluni tumyara'arteggun. Tua-i-llu-gguq uumek negairpall'ermek tekitelliniuq. Negairpall'er. Tua-i-ll' negairpallraam taum tekicani eluciraralliniuq, qanyuilameng-llu cat ciissit. Eluciraraani taum, pilliniuq ukineq una, ukineq. Ak'aki-w' tua-i camna camani ellatun ayuqluni. Ellauluni tua-i tangvallra.

Atam kalevteqataami tunuminun maavet elucirarani, tunuanun [piluni] qeskiini, negairpall'er imna atralliniuq, atrarturalliniuq. Imumek iciw' negairet ilavkungqelriit. Atraumalliniuk.

Tua-ll' tut'elliniuk imuggun iqvaryaramegteggun, iqvaryaramegnegun, yaatmegnegun. Tuc'ami tua-i atam imna negairpak ataam tayima mayullinilria tamana uskuratek aturluku.

Tua-i-ll' kinguani iterluni pilliniuq, ak'a tua-i maurlurlua tuqullrullinilria. Tua-i tuquluni. Imkucicetun taugaam augkucetun pivkenani. Tua-i tuqullrani, tuqumaluk' tangrramiu, qaill' picirkaunani tua-i qaillun-llu yuullerkani nalluluku, kiimelami-llu.

Qiagura'urlulliniluni tua-i ketiini wani. Qaigura'urlurraarluni taqngami anlliniluni. Anngami pilliniuq, "Qaillun atak wii piqerlii? Yaqulgulua taugaam wii pikuma assiryartuq."

Tua-i-ll' nacaqerluni kuimegnun unavet angllulliniluni. Imkuuluni tuullguluni piiyaaqell' . . . Qaill' imat'am ayuqell'? Tuullguluni pugngami qalriayaaqellria tuyeraaraluni qalrialliniuq. "Tuyer, tuyer." Iciw' tua-i, tusairnaraat-qaa nallunritaten, qaleqcuucuayagaat?

Qaleqcuucuaraat. Tamakut-qaa tangeqsaitaten?

Arnaq: Tanglaryaaqellikenka-w'.

Apaqutaq: Ii-i. Mik'nateng tua-i qaleqcuucuayagaat.

Tua-i-ll' qalrialuni tuaten puggliniuq, "Tuyer, tuyer!" Tuamtell' angllunqiggluni, "Ciin makuusia?" Tuamtall' tamakuuluni yaqulguluni cucukellmitun pugyugluni-am piyaaqell'. Imutun-am qalrialuni tusairnarauluni, "Tuyer, tuyer!"

Waten ciuqlirmi umyuarteqsaaqellruuq angllullermini. Teggalquq una kuigem iluani. Taunguluni piyungermi, taugken tang uitaciqluni pekcuunani. Taugaam tamakuuluni yaqulguluni pugqataryaaqellriim ciuqlirmek, qalrialuni tusairnarcetun puggliniluni.

Then he dove for the second time, not wanting to be that kind [of bird], and when he came out of the water, he was still [a grebe]. Then he [gave up and] said, "I'll just be [a grebe] so future hunters will hardly catch me." [*chuckles*] So he kept his new guise and remained [a grebe].

Though hunters rarely catch them, I have hunted and caught them myself. [*laughs*]

This is how long this legend is.

Tuamtell' kinguqliliriluni tamakuuyuumiinani pugyaaquq-am, tamakuuluni. Tua-ll' pilliniuq, "Aa tua-i makuugurlii tua-i akwaku kinguliat pitaqvaka-
yuitniaraatnga." [*ngelaq'ertuq*] Tua-i tamakuuguralliniluni.

Pitaqvakayuilengraitki wii taugaam pitaqetuanka tusairnaraat. [*ngel'artuq*]

Tua-i waten man'a quliraq taktauq.

ANIMALS RECIPROCATE

<e> *Care of Fish and Food* &

Joshua Phillip and Rachel Sallaffie, Tuluksak, June 1988

Rachel Sallaffie: The traditional rules.

Joshua Phillip: And these rules of long ago; the first and the most important rules. A couple with children, the rule that they have is to take good care of fish and food.

And their way of taking care of fish; when they were down working on fish, they told them to clean the area where they had been working on fish when they were done. They told them not to leave it messy. That is the way to take care of this fish that is going to provide strength. They told them to take good care of it, instead of just leaving things as they are when one is done.

That is the way to care for things.

And then again, [to have the fish come out tasty,] they continually tried to keep the fish in good condition. After hanging them to dry . . . Also after hanging them, they would do this to them before very long. While they were hanging, they moved them just a little bit. They called the process *yuupiggluki* [shifting fish that had been hung to dry so that raw parts would dry].

They say the skin underneath on which it was draped over [the hanging rack] doesn't dry right away. So they say to move it just a little bit as soon as the outside has dried a little. This is what they called *yuupiggluku*. And then that [skin underneath] will dry up.

They say if that isn't done to it, the sun will cook it and cut it through there or the blow flies will lay their eggs there; maggots will appear at that spot. When they took care of fish, they tried to let them dry in the best possible way so that they would be tasty fish.

UNGUNGSSIT IMARPIGMIUTAAT-LLU AKINAUTULLRAT

❧ *Neqem Auluksaraa* ❧

Maqista Maayaaq-llu, Tuulkessaaq, June 1988

Maayaaq: Nutemllaat alerquutet.

Maqista: Makut-llu maa-i nutemllaat alerquutet; arcaqerluku atam ciuqlirmek alerquutet makut. Ukuk nulirqellriik yuglutek, tua-i-llu alerquuterlutek neqet elluarrluki aulukesqelluki.

Man'a-llu neq'liuryaraat; neqnek qaqiutaqata, caarkairtaqata, kenagcesqelluku neqnek man' calivikellrat. Tangniicesqevkenaku. Tamaa-i aulukiyaraq mat'umek piniutekaatnek neqmek. Elluarrluku pisqelluku, peggnginarpek'naku.

Tamaa-i aulukiyaraq.

Tuamtallu neqet assircetengnaqerrlainarluki. Kinercirraarluki . . . Cali-llu agartaqamegteki ak'anurrlivkenaki cali waten piaqluki. Waken agamallratnek waten ellma nugtaqaniirluki. Waniwa-gguq yuupiggluki.

Kan'a-gguq-am waten tevingallrat tamaa kinyuituq. Taugaam-gguq man'a qaingat kinqaqan, tauna egmian ak'anun pivkenaku nugtaqaniirluku. Waniwa-gguq yuupiggluku. Tauna-ll' imna kinerluku.

Tuaten-gguq pinrilkuni, tuaggun akertem kepluku wall'u paralurciqaa; tuaggun paraluayaarluni. Elluarrluki waten kinercetengnaqluki pilallrulliniit neqet aulukaqamegteki, assirluki neqngullerkaat pitekluku.

325

Rachel Sallaffie: Talk about the admonishments and rules; people who caught at all times.

Joshua Phillip: Fish was also most important to them. There is also a rule: you are not to leave an old piece of fish you see just laying around on the ground alone. You are to immediately take it and dig a spot for it and bury it where a person isn't going to be walking on it; this applies especially to fish.

And then the ones who caught all the time, they were called *piculit* [those who are good at catching], or *neqculit* [those good at catching fish] or *melqulegculit* [good hunters of fur-bearing animals]. They also want those [caught] to be well taken care of and for [people] not to make a mess of them.

They say some of the men, after being good at catching, he is good at catching easily and there is always food in the place where he goes. They say if his wife doesn't take good care of [things that he caught] when he brings them home, her husband, after being good at catching, he will stop catching. If she doesn't take good care of them, she makes a mess out of the fish or the other fur animals he gets, if she doesn't take good care of them, they say her husband will stop catching after being good at catching.

They want that woman, that wife of his, to take good care of everything. They want her to take good care of what her husband caught, the fish or fur-bearing animals. And she must never allow them to be where people would step on them. And she must never allow their bones to be where people walked around. She must always put them away.

And they used to say this to them. They said they should put away the fish by digging a pit for it and burying it. But they said one that isn't an animal from the water, a land animal, they should throw away the bones of land animals in the water, either in a river or a lake. They took care of those in opposite ways [remains of water creatures buried in the land and remains of land creatures thrown in the water].

They always put their bones or their furs away instead of leaving them there to get messy.

And again, their houses, even though their floors were soil floors, they never allowed it to get covered with debris. They always swept it. And they would always sweep out the charcoal from their fire pits.

And again, they had this rule. They said a man who arrives with food that is going to sustain them, as soon as he reaches his house, it is said the things he caught are no longer his. They say his wife receives them and will now own them and will take good care of them. This wife of his is supposed to take really good care of them because they are hers.

It is said that they belong to the man as he takes them home, and when he arrives with them, he leaves them to his wife; they now belong to his wife. She must take good care of them.

Maayaaq: Qanrutekluku inerquutet cali alerquutet; yuut piquralriit kesianek.

Maqista: Cali-am man' ciukluku neqa. Waten alerquuterluni: neqalleruar-gguq tangrrinaryaqunaku waten cailkami uitalria. Egmianun-gguq teguluku natmun yuum tutmallerkaqenrilkiinun elakaulluku; arcaqerluki-am neqet piluki.

Tua-i-llu waten piquralriit piculinek aterluteng, neqculinek-llu, wall'u melqulegculinek. Tamakut-am cali elluarrluki cali aulukesqumaluteng uqlautevkenaki.

Waten-gguq angutem ilii picurraarluni, tua-i piculuni piqayuluni, ciunra-llu tamarmi neqtarluni. Uum-gguq-am nulirran tekiutaqaki elluarrluki auluksuilkaki, imna tauna uinga picurraarluni picuiruciiquq. Aulukcurlakaki, aulukcurlagluki, uqlaucugluki wall'u neqet, wall'u allat pitai melqut, aulukcurlakaki, uinga-gguq picuiruciiquq picurraarluni.

Ca tamalkuan assirluku pisqumaluku uumun arnamun, taumun nulirranun. Aulukesqumaluki uingan pitai assirluki-llu neqet wall'u melqulget. Tutmallermi-llu uitavkayuunaki. Enrit-llu cali tutmallermi uitavkayuunaki. Qemagngarrlainarluki.

Waten-llu pituluki. Neqa-gguq nunamun elaulluku, qemaggluku. Taugken-gguq mermiutaunrilnguq, nunamiutaq, nunamiutaam enra mermun eggluku, kuigmun wall'u nanvamun. Mumigullukek taukuk auluklukek.

Wani uitallratni uqlautnguvkenaki tamakut, enrit wall'u cat melqurrit, tamakut qemagngarrlainarluki.

Tuamtallu eneteng, nunarrlainaungraata carangllugtangqessuunaki. Kagirrlainarluki. Kenillerteng-llu cali kangipluit kagirrlainatuluki.

Tuamtallu waten alerquuterluteng. Angun-gguq una neqnek tekiurqellria wavet neqkaitnek aulukutekaitnek, eneminun-gguq wavet, eneminun tekitaqami, elliin pikenrilarai angutem. Uum-gguq taugaam nulirran akurturluki piksagutelarai nutaan aulukluki elluarrluki. Elluarrluki tua-i aulukarkauluki elliin pikngamiki uum nulirran.

Wani-gguq ut'rusnginanerminiki angutem piktui, nuliaminun-llu tekiucamiki peggluki; nulirran piksagulluki. Elluarrluki taugaam aulukarkauluki.

That is the way to take care of fish and the way good hunters take care of them. One is not supposed to make a mess out of it, but take good care of everything.

They say if one is like that, if a couple takes good care of things, of fish and small fur-bearing animals, her husband will not become a poor hunter or a poor fisherman. That is also one of the sayings.

And they say during those times back then, they used to go through famine at times. They would go hungry. Food would be scarce. At that time, before going hungry, some who were able to would buy some food for the spring season from someone who was a good hunter. They would buy some from a couple who had plenty of food to tide them over until summer.

Then they would go through famine. There would be no fish. There is also the following teaching. They say if a couple has a lot of food during the time that they are going through a famine, they say if people are going hungry, they are never to sell food to one who is hungry. They should only give them away.

After having sold during that time when they weren't hungry, they are told not to sell any [food] during the time that they are hungry, but to give them away. They are to try to give it away equally to the people and not mention repayment. That was the instruction.

It is said that some of them do this. Although they are hungry, they pay for those things; they let them pay with their canoes or kayaks for something that is enough for dinner. Some of them do that, even though they are told not to do that.

Then they say famine will pass. They say when famine passes, even though her husband had been a good fisherman or a good hunter before that time, when that famine passes, her husband will become a poor hunter, even though he had been called a good hunter.

They say this is what they do. At that time when there was a famine, people exchanged their things like kayaks for food to eat for dinner. They say even though they were not happy [for the exchange], they did that. And because they were not happy, [the ones who sold food] became poor hunters, because he let them exchange something for food when they were hungry.

But that one who gave away without letting them pay for [food], when they are no longer going hungry, he becomes a better hunter and lives a life with less wants. They say that is the way to take care of things through this old custom that has been in existance for a long time.

And again, it is said they'd say to the young girls, "If you are going to meet a boy or a man, don't pass him on his windward side."

And there is advice for a boy, not to pass a young girl on her leeward side.

These are the teachings. A boy was not to pass a girl on her leeward side, only on the windward side.

Tuaten tua-i man'a aulukiyaraq neqnek, piculit-llu aulukiyaraat. Uqlautevkenaku assirrlainarluku ca tamalkuan aulukluku.

Tuaten-gguq ayuqekuni, ukuk nulirqellriik makunek canek elluarrlutek aulukikunek, neqnek ungungssiarnek-llu makunek melqulegnek, uinga-gguq picuirusngaituq neqcuirusngaunani-llu. Tuaten cali qanruyuterluteng.

Tua-llu-gguq cali pivakarluteng avani cangerlagluteng cali kaigyaramek. Kainiqtuluteng. Neqa amllessuunani. Waten-am cali tamaani-gguq ciungani kaigpailegmeng, ilait tuaken piqayulimek, neqculimek-llu, neqnek kipurqetuut neqkameggnek up'nerkami. Kiagnatkaanun atu'urkameggnek [taukugnek] neqaucilriignek kipurqetuut.

Tua-llu-gguq kaituut. Neqa piinani. Alerquuterluni-am waten cali. Tamatumgguq kaillrata nalliini, ukuk nulirqellriik neqauciqunek, neqauteliqunek kaikatagguq yuut, agu-gguq akilirluki tunyaqunaki taumun kailriamun. Taugaam cikiutekluki.

Tamaani kainritellratni tun'iturraarluni, tuani-gguq kaikata akilirluki tunyaqunaki, taugaam cikiutekluki. Yuut pitatekengnaqluki neqkaitnek cikirturluki akimek-llu qaneqsaunani. Tuaten alerquuterluni.

Tua-llu-gguq-am ilii waten pilartuq. Kaingraata akilirluki kipurqaqluki; aguutaitnek, wall'u qayaitnek-llu atakutarkayanrat akilircetaqluku. Tamana inerquutekengramegteggu-am ilait tuatnalalliniut.

Tua-i-llu-gguq kaigyaraq pellugciquq. Kaigyaraq-gguq pellugaqan imkut, taum-gguq uinga neqcullruyaaqeciquq, wall'u piculuni, tamana-gguq kaigyaraq pellukan, uinga picuiruciiquq, piculimek atengqerraarluni.

Waten-gguq-am piut. Tamakut-gguq-am imkut kaillermeng tamaani nalliini cameggnek naverrluku, qayateng-llu atakutarkayanermeggnun neqmun tun'aqluki. Quyaksaileng'ermeng-gguq tamakut tuatnalartut. Tamatum-gguq quyanritellrata picuirucet'larai tamakut kaigluki akilirturluki tun'ilallret neqkaitnek.

Imna-gguq taugken cikirturilleq akilirceteksaunaki, kainriraqata-gguq nutaan picurikanirluni nuqlitenritkanirluni-llu pituuq, yuulartuq. Tamaa-i-gguq tamana aulukiyaraq nutemllarkun maaggun.

Tuamtallu-gguq ayagyuat nasaurluut waten qanrut'larait, "Tan'gaurlurmek wall'u angutmek pairkengqataquvet asguakun kituryaqunaku tan'gaurluq wall' angun."

Tuamtallu tan'gaurluq cali qanruyuterluni neviarcaraam uqrakun kituusqevkenaku paireskaku.

Maa-i makut alerquutet. Tuaten nasaurluq uqrakun kituusqevkenaku tan'gaurlurmun, asguakun taugaam.

It is said during the time they didn't have any soaps, people were strong smelling. During this time, when one passes a young lady, her leeward side smells nice, it smells of perfume.

They say that back in the time of our ancestors, the passing of a female wasn't like that. She had a different odor. The young girls are not like that at the present time. Their leeward sides only smell of perfume.

Those people of the past, when they didn't have any soaps, they bathed like this. They first washed in aged urine that was very strong; they used that as soap. That aged urine is very strong; it is even stronger than Clorox.

It even washes dirt off right away. Dirt is not going to remain on the skin or on clothing. And if a cloth had any designs on it, and it was put into the aged urine, all of its designs came off. That aged urine is stronger than Clorox. A person would not be able to breathe in the fumes because it was so strong. And his eyes would quickly sting from the aged urine.

Rachel Sallaffie: What are some legends that would help people? And [must they] keep in mind those admonishments and rules?

Joshua Phillip: Those legends, *qanruyutet* [instructions] . . .

When one of the people was relating a legend, I said the following to him. When he said, "I have forgotten some of it. It is okay if I don't relate this legend."

And then I said to him, "Go ahead and insert anything you think in the parts that you don't remember."

The one who I asked [to insert portions] quickly answered me, "Well, if I just added anything to the story, a legend will no longer be a legend; it will no longer be. Because it was given just any ending, the legend will no longer be a legend."

๛ *Common Loon Story* ๛

Elsie Tommy and Marie Meade, Anchorage, June 1992

Elsie Tommy: I also heard a story, the story I heard a long time ago.

There was a woman. In the spring, like now, she got ready to go and gather food, putting on her waterproof boots and her belt, she left with a pack on her back. When she found eggs she put them away in her pack.

Along the way, when she found common loon eggs — there were two of them she was about to pick up — a common loon suddenly landed in front of her and yelled at her, "*Aa-aa-aa, aa-aa-aa,* would you please leave my poor children there. We do grieve for the loss of our children just like you do because we are aware and can feel no differently than you."

Tamaani-gguq miilaitellermeggni teptullruut yuut. Mat'um nalliini neviarcar kitulriani uqra narnirqelartuq, imkunek *perfume*-arninaqluteng.

Avani ciuliamteni tuaten ayuqellrunrituq-gguq arnam kitullra. Allay'ugmek tepengqelartuq. Mat'um nalliini tuatnanritut nasaurluut. *Perfume*-arninarqelartut taugaam uqrit.

Augkut miilaitellermeggni waten-llu ervuqatuluteng. Ciumek teq'iciramun imumun tukniqapiarmun; miilaqluku tamana. Tamana teq'iciraq waten pinirtauq; Clorox-aam-llu tukninqaa teq'iciraq.

Ca, iqaq-llu, egmian augaartetuluku. Iqaq amim qaingani wall'u lumarram qaingani, uitangaunani. Qaralingqerraarluni-llu lumarraq akureskuni teq'icira-mun, qaralii aug'ararkauluteng tamarmeng. Clorox-aam tuknineqluku taman' teq'iciraq. Puyuani taugken yuk anertevkarngaunani watqapik, tukniqapiggluni. Iik-llu qatliagarkaulutek teq'iciramek.

Maayaaq: Cat qulirat piugat ikayurarkauluki yuut? Cali umyuaqerkauluki tamakut inerquutet wall' alerquutet?

Maqista: Augkut qulirat, qanruyutet . . .

Waten-am iliit qulirillrani piaqa. Waten qanellrani, "Ilii tang nallu-yagusngatlinikeka. Mat'umek qulirinrilngerma canrituq."

Tua-ll' piaqa, "Aren, umyuarpet piuyukellrakun iquliraqluku nalluyagutelten pikiki."

Imum-am ellimellma kiugartaanga waten, "Aren, tuaten-wa piciatun iqu-lilaqumku qiliraq quliraunrirciquq; piunrirluni tua-i. Piciatun imum tamatum iqulillran, quliraq-llu quliraunrirciquq."

৯ *Tunutellgem Qanemcia* ৯

Nanugaq Arnaq-llu, Anchorage, June 1992

Nanugaq: Cali taumek qanemcimek niitellrulrianga, ak'a avani qanemciq tauna niitelqa.

Tauna-gguq arnaq. Waten up'nerkami makiraqataami uptelliniluni ivrucirluni, tua-i naquggluni-llu, waten-ll' atmagluni ayaglun' tua-i. Kayangunek tekitaqami tua-i teguaqluk' issratminun ek'aqluki.

Tua-i pivakarluni tunutellgem kayanguinek tekicami-am tua-i — malruulutek tua-i teguqatarlukek — tunutellek ciuqerranun mip'allalliniluni aarpagluk', "Aa-aa-aa, aa-aa-aa, irniagka atam taukuk uitatqaurluqerkek. Elpecicetun tang irniamtenek qivrularyaaqelriakut, allakaunrilngurmek elpecicetun ellang-qerrngamta."

Then the woman looked at it for a moment. "If you don't take them I will grant you a long life which will also be granted to your children. And your children will also pass down this [long life] to their own children." [The common loon] told her that.

She placed the eggs that she had taken back in the nest and said, "I will not take them for I gratefully accept the gift of life you have granted me." The common loon agreed with her.

Then she turned and placed all the eggs she had gathered back in their nest. She returned home with an empty pack.

Then when she got home her mother said to her, "Why haven't you found any eggs? I thought there were many eggs out there."

Then she said, "I did find some eggs, but I returned them when the common loon told me something which would help me. Truly, the gift of [long] life I will be given, and the [long] life that will be given to my siblings, I have gratefully accepted. You know, we mourn over the loss of our family members. That way we all may not grieve over loss but live until the end."

They say that person who was spoken to by a common loon had a long line of generations. There is one who is alive over there now, the last one, a little woman.

❧ *Swallows* ❧

Martha Mann with Julia Azean and Marie Meade, Kongiganak, July 1994

Marie Meade: They tell people not to ever bother swallows.

Martha Mann: That Mancualler, one time the swallows made mud nests on the exterior wall of the school. Mancualler at that time had not gotten a wife. That guy named Mancuaq who was raised by Paniluar. After the little eggs hatched . . . I stopped for a moment when I was getting some water, I saw him standing there holding a stick. Oh my, then he began striking the nest, and soon the little birds fell down on the ground. Oh my.

Julia Azean: How frightening.

Martha Mann: The little birds that had just hatched with no feathers at all looked like dried fish on the ground.

Julia Azean: Poor things.

Martha Mann: The others around told him not to do it. They say that swallows [are sensitive and] don't like to be bothered. Then [when the parents] became protective of their young, not targeting us, they began to fly around and dive down at that one who destroyed [their nest] as if they were trying to get in his eyes.

Tua-i-ll' taum tangvakalliniluk' arnam taum. "Tegunrilkuvkek nunulirciqam-ken akwarpak unguvakarpenek, irniarpenun kinguvarluni. Irniarpet-llu aturluku cali tamana cali kinguvarluni irniarkaitnun." Tuaten tua-i qanrutliniluku.

Tua-i-am taukuk teguyaaqellregni ellilukek tua-i qanerluni tua-i, "Tua-i kitaki tegunrillakek nunuliutekan tamana unguva wiinga-llu quyakluku akurtuuma-niarqa." Taum tunutellgem angraluku tua-i.

Tua-i-ll' tamakut imkut kayangut avurturallni tua-i enaitnun elliuralliniluk' qaqilluku tua-i. Uterrluni-ll' issratni imaunaku.

Tua-i-ll' tekican pillinia aaniin, "Qaillun pilriaten kayangutenricit? Kayangut-ggem amllertut."

Tua-ll' pilliniuq, "Tua-i-wa kayangucaaqelrianga kayangut ellilaqenka ika-yuutekamnek tunutellgem qanrucanga. Ilumun unguvamek cikirciullerkamtenek, anelgutenka-llu unguvakaitnek cikiumallerkaitnek quyalua. Iciwa ilaput tuquaqata qivruaqelriakut. Tuaten tua-i qivruqayuunata iquklilluta iquklicugluta."

Tua-i-gguq tauna tua-i tunutellgem taum qanrutellra tua-i ilakelriit-gguq tua-i kinguvallruut tua-i. Ama-i amna atauciq unguvauq, nangneqlikacaaq, arnacuayaaq mik'nani.

❧ *Kauturyaraat* ❧

Mass'aluq, Anglluralria, Arnaq-llu, Kangirnaq, July 1994

Arnaq: Qaillukuaqalaasqevkenaki kauturyaraat.

Mass'aluq: Imna-am Mancualler, elitnaurviim qacarnerakun kauturyaraat nel'ilriit marayanek. Nulirtuqsaunani taun' Mancualler. Imna Mancuaq Panilua-raam im' anglicaraa. Tamakut-am imkut tuk'riata . . . Mertarlua wii arulaiqallemni, piunga muragaq-wa tegumiara. Aren, tamakut tang imkut nek'ek kauturyaraak kaugturlukek igtut. Aren.

Anglluralria: Ila-i.
Mass'aluq: Tuar tang unani tuk'naayagaat neqerrluaraat melqungeksaunateng.

Anglluralria: Akleng-atagnaa.
Mass'aluq: Makut inerquayaaqaat. Makut-gguq ilangciaraasqumamanritut kauturyaraat. Tuar tang kusgullermeggni, wangkuta-ll' pivkenata, tauna taugaam navguilleq, tuar tang iigken'gun itsaalriik. Kaugtussaangraacetek kaugturce-teksaunatek. Keggmarluku tuaten kegginaakun.

Although he tried to strike them, they didn't let him strike them. They were biting his face, too.

Julia Azean: How frightening. Poor.

Martha Mann: Someone told him that they were very dangerous and shouldn't be bothered. [He retorted,] "They're merely birds and aren't dangerous at all!" At that time he was young and robust. He scoffed at them. Then he began hitting the baby birds, and he killed them.

Then as he got older he married Uyangqulria. Then when she had children, and whenever their babies got bigger, they would die. And sometimes two of their children would die at once. One time he said that swallows [were very powerful beings and] should not be harmed.

Julia Azean: His child Caingilnguq is still alive. And that person, I think Caingilnguq is the only one left.

Caingilnguq who is married to Uyangqulria, and Caingilnguq is their child. He's the only one left alive.

Martha Mann: His childen started to die one after the other.

✍ *Those with Healing Hands* ✍

Elsie Tommy with Marie Meade, Anchorage, June 1992

Elsie Tommy: Also Cukiq before she died . . . You know the voles, if we uncover and find furry caterpillars or hairless caterpillars inside mouse store houses, we'd take our *qaspeq* [hooded cloth garment] skirt and cover them, then one would do this [holding our hands palms up over our cloth garments]. They would instruct us to do this and stay for a while. We wouldn't do this.

Taking her hands to the insects, she would cover [the insects] with the skirt of her *qaspeq,* and place [her hands] on top like this [palms up].

[She would place her hands] on their backs [palms up]. They said that when they penetrated into the hands, the hands would tingle. Her arms would also feel tingling. They say those with [healing] hands would be able to suck out a person's illness.

I myself, also, I watched Asaun's mother when we were staying at Alarneq when Aapekniiq [healed] her. At that time she had an illness in her spine, back between her shoulder blades and all the way up to the top and down to above her waist.

I saw someone who Aapekniiq worked on with her hands.

When she was about to work on her she asked if we had some *ayuq* [Labrador tea]. We gave her some *ayuq* since we had a supply of *ayuq*.

Anglluralria: Ila-i. Akleng.

Mass'aluq: Pia, makut-gguq alingnarqut qaillukuaresqumanritut. "Tua-i yaqulguameng-w' alingnarqenrilnguut!" Imumi tua-i cayunaitellmi nalliini. Tua-i qumlikluki. Tamakut-ll' imkut irniakek kaugluki tua-i yaa-i tuquqluki.

Tua-i-ll' atam piinanermini nuliangelria imumek Uyangqulriamek. Cunaw' irniangaqam', angliaqata, tuqunaurtut. Malruuluteng-llu waten tuqunaurtut. Caqerluni qanertuq, kauturyaraat-gguq makut cayunaitelliniut.

Anglluralria: Augna-w' ava-i Caingilnguq irniara call' unguvalria. Augna-w' call', aren kiimelliryugnarquq Caingilnguq.

Caingilnguq Uyangqulriamek nuliarluni, Caingilnguq-wa yuak. Tayim' kiimi uitanguq tauna.

Mass'aluq: Aren tua-i tuquurangkilit irniari.

❧ *Unatengqellriit* ❧

Nanugaq Arnaq-llu, Anchorage, June 1992

Nanugaq: Cali imkunek tayim' Cukim tuquvailegmi . . . Iciw' uugnaraat, avelngaat enaitni pakikengkumta uguguanek, melqurripcernek wall', waten qasperput taukunun patuqaulluk' tua-i-llu waten piqerluni. Waten piqerluta uitauraasqelluta. Waten pivkenata.

Unatni tua-i taukunun ciissinun, qaspemi, akulleraminek patuqerluki, tua-ll' qaingatnun waten piqerluki.

Neverrluki. Tua-llu-gguq tamakut pulakuneng unatnun, unatet kakilacagarluteng. Kakiayaarlutek tallik-llu. Tua-i-gguq yuum apqucia tamakut melugluku aug'atulqaat call' unatellget.

Wiinga cali, Atsautem tayim' aaniin, aaniinek tangvallruunga, Alarnermi uitaluta, Aapekniim wani pillrani. Tuani qemirrluminek apqucirluni, pam'um keggasgegmi akuliigni pikna ngelkarrluku, kan'a-ll' qukami qulii.

Aapekniim caavtaallrani tangssullruaqa.

Tuani piqataamiu piakut ayuutengqellemtenek apqaurluta. Ayuutengqerrngamta ayumek piluku.

When she asked we gave her three *ayuq* plants. Then the third one, she placed them down, and when she took the third plant, she [brushed it on both of her palms] and put it aside separate from the other two.

Then she placed her hands on her back. And she left them there for a while. When she moved them sideways her flesh, her skin would do this [adhere]. And when she moved them over this way [the skin] would move this way. And when she moved them over this way, [the skin] would move this way.

She moved her hands across. These [hands] couldn't [come off]. And after she left them there for a while when she lifted her hands, the skin [of the patient] came up stuck to her hands.

Marie Meade: When she lifted up her hands.

Elsie Tommy: Yes, when she lifted them. Her hands were stuck to her skin. They were glued here.

After she did this, she [put her hands] down again. She massaged sideways back and forth. Her flesh followed the movement of her hands. It was following the movement back and forth.

After she did that, when she'd lift [her hands], the flesh would be glued here. [*chuckle*]

It was amazing to watch her work. I thought, "I wonder how [her hands] are going to come off [the skin] when they are glued."

Then finally she asked someone to place the other two *ayuq* plants down there on this part of her body [base of the neck].

Marie Meade: In front of her hands.

Elsie Tommy: Yes. She asked someone to place them at the front of her hands, the two of them. And the one [*ayuq* plant] she had used already was over there. Then when they placed the two *ayuq* plants there, after a short while, [she moved her hands forward] on top of the plants.

Marie Meade: [She moved her hands] forward?

Elsie Tommy: Yes, she moved both [her hands] forward [over] those two *ayuq* plants . . .

Marie Meade: Did she [move her hands] over the top of those two *ayuq* plants?

Elsie Tommy: When they placed the two *ayuq* plants there, after a moment, she moved [her hands] this way over them and detached them. They say that since she had furry-caterpillar hands, she used *ayuq*.

Marie Meade: Ayuq would help her in her work.

Elsie Tommy: Yes. And the kind of insects which aren't furry. You know those insects which don't have any fur, the light-colored ones with many legs. They say if someone has those kinds of hands they would use salmonberry leaves.

Marie Meade: The [salmonberry leaves] would help them in their work.

Elsie Tommy: Yes. If they prepare to use [their hands] to work on someone's body, they [wiped their hands] with salmonberry leaves.

Tua-i-ll' ayunek pingayunek waten tungcian, tunluki. Tua-i-ll' pingayuat, elliluki, pingayuat teguamiu unatminun waten piqtaarluk' tua-i-ll' allakaqerluk' elliqerluku.

Tua-i-llu tunuanun unatni patkarluk' waten elliqerluki. Tua-i ellimaurluki. Canivaryaaqaqani kemga, kemga man'a waten piaqlun', amia piaqluni. Ukatmurtaqani ukatmun piaqluni. Ukatmurtaqani ukatmun piaqlun'.

Arvialuni. Ukut pisciiganateng. Tua-i-ll' imumek uitaurarraarluni, kevegyaaqngaku, kemga malikluku amia man'a nangerrluni.

Arnaq: Unatni waten mayurtellermini.

Nanugaq: Ii-i mayurcaaqellrani. Amianun nepesngaluteng unatai. Maavet nepesngaluteng.

Waten tua-i pirraarluk', tuamtell' atrarrluki. Tua-i canivaqtaarluku. Kemga amia man' malikurluku. Maligutqapiarluni, utqetaarluni [amia].

Tua-i tuatnarraarlun', kevegyaaqaqateng, amir' maani nepesngaaqluni. [*ngelaq'ertuq*]

Irr'inaqlun' tangvallra. Umyuarteqelqa, "Qaill'-kiq tayim' nepingaluki ukut aug'arniartat."

Tua-ll'-am piuraqerluni-am qanertuq, kitak'-gguq kankuk, ayuk kankuk ukucianun, waten ukucianun elliqaqerlik.

Arnaq: Ciuqerritnun unatain.

Nanugaq: Ii-i. Ciuqerritnun unatmi elliqaasqellukek, malruulutek. Ingna-w' yaa-i atullra. Tua-i-ll' taukuk tua-i ayuk elliqaitkek, uitauraqerluni qaingira'arrlukek.

Arnaq: Ciutmun?

Nanugaq: Mm-m, ciutmun tua-i taukuk ayuk . . .

Arnaq: Qaingagnegun-llu-q' taukuk ayuk?

Nanugaq: Ayuk taukuk waten elliqaitkek uitauraqarraarlun', tua-ll' ukatmun qaingira'arrlukek aug'arlukek. Tua-i-gguq-wa unatengqerrami uguguanek, tamakunek aturlun' ayunek.

Arnaq: Ayut ikayuraqluku.

Nanugaq: Mm-m. Tuamtellu imkunek ciissinek melqurrunateng. Tua-i melqurrunateng iciw' imkut ciissit, ipilirluteng qaterluteng pitulriit. Cali-gguq unatekaqamegteki, naunrakutanek imkunek pellukutanek-gguq aklungqertut tamakut.

Arnaq: Ikayuqluki.

Nanugaq: Mm-m. Tua-i yuum qainganun atuqataqunegteki, naunraam pellukutaanek [perriqerluki unatai].

Marie Meade: They rubbed it on their hands.

Elsie Tommy: Yes. And two of them would be used to pry off [the hands].

Marie Meade: The salmonberry leaves would also be good?

Elsie Tommy: Those kinds of insects that they called *melqurripceret*, they say since those *melqurripceret* stay on those kinds of plants, [the plants] helped them in their work for prying off [the hands].

And [ones with] furry-caterpillar [hands] use *ayuq*. It is because they like to stay on *ayuq* plants.

They still see them sometimes these days.

[The mouse cache] would be filled with all furry caterpillars. They would be lined up. They looked like they were boiling.

Marie Meade: Did you see them?

Elsie Tommy: Panruk and me, at Kuingiartelleq, her late grandmother would bring us out in fall gathering mouse food.

We did find a mouse cache like that. Our hatchet fell. After preparing it, together side by side, she was here and I was here. Oh, [it was filled with] insects! [*chuckle*]

Marie Meade: Then you poor ones both got scared.

Elsie Tommy: Yes. We suddenly covered it. We ran away. [*chuckle*] Then we came up to our late aunt. We were running out of breath. [*chuckle*] [Our aunt said,] "What's wrong with you two?" We told her that we had uncovered some insects [from a mouse cache]. Then [she said,] "Oh my goodness! They probably fled already! They would have given you magnificent hands! They would have assisted you greatly!"

We brought her over. That [mouse cache] that we had quickly covered back up, I uncovered it with the back of the hatchet; it was totally empty. There were holes in the bottom. Apparently, they had gone inside [those holes]. Right then and there, that person really regretted the loss. She regretted our lost opportunity. She said they were supposed to be our healing hands.

After that I said to Panruk, poor Panruk sometime, "I'm glad we didn't happily welcome those dreadful things that Cukiq told us about." [*chuckle*]

Marie Meade: Oh gosh. A missed opportunity.

Elsie Tommy: She probably would have instructed us to do the proper action if she had been nearby. But we were afraid of them.

Also in the summer, in spring, down at Merr'aq, Panigkaq and the rest of us would play right above our place. We were all young girls then. One time we uncovered and found the kind [of insect] with no fur in a [mouse cache].

There were many insects with no fur.

Marie Meade: What a missed opportunity.

Arnaq: Perriqerluni.

Nanugaq: Mmm. Taukuk-llu call' ekitessuutekek cali.

Arnaq: Pellukutat-llu-q' assirluteng?

Nanugaq: Ciissit-gguq tamaa-i tamakut melqurripcernek atengqelallret, tamakut melqurripceret-gguq tamakuni uitatuata, tamakunek ikayungqertut, ekitessuuterluteng.

Uguguat-ll' imkut melquyagalilriit ayunek. Ayuni-gguq-wa uitauratuata.

Maa-i call' tangtuut cam iliini.

Uguguarrlainarnek atam imangqetuut tua-i uguguarrlainarnek tua-i. *Line*-arluteng. Tangvallrit qallarvayagarnganateng.

Arnaq: Tangellruaten?

Nanugaq: Wangkuk wani Panruk-llu, Kuingiartellermi, maurluirutiin tayima uksuarmi ayagataqlunuk pakissaagullunuk.

Tuaten tua-i pakikengyaaqlunuk. Qalqapagarpuk igtuq. Tua-i pirrarrluk' tua-i, akiqliqlunuk waten, ellii wanlluni, wiinga-ll' wani. Aren tua-i ciissinek [imarluni]! [*ngelaq'ertuq*]

Arnaq: Akleng alingallaglutek tamarpetek.

Nanugaq: Ii-i. Paturlerulluku. Aqvaqurlunuk. [*ngelaq'ertuq*] Tekiarcamegnegull' anaanairutvuk. Anertevkarlunuk. [*ngelaq'ertuq*] "Qaill' picetek?" Ciissinek pakikengnilunuk. Tua-i-ll', "Aren ataki! Ak'a-w' qimallilriit! Unatekaqegtaaratek! Ikayurkaqegtaaratek!"

Agulluk'. Tauna im' paturlellerpuk, im' wiinga-am aug'umek qalqapiim tunucuanek tuani pakigarrluku; imangssagaunan'. Unkut-wa terr'ani kapuqlayagaat. Tamaavet itellrullinilriit. Tuani cunaw' im' tauna uurcarak'acagarluni. Tua-i-gguq uurcarallunuk. Unatekapuk-gguq.

Tua-ll'-am Panruk, Panrugeurluq cam iliini piaqa, "Anirta Cukim carayagnek augkunek pillranikuk quyaqallrunritukuk." [*ngelaq'ertuq*]

Arnaq: Iiren. Qessanaq.

Nanugaq: Canimelkuni-w' elliin pivkaryallrullikiikuk. Wangkuk taugaam alikluki.

Cali kiagmi, up'nerkami Merr'armiuni kanani Panigkaq-llu tayima kiatemteni tua-i caaqelriakut. Nasaurluuluta. Pivakarluta-am tamakucinek melqurrunateng pakikengluta.

Melqungssagaunateng tua-i ciissirugaat.

Arnaq: Qessanaq.

Elsie Tommy: They were all in a line. They were boiling. We suddenly covered them up. Then her mother again regretted our loss, the three of us [and our loss], "They would have been wonderful hands for you. How frustrating it is that they would present themselves to those who would not take them! They should offer themselves to those who would accept them, [*chuckle*] those who will take them and welcome them."

Marie Meade: They have come to you again and again. How unfortunate that you didn't accept.

Elsie Tommy: Panigkaq, too, will remember the ones we uncovered [from a mouse cache].

ꝛ *The Strength of a Poor Person's Mind* ꝗ

Andy Kinzy with Marie Meade and Ann Fienup-Riordan, St. Marys, February 1993

Andy Kinzy: And also this, the rationale behind helping the needy and disadvantaged. The known fact of the strength of the mind of a person who is in need and has no one to help him. What is it that makes the mind of a person who is impoverished so strong?

I've heard talk from people, including talk from priests that God resides in people who were poor and impoverished.

Now, if I see an impoverished person in need of help and I give aide, if he helps him, the one who is with him always, the all-powerful one, is the one who would be the most grateful for the action. And when he gets filled with joy, the one who abides by him always, the all-powerful one will push him in the direction of goodness.

I personally experienced the power of a poor person's mind.

One time when the days were getting long like this I was at Nanvarnaq. But in Chevak there was . . . You've heard of Miissaa. He was there taking care of George Sheppard's store.

The word came that he wanted me to go seal hunting with him down below Qissunamiut. [When I got the message] I went to see him the next day. We began traveling down to the coast.

And just as we were passing Qissunamiut the weather got bad, and it got wet.

That person didn't go against my judgment. I told him that if we insisted on traveling in bad weather we would not be able to function well if we traveled to the ocean shore. We decided to go back.

Nanugaq: *Line*-aumaluteng. Qallarvagluteng. Paturlerluki. Tayim' aaniin cali tua-i uurcaralluta tua-i pingayuuluta, "Unatekaqegtaaraci. Canun pakikengevkalartat! Aturarqestekameggnun-llu pakikeng[evkalarlit], [*ngelaq'ertuq*] aturtekameggnun ciuniurtekameggnun."

Arnaq: Pilaryaaqellinikiitgen. Qessanaq.

Nanugaq: Panigkam-llu tua-i nallunrilkai tayim' pakikengelput.

❧ *Naklegnarqelriim Umyugaan Kayutacia* ☙

Qut'raacuk, Arnaq, Ellaq'am Arnaan-llu, Negeqliq, February 1993

Qut'raacuk: Cali una wani waten ilaminek, mat'umek-wa ikayuanarqelriamek iqulek una. Una wani naklegnarqelria ikayurtailnguq umyugaa kayullra. Cam tauna umyugaa kayuvkartau naklegnarqelriim?

Niitelartukut, iliini niigarteqerlartua wii maaken agayulirtenek-llu Agayun naklegnarqelriani taugaam uitaniluku.

Tua-llu tauna naklegnarqelria ikayuanarqekan-ll' ikayuakumku, ikayuakuniu, imna taugaam nayurtii, camek caprilnguq, quyalirarkaugarput-gguq. Taugken quyakuni, camek caprilucimitun elluam taugaam tungiinun cingqerarkaugaa im'um wani nayurtiin.

Tua-i man'a naklegnarqelriim umyugaan kayutacia naspetellruaqa wii tungaitqapiggluku.

Cam iliini-am waten watuami erenret takliluki Nanvarnami uitatulua. Chevak-ami taugken imumek . . . Niitela'arci Miissaa. Taumek yungqerrluni George Sheppard-am laavkaara nayurluku.

Tuyurtequagaanga Qissunamiut ketiitnun qamigaucuglua. Tua-i unuaquan tua ullagluku tua. Ayaglunuk ketetmun.

Qissunamiut-am kituqerluki cella assiirulluni, mecungnaringluni tuaten.

Umyuaqa narurtaanrilmia taum. Piaqa wangkuk elluaciqngaitnilunuk waten cella assiunaku, imarpiim ceniinun camavet ayakumnuk, egmian pingnaqkumegnuk. Utertetngurrlunug-am.

And when the conditions became wet, since I didn't have gear to keep me dry I stopped at Qissunamiut, even though he continued up toward his village of Chevak.

I got weathered in for three days in that place. It wasn't fun staying there. In three days nine people died there. Apparently, I had gotten there when the village was affected by bad luck.

During the evening an old man came in. When he came in I asked my host to make some tea from my grub box and had him drink some tea. He would come in every day like that. When he came in I would ask my host to make hot water for tea. I would ask her to include him in the tea drinking. It was at that time that I personally experienced the strength of the mind of one without a provider.

Then on the third day . . . It was the day before I left. The old man stayed late into the night. Eventually my host got tired and wanted to go to bed. When they began to ready themselves to retire for the night, he moved closer to me. He moved closer and whispered in my ear. He asked me if I had .30-'30 shells to spare. He said that even three shells would do. I gave him the whole box of shells. As he took [the box] he dropped his head down. Then after a moment he lifted his eyes filled with tears, when the poor thing suddenly got happy. And he didn't thank me. He went to the door. And right before he opened it he turned his head back toward me. He said, "Don't mind it. When you go it will be replaced."

In the morning, early in the morning I went out and checked the weather and found thick clouds in the sky. One was able to see in the distance, but it was very gray. I was going to travel up to Chevak with a young *nukalpiaq* from Qissunamiut named Uruvak. As I was leaving they were very . . . I wasn't acquainted with my traveling companion. Then just as I was leaving Qissunamiut I saw tracks of a white fox. My thoughts were very strong in wishing to follow the tracks for a while. I was very determined. Then after I secured the [sled's] hook I began following its tracks.

It was probably the distance between here and the hall over there. I think that was how far I walked from my sled. The tracks I was following were zigzagging, and it would even go back over its tracks again. You can't see white foxes when it's overcast.

Apparently, the one I was tracking was sitting right in front of me, and I had not been able to see it. While I went back and forth examining its tracks [I saw something], and as I focused my eyes, I saw a white fox staring at me with its head tilted to the side. It was right up close. I looked at it up close. Since it wasn't caught in a trap, my gun here on the side . . . I didn't even lift it to aim, but I just lifted it up enough to . . . It was because [the fox] was right by my side. And as soon as it came down I quickly removed its skin and left. I had seen my traveling companion passing by beyond where my dogs were sitting and heading up there.

Mecungnaringan, mecungniurcuutailama-llu wii tuavet Qissunamiunun arulairlua, ellii kitungraan kelutmun Chevak-amun nunaminun tuavet.

Pingayuni-am ernerni, *three days,* capuraulua tamaani. Atam tua anglanarqenritellriit tang taukut. *Three days nine*-anek yugnek ilangartellriit. Nunallullratgguq, nunallullrat cunawa nall'arrluku.

Atakuaraumainanrani itertuq angukar una. Itran tua-i taquarramnek caayurrarnek caayulivkarluku iqukevkarluku yuurqercelluku. Tua-i unuaquaqan it'eqluni. Itraqan tua-i caanilivkaqluku taun' tukuqa. Tauna iqukevkaqluku. Castailnguum umyugaa tuani naspetellruaqa.

Uumi tua-i pingayuatni . . . Waniwa unuaqu ayagciqlua. Atakurpak uitauq imna angukar. Kiituani ukut tukunka inarcungut. Inarcunga'arcata waten taikanirtuq canimnun wavet. Taikaniqerluni ciutemnun pus'arrluni agyumiqaraanga. Pingayurraungraata-gguq-qaa *.30-'30 shells* pisciigatqapigtaqa. Ilangarcimanrilnguugnek, qanrulluk' tuaten piaqa taukunek pisqelluku. Teguamikek atam pus'artuq. Pusngauraqerluni ciugartuq alluvilliiurqurlulliuq-llu quyaqaurlullermini. Quyanritaanga-llu. Amik ugna ullagaa. Ikirteqataamiu takuyaraanga kiavet. Pianga, "Ilangcinrilgu. Ayakuvet cimingeciquq."

Unuakumi, unuakuayaarmi anngama cella piaqa amirlurpagluni. Taugaam cella kiarnaqsaaqluni, amirlurpagluni taugaam. Iliitnek taugken taukut Qissunamiut nukalpiaratnek-gguq uumek Uruvagmek malilirlua tag'qatarlua Cev'amun. Angli taukut ayiima . . . Maligkauteka-ll' taun' nalluluku tayim'. Ayiima angli uniteqerluki Qissunamiut qaterliarmek, *white fox,* tumainek tangerrlua. Umyuama qam'um arulairutesciiganaku tumaikun ayacuaqernalua. Cagnitqapigtua pinritesciiganii tua. *Hook*-aqa tutmaulluku asvairingnaqluku pirraarluk' tumaikun tamaaggun ayaglua.

Kan'a-kiq, ingna *hall*-aq cangata. Tuaten-kiq unitetalliagka ikamragka. Imna tum'artelqa tua-i utertaaqapiarlun' tumni-ll' ataam kana'aqluki. Amirluluku *white fox* nallunatuut, tangerrnaqsuitut.

Cunaw' una wani tum'artelqa wani ciuqamni aqumgavkarluku tangssuunaku. Cam iliini utertaarpakarlua taum' tumaikun, cameg imumek [tangrrama] piqertua qaterliaraam irirrarmi waten tangvaurqiinga. Canirrarmi waten. Wavet tua-i suvriryaaqluku. Kapkaanaq'ngaunritlinian nutka man'a . . . Waten-llu pivkenaku, qinrutevkenaku, mayuqaniqerluku taugaam waten piqerluku . . . Wanlan canimni. Egmian tua-i nengqercan, amia matartelaaggaarluku taugken ayaglua. Imna-w' aipaqa maligkauteka augg'un, yaatiitgun qimugtema, kelutmun tayim' kitullruluni.

When he got there he had told the storekeeper that I was so confident in my abilities as a person from the inland region. He asked him how I thought that I was going to catch a white fox by tracking it on a cloudy day. [*laughter*]

The storekeeper there had always been friendly to me and chatted with me freely about anything. When I arrived the person who was to be my traveling companion was already there at the store. Apparently when he got there he had criticized me, saying how I had such confidence in my abilities as a person from the inland region. He had wondered why I had tracked the animal and how I had expected to catch a white fox on a cloudy day.

Just as I entered Miissaa blurted out at me while [my traveling companion] was there, "Did you catch the animal you tracked?" Then I blurted back in the same stern tone of voice, "I certainly caught it when I tracked it down." [*chuckle*] I brought it in and handed it to him to dry. Apparently, [I had said that] right in front of the person who had ridiculed me. [*laughter*]

Amazing things happened after that. And all during the fall time . . . The next day when I went back up to my place at Nanvarnaq, the *taluyacuaraat* [little animal traps] . . . Before that time I had checked them again and again, but they had not gotten anything. I dug the snow with a shovel intending to take them out. When I got to them, after removing the cover, I reached down and lifted them, that one down there was very heavy. Then I said to myself, "Did [the trap] below fill with soil?"

When I pulled it up, I found seven mink and several muskrat in the trap. It was loaded jammed tight. Again at that time, I remembered the man who had said that the gift would be replaced when I hunted. Then all during spring an animal would be available for me to catch every time I went out hunting. And all the animals I saw were always accessible and ready to be caught. I've assumed that perhaps the old man's determination was very profound at that time. The time when he said that when I went [the box of shells] would be replaced with something else.

The way I understand it, I suspect that he wasn't the only one who had made me successful [at hunting]. During the time nine people died, the coffins they constructed were just driftwood and not wood planks. I happened to have with me a one-yard piece of thick, white cloth. And since the couple I saw looked so very dejected and sorrowful and the others didn't seem to care much to offer help toward them, I had someone place the one yard of cloth on the head [of the deceased]. Apparently the two were very poor. Those two were very grateful when I had someone place the whole cloth on [the deceased].

I've always thought that perhaps my belief in offering kindness and help to the impoverished and those who were less fortunate has helped me to bypass ill fortune ahead of me. I've lived through some dire situations several times that

Tekicami tauna laavkaam yua pillia, cakneq-lli-gguq wangni nuna-miungunitekvaa. Qayuwa-kiq-gguq qaterliarrnalua amirlurpagmi tum'arcia qaterliarmek. [ngel'artut]

Taum tua-i laavkaam yuan taum pilarmiamia, qanyunaklarmiamia. Maaten tekitua tamaantelliniluni laavkaami tauna maligkauteka. Cunaw' itrami qa-curqurlullianga, cakneq-lli-gguq wangni nunamiungunitekvaa. Qayuwa-kiq-gguq qaterliarrnalua amirlurpagmi tum'arcia.

Itrucimtun-am Miissaam tamaanelnginanrani pileryagaanga-am, "Tua-llu-qaa tua tum'artellren pitaqan?" Qanellra tegtaciluku piaqa, "Tum'arcamku-wa pitaqekeka." [ngelaq'ertuq] Itrulluku-llu elliinun kinerciisqelluku. Taum qacur-qestema takuani cunawa. [ngel'artut]

Atam tua-i tuani iillanarqelria. Uksuarpak-llu . . . Unuaquan kelutmun nunam-nun ayagngama, Nanvarnamun utercama cayugnailan taluyacuaraat . . . Catqa-yuunateng takuqtangramteng taum ciungani. Qanikciurluki yuunaluki. Tekicamki camavet patuit aug'arraarluki ikuggsaaqanka, ik'ikik' cam. Piunga, "Nunamek-qaa camkut imangut?"

Nugtanka taluyacualleraat imkut seven-anek imarmiutarnek imarluteng, qavcinek-llu kanaqlagnek. Kevipiggluteng tua-i kevilliut. Atam tua-i umyua-qerreskeka-am cali tuani cali imna ayakuma cimingeciqniluki qanlleq. Cunawa tua-i up'nerkarpak ayalqa tamarmi pitarkangqerrlainarluni. Arenqigglainarluteng-llu makut tangellrenka. Umyugaa cagniqertellruyukluku tang taum paqnaklaqka. Ayakuma cimingeciqnilukek qanlleq.

Taurrlainarmun cali pinricuklua tuaten nakercivkanricuklua umyuartequa. Tuani tua-i nine-anek ilangarutmeggni, ilangarutiitni tuskanek-llu caqukiuyuu-nateng, muragglainarnek taugaam. Caqerlua-ll'-am tuani qatellriarrarmek one yard-arrarmek qaternitkautmek avaqlirrangqertua. Ukuk tua-i atauciik aren-qiateurlussiyaagpakaagnek cakneq anagullutek, tua-i elluarrlutek piman-ritsiyaagpakaagnek, imna tulvaarrakuyuk one yard-arraq nasqurran nekaanun elliqertelluku amllertacirraatun. Cunawa yuurlurmilriik naklegnaqmilriik, yuk tauna nall'arrluku. Quyaurlullruuk cali taukuk cakneq taumek tua-i amller-tacirraatun elliqervikevkallemni.

Atam tua-i tamaaggun naklekingnaqucim, naklekingnaqucima uum wani tangnerrlukevkenaku yuk, picurlagnaq man'a pellugcet'laryukluku-llu um-yuarteqlartua. Ilii pelluyunailengraan pelluglarqa qavcirqunek. Tamakunun-am

seemed impossible to get through at the time. I've always thought that those people's feelings of gratitude helped me to survive. I've thought that perhaps it is truly a good thing to always extend ourselves toward the less fortunate instead of ignoring them.

wii quyaqallernun umyugaitnun umyuartequtela'arqa pinarqelria man'a pe-
lluglallemnek. Ilumun waten tangrrinarpek'naku-gguq pingnaqurallra taugaam
assinrupigcukluku umyuarteqlartua.

NOTES

1. A number of Yup'ik and non-Native scholars have worked over the years to document Yup'ik narrative traditions. For a summary of these efforts see Fienup-Riordan 2007a:1–6, "Central Yup'ik and Cup'ig Narratives."

2. Jents Flynn of Tununak also told how Raven created mosquitoes when he became drowsy and wanted to wake himself up (Orr et al. 1997:251).

3. In his 1991 rendition, Jack Williams also included the story of Aacurlir, describing how her husband left her for two *ircenrraat* women. Taking the form of a polar bear, Aacurlir destroyed them all.

4. See Fienup-Riordan 1983:175–188, 1994:3–10, and 2007b:17–19 for detailed discussions of this story. Translations also appear in Fienup-Riordan and Meade 1994:57–74 and Fienup-Riordan 2000:58–81.

5. Another Yup'ik version of the story of Atertayagaq, but without English translation, appears in Fredson et al 1999.

6. Many accounts of *ircenrraat* have been recorded, including those by Henry Alakayak of Manokotak (Meade and Fienup-Riordan 20005:288–299), Frank Andrew (2008:400–405), Kay Hendrickson of Mekoryuk (Meade and Fienup-Riordan 1996:47), and John Phillip (Rearden and Fienup-Riordan 2016). Margaret Lantis (1946:301) described "i'xcit," each with one side of its face awry, mouth pulled up on one side and one eye squinting. I have also written briefly about them, based on what elders have shared (Fienup-Riordan 1994:63–76; 1996:72–76; 2005:234; 2016:182–202).

7. This story has also been recorded from Frank Andrew (2008:386–399) and Billy Lincoln (Fienup-Riordan 1994:67–74).

8. Paul John also told a story of small people who grew large as they slept (Shield and Fienup-Riordan 2003:132–135). And Frank Andrew included a similar story as one episode in his long story "Anakalii Ner'aqallii/I Have Eaten My Mother" (Andrew and Rearden 2007:79).

9. For detailed discussions of the traditional Yup'ik ceremonial cycle, see Fienup-Riordan 1994:211–355 and Barker, Fienup-Riordan, and John 2010:37–49.

10. This is the end of the first part of the 1976 recording and the beginning of the 1991 recording.

11. In this second recording, Jack Williams is speaking to two non-Native researchers—Robert Drozda and Bill Sheppard—working on Nunivak Island. Although neither spoke Cup'ig, they had asked Hultman Kiokun (the village land planner and Jack Williams' son-in-law) to ask Jack to tell the story entirely in Cup'ig for the recording. After the recording session began, Kiokun left, and Drozda and Sheppard carried on without him.

12. From this point until the story's end, we have used the 1976 recording. The two versions of the story that Jack told are similar in many respects but end with different "episodes." We felt that the ending of the 1976 version was clearer and easier to understand.

13. This is a literal translation of the words the men sang. The original English version of the song is as follows:

Verse:

When I fear my faith will fail, Christ will hold me fast.

When the tempter would prevail, he will hold me fast.

Chorus:

He will hold me fast. He will hold me fast.

For my Savior loves me so, He will hold me fast.

Verse:

When I fear my faith will fail, Christ will hold me fast.

For my love is often cold, he must hold me fast.

Verse:

Precious in his holy sight, He will hold me fast.

Those He saves are His delight. Christ will hold me fast.

Verse:

He'll not let my soul be lost. He will hold me fast.

For my life He bled and died. He will hold me fast.

COLLECTION NOTES

All stories marked with an asterisk are available as audio recordings in the Yup'ik Atlas at http://eloka-arctic.org/communities/yupik/atlas.

First Ancestors

There Are Many Stories. Ann Fienup-Riordan tape collection. Tape 108, pages 24–32. Interview with Dennis Panruk by David Chanar. Chefornak. December 17, 1987.

Short Raven Legends. Ann Fienup-Riordan tape collection. Tape 108, pages 33–41. Interview with Dennis Panruk by David Chanar. Chefornak. December 17, 1987.

*Raven Legends. Ann Fienup-Riordan tape collection. Tape 68, pages 22–36. Interview with Frances Usugan by Cathy Moses and Ann Fienup-Riordan. Toksook Bay. July 22, 1985.

A Poor Young Lad. Ann Fienup-Riordan tape collection. Tape 71, pages 38–40. Interview with Magdalene Sunny and Tim Agagtak by Ruth Jimmie and Ann Fienup-Riordan. Nightmute. July 17, 1985.

First Ancestor. CEC tape collection. Nelson Island Project, Nelson Island Circumnavigation, Tape 8, pages 258–261, 270, and 282–285. Paul John, Michael John, and Simeon Agnus with Anna Agnus, Martina John, Joe Felix, Theresa Abraham, John Roy John, Rita Angaiak, John Walter Sr., John Walter Jr., June McAtee, Steve Street, Tom Doolittle, Ruth Jimmie, David Chanar, Alice Rearden, and Ann Fienup-Riordan. Umkumiut, Nelson Island. July 20, 2007.

How Nunivak Came to Be Inhabited. Ann Fienup-Riordan tape collection. Tape 45, pages 9–29, continued on Tape 40, side B. Interview with Jack Williams from Mekoryuk. Nelson Island High School, Toksook Bay. November 19, 1976; Robert Drozda tape collection. Interview with Jack Williams by Robert Drozda and Bill Sheppard. Mekoryuk. July 26, 1991.

Humans and Animals

Sparrow Story. Ann Fienup-Riordan tape collection. Tape 71, pages 41–43. Interview with Magdalene Sunny and Tim Agagtak by Ruth Jimmie and Ann Fienup-Riordan. Nightmute. July 17, 1985.

Muskrat and Grebe. Ann Fienup-Riordan tape collection. Tape 7/8/1994, pages 46–48. Interview with Martha Mann by Marie Meade and Julia Azean. Kongiganak. July 8, 1994.

Red Fox and White-fronted Goose. CEC tape collection. Tape 6/11/2003, pages 12–15. John Alirkar of Toksook Bay with Theresa Moses, Simeon Agnus, and Anna Agnus. Umkumiut Culture Camp. June 11, 2003.

Caribou Boy. CEC tape collection. Tape 6/11/2003, pages 41–45. John Alirkar of Toksook Bay with Theresa Moses, Simeon Agnus, and Anna Agnus. Umkumiut Culture Camp. June 12, 2003.

One Who Speared a Human. Ann Fienup-Riordan tape collection. Mask Exhibit Tape 1/1996, pages 1–15. Interview with Dick Anthony of Nightmute by Marie Meade. Toksook Bay. January 23, 1996.

Our Father Was Saved by a Dog. Ann Fienup-Riordan tape collection. Tape 7/8/1994, pages 22–24. Interview with Martha Mann by Marie Meade and Julia Azean. Kongiganak. July 8, 1994.

Ayugutarin. Ann Fienup-Riordan tape collection. Tape 70, pages 1–9. Interview with Tim Agagtak by Ruth Jimmie and Ann Fienup-Riordan. Nightmute. July 17, 1985.

Small One Who Drifted Away. CEC tape collection. Tape 10/2006, pages 8–45. John Phillip of Kongiganak with Roland Phillip, George Billy, Alice Rearden, Mark John, and Ann Fienup-Riordan. Bethel. October 12, 2006.

Grandmother and Grandchild

Grandmother and Grandchild. Ann Fienup-Riordan tape collection. Tape 162, pages 32–38. Interview with Elsie Tommy of Newtok by Marie Meade. Anchorage. June 9, 1992.

One Who Changed the Weather. Ann Fienup-Riordan tape collection. Tape 43, pages 11–14. Interview with Lucy Inakak by Eliza Orr. Tununak. May 1976.

One Who Transformed into a Water Beetle. Ann Fienup-Riordan tape collection. Tape 43, pages 14–26, continued on Tape 42, pages 14-17. Interview with Stephanie Nayagniq by Eliza Orr. Tununak. May 1976.

Long Nails. Ann Fienup-Riordan tape collection. Tape 42, pages 17–21. Interview with Stephanie Nayagniq by Eliza Orr. Tununak. May 1976.

The Little Needlefish. CEC tape collection. Tape 7/01/2002, pages 3–5. Wassillie Evan of Akiak with Annie Jackson and Peter Galila. Akiak Culture Camp. July 1, 2002.

When Extraordinary Beings Were Present

Ircenrraat Stories. Ann Fienup-Riordan tape collection. Tape 68, pages 1–10. Interview with Frances Usugan by Cathy Moses and Ann Fienup-Riordan. Toksook Bay. July 22, 1985.

Ircenrraat and Inglugpayugaat. Ann Fienup-Riordan tape collection. Tape 141, pages 44–51. Interview with Mary Napoka by Rachel Sallaffie and Ann Fienup-Riordan. Tuluksak. May 9, 1989.

*Those Pretending to Arrive. Ann Fienup-Riordan tape collection. Tape 68, pages 10–13. Interview with Frances Usugan by Cathy Moses and Ann Fienup-Riordan. Toksook Bay. July 22, 1985.

*Person Who Came Upon Wolf Pups. Ann Fienup-Riordan tape collection. Tape 163, pages 32–36. Interview with Dick Andrew by Marie Meade and Ann Fienup-Riordan. Bethel. August 16, 1992.

*At Cuukvagtuli. Ann Fienup-Riordan tape collection. Tape 141, pages 51–54. Interview with Mary Napoka by Rachel Sallaffie and Ann Fienup-Riordan. Tuluksak. May 9, 1989.

*One Who Became What He Saw. Ann Fienup-Riordan tape collection. Tape 43, pages 1–5. Interview with Theresa Hooper by Eliza Orr. Tununak. May 1976.

Spirit Helpers

*Neryull'er. CEC tape collection. Warfare Gathering, Tape 6, pages 253–258. Nick Andrew of Marshall with Paul John, Paul Kiunya, John Phillip, Annie Blue, Alice Rearden, Marie Meade, and Ann Fienup-Riordan. Anchorage. October 26, 2006.

*One Who Stole Spirit Helpers From a Powerful Shaman. CEC tape collection. Tape 4/18/2012, pages 132–142. Interview with Raphael Jimmy and Sophie Lee by Alice Rearden, Mark John, and Ann Fienup-Riordan. Anchorage. April 18, 2012.

Other Worlds

*Pamalirugmiut. Ann Fienup-Riordan tape collection. Tape 162, pages 9–12. Interview with Elsie Tommy of Newtok by Marie Meade. Anchorage. June 9, 1992.

Ones Who Went Beneath. Ann Fienup-Riordan tape collection. Tape 7/8/1994, pages 1–6. Interview with Martha Mann by Marie Meade and Julia Azean. Kongiganak. July 8, 1994.

Woman With Long Hair. Ann Fienup-Riordan tape collection. Tape 70, pages 10–12. Interview with Magdalene Sunny and Tim Agagtaq by Ruth Jimmie and Ann Fienup-Riordan. Nightmute. July 17, 1985.

Qanikcaartuli. Ann Fienup-Riordan tape collection. Tape 163, pages 12–24. Interview with Dick Andrew by Marie Meade and Ann Fienup-Riordan. Bethel. August 16, 1992.

Animals Reciprocate

Care of Fish and Food. Yupiit Nation tape collection. Tape 23, pages 7–15. Interview with Joshua Phillip by Rachel Sallaffie and Ann Fienup-Riordan. Tuluksak. June 1988.

*Common Loon Story. Ann Fienup-Riordan tape collection. Tape 162, pages 39–40. Interview with Elsie Tommy of Newtok by Marie Meade. Anchorage. June 9, 1992.

*Swallows. Ann Fienup-Riordan tape collection. Tape 7/8/1994, pages 43–46. Interview with Martha Mann by Marie Meade and Julia Azean. Kongiganak. July 8, 1994.

Those with Healing Hands. Ann Fienup-Riordan tape collection. Tape 162, pages 24–31. Interview with Elsie Tommy of Newtok by Marie Meade. Anchorage. June 9, 1992.

*The Strength of a Poor Person's Mind. Ann Fienup-Riordan tape collection. Tape 189, pages 15–20. Interview with Andy Kinzy by Marie Meade and Ann Fienup-Riordan. St. Marys. February 28, 1993.

GLOSSARY

Note: In the Yup'ik lauguage, nouns ending in "q" are singular, nouns ending in "t" are plural, and nouns ending in "k" are dual.

agiirrnguat those pretending to arrive

akutaq festive mixture of berries, fat, boned fish and other ingredients; lit., "a mixture"

angalkuq / angalkut shaman / s

anuurluqelriik grandmother and grandchild, lit., "grandmother-related ones" from *anuurluq* (grandmother)

ayuq / ayut Labrador tea plant / s

cingssiiget small persons with pointed heads

ciuliaqatuut first ancestors

evunret piled ice

igcaraq / igcarat underground entryway / s

iinruq / iinrut amulet / s, medicine / s

iluraq / ilurapak male cross-cousin of a male

inglugpayugaat ones that have one of something, from *inglu-*, "other one of a pair"

ircenrraq / ircenrraat other-than-human person / s

itqiirpak / itqiirpiit lit., "big hand"; huge hand / s with mouths on each fingertip, said to rise from the ocean as a flaming red ball

nin'amayuk / nin'amayuut herring aged in seal oil

nukalpiaq / nukalpiat great hunter / s, accomplished hunter / s and provider / s

nukalpiar / nukiar (Cup'ig) rich person

nukalpiartaq very accomplished hunter

qanemciq / *qanemcit* story / stories, from *qaner-*, "to speak"

qaneryaraq /*qaneryarar* / *qaneryarat* oral instruction / s; word / s of advice, lit., "that which is spoken"

qanruyun /*qanruyutet* oral instruction / s

qasgi / *qaygi* / *qasgit* communal men's house / s

qatngun / *qatngutkellriit* spouse exchange partner / s

qatngutek / *qatngutkellriik* two who share everything they possess, including their wives

qulingssaaq / *qulingssaat* short *quliraq* / *qulirat*

quliraq / *quli'ir* / *qulirat* legend / s, traditional tale / s

tuunraq / *tuunrat* spirit helper / s

uiteraq red ocher

yuk / *yuut* person / people

REFERENCES

Ager, Lynn Price. 1971. *The Eskimo Storyknife Complex of Southwestern Alaska.* Masters Thesis, University of Alaska Fairbanks.

Amos, Muriel M. and Howard T. Amos. 2003. *Cup'ig Eskimo Dictionary.* Fairbanks, AK: Alaska Native Language Center, University of Alaska.

Andrew, Frank. 2008. *Paitarkiutenka/My Legacy to You.* Seattle: University of Washington Press.

Andrew, Frank, and Alice Rearden. 2007. "Aanakallii Ner'aqallii/I Have Eaten My Mother." In: *Words of the Real People: Alaska Native Literature in Translation.* Ann Fienup-Riordan and Lawrence Kaplan, ed. pp. 68–83. Fairbanks: University of Alaska Press.

Barker, James, Ann Fienup-Riordan, and Theresa John. 2010. *Yupiit Yuraryarait/Yup'ik Ways of Dancing.* Fairbanks: University of Alaska Press.

Becker, A. L. 2000. *Beyond Translation: Essays toward a Modern Philology.* Ann Arbor: University of Michigan Press.

Curtis, Edward S. 1930. *The North American Indian, Being a Series of Volumes Picturing and Describing the Indians of the United States, the Dominion of Canada, and Alaska,* Vol. 20. Johnson Reprint, New York, 1970.

Cruikshank, Julie. 1990. *Life Lived Like a Story.* Lincoln: University of Nebraska Press.

Dauenhauer, Nora Marks and Richard Dauenhauer. 1999. "The Paradox of Talking on the Page: Some Aspects of the Tlingit and Haida Experience." In: *Talking on the Page: Editing Aboriginal Oral Texts.* Laura Murray and Keren Rice, ed. pp. 3–42. Toronto: University of Toronto Press.

Drozda, Robert. 1994. *Qikertamteni Nunat Atrit Nuniwarmiuni: The Names of Places on Our Island Nunivak.* Nunivak Island Place Name Project. Draft Manuscript. Mekoryuk IRA Council, Nunivak Island, Alaska.

———. 2007. Introduction to "Sibling Brothers." In: *Words of the Real People: Alaska Native Literature in Translation.* Ann Fienup-Riordan and Lawrence Kaplan, ed. pp. 102–105. Fairbanks: University of Alaska Press.

Fienup-Riordan, Ann. 1983. *The Nelson Island Eskimo.* Anchorage: Alaska Pacific University Press.

———. 1988. *The Yup'ik Eskimos as Described in the Travel Journals and Ethnographic Accounts of John and Edith Kilbuck, 1885–1900.* Kingston, ON: Limestone Press.

———. 1991. *The Real People and the Children of Thunder: The Yup'ik Eskimo Encounter with Moravian Missionaries John and Edith Kilbuck.* Norman: University of Oklahoma Press.

———. 1994. *Boundaries and Passages: Rule and Ritual in Yup'ik Eskimo Oral Tradition.* Norman: University of Oklahoma Press.

———. 1996. *The Living Tradition of Yup'ik Masks: Agayuliyararput/Our Way of Making Prayer.* Seattle: University of Washington Press.

———. 2000. *Hunting Tradition in a Changing World: Yup'ik Lives in Alaska Today.* New Brunswick, NJ: Rutgers University Press.

———. 2000 (ed.). *Where the Echo Began and Other Oral Traditions from Southwestern Alaska Recorded by Hans Himmelheber.* Fairbanks: University of Alaska Press.

———. 2005. *Wise Words of the Yup'ik People: We Talk to You Because We Love You.* Lincoln: University of Nebraska Press.

———. 2007a. "Central Yup'ik and Cup'ig Narratives." In: *Words of the Real People: Alaska Native Literature in Translation.* Ann Fienup-Riordan and Lawrence Kaplan, ed. pp. 1–6. Fairbanks: University of Alaska Press.

———. 2007b. *Yuungnaqpiallerput/The Way We Genuinely Live: Masterworks of Yup'ik Science and Survival.* Seattle: University of Washington Press.

———. 2016. "The Past Is Old, the Future Is Traditional: *Ircenrraat,* the DOT, and the Inventiveness of Tradition." In: *A Practice of Anthropology: The Thought and Influence of Marshall Sahlins.* Alex Golub, Daniel Rosenblatt, and John D. Kelly, eds. pp. 182–202. Montreal and Kingston: McGill-Queens University Press.

Fienup-Riordan, Ann, and Marie Meade. 1994. "The Boy Who Went to Live with the Seals." In: *Coming to Light: Contemporary Translations of the Native Literatures of North America.* Brian Swann, ed. pp. 57–74. New York: Random House.

Fienup-Riordan, Ann, and Alice Rearden. 2012. *Ellavut: Our Yup'ik World and Weather: Continuity and Change on the Bering Sea Coast.* Seattle: University of Washington Press.

———. 2016. *Anguyiim Nalliini/Time of Warring: The History of Bow-and-Arrow Warfare in Southwest Alaska.* Fairbanks: University of Alaska Press and the Alaska Native Language Center.

Fienup-Riordan, Ann, and Lawrence Kaplan, ed. 2007. *Words of the Real People: Alaska Native Literature in Translation.* Fairbanks: University of Alaska Press.

Fredson, Alice, and Mary Jane Mann, Elena Dock, and Leisy T. Wyman. 1999. *Kipnirmiut Tiganrita Igmirtitlrit/Qipnermiut Tegganrita Egmirtellrit (Legacy of the Kipnuk Elders).* Fairbanks: Alaska Native Language Center.

Green, Esther. 1976. "The Boy Who Turned into a Swallow." *Kaliikaq Yugnek* (Bethel Regional High School). 2(2):45.

Hymes, Dell. 1981. *"In Vain I Tried to Tell You": Essays in Native American Ethnopoetics.* Studies in Native American Literature 1. Philadelphia: University of Pennsylvania Press.

Jacobson, Steven A. 1984. *Yup'ik Eskimo Dictionary.* Fairbanks: Alaska Native Language Center, University of Alaska.

———. 1995. *A Practical Grammar of the Central Alaskan Yup'ik Eskimo Language.* Fairbanks: Alaska Native Language Center, University of Alaska.

———. 2012. *Yup'ik Eskimo Dictionary, Second Edition.* Fairbanks: Alaska Native Language Center.

Krauss, Michael E. 2007. "Native Languages in Alaska." In: *The Vanishing Voices of the Pacific Rim.* Osahito Miyaoka, Osamu Sakiyama, and Michael E. Krauss, ed. Oxford: Oxford University Press.

Lantis, Margaret. 1946. "The Social Culture of the Nunivak Eskimo." *Transactions of the American Philosophical Society* (Philadelphia) 35:153–323.

———. 1953. "Nunivak Eskimo Personality as Revealed in the Mythology." *Anthropological Papers of the University of Alaska* 2(11):109–174.

———. 1990. "The Selection of Symbolic Meaning." *Hunting, Sexes and Symbolism.* Ann Fienup-Riordan, ed. Supplementary issue of *Études/Inuit/Studies* 14(1–2):169–189.

Mather, Elsie P. 1985. *Cauyarnariuq/A Time for Drumming.* Alaska Historical Commission Studies in History No. 184. Bethel, Alaska: Lower Kuskokwim School District Bilingual/Bicultural Department.

———. 1995. "With a Vision Beyond Our Immediate Needs: Oral Traditions in an Age of Literacy." In: *When Our Words Return: Writing, Hearing, and Remembering Oral Traditions of Alaska and the Yukon.* Phyllis Morrow and William Schneider, eds. pp. 13–26. Logan: Utah State University Press.

McGill, Lillian Michael. n.d. *Akaguagaankaaq.* Told by Olinka Michael, illustrated by Teri Sloat. Bethel, Alaska: Bilingual Education Center, Bureau of Indian Affairs.

Meade, Marie and Ann Fienup-Riordan. 1996. *Agayuliyararput, Kegginaqut, Kangiit-llu/Our Way of Making Prayer, Yup'ik Masks and the Stories They Tell.* Seattle: University of Washington Press.

———. 2005. *Ciuliamta Akluit/Things of Our Ancestors: Yup'ik Elders Explore the Jacobsen Collection at the Ethnologisches Museum Berlin.* Seattle: University of Washington Press.

Miyaoka, Osahito, and Elsie Mather. 1979. *Yup'ik Eskimo Orthography.* Bethel, AK: Kuskokwim Community College.

Morrow, Phyllis. 1994. "Oral Literature of the Alaskan Arctic." *Dictionary of Native American Literature*. Andrew Wiget, ed. pp. 19–26. New York: Garland Publishing.

———. 1995. "On Shaky Ground: Folklore, Collaboration, and Problematic Outcomes." In: *When Our Words Return: Writing, Hearing, and Remembering Oral Traditions of Alaska and the Yukon*. Phyllis Morrow and William Schneider, eds. pp. 27–51. Logan, Utah: Utah State University Press.

———. 2007. "Introduction to 'Yaqutgiarcankut/Yaqutgiarcaq and Her Family.'" In: *Words of the Real People: Alaska Native Literature in Translation*. Ann Fienup-Riordan and Lawrence Kaplan, ed. pp. 7–11. Fairbanks: University of Alaska Press.

Morrow, Phyllis, and Elsie Mather. 1994. "Two Tellings of the Story of Uterneq: The Woman Who Returned from the Dead." In: *Coming to Light: Contemporary Translations of the Native Literatures of North America*. Brian Swann, ed. pp. 37–56. New York: Random House.

Moses, Leo. 1999. "The Mind's Power." In: *Alaska Native Writers, Storytellers, and Orators: The Expanded Edition*. Jeane Breinig and Pat Partnow, ed. pp. 80–88. *Alaska Quarterly Review*, University of Alaska Anchorage.

Nelson, Edward William. 1899. *The Eskimo about Bering Strait*. Bureau of American Ethnology Annual Report for 1896–1897, Vol. 18, Pt. I. Washington, D.C.: Smithsonian Institution Press (Reprinted 1983).

Orr, Eliza Cingarkaq and Ben Orr. 1995. *Qanemcikarluni Tekitnarqelartuq/One Must Arrive with a Story to Tell: Traditional Narratives by the Elders of Tununak, Alaska*. Fairbanks: Alaska Native Language Center, University of Alaska.

Orr, Eliza Cingarkaq, Ben Orr, Victor Kanrilak, Jr., and Andy Charlie, Jr. 1997. *Ellangellemni . . . /When I Became Aware . . . .* Fairbanks: Alaska Native Language Center, University of Alaska.

Oswalt, Wendell. 1963. *Mission of Change in Alaska: Eskimos and Moravians on the Kuskokwim*. San Marino, Calif.: Huntington Library.

———. 1964. "Traditional Storyknife Tales of Yuk Girls." *Proceedings of the American Philosophical Society* 108(4):310–336.

———. 1990. *Bashful No Longer: An Alaskan Eskimo Ethnohistory, 1778–1988*. Norman: University of Oklahoma Press.

Rearden, Alice, Marie Meade, and Ann Fienup-Riordan. 2005. *Yupiit Qanruyutait/Yup'ik Words of Wisdom*. Lincoln: University of Nebraska Press.

Rearden, Alice, and Ann Fienup-Riordan. 2011. *Qaluyaarmiuni Nunamtenek Qanemciput/Our Nelson Island Stories*. Seattle: University of Washington Press.

———. 2013. *Erinaput Unguvaniartut/So Our Voices Will Live: Quinhagak History and Oral Traditions*. Fairbanks: Alaska Native Language Center.

———. 2014. *Nunamta Ellamta-llu Ayuqucia/What Our Land and World are Like: Lower Yukon History and Oral Traditions.* Fairbanks: Alaska Native Language Center.

———. 2016. *Ciulirnerunak Yuuyaqunak/Do Not Live Without an Elder: The Subsistence Way of Life in Southwest Alaska.* Fairbanks: University of Alaska Press.

Reed, Irene, Osahito Miyaoka, Steven Jacobson, Pascal Afcan, and Michael Krauss. 1977. *Yup'ik Eskimo Grammar.* Fairbanks: Alaska Native Language Center, University of Alaska.

Ruppert, James and John W. Bernet. 2001. *Our Voices: Native Stories of Alaska and the Yukon.* Lincoln: University of Nebraska Press.

Sarris, Greg. 1993. *Keeping Slug Woman Alive: A Holistic Approach to American Indian Texts.* Berkeley: University of California Press.

Shield, Sophie and Ann Fienup-Riordan. 2003. *Qulirat Qanemcit-llu Kinguvarcimalriit/ Stories for Future Generations: The Oratory of Yup'ik Eskimo Elder Paul John.* Seattle: University of Washington Press.

Sonne, Birgitte. 1988. *Agayut: Nunivak Masks and Drawings from the 5th Thule Expedition 1921–24.* Collected by Knud Rasmussen. Report of the 5th Thule Expedition, Volume X, Part 4. Grafodan Offset, Denmark: Gyldendal.

Swann, Brian. 1994. *Coming to Light: Contemporary Translations of the Native Literatures of North America.* New York: Random House.

Tedlock, Dennis. 1983. *The Spoken Word and the Work of Interpretation.* Philadelphia: University of Pennsylvania Press.

Tennant, Edward A., and Joseph N. Bitar, ed. 1981. *Yupik Lore: Oral Traditions of an Eskimo People.* Bethel, Alaska: Lower Kuskokwim School District Bilingual/ Bicultural Department.

Wassilie, Marie. 1978. "The Raven." *Kalikaq Yugnek,* Vol. IV (spring). pp. 99–101. Bethel, AK: Bethel Regional High School.

White, Natalia, Elsie Mather, and Phyllis Morrow. 2007. "Yaqutgiarcankut/ Yaqutgiarcaq and Her Family." In: *Words of the Real People: Alaska Native Literature in Translation.* Ann Fienup-Riordan and Lawrence Kaplan, ed. pp. 7–29. Fairbanks: University of Alaska Press.

Woodbury, Anthony C. 1984a. "Eskimo and Aleut Languages." In *Arctic,* Vol. 5, *Handbook of North American Indians.* David Damas, ed. pp. 49–63. Washington, D.C.: Smithsonian Institution Press.

———. 1984b. *Cev'armiut Qanemciit Qulirait-llu/Eskimo Narratives and Tales from Chevak, Alaska.* Fairbanks: Alaska Native Language Center, University of Alaska.

———. 1987. "Rhetorical Structure in a Central Alaskan Yup'ik Eskimo Traditional Narrative." In: *Native American Discourse: Poetics and Rhetoric,* Joel Sherzer and

Anthony C. Woodbury, ed. pp. 177–239. Cambridge: Cambridge University Press.

Woodbury, Anthony C. and Leo Moses. 1994. "Mary Kokrak: Five Brothers and Their Younger Sister." In: *Coming to Light: Contemporary Translations of the Native Literatures of North America*. Brian Swann, ed. pp. 15–36. New York: Random House.

Worm, Mary. 1986. "The Crow and the Mink" (transcribed and translated by Elsie P. Mather and Phyllis Morrow). In *Alaska Native Writers, Storytellers, and Orators. Alaska Quarterly Review* 4(3–4):46–58.

INDEX